Philosophy in the Condition of Modernism

Ana Falcato · Antonio Cardiello
Editors

Philosophy in the Condition of Modernism

Editors
Ana Falcato
Institute of Philosophy of Nova
    (IFILNOVA)
New University of Lisbon
Lisbon, Portugal

Antonio Cardiello
Institute of Philosophy of Nova
    (IFILNOVA)
New University of Lisbon
Lisbon, Portugal

ISBN 978-3-319-77077-2   ISBN 978-3-319-77078-9   (eBook)
https://doi.org/10.1007/978-3-319-77078-9

Library of Congress Control Number: 2018934651

Cover credit: Manuel Lopez Sosa/EyeEm

Printed on acid-free paper

This Palgrave Macmillan imprint is published by the registered company Springer International Publishing AG part of Springer Nature
The registered company address is: Gewerbestrasse 11, 6330 Cham, Switzerland

Acknowledgements

We have many people to thank for the conception, preparation and final editing of this book.

There are direct and indirect intellectual debts which we would like to address at the outset. First, we would like to express our gratitude to the always-inspiring masterfulness of Stephen Mulhall's non-conformist philosophical writing, as well as his teaching. It was also through reading his books and essays that we re-discovered the powerful thought of an older master, Stanley Cavell—a true writer-philosopher—whom we first encountered while studying Wittgenstein's *Philosophical Investigations* in 2007, and whose work inspired us to approach this masterpiece in the history of philosophy as a stage drama.

The IFILNOVA provided the indispensable institutional support that made this project feasible and gave us access to a hub of philosophical inspiration and criticism.

Without the financial support of the Alexander von Humboldt Foundation and the FCT (Portuguese Foundation for Science and Technology), we would not have been able to obtain the means that enabled this project to see the light of day and that allowed us to develop the professional network to which the remarkable team of colleagues and friends who have collaborated on this project belong. We hereby express our gratitude for their financial support.

Thanks also go to everyone at Palgrave Macmillan, especially to Brendam George and April James, for their editorial advice and their unwavering support.

Finally, we would like to express our gratitude to all the authors who contributed their many wonderful texts to this project. This volume is dedicated to you.

Contents

Editors and Contributors

About the Editors

Ana Falcato is a Post-Doc Research Fellow in Philosophy at the IFILNOVA of the New University of Lisbon. At the moment, she is conducting an individual project on the novelistic and critical output of the South-African Nobel Prize Winner J. M. Coetzee. She has published work in *Studies in the Novel, Kant-Studien, Hypatia: A Journal of Feminist Philosophy* and *Wittgenstein-Studien*. She is currently editing a book of essays on *Intersubjectivity and Values* with Cambridge Scholar Publishing.

Antonio Cardiello is an FCT post-doctoral research fellow at IFILNOVA, where he collaborates with CultureLab (specifically with the research group "Questions of Subjectivity: Philosophy and Literature"). His areas of expertise cover comparative approaches to Eastern and Western philosophical traditions and Fernando Pessoa's philosophy, focusing especially on its Neopaganism. He has joint responsibility for the digitization of Fernando Pessoa's Private Library (online since 2010). Relevant publication include: *Una Stirpe incognita*

(EDB Edizioni, 2016), the co-edition of *Nietzsche e Pessoa. Ensaios* (Tinta-da-china, 2016) and the first critical edition of *Obra Completa de Álvaro de Campos* (Lisboa: Tinta-da-China, 2014).

Contributors

Charles Altieri is Rachel Stageberg Anderson Chair of English Literature at UC Berkeley. He teaches primarily courses in twentieth poetry and poetry and the visual arts, as well as courses in intersections between philosophy and poetry. Author of several books, his latest are *Wallace Stevens and the Demands of Modernity*, and *Reckoning with Imagination: Wittgenstein and the Aesthetics of Literary Expecrience*.

Alice Crary is Associate Professor and Chair of the Philosophy Department at the New School for Social Research (New York). Her research interests include moral philosophy, Wittgenstein, philosophy and literature, feminism and philosophy, cognitive disability, and philosophy and animals. She is the author of *Beyond Moral Judgment* (Harvard University Press, 2007) and *Inside Ethics: On the Demands of Moral Thought* (Harvard University Press, 2016), and co-editor (with Rupert Read) of *The New Wittgenstein* (Routledge, 2000).

Michael D'Arcy completed his Ph.D. at Cornell University and is currently Associate Professor of English literature at St. Francis Xavier University (Nova Scotia, Canada). His research interests include twentieth-century British, Irish, and Anglophone literature; media studies; film and visual culture; and literary theory. He is the co-editor (with Mathias Nilges) of *The Contemporaneity of Modernism: Literature, Media, Culture* (Routledge, 2016). His other work (published or forthcoming) includes: "'Blind Representation': On the Epic Naiveté of the Cinema," in *Postmodern Culture* (Johns Hopkins University Press, 2015); "To Burn or Not to Burn: Modernism's Photographic Exposures," (in *The Contemporaneity of Modernism*); "Beckett's Trilogy and the Deaths of (Auto)biographical Form," in *Samuel Beckett Today/Aujourd'hui* 26 (2014); "Influence," in *Samuel Beckett in Context* (Cambridge University Press, 2013); and "Indifferent Memory: Beckett, Naipaul, and the Task of Textuality," in *The Journal of Beckett Studies* 19.1 (2010). He is currently completing a monograph titled *The Slow Novel: Late Modernism and the Adventure of Narrative Stupidity*.

María José Gámez Fuentes holds a Ph.D. in Critical Theory and Cultural Studies from the University of Nottingham, where she also worked as a Teaching Assistant. She has written widely in Spanish and English both on women and motherhood in Spanish Cinema and on the representation of gender violence. Currently she is Associate Professor at the Department of Communication Sciences at Universitat Jaume I of Castellón (Spain). She channels her research on Gender and Cultural studies through the Institute for Social Development and Peace and the Institute for Feminist Research of that university. Her latest work engages with feminism and the politics of representation with special interest on how to transform cultural and structural violence against women. Her contributions have been published in *Social Movement Studies, International Journal of Iberian Studies, Peace Review, Cineaste, Hispanic Research Journal* and *Journal of Spanish Cultural Studies* among others.

Jonathan Gilmore teaches philosophy of art at the City University of New York. Most recently, he was a 2013–2014 National Endowment for the Humanities Fellow. He taught for several years in the Philosophy Department at Yale University and, before that, in the Philosophy Department at Princeton University, where he was a Cotsen Postdoctoral Fellow in the Society of Fellows. He is the recipient of NEH, Whiting, Mellon, and other national fellowships and awards. He is the author of *The Life of a Style: Beginnings and Endings in the Narrative History of Art* (Cornell University Press, 2000) and has published several articles on aesthetics, the history and historiography of modern art, science and art, the nature of the imagination, freedom of expression, criticism, and twentieth-century European philosophy. His art criticism has appeared in *Artforum, Art in America, ArtNews, Tema Celeste*, and *Modern Painters* and he is the author, most recently, of a monograph essay on the artist Sarah Sze, the American Representative to the 2013 Venice Biennale.

Garry L. Hagberg is the James H. Ottaway Professor of Philosophy and Aesthetics at Bard College, and has in recent years also held a Chair in the School of Philosophy at the University of East Anglia. Author of numerous papers at the intersection of aesthetics and the philosophy of language, his books include *Meaning and Interpretation: Wittgenstein, Henry James, and Literary Knowledge*; and *Art as Language: Wittgenstein, Meaning, and Aesthetic Theory*; his *Describing Ourselves: Wittgenstein and Autobiographical Consciousness* appeared with Oxford University Press in 2008 (paper 2011). An edited collection, *Art and Ethical Criticism*, appeared in 2008 with Blackwell (paper 2011, Wiley-Blackwell), and he is co-editor of *A Companion to the Philosophy of Literature* (Wiley-Blackwell, 2010) and Editor of the journal *Philosophy and Literature*. He is presently writing a new book on the contribution literary experience makes to the formation of self and sensibility, *Living in Words: Literature, Autobiographical Language, and the Composition of Selfhood*, and editing a volume *Fictional Characters, Real Problems: The Search for Ethical Content in Literature*.

Katerina Kitsi-Mitakou holds degrees in English Studies from the Aristotle University of Thessaloniki (BA Honours, Ph.D.) and Leeds University (MA in Theatre Studies). She is Associate Professor in English Literature and Culture in the School of English, Aristotle University of Thessaloniki. She has been teaching and publishing on Realism, Modernism, and the English novel, as well as on feminist and body theory.

Alexander Kozin (Ph.D. in Philosophy of Communication, 2002, SIUC) is Honorary Research Fellow at the Centre for Literature and Philosophy, University of Sussex, UK. Before that he was Research Fellow at the University of Edinburgh, where he specialized in visual communication. From 2003 to 2008 he tenured at Freie Universitaet Berlin, where he participated in a DFG-funded post-doctoral international project "Comparative Microsociology of Criminal Defense Proceedings." His most frequently practised methods are based on phenomenology and include ethnomethodology, conversation analysis, ethnography of communication, discourse analysis, and semiotics.

He has published in *Semiotica, Discourse Studies, Law and Critique, American Journal of Semiotics, Sign Systems, Text and Talk, Janus Head, Comparative Sociology*, and other academic journals. He also co-authored a book on the ethnographic study of law in America, Germany, and England. Currently, he is working on a book project, "On the Exceptional Status of Alien Modalities in Husserl's Phenomenology." His current research interests include a project on the construction of space in Kafka's works on the law and a study of postcolonial literature in light of Husserl's xenology, where authors such as Kipling, Maugham, Conrad, and Bowles will be analysed.

Michael Levenson is William B. Christian Professor of English at the University of Virginia and author of *A Genealogy of Modernism* (Cambridge University Press, 1984), *Modernism and the Fate of Individuality* (Cambridge University Press, 1990), *The Spectacle of Intimacy* (Princeton University Press, co-author Karen Chase, 2000), and *Modernism* from Yale University Press (2011); and editor of the *Cambridge Companion to Modernism* (2000, 2nd edition, 2011). Professor Levenson has published essays in such journals as *ELH, Novel, Modernism/Modernity, The New Republic, Wilson Quarterly, Raritan*; among his public lectures are those at Harvard, Yale, University of Chicago, Johns Hopkins, Berkeley, and Oxford University

Laura María Lojo Rodríguez is Senior Lecturer in English Literature at the Department of English Studies, University of Santiago de Compostela (Spain), where she teaches Literature(s) in English, Literary Theory and Gender Studies. She is currently the supervisor of the research group "Discourse and Identity". Her most recent publications include: *Moving across a Century: Women's Short Fiction from Virginia Woolf to Ali Smith* (Bern: Peter Lang, 2012), "'The Saving Power of Hallucination': Elizabeth Bowen's "Mysterious Kôr" and Female Romance" (*Zeitschrift für Anglistik und Amerikanistik*, 2014) and "Unveiling the Past: Éilís Ní Dhuibhne's 'Sex in the Context of Ireland'" (*Nordic Irish Studies*, 2014). Lojo is also a member of the research project *Women's Tales: The Short Fiction of Contemporary British Writers 1974–2013* (FEM2013-41977-P).

Rebeca Maseda García is Associate Professor at the College of Arts and Sciences in the University of Alaska at Anchorage. She has an extensive record of publications (as well as grants, conference presentations, guest lectures, etc.) on film and gender, and language learning. Throughout her career she has delved into contentious issues pertaining to the relationship between gender and Feminism(s). Her last research focuses on cinematographic representations of violence and trauma: the possibility of depicting trauma, and alternative modes of representation that avoid traumatization, victimization, voyeurism, aestheticization, and trivialization.

Stephen Mulhall is a Professor of Philosophy, and a Tutorial Fellow of New College, Oxford. His two main areas of research are the philosophy of Wittgenstein, and some of the key figures in the Franco-German traditions of philosophy arising from Kant—especially Heidegger, Sartre, Nietzsche and Kierkegaard. His publications include: *The Self and Its Shadows: A Book of Essays on Individuality as Negation in Philosophy and the Arts* (Oxford University Press, 2013), *The Wounded Animal: J. M. Coetzee and the difficulty of reality in literature and philosophy* (Princeton University Press, 2009), *On Film* (Routledge, 2008), *Heidegger and "Being and Time"* (Routledge, 2005), and *Inheritance and Originality* (Oxford University Press, 2001).

Mathias Nilges is Associate Professor of English and Critical Theory at St. Francis Xavier University in Canada. With Emilio Sauri he is the editor of *Literary Materialisms* (2013), with Nicholas Brown, Josh Robinson, and Neil Larsen of *Marxism and the Critique of Value* (2014), and with Michael D'Arcy of *The Contemporaneity of Modernism* (2015). His essays have appeared (and are forthcoming) in journals such as *Callaloo, Textual Practice, American Literary History, Postmodern Culture,* and *NOVEL*. His monograph *Nostalgia for the Future: The Time of the Contemporary American Novel* is currently under review. With Emilio Sauri and Sarah Brouillette he is the editor of a forthcoming collection of essays titled *Literature and the Global Contemporary.*

Jerónimo Pizarro is a professor at University of the Andes, chair of Portuguese Studies at the Camões Institute in Colombia and Hispanic

Literature and Portuguese Linguistics. He completed a Ph.D. at Harvard University (2008) and Lisbon University (2006). He already has seven volumes in the critical edition of Pessoa's work, the first one being *The Book of Disquiet* [*Livro do Desassossego*]. He published in 2010 *Fernando Pessoa's Private Library* [*A Biblioteca Particular de Fernando Pessoa*], co-authored with Patricio Ferrari and Antonio Cardiello; the three scholars coordinated the digitization of the poet's library with the support of the Casa Fernando Pessoa. In 2011 he edited, with Steffen Dix, the collection *Portuguese Modernisms in Literature and the Visual Arts*. He also coordinated two new series in Ática, Fernando Pessoa's historical publishing house: 1. *Fernando Pessoa | Work*, and 2. *Fernando Pessoa | Essays*.

Rupert Read is Reader in Philosophy at the University of East Anglia. His *Film as philosophy: essays on cinema after Wittgenstein and Cavell* (edited book, jointly edited with Jerry Goodenough; London: Palgrave Macmillan, 2005) helped bring the attention of the academic world to the possibility of reading films philosophically. His own contributions to that volume are: 'What theory of film do Wittgenstein and Cavell have?' and '"Memento': a philosophical investigation". The book as a whole (and its ruling idea of 'film AS philosophy', which was his own conception), wins praise on the back cover for representing "a wholly new view of the relationship between image and thought" and as calling "for course development". Read has more recently published on 'Melancholia' (in *Sequence*) and repeatedly as part of the 'Thinking Film collective' (thinkingfilmcolleactive.blogspot.co.uk). Read is now working on a book entitled 'Film as freedom'. He is co-editor of the epochal '*The New Wittgenstein*' collection (2000), published with Routledge. His monographs are *Kuhn* (Polity, 2002; this book develops a Wittgensteinian interpretation of Kuhn, for the first time), *Applying Wittgenstein* (Continuum, 2007), *Philosophy for Life* (Continuum, 2007), *There Is No Such Thing as a Social Science* (Ashgate, 2008; this book makes a Winchian/Wittgensteinian argument to the conclusion stated in its title), *Wittgenstein Among the Sciences* (Ashgate, 2012) and *A Wittgensteinian Way With Paradoxes* (Rowman and Littlefield (Lexington), 2013).

Bartholomew Ryan is a researcher and coordinator of the CulturLab at the Nova Institute of Philosophy (IFILNOVA) at the Universidade

Nova de Lisboa. His academic and creative works orbit around the central motif of 'transformation,' which takes into account the masks, journeys and (multiple) identities that define the modern human condition. Amongst his various publications, his books include *Nietzsche and Pessoa: Ensaios* (editor, 2016), *Nietzsche and the Problem of Subjectivity* (editor, 2015), and *Kierkegaard's Indirect Politics: Interludes with Lukács, Schmitt, Benjamin and Adorno* (2014). He has also taught at Bard College of Berlin, Universidade de Lisboa, Lady Margaret Hall at Oxford, and University of Aarhus. He studied at Trinity College Dublin (BA), University College Dublin (MA), and Aarhus University (Ph.D.). He is also the composer and leader of the international music project *The Loafing Heroes*.

Tanja Staehler (Ph.D. 2003, University of Wuppertal) is Reader in Philosophy at the University of Sussex and Co-Director of the Centre for Literature and Philosophy. Her research areas are Plato, Hegel, Phenomenology, and Continental Aesthetics. She has published a monograph on Hegel and Husserl in Kluwer's *Phaenomenologica* series: *Die Unruhe des Anfangs. Hegel und Husserl über den Weg in die Phänomenologie* (2003). Her second monograph is entitled *Plato and Levinas: The Ambiguous Out-Side of Ethics* (Routledge, 2010) and discusses the relationship between ethics and aesthetics. She has published articles on phenomenological methodology, history, culture, and dance (Pina Bausch). Currently, her research focuses on the embodied experiences of pregnancy, birth, and being with infants, utilising also literary resources.

1

Introduction: Philosophy and Literary Modernism—An Old Problem Finally Made New

Ana Falcato and Antonio Cardiello

Although approximately two-and-a-half-thousand years separate the birth of philosophy and the emergence of literary modernism in the last decade of the nineteenth century, these forms of spiritual creation face overlapping problems, however opposite their methods. Both philosophical works and modernist literary texts are characterised by reflexive density, which is typically made a self-standing topic and which thus allows for meta-reflection—a feature with a highly relevant linguistic impact, as we shall see in what follows. As such, the works of philosophy and the texts of modernism share what Michael Levenson has aptly termed 'forms of creative violence' (Levenson 1999: 2).

To take an example of 'creative violence' from one of the most radical methods of inquiry developed by twentieth-century philosophy, i.e. hermeneutics, in *The Beginning of Philosophy*, Hans-Georg Gadamer exercises a certain 'interpretive violence' against the famous passage from

A. Falcato (✉) · A. Cardiello
Institute of Philosophy of Nova (IFILNOVA),
New University of Lisbon, Lisbon, Portugal

© The Author(s) 2018
A. Falcato and A. Cardiello (eds.), *Philosophy in the Condition of Modernism*,
https://doi.org/10.1007/978-3-319-77078-9_1

1

Metaphysics A, where Aristotle discusses the methodological shift opened by the causal paradigm deployed by the Presocratics, referring to Thales as the first philosopher to propose an entirely new explanatory tool to account for the origins of the universe. Gadamer writes:

> Basically, our discussion is trying to show that we are standing here at the origin of doxography. [...] For example, when Aristotle begins to speak in the *Metaphysics* of the first conception of cause and says that Thales proposed this and that Thales was the first thinker who did *not simply recount myths but also made use of evidence,*[1] then we must understand that by 'cause' he meant matter. (2000: 80)

Strictly speaking, Aristotle is not discussing the myths recounted by the poets and cosmologists whose work precedes the Milesians, but rather unfolding the specificity which comes from the attempt to explain the whole universe as stemming from a single cause. And yet, the hermeneutic freedom exercised by Gadamer himself will remind the attentive reader of the opposite theoretical hypothesis suggested by T.S. Eliot, who, when he reviewed Joyce's *Ulysses* for *The Dial* in November 1923, wrote the following:

> Mr. Joyce's parallel use of the Odyssey has a great importance. It has the importance of a scientific discovery. No one else has built a novel upon such a foundation before: it has never before been necessary. If [Ulysses] is not a novel, that is simply because the novel is a form which will no longer serve; it is because the novel, instead of being a form, was simply the expression of an age which had not sufficiently lost all form to feel the need of something stricter. [...] Instead of the narrative method, we may now use the mythical method.[2] (Eliot 1975: 178)

Comparing these two remarkable passages, we seem warranted to conclude that both the philosophical method and the modernist method represent radical breaks with a given tradition.[3] And at the same time, one can detect a form of arrogance in any attempt at categorization that speaks of *a* philosophical method alongside *a* modernist method. Regarding the latter, and in reference to the last excerpt quoted above, it is certainly worth bearing in mind that in this passage, Eliot is only reviewing *one* work from a vast list that scholars now consider the modernist canon. The cultural impact of *Ulysses* and its immediate standing as a hallmark of modernism certainly remains indisputable—just as Joyce had predicted—but equally indispensable to the constitution of something like a modernist canon are: *Mrs. Dalloway, To the Lighthouse, The Waste Land* and *The Cantos*. This observation about different forms of radical rupture, which do not ask to be systematized and ultimately cannot bear systematization, leads to a second strand of reflection on the intertwinement of modernism and philosophy, this time strictly derived from the field of philosophical criticism. In a book that is highly relevant to the present study, *Modernism and the Language of Philosophy* (2006), Anat Matar develops a historic-philosophical hypothesis for justifying the emergence of literary modernism in the last quarter of the nineteenth century, which she encapsulates in the following statement:

> I see modernism as emerging from a unity of two philosophical insights, which matured in the nineteenth-century. The growing awareness of the loss of (or, alternatively, liberation from) the transcendent, stabilizing factor that enabled realist metaphysics led to novel conceptions of philosophy and of language alike. (2006: 7)

Matar's methodology is strictly philosophical, and it aims at identifying, from within the evolution of modern philosophy itself, the conditions for the possibility of literary modernism as a radical artistic breakthrough. Besides making a conciliatory effort to bring together the analytic and the so-called continental traditions in philosophy, the author conceives of the anti-dogmatic obsession with language which typically characterizes modernist works as the logical consequence of a general disbelief in the existence of a metaphysical reality which transcends the subject and the very language she uses to describe the world as she perceives it. Matar does not content herself with diagnosis, however. A careful analysis draws her to the conclusion that the modernists replaced one dogmatism with another, by which she means that the most prestigious modernist artists swapped a linguistic for an essentialist form of dogmatism, whereas, she claims, only a thorough reflection on the ludic, performative and non-static character of human language can make room for a modernist overcoming of modernism.

A second—and arguably better-known—platform for dialogue between philosophy and modernism can be found in the texts of Stanley Cavell (cf. 1969, 1971) and is fundamentally indebted to both an assessment of the Wittgensteinian notion of 'criteria' and a highly original interdisciplinary borrowing of key concepts introduced by the American art critic Michael Fried, originally applied to the evolution of modern European painting.[4] Cavell discusses and refines these concepts, suggesting that they are instrumental in working out an unconventional mode of writing and practicing philosophy. In a crucial passage from 'A Matter of Meaning It', included in the volume *Must We Mean What We Say?*, Cavell writes the following about the philosophical puzzle facing modernist artist and modern art critics alike:

> The task of the modernist artist, as of the contemporary critic, is to find what it is his art finally depends upon; it doesn't matter that we haven't a priori criteria for defining a painting, what matters is that we realize that the criteria are something we must discover, discover in the continuity of painting itself. But my point now is that to discover this we need to discover what objects we accept as paintings, and why we so accept them. (2002: 219)

An implicit message in this proposal of a permanent upgrading of the standing *criteria* which allow a modern viewer to *recognize an artwork as such* concerns the fact that pretty much the same can happen to the philosophical text itself. Stanley Cavell's texts are systematic disruptions of the common understanding held by a philosophical community concerning what an essay or dissertation in the discipline can reasonably be. Thus, the dynamic that inheres in linguistic playfulness, and which according to Matar is the untrodden path that makes the de-dogmatization of modernism possible, finds in the work of Stanley Cavell a highly significant instantiation—and this at two distinct levels. On the one hand, as the above passage shows, he clearly refuses to accept formal criteria which would bind together all modern artworks; on the other hand, his prose embodies the very denial of criteria, as applied to philosophy, for which he stands when discussing modern art.

A further way to instantiate Matar's claims about the de-dogmatization of contemporary philosophy—a path she clearly doesn't take—was immediately pointed out when the book was first critically assessed. In a review of *Modernism and the Language of Philosophy*, published by *Notre Dame Philosophical Reviews*, Fabrice Pataut wrote the following: 'One fruitful way to open the dialogue Matar wishes to establish would be to consider acts of thought pertaining to the domain of fiction' (2006).

This clearly addresses Matar's failure to weigh the historical and conceptual relations between modernism and philosophy, but it is not a critique one could possibly level at Stanley Cavell's *oeuvre*, which includes books of essays and monographs that critically assess the works of writers like Shakespeare, Kierkegaard, Beckett, Thoreau, Emerson, Ibsen and J.M. Coetzee. And in ways that often run parallel to the Cavellian approach to the two fields of inquiry, the present book also fully addresses this demand for companionship between fiction and philosophical analysis.

Our aim is thus to provide a timely contribution to the vast debate between two traditionally rival disciplines—a debate that is already firmly rooted in much academic philosophy as it is currently practiced—and to make that re-gathering both explicit and self-conscious. Following the cry for novelty and rupture with the weary tradition of realism, which has defined modernism since its inception (and, in the case of contemporary philosophy, in a way that is further complicated by the presence of a split between *two traditions*), this book also challenges settled modes of writing and practicing philosophy and criticism. Acknowledging already-trodden paths that have this reconciliatory aim in mind, along with aspects that went amiss in such efforts and were rightfully pointed out—like Pataut's main critique of Matar's book—this volume not only incorporates a generous dialogue with poets and novelists but recognizes and adapts the general point that Michael Fried has been making for over forty years in the field of art criticism. For our present purposes, the key figure whose vital importance and standing presence neither philosophy nor criticism can justifiably ignore is the reader herself. Not, of course, in the trivial sense that 'the text is there to be read', but rather in the sophisticated and self-reflective sense that the text must find the means of acknowledging the reader's presence to it, from the inside.

Doing justice to recent critiques of the unnecessary technicality of philosophical vocabulary—a critique explicitly addressed to all authors who aspire to publish in the most prestigious scientific journals in the discipline—the essays collected here combine analytic rigour with the omission of needless technical jargon. The appeal to the critical, sharp eye of the reader begins with style itself, which imposes its own demands (which are far from being strictly cognitive). However, given the still-common use of technical jargon, validated as a scientific language, this book itself undertakes a *radical problematization* of the status of the typical academic essay, carried out via a creative dialogue with different artistic practices—a dialogue which is not meant to assimilate them, but rather to respect differences and individually assess them. As our reader shall see, in all the texts collected here, his or her role is confirmed from within the text itself—a form of interpellation which characterizes both modern art and the modern text. This happens via technical means which structurally oppose the very trick identified by Michael Fried as a crucial move in modern painting: the critical presence of the reader him- or herself is made explicit not through the *fiction of his absence* but rather by being *explicitly stated.*

More widely acknowledged in the chapter on dystopias of the self, this is, we believe, a structural feature of all the essays that make up this volume, and one which we view as a characteristic trait of every text that exists in the condition of modernism. Foregrounding the medium in which it exists, the text radically acknowledges the presence of its reader from within. Because this acknowledgement is in each case singular, *our* reader will find as many such strategies as the texts we gather in this collection.

Split into five major parts, this volume addresses the broad topics of 'Writing Philosophy', 'Language and Contents', 'Modern Topics', 'Historical Perspectives' and 'Dystopias of the Self'. Key conceptual problems which have preoccupied modernist writers and contemporary philosophers alike, including language, selfhood, solipsism, death and temporality, are explored in great detail with a view to disclosing how literary modernism bore the influence of traditional philosophy and how philosophy, now facing a new period of crisis, might incorporate certain technical lessons from twentieth-century modernism.

Besides providing the reader with new insights on modernist writers and their sometimes troubled relations with traditional philosophy, as well as contributing to a fresh, broad understanding of what writing philosophy can be, the papers we gather here also leave many unanswered questions at these two main thematic junctures, thus offering promising prospects for future comparative research between philosophy and the modernist movement in the arts.

The remainder of this introduction will discuss key aspects addressed by the essays in the order in which they appear in the volume and will consider how they provide new ground for thinking about these topics in the future.

Part I: Writing Philosophy

The volume opens with Michael Levenson's 'Habit, Labour, Need and Desire', an essay based on a public lecture given in 2014 at the Willson Center for Humanities and Arts at the University of Georgia. Levenson's overarching argument is meant to bridge what is certainly one of the most important conceptual keys for the late Sartre and his well-known attempt to bring together Marxism and Existentialism in the *Critique of Dialectical Reason*—namely the rich meaning implied in the idea of 'need' (*rareté*)—with its rebuttal by structuralists at the beginning of the 1960s. The article also considers the ontological space this debate may open for locating historically the creativity which the daily shaping of materials of life itself shares with the creation of a work of art. A rich interpretation of Freud's 'A Child is Being Beaten' is key to this turning away from the Sartrean paradigm, moving from lack to productivity. Despite using the term 'art' only twice in the 1919 essay—to refer to his patients' tendency to daydream and construe new sadomasochistic phantasies when reading *Uncle Tom's Cabin*—what Freud's interpretation does, Levenson claims, is to track the shaping and labouring of desire itself, thus showing not only that desire is not static but that, even when it follows habitual paths in daily life, it does so by reforming them. In the last part of the essay, Levenson briefly examines the relevance of Walter Benjamin's analytic shift, at the end of *The Work of Art in the Age of Mechanical Reproduction*, from cinema to architecture. Benjamin's remarkable feat in the closing chapter of the book is to show how, in architecture, *the optical apprehension* of the work is structurally inseparable from the habit of using buildings, and how the first can only be accomplished by what he terms a corresponding 'tactile appropriation'. Levenson concludes the essay by suggesting that the subjective axis of need and desire—but also of *habit*—incorporates an undisguisable creative pull alongside the pull of survival, to the extent that, in carrying the individual into the future, it takes him to the social sphere, where that progress is made possible. Interestingly, this move may be seen as landing us back onto Sartrean ground and the dialectical model in which *need* is presented as the fundamental drive impelling individuals to fight both the environment and other human agents.

The next chapter, Rupert Read's 'Wittgenstein as Unreliable Narrator/Unreliable Author', begins by tackling the famous paragraph 133 of the *Philosophical Investigations*, in which a supposedly non-essentialist philosophical method is put forth. Anchored in a resolute reading of Wittgenstein's philosophy, which consistently refuses to accept a strict division between the framework of the *Tractatus Logico-Philosophicus* and the one developed in the *Philosophical Investigations*, as well as the positing of a substantial category of non-sense in the first work, in this essay Read applies that very procedure to the temptation to substantialize the 'end of philosophy' thesis supposedly advanced in §133. What Read primarily argues is that a non-metaphysical interpretation of PI 133 does not undermine the resolute readers' fundamental stance on Wittgenstein's philosophy—on the contrary, it confirms it. What is at stake is not a commitment to an overall, positive method that would enable us to handle all philosophical problems, not least amongst them the very drive motivating us to philosophize in the first place. On the one hand, investing seriously in the pursuit of a method for solving all sorts of philosophical problems would be akin to standing for a metaphysical counterpart to the discovery of a logical calculus that would enable us to map out language and reality in a gapless manner. On the other hand, when it comes to Wittgenstein's comment in the famous passage from PI 133 to the effect that 'there is not *a* philosophical method, though there are indeed methods, like different therapies', to view him as *arguing for* an ultimate ground from which to solve all philosophical riddles is not only to commit him to a belief in the substantial character of such problems but furthermore, and in that very gesture, to continue the philosophical practice itself—which utterly contradicts a literal interpretation of the section in toto.

In the second part of the paper, and relying on the modernist notions of the 'unreliable narrator' and the 'unreliable author', Read briefly adapts the anti-substantialist proposal sketched above to an interpretation of such films as Resnais' *Hiroshima Mon Amour*, Bergman's *Persona*, Fincher's *Fight Club* and Nolan's *Memento*, which are here taken as Wittgensteinian 'objects of comparison'. The paper doesn't elaborate much on this last point, however, and considering Wittgenstein's professed fascination with American movies and, on his own account, the therapeutic role played by cinema in his philosophical obsessions, this is certainly worth pursuing in further research.

Part I closes with Ana Falcato's 'Embodied Ghosts: Coetzee's Realist Modernism', in which the polemic issue of conveying any genuine ethical idea in dry, academic prose is raised and discussed with an eye to a relatively recent dialogue between a group of Anglo-American philosophers and J.M. Coetzee's novelistic output. The essay focuses on Coetzee's book from 2007, *Diary of a Bad Year*, mostly because of the impressive strategy used by the writer for highlighting the writing process itself. It is first argued that the graphic page split introduced by the author serves various purposes and is far from being a mere stylistic whim. The next steps in the argument follow a highly stimulating interpretation of this formal strategy developed by Jonathan Lear, from which two main conclusions can be extracted: First, it is only by seemingly giving up on his well-known qualms about ascribing power and clearly positioning the voice of the narrator that Coetzee can emulate the expression of strong ethical commitments in fiction. However, it is his usual explicit mistrust of the supposed authority of the voice of the author that permits him to embed such views in a broader narrative universe that has been designed, among other things, to question their force and truth. All in all, it is Coetzee's aesthetic allegiance to some of the pioneering figures of high European modernism that gives him the tools to write a book that problematizes the merits of traditional normative ethical theorizing and the snobbishness of an opinionated form of journalism which aims at transmitting the ultimate truth about a globalized, fragmented world it has no means of accessing.

Part II: Language and Contents

Part II, 'Language and Contents', explores how linguistic formulations, in both the literary work and the philosophical essay, can gesture towards themselves when either imaginary plots and the lives of fictional characters are described or specific positions are argued for. Elaborating on the different ways in which the human mind can have access to a reality that transcends it, contributors to this section discuss how language can be made to accomplish this, either by being rendered transparent by authors, by being pointed out, or through a dynamic mixture of both strategies.

The fifth chapter, Garry Hagberg's 'The Medium Itself: Modernism in Art and Philosophy's Linguistic Self-Analysis', takes an approach to Modernist Art which concentrates on the different mediums used for representing a subject rather than on modernist topics per se. From a philosophical standpoint, Hagberg's hypothesis is inspired by Wittgenstein's late work, with special reference to his remark that 'language is itself the vehicle of thought' (*Philosophical Investigations*, §§ 329–330). The author opens his analysis with a thorough examination of the Private Language Argument, denouncing common misinterpretations of this odd puzzle, which was originally meant to highlight the publicity of language in a most unconventional linguistic framework. Already at the end of first section, after quoting paragraph 293 of the *Investigations* (where Wittgenstein decries the privacy of a language meant to account for sensations), and even before discussing specific modernist works of art, Hagberg suggests that Wittgenstein's complex argument can be read as replacing a Romantic linguistic paradigm with a modernist one. In the second and third sections of the paper, Hagberg develops insightful interpretations of modernist artworks, such as Matisse's *The Green Stripe* (*Portrait of Madame Matisse*), André

Derrain's *La Jettée à L'Estaque*, the Looshaus in Vienna, Schoenberg's Chamber Symphony No 1, Opus 9, and—of special interest to the Wittgensteinian interpretive framework deployed throughout the paper—Joseph Kosuth's *One and Three Chairs* (an iterable installation consisting of a chair, a photograph of that chair on each and every occasion it has been put on display, and a dictionary entry for the word 'Chair'). Hagberg suggests that these pieces fit the late Wittgenstein's understanding of human language remarkably well, not just because they leave the materials which make them up outwardly exposed, thus undermining any philosophical temptation to turn their meanings into irremediably private entities, but also because they can only be properly assessed in the context of a culture which either enables their production or is ready to welcome the challenge to traditional formal standards that they pose.

In Chapter 6, 'Encountering the Alien: Paul Bowles on Death and Madness at the Edge of the World', Tanja Staehler and Alexander Kozin venture a phenomenological analysis of Paul Bowles' *The Sheltering Sky*. Relying both on the conceptual schemata of traditional phenomenologists and on a more recent strand in the discipline, 'xenology'—a descriptive means of analysing the encounter between the alien world and the subjective, familiar world—Staehler and Kozin interpret both Bowles' literary piece and, briefly, Bernardo Bertolucci's adaptation of it to cinema in the 1990s, as portraying an entirely disturbing inter-subjective experience, whereby the self is alienated from its life-world by means of a dramatic cultural clash. The endpoint of this disturbing experience is not merely the deprivation of one's known life-world but radical self-mutation: the subject turns himself into an alien.

The first part of the essay expounds two classical phenomenological analyses of the experience of radical alterity, or alienness: first in Husserl's description of the radical obstacle that the alien [*Das Fremde*] poses to the constitution of a common cultural world, and then in Heidegger's interpretation of the dual and shifting nature of the Greek concepts of *aletheia*, *daimôn*, *Eros* and *Thanatos*. In the second half of the essay, Staehler and Kozin apply the main tenets of this descriptive method to a highly original reading of *The Sheltering Sky*. In the story of Kit, Port, Tunner and the Arabs they meet in Tangier, the alien presence intrudes upon the world-experience and shocked sensibility of the travellers (which Bowles forcefully distinguishes from the *tourists*) in such a self-erasing manner that the protagonist couple (Port and Kit) end up surrendering: to Death, to Love. When Port dies of typhoid, Kit leaves the corpse behind in the French barracks and escapes into the desert, where she joins a caravan and gives herself up to extremes of sensual pleasure. The last part of the novel, Staehler and Kozin claim, intimates that an utter surrender to the alienating power of Eros is self-fulfilling precisely to the extent that it is self-disruptive.

The phenomenological reading of Bowles' novel seems to lend more support to Heidegger's openness to what transcends the human than to Husserl's difficulties with the assimilation of the alien world into one's own. Two points are worth stressing, however: for an author as utterly unconcerned with the claims of subjectivity as Heidegger was, overcoming it cannot exactly be framed as a challenge; on the other hand, and as both Bowles' novel and Bertolucci's motion picture show in great detail, the price one pays for such self-transcendence is incredibly high. Finally, one point the essay doesn't tackle—mentioning the movie and Paul Bowles' participation in it only briefly in the first section—is the ultimate overpowering of Eros by Thanatos in Bertolucci's movie, with the intimation of a sky-ending experience and with Paul Bowles' voice itself closing the picture. This is certainly a good starting point for further research on xenology, as applied to different art media.

Alice Crary's 'Stories to Meditate On: Animals in Gaita's Narrative Philosophy' discusses Raimond Gaita's unusual conception of philosophy *as a vocation*—unusual within the contemporary academic mainstream, that is—and relates this understanding of what philosophy should be with his equally unorthodox stance toward academic animal rights movements. In several books and essays from the end of the 1990s onward, Gaita counters the criterial weight animal rights advocates ascribe to individual properties when determining the moral status of a creature, claiming that such a method leaves these supposedly radical ethical theorists with a view of the animals they claim to defend which is at least as distorted as the view of the human mind they openly endorse. Relying on a constitutively materialist understanding of the mind, mainstream animal rights campaigners forsake the subjective, live dimension of interaction with other human beings and animals and, tacitly or explicitly, advocate a method for ascertaining the relevant mental property, or set of properties, from a transcendent standpoint, making direct contact with the creature whose ethical status is under scrutiny redundant. Gaita dismisses this consequentialist and scientistic way of ascertaining the ethical status of any creature whatever mostly due to its phenomenological poverty, claiming that there are forms of judgement that, although 'undistorted by feeling', are not 'uninformed by feeling' (1998: 89). He—and Crary with him—counters this exteriorized model for ascribing mental properties with a certain reading of Wittgenstein's philosophy of mind, mostly developed by Peter Winch, according to which full ascription of mental states follows affective response—not vice versa. In the last part of the essay, Crary discusses a further point of Rai Gaita's philosophical project: his unstinted enthusiasm for fiction and personal life stories as narrative tools ethics cannot do without. These two features of Gaita's distinctive approach to ethics and to philosophy more broadly construed—a non-materialist, phenomenologically rich view of human and animal mental lives, and a narrative approach to ethics—are of course deeply intertwined. Not only is a rich narrative rendering of human and non-human ethically relevant experience better equipped to convey its more intricate details and complexities, but the liveliness of narrative prose is one of the most effective means of dislodging the assumption of an ethically inert presentation of human and non-human settings. Without openly stating it, both Gaita and Crary are challenging the self-proclaimed radicalism and moral courage of renowned animal-rights campaigners. When trying to set out decision procedures on the basis of fixed individual properties supposedly shared by all moral agents without taking into account their singular expression and direct enactment by individual actors in the moral realm, these activists run the risk of falling for a kind of categorizing prejudice which doesn't differ much, in form, from the *speciecist* prejudice they first levelled at meat-eaters and at those who subject non-human animals to all sorts of unfair treatment.

Part III: Modern Topics

Part III, 'Modern Topics', opens with Laura Lojo-Rodriguez' provocative text 'Thought in America and for the Americans: Victoria Ocampo, *Sur* and European Modernism', which presents and evaluates the mediating role played by the Argentine writer in implementing some of the main insights of European high modernism in South America during the inter-war period. Two intellectuals from the Old Continent—José Ortega y Gasset and Virginia Woolf—played the role of supporter and leading inspiration, respectively, while Waldo Frank provided Ocampo with a more integrative notion of America itself. In each section of the article, Lojo-Rodríguez explores the pluralistic and innovative character assumed by *Sur* since its first issue, printed in Buenos Aires on the first day of 1931 and boasting an editorial board with the likes of Jorge Luis Borges, María Rosa Oliver, Pierre Drieu de la Rochelle, Waldo Frank, and José Ortega y Gasset, among others. The intellectual stakes were doubtlessly high, and so was Ocampo's concern to use the modernistic spirit of the magazine to overcome certain intellectual prejudices still harboured by most of its male associates. One such prejudice was the public use of genres like the letter and the essay as means of establishing cross-cultural dialogue and imparting universal ideas. Funnily enough, the epistle would also serve Ocampo in denouncing the most deeply rooted Eurocentric prejudices which, in one way or another, inhabited the minds and informed the discourses of her most cherished spiritual mentors—like Virginia Woolf herself. In the last part of her essay, Lojo-Rodríguez significantly points out that it was actually in South America, not Europe, where the first leading woman intellectual—Victoria Ocampo—was elected member of a national academy of letters. Whether due to her own premature death or to a deeply entrenched set of intellectual and geographical prejudices, which most likely prevented the conscious acknowledgement of her place in the literary milieu of which she was the centre, this was a form of public recognition never bestowed on Virginia Woolf.

The next essay, by Katerina Kitsi-Mitakou—'"But She Loved Her Roses (Didn't That Help the Armenians?)": Resisting Facts, Inventing Forms, Negotiating History'—disputes the standardly accepted view on the animosity against philosophy generally harboured by the literary modernists. Her analysis focuses on two major novels by Virginia Woolf—*To the Lighthouse* and *Mrs. Dalloway*—and her central claim is that Woolf found a great deal of inspiration in such classic philosophical topics as the split between subject and object and the refutation of idealism. Specifically, in *To the Lighthouse*, not only is the idealism of Mr. Ramsay not ignored, but his own theories map out the difficult character construction that Woolf elaborates on in her essays, conferences, discussions and diaries. Kitsi-Mitakou examines at length how Woolf systematically explored the literary technique of the 'narrated monologue', through which a character's singular thought can be explored without using traditional dialogue. This technical device allowed her to develop kinds of narrators who, moving in and out of the mental universe of different characters, not only do not endorse individual experiences, but do not even allow the reader to imaginatively conceive of individual characters with concrete, first-personal thoughts.

The last part of the essay articulates the narrative pliancy allowed for by this very technique with the problematization, developed by Fredric Jameson, of the kind of Marxist historicism argued for by Benjamin and Luckács, here applied to the infamous Armenian Question (as it is confusedly alluded to in *Mrs. Dalloway*). In *The Political Unconscious*, Jameson argues that a form of social commitment is present in the rhetoric of modernism; that is to say, the historic-political dynamic is not overcome but *textualized*. The reference to Clarissa Dalloway's love of roses alongside a confused mention of the Armenian Question (*prima facie* interpretable as a sheer sign of aesthetic carelessness and irresponsibility) could well be interpreted, Kitsi-Mitakou claims, as the emergence of a political unconscious within Woolf's text. The articulation of the technique of 'narrated monologue' and the emergence of a political unconscious, linguistically deployed by the novel itself, is at least interpretable as a subliminal form of social compromise in Woolf's texts.

Next comes an essay by María José Gámez Fuentes and Rebeca Maseda García, 'Virginia Woolf and The Hours (Stephen Daldry, 2002): Virginia Woolf, Popular Culture and the Subject of Feminism', which discusses the importance of the contemporary debate on the place of women in post-modern culture. They propose a post-structuralist reading, split into five stages, of the 2002 movie *The Hours*, a piece where the Woolfian modernist conception of feminine subjectivity is re-enacted and which 'manages to re-signify old feminist struggles within new paradigms of identity politics via popular culture'. The movie, directed by Stephen Daldry, adapts the homonymous novel by Michael Cunningham and takes inspiration from Woolf's own life during the time when she was writing *Mrs. Dalloway*, narrating the story of how writing the novel impacted her life, as well as the (fictional) impact she had on two other women. Split by the parallel montage of three distinct narrative times, spanning three distinct historical moments, the lives of the three women are brought together in a single book.

The decision to divide the essay into five sections is itself key to Fuentes and García's theoretical proposal, inspired as it is by the kind of post-structuralism envisioned by Judith Butler as the best conceptual tool for tackling issues related to subjectivity, gender and sex. The separation of categories such as sex and gender is abandoned and replaced by an interactive model which enables us to think of both as a set of practices and discursive paradigms which empower given social strata while disempowering others.

Whereas the first section in the essay underlies the direct but problematic connection which can be drawn between post-modernism and different feminist paradigms, and which has been put forth by Craig Owens, Derrida and Alice Jardine, the remaining sections deal with a retrospective analysis of Daldry's movie and all the different ways in which any critical reading can detect in the film itself the workings of a creative process akin to Virginia Woolf's visionary genius. Backed up by solid arguments and a rich narrative texture, Fuentes and Garcia's essay deploys a complex set of relations, which allows them to first identify and then deconstruct problems of subjectivity, gender and social conditioning as they are faced by the central female characters of *The Hours*. They end up conferring on the movie itself the very status of a work 'beyond any bipolar categorization of modernism versus postmodernism'—a status also attributed to Virginia Woolf's oeuvre. For Fuentes and García, if a movie like *The Hours* can incorporate the post-modern renunciation of the single point of view while opting instead for the multiplicity of interpretations of what it means to be a woman, showcasing the performative possibilities of language itself and the vulnerability of gender in daily life, where the most intimate questions about the meaning of life, about crises of identity—not least of all, about sexual identity—generate anxiety rather than meaningful answers in a patriarchal society, this is because those very moves are part and parcel of a worldview we have inherited from Virginia Woolf and which the movie highlights with acute realism.

Part IV: Historical Perspectives

Part IV deals with the issue of historical perspectives, balancing the positive accomplishments in the realm of fiction with the often philosophical or critical frameworks which either incite them or provide feasible reconstructions of their rationale. In the first essay, 'Finance Capital and the Time of the Novel, or Money without Narrative Qualities', Mathias Nilges praises the highly sophisticated ways in which fiction over the last fifteen years or so, as against philosophical criticism, has provided us with effective imaginative solutions for the crisis of finance capitalism. A crucial passage in the paper bears the value of a theoretical diagnostic and follows a careful examination of Richard Sennett's views—as exposed in *The Culture of New Capitalism*—on the contradictory tensions which define contemporary society. Nilges writes: 'The result of the new capitalism […] is the inability to formulate narratives of the future, since the present is determined by "unstable energy" that does not allow for stable teleologies'. At the heart of this incapacity is what Nilges describes as the logic of the finance—or, better, the financialized—imagination. What defines the latter, he claims, is a structural incapacity to move into the future, to project unknown scenarios, and a tendency to instead stretch back into more manageable settings from a recoverable past, often surrounded by an aura of nostalgia. The problem, of course, is that this very course undermines the logic of finance capital. Nilges documents this short-circuiting of the logic of finance capital with many critical sources, ranging from the classic work of Bloch and Adorno, Fredric Jameson's critique of utopian thought in the 1990s, and more recent work by Paul Virilio, Bernard Stiegler and Jacques Rancière. At the end of the essay, Nilges sketches a possible way out of this imaginative failure. Borrowing a concept from Paul Ricoeur's *Time and Narrative*, expressed by a word he chose to leave in the German original—*Vergegenwaertlichen*—Nilges suggests that one possible way to overcome the contradictory impasse facing the financialized imagination is to consciously make present, in narrating it, the very episteme of finance capitalism, no matter how strange the latter turns out to be. Curiously enough—having referred to Don DeLillo's work at the beginning of the essay—Nilges does not at this point go back to the narrative method used in *Cosmopolis*, a method which precisely matches—often in a way that overwhelms the reader—this strategy of presentification. A thorough analysis of this novel, key to the topic of finance capital and the scarce imaginative paths this historical moment still allows us to take, certainly constitutes a worthy topic of future research.

In Chapter 12, 'Marianne Moore and the Logic of "Inner Sensuousness"', Charles Altieri links the impact of Moore's poetry on the reader's consciousness with the Hegelian notion of 'inner sensuousness' (or 'inner subjectivity'), presented in the *Lectures on Aesthetics*. Altieri's purpose in establishing this connection is to counter the main tenets of recent approaches to materialism, when these are applied not only to biological but also to sociological, environmental and cultural phenomena. In the first part of the essay, Altieri refers to a work by Diana Coole and Samantha Frost, titled *New Materialisms: Ontology, Agency and Politics*. Coole and Frost write about what is distinctive about new materialism: 'The prevailing ethos of new materialist ontology [...] avoids dualisms [...]. For materiality is always something more than "mere" matter: an excess, a force, vitality [...] that renders matter self-creative, productive' (8, 9). A sharp analysis of three poems by Marianne Moore—'Egyptian Pulled Glass Bottle', 'A Grave' and 'An Octopus'—leads Altieri to a conclusion that clashes structurally with the new materialists' view. In modernist poetry (specifically in Moore's Poetry), he claims, what the reader experiences is not sensual and material aspects displaying a spirituality of their own but the sensuous becoming itself *spiritualized*. Just like the reconciliation of Spirit with itself which, in Romantic art, internalizes the sensuality characteristic of Greek art without giving up on that moment of exteriority—which self-consciousness makes its own—modernist poetry has the means to explore highly sophisticated formal devices (which Altieri aptly terms 'retinal'), pointing consciousness toward the way out of them, toward its interiority. What Altieri's rich phenomenological analysis of Moore's poems shows is how, in the best modernist poetry, and even if through such spatial devices as rhythmic, syllabic composition or the uncommon design of stanzas, Thinking comes alive.

Michael D'Arcy's 'Intimidated Thought: The Novelistic Conditions of Modernism' discusses the conclusion of a recent book by C.D. Blanton (*Epic Negation: The Dialectical Poetics of Late Modernism*), in which the claim that any literary form concerned with totality could ever remain purely literary is countered. D'Arcy examines the scenario of modernism's absent totality and its philosophical background, calling, alongside Benjamin, for the linguistic reorientation of philosophy—that is to say, for a shift from 'the scenario of knowledge and its limitations, organized around the subject-object problem', to 'a linguistic scenario of reading, commentary and citation'. This linguistic reorientation of thought in twentieth-century Marxist literary theory constitutes the theoretical camp where D'Arcy analyses problems of narrative form and the dilemmas of reading they engender (according to Theodor Adorno). The chapter begins with a critical reassessment of Fredric Jameson's *The Antinomies of Realism*, where the Marxist political theorist, invoking Barthes' 'The Reality Effect', quotes the latter's observation that 'the irreconcilable divorce between intelligibility and experience, between meaning and existence, can be grasped as a fundamental feature of modernity'. It then turns to the work of Adorno, for whom the proliferation of description and digression works to supplement narrative discourse rather than to dissolve it. On the question of excessive detail or description, Adorno implicitly agrees with Lukács' point that such excess anticipates modernism. For D'Arcy, this involves a transformation of philosophy according to a linguistic orientation of thought, since philosophy itself is now reoriented as a practice of reading and reflecting on language. In short, the problem of knowledge is reconceived as one of reading and narrative form, and the excessive detail or description of proto-modernism is understood according to the ideal invoked by Adorno in 'Why Still Philosophy?'

The final chapter of Part IV, Jerónimo Pizarro's 'A Quotation from Seneca is Missing: About a So-Called Poem for Children', excavates the origins of one of the most misinterpreted poems Fernando Pessoa ever wrote. Composed in March 1935, only eight months before the poet's death, 'Liberty' was censured by the fascist Portuguese regime which had come to power the previous year. The poem circulated clandestinely in several literary circles until 1937, when its publication was finally allowed in the journal *Seara Nova*. Taking his interpretive cue from the famous triadic hermeneutic model which, for Umberto Eco, should constitute the springboard for all contemporary criticism—i.e. the author's intention, the intention of the text, and the intention of the reader—Pizarro construes an alternative reading of the piece, which he traces back to the compositional process itself. Particular emphasis is first laid on the choice made by different editors to include 'Liberty' in anthologies of poems and texts for children, due to the candour of its language and the apparent simplicity of its verse structure. What this straightforward reading leaves out, however, is the subtle political satire that Pessoa was drawing, the object of which was the emergent political scenario in Portugal at the time.

The enlightening contributions of two of Fernando Pessoa's most important political scholars—Luís Prista and José Barreto—are relied on by Pizarro in the presentation and justification of his more refined stance on the poem. Together, these authors make a double claim about this problematic late piece by Pessoa. On the one hand, they stress the need to keep sight of Pessoa's standing opposition to the historical-social context Portugal was facing at the time immediately before his death, and especially his deep antipathy towards António de Oliveira Salazar, the leader of the conservative regime. In private messages—and arguably also in the poem under analysis—Pessoa had already begun to oppose Salazar in the name of freedom of speech and the dignity of the human being. On the other hand, there is rich symbolism in certain stretches of the poem itself—mostly encrypted—but it is precisely from these passages that it is possible to extract proof of the direct link between the lyrical composition and the political and cultural events which are believed to be at the poem's origin.

The greatest merit of this essay lies in freeing Pessoa's late poetry from a host of false conjectures which had previously been imposed as the correct approach to Pessoa's work, both from a formal and from an intellectual point of view.

Part V: Dystopias of the Self

In the final part of the volume, we pay close attention to the way in which the subject of different forms of artistic representation can, in turn, be shaped and deformed by artistic experience itself, beginning with Stephen Mulhall's long essay on William Golding's *Darkness Visible*.

'The Well Is Not the World: William Golding's Sense of Reality in *Darkness Visible*' constitutes a dialectic *tour de force* with Golding's astonishing capacity to deploy a deep and troubled sense of reality in his novels, which in many ways overcomes the empirical force of reality itself. Formally, Mulhall relies once more on the basic tenets of a thesis he had previously defended about J.M. Coetzee's novels (cf. Mulhall 2009); this being an isolated article, however, he narrows down his analysis to the peculiarities of one specific piece written by Golding in 1979, from which he quotes extensively. His point of departure is an article by Barbara Everett, collected in *William Golding: The Man and his Books*, which highlights the *impenetrability* to criticism that is so typical of William Golding's novels, a feature about which Everett writes the following: 'The novels dissolve, on the one hand, into their own critique, which the interested can only re-echo; and on the other, they take the form of theory's opposite, an undiscussable whole world peculiarly substantial in itself, thingy and definitive' (Everett 1986). Although in complete agreement with Everett's reading of the main impact of the novel's prose upon its readers as 'thing-like', Mulhall wants to dispute the idea of an overall impenetrability to criticism. His positive claim about *Darkness Visible* itself and the possibility of critically assessing it is twofold. To the extent that Golding so successfully (and dramatically) portrays scenes of pure evil in his prose, he replicates it (the divide between represented reality and reality itself is blurred), and the critics who dare not assess it are perhaps responding to Golding's intimation that *writing evil multiplies it*—makes it visible, so to speak. At the same time, those critics might be taken to suggest that Golding shouldn't have written such a brutal masterpiece. On the other hand, Mulhall claims, criticism that dares to immerse itself in textual analysis, quoting from the novel and unearthing buried messages, again faces a double challenge. Not only does it fall prey to a mimetic threat similar to that faced by the writer, thus adding up to the visibility of evil to which Golding alludes, but it still risks, by revealing through literary commentary the undistinguishable nature of depicted evil and evil proper, neutralizing the latter by means of a critical artefact where their identity is affirmed. Both writer and critic seem to face a true moral quandary.

Mulhall's chapter suggests, but does not itself pursue, a further undeveloped avenue of research when it comes to this puzzling overlap between a literarily-engendered sense of reality and reality itself: a comparison between Golding's work and the work of J.M. Coetzee. The two novelists manage to blur the 'representative divide' explained above by relying on entirely different writing styles. Whereas Coetzee's prose is sober and minimalist, Golding uses highly dramatic, even exacerbated language. And yet, both convey experiences of dramatic evil which the reader must *live through* rather than imagine. What does this difference say about the paper's main thesis—i.e. that a sense of reality deployed in literary language can overcome reality itself? Does it constitute a powerful tool of literary language, independent of style and temperament? Or rather, is it that the heterogeneity of the historical and geographic conditions in which these two novelists were born and raised couldn't *but* result in their working in such different literary registers?

Continuing the theme of the reliability of depicted topics, Jonathan Gilmore's chapter explores one type of *tension*, which persists in modern theories of art, between a model of continuity with nature and another which underlies art's discontinuity with the natural realm. The notion of 'pictorial decorum' as an ultimate achievement of a depictive relation between subject and medium simultaneously opens up the possibility of conflict between the subject of a work of visual art and the way in which that subject is portrayed, as in cases where the subject does not warrant how it has been depicted, which are thus violations of decorum.

Gilmore gets his theoretical bearings from historical figures as diverse as Hegel, Flaubert, Nabokov, Collingwood, Wittgenstein and, of course, Horacio and his *Ars Poetica*. The author acknowledges and discusses three types of violation of pictorial decorum: (i) expressive failures; (ii) cognitive failures; and (iii) moral and political failures. Lack of expressive fit or expressive failure is defined as an inadequate deployment of style in relation to the depicted subject, the unfittingness of a flawed articulation of the subject, and the representative means with which the artist operates. This is mostly a matter of technical inadequacy. Cognitive failure, on the other hand, arises from a representation of the subject which motivates false beliefs about it or elicits inadequate responses. As with expressive failure, it demands of the spectator a preconception of the depicted subject itself, but the burden of proof here lies with the subject rather than the expressive device, which may distort its acknowledged intrinsic features. Finally, moral and political failure originates in a lack of agreement between the salient formal features of a work and a set of normative standards typically shared by those members of a community that make up its public. The determining pole for the diagnosis of this kind of inappropriateness of artistic depiction is thus the audience.

Gilmore admits that 'those different types of decorum—expressive, cognitive, moral or political—may be interdependent'. However, what he mostly has in mind is a single picture's simultaneously failing to properly convey its subject on expressive, cognitive and moral grounds (as when fifteenth-century European artists, having absorbed the highest standards of classical art, projected them onto unwarranted depictions of Christ, for example, and their failure was then diagnosed on different fronts). But perhaps one can trace another kind of articulation among the three modes of failure, e.g. a genetic model which justifies the more complex lack of fit on the basis of the less complex and thus views the cognitive failure as arising from the merely expressive one and political failures as originating in a judgement about the cognitive content of a depiction. Gilmore's broad stance toward the notion of pictorial decorum would itself warrant such an approach, since he understands failures of decorum as a function of the point and purpose of the artwork in question.

The closing chapter, Bartholomew Ryan's "'Navegar é preciso, viver não é preciso': The Interior, Impossible Journeys of Kierkegaard and

Fernando Pessoa", is a new contribution to a line of research initiated in the 1970s with the seminal work of Eduardo Lourenço, the main purpose of which has always been to establish an ideal dialogue between the thoughts of the Danish philosopher and the Portuguese poet. Opposing some leading ideas defended in previous studies on this topic, Ryan interprets, from a modernist standpoint, the relationship and possible influences between the works of Kierkegaard and Pessoa. In particular, Ryan focuses on the subject of the interior journey made by both thinkers, a journey consisting mainly in living 'more intensely, more widely and more turbulently than those who live externally' (Pessoa 2015: 373), of which their pseudonyms and heteronyms can be seen as the most concrete expression. The path taken by Kierkegaard and Pessoa on their inner journeys invariably traverses the abyss of human consciousness, finally leading to a disaggregation and subsequent reconfiguration of the self. Unfortunately, and as Ryan points out, such an enterprise is doomed to fail due to the ontological finitude both authors recognize in the subject itself. The structure of the paper, moreover, reflects this journey. In the first three sections, Ryan deals with the 'Imagination' and the influence that the epic adventures of the explorer Peter Wilhelm Lund and Portuguese sailors from the fifteenth and sixteenth centuries had on Kierkegaard and Pessoa, respectively. The two final sections are devoted to the tragic figures of Don Quixote, Faust and Hamlet, who experienced internal journeys with catastrophic consequences, amounting to existential shipwrecks. Ryan interprets these figures as literary and stylistic models whose impact on Kierkegaard's and Pessoa's work is evident.

Conclusion

What specific questions regarding philosophy and aesthetic modernism do the seventeen essays gathered in this volume address, and what possible avenues for future research does the book effectively open? At the outset of this introduction, we highlighted the fact that this project introduces two entirely original elements into the ongoing debate between philosophy and literary modernism. On the one hand, a rupture with a weary tradition of presenting philosophical questions and findings in a standardized essayistic form should find new ways of engaging the intellectual curiosity of the reader; on the other hand, it is suggested, such a move might be initiated by (re)drawing attention to concrete works of fiction. Careful examination of the most important ideas put forth in these seventeen essays have shown us that the two insights are indeed related. Philosophical discussions of works of fiction do challenge readers of philosophy, and by re-invoking the words of Stanley Cavell on the dilemmatic condition of the modern, we can understand why:

> The essential fact of (what I refer to as) the modern lies in the relation between the present practice of an enterprise and the history of that enterprise, in the fact that this relation has become problematic. [...] But 'the past' does not in this context refer simply to the historical past; it refers to one's own past, to what is past, or what has passed, within oneself. One could say that in a modernist situation 'past' loses its temporal accent and means anything 'not present'. Meaning what one says becomes a matter of making one's sense present to oneself. (2002: xviii)

The problem, in philosophy as in life, is that historical mental habits are extremely hard to break, and this systematic self-questioning of the discipline's foundations and standards of practice, by once again inviting to its forums a traditionally unwelcome guest, is already a test of the resilience of the normal reader of philosophy. Careful examination and critical assessment of the highly complex essays in this book has proved to us that there is perhaps no better way to make the philosophy reader's sense textually present to itself than by bringing to his attention once again what some of his most capable colleagues have to say about their archenemy.

Notes

1. My italics.
2. The contrast hereby established is purely illustrative; getting into the contextual details of Gadamer's and Eliot's meaning falls beyond the scope of the present introduction. However, a brief allusion to the

critical direction animating each remark seems appropriate. Gadamer's hermeneutic purpose is to establish a 're-appropriation' of the beginning of Western philosophy (and even Western culture), locating it in the works of Plato and Aristotle rather than the Presocratics, and the ultimate aim of his analysis is a genetic one. When Eliot refers to 'the mythical method' first deployed by Joyce, what he has in mind is the consummation, with *Ulysses*, of an utter dismantling of the socially-mimetic capacity of the novel as a genre.

3. Robert Pippin defines the latter, precisely because of its dissatisfaction with modernity, as a 'Culture of Rupture' (1999: 29).

4. It is first in *Absorption and Theatricality: Painting and Beholder in the Age of Diderot* (1980) that Fried develops a highly complex, dialectic account of the ever more sophisticated techniques French painters were almost compelled to use when the sheer presence of a beholder standing in front of the painting, admiring it, could no longer be taken for granted. Following Diderot, who in his writings on art from the 1750s and 1760s criticizes French theatre and the theatrical effect of representations made for the public in general, Fried will elaborate a hermeneutic model for French art produced in this period (mainly by Greuze and Chardin), according to which it is in scenes depicting characters that are deeply self-absorbed, and so seemingly oblivious to the presence of a beholder, that both presence and enthrallment by the latter are still attainable.

References

Cavell, S. 2002. *Must We Mean What We Say?* Cambridge: Cambridge University Press.

Eliot, T.S. 1975. *Selected Prosed of T.S. Eliot*, ed. and with an Introduction by Frank Kermode. New York: Harcourt.

Everett, B. 1986. Golding's Pity. In *William Golding: The Man and His Books*, ed. J. Carey. London: Faber and Faber.

Fried, M. 1980. *Absorption and Theatricality: Painting and Beholder in the Age of Diderot*. Berkeley: University of California Press.

Gadamer, H.-G. 2000. *The Beginning of Philosophy*. New York: Continuum.

Gaita, R. 1998. *A Common Humanity: Thinking About Love and Truth and Justice*. London: Routledge.

Levenson, M. (ed.). 1999. *The Cambridge Companion to Modernism*. Cambridge: Cambridge University Press.

Matar, A. 2006. *Modernism and the Language of Philosophy*. London and New York: Routledge.

Mulhall, S. 2009. *The Wounded Animal. J.M. Coetzee and the Difficulty of Reality in Literature and Philosophy*. Princeton, New Jersey: Princeton University Press.

Pataut, M. 2006. Review of 'Anat Matar, Modernism and the Language of Philosophy, Routledge, 2006'. In *Notre Dame Philosophical Reviews*. Web. 31 July, 2017.

Pessoa, F. 2015. *The Book of Disquiet*, trans. and ed. Richard Zenith. London: Penguin Books.

Pippin, R. 1999. *Modernism as a Philosophical Problem*. Oxford: Blackwell.

Part I

Writing Philosophy

2

Habit, Labour, Need and Desire

Michael Levenson

Habit is itself a term *habitual,* close to us, moving as regular currency, but obscure in its familiarity. We think we know what it *is* and *means.* And if we are modernists, or scholars of the modern, we instinctively regard habit as an enemy of the arts, of free play, of imaginative release. Spontaneity loses itself in the rhythm of repetition, the re-enactment of the same that puts consciousness to sleep.

This chapter is a reflection on a constellation of concepts, practices and experiences, under the heading of 'Habit, Labour, Need and Desire'. The effort is to make an effort: to try to open some central ideas to different lights and to new relations among themselves—and then to ask how these ideas might bear on our grasp of the work of art. Needless to say, this represents a conceptual net too vast for a single essay. But what's the point in travelling over distances, if you don't carry some heavy baggage? I am trying to find a way to get deeper, to ask harder

M. Levenson (✉)
University of Virginia, Charlottesville, USA
e-mail: michael.levenson@virginia.edu

© The Author(s) 2018
A. Falcato and A. Cardiello (eds.), *Philosophy in the Condition of Modernism,*
https://doi.org/10.1007/978-3-319-77078-9_2

questions of myself, and to open thought to view as I make the attempt. I like being vulnerable in public.

Modernism, as a culture of novelty, set itself against dead habit—*cliché*, formula. Russian Formalism of the 1920s gave it a classic statement. So, Viktor Shklovski identifies defamiliarization as the central principle of art, and in one aspect or another, this was the orthodoxy of Modernism. Only when we break the hard shell of routine will we glimpse the radiant world. Or in Shklovski's canonical terms:

> Habitualization devours works, clothes, furniture, one's wife, and the fear of war. "If the whole complex lives of many people go on unconsciously, then such lives are as if they had never been."[1] And art exists that one may recover the sensation of life; it exists to make one feel things, to make the stone stony. The purpose of art is to impart the sensation of things as they are perceived and not as they are known. The technique of art is to make objects 'unfamiliar,' to make forms difficult, to increase the difficulty and length of perception because the process of perception is an aesthetic end in itself and must be prolonged.[2]

Against this background, let us ask again: what does the habitual have to do with the aesthetic? This question generates other questions, and I mean to approach them through what may seem historical indirection, but what is, in fact, a main thoroughfare of my essay. The act of indirection is to look back fifty years—almost exactly fifty years, back to the moment of the early 1960s. This was when Jean-Paul Sartre published the *Critique of Dialectical Reason*—a work that offered itself as nothing less than a final synthesis in European Philosophy and a solution to the problem of history. The long introduction to the work was published separately under the title *Search for a Method*; it laid out the broadest frame of the *Critique*, namely and notoriously, to accommodate Marxism and Existentialism—or, still more ambitiously, Marxism, Psychoanalysis and Existentialism; to offer, that is, a theory of class, of the family, and of individual freedom. The *Critique* itself, in over a thousand pages of amphetamine-incited writing, remains one of the great under-read or never-read books of twentieth-century philosophy.

It occupies something of the place that *Finnegans Wake* occupies in modern literature. Namely: later. Not now, I'll read it later.

All of the work is formidable, all of it interesting. Here I want to explore only its beginning, which is where it is most formidable. In the 1950s, Sartre's career brought him from a theory of radical freedom toward the radical politics of Marxism. But the change wasn't a recanting or an abandonment. The ambitious aim in the *Critique of Dialectical Reason* is how to preserve subjectivity as a starting point and then to find a way beyond the self, toward others, and into History. How is it that individuals, thrown into the world one freedom at a time, can find their way into shared projects and relations? How do free individuals join together in purposive groups with an historical mission?

The first volume of the *Critique* appeared in 1960, and among its most attentive early readers was Claude Levi-Strauss, who had become the leading theorist of a new anthropology and had recently achieved his own prominence. Through the fifties, Levi-Strauss was engaged in a different act of synthesis: namely, the integration of linguistics and anthropology. The celebrated claim is that the structure of language mirrors the structure of social form, and that these deep ordering structures go beyond the reach of human will. It's a claim that interested Sartre, who devoted key pages in his *Critique* to reflections on the new structural anthropology and its bearing on his own project.

In the year 1961–1962, those fifty odd years ago, Levi-Strauss was preparing his next major text, *La Pensée Sauvage* (The Savage Mind). During the time he was composing the work, he was also leading a group of students through a year-long reading of Sartre's new book. The result of the seminar was the final chapter of *The Savage Mind*, a long relentless critique of the *Critique*, which challenged its deepest assumptions.

For Sartre, the beginning of the answer to the central question—how do individuals join with others, how do they develop a sense of social mission—was to deepen our understanding of *need*. This is our first condition, that we are creatures of need in a universe of scarcity. We lack, and so we need. We are driven to overcome our lack through a primal encounter with the world, the world of food, and water, and wood.

And because we depend on the materials of the world to satisfy our need, we come to know ourselves as material creatures—as well as free agents. Need is *where mind meets body*. So, as we struggle to survive, we come to recognize that our survival cannot be a set of isolated acts, grabbing this, eating that. Survival must be a project of mind and body—"project" being as central a concept as any in Sartre. To make a project of survival, writes Sartre, is to bring our various acts into a unity—our sensations, our encounter with the world, our breathing, our eating. We don't flail blindly. We come to understand 'hunger', for instance, as a name for basic needs, and we organize our sensations, concepts, and acts to avoid the perpetual threat of our hunger. We make a project of overcoming scarcity.

This is when we encounter the others, other human beings. We meet one another on the basis of need. The self finds that Others too are making projects of survival; their paths intersect with ours—they may be parents or siblings, or strangers—but we recognize that we have company in our struggle with lack. Further, as we discover others, other hungry human beings, we begin to live a past and a future, we enter the movement of history, we finally become conscious of its shape.

As Sartre clinchingly puts it, 'Everything is to be explained through need' (2004: 80). Need explains everything, because it sets in motion the passage from our individuality, our individual bodies and our separate freedoms, to our life with others, in the long historical project of settling accounts with scarcity—arriving, at last, at a time when we overcome the terrible limits of our need.

This becomes the first point of contention raised in *The Savage Mind*. What is this need, asks Levi-Strauss, that is supposed to lie at the root of our being and that is said to explain everything? In fact, he insists, you find something quite other in what he ironically names the Savage Mind—that is, the attitudes of the pre-modern peoples studied by anthropology. When you travel among those we should call 'prior', not 'primitive', what you discover is a life beyond, or before, need. Apart from our hunger and thirst stands the working of curiosity, the mere sheer fascination with the spectacle of the world's diversity, the thoughtful pondering of its textures and its tastes. Or, as Levi-Strauss puts it in a taut rebuttal to Sartre:

The universe is an object of thought at least as much as it is a means of satisfying needs. (1966: 3)

And: 'Animals and plants are not known as a result of their usefulness; they are deemed to be useful or interesting because they are first of all known' (1966: 9). The telling claim is that contemplation is as fundamental as interest. The satisfaction of recognizing structure is more basic than the power of need. Again, from *The Savage Mind*: 'Classifying, as opposed to not classifying, has a value of its own, whatever form the classification may take' (idem, ibidem).

To take this view is to strike at the root of Sartre's position—not only because it unsettles the priority of need, but also because it rejects the centrality of free individual consciousness on which Sartrean philosophy rests, on the grounds that: 'He who begins by steeping himself in the allegedly self-evident truths of introspection never emerges from them' (1966: 249).

There in 1961–1962 it erupted: the struggle of competing presuppositions: structure *or* consciousness, curiosity *or* need, classification *or* history. It was a deep conflict of assumptions and methods, and just as much, a conflict over the aims of a philosophical vocation, and the claims of politics. At an unsteady moment in the twentieth-century, when anti-colonialism, and especially Algeria, made questions of theory very practical—this is when lines of debate were refined and prepared and sharpened. But no sooner had it flared then it faded. What is striking about the episode is its depth and vehemence, and then its disappearance. We have had, in effect, a half century of forgetting. We forgot that we meant to struggle over the claims of consciousness and history, contemplation and need. The intellectual and practical reason of the twentieth century had arrived at a crux where differences had shown clear, and at just that moment, the conversation was deferred. Deferred because of *differance*—that is, because, or substantially because, a third term intervened between the contending couple and displaced their argument, until it seemed naïve, and then obsolete. Derrida was writing quietly when Sartre and Levi-Strauss were vying noisily. But in a very few years, certainly by the middle 1960s, the very terms articulated by Sartre and Levi-Strauss were under wide erasure.

The double force of deconstruction's emergence was to annul the privilege of consciousness and to confound the coherence of structure. The founding assumptions of both Sartre and Levi-Strauss were challenged and overturned—challenged and overturned through the virtuosity of Derrida and deconstruction.

This turn was critical, trenchant, and un-cancellable. But it had the effect of foreshortening the struggle between Sartre and Levi-Strauss, existential Marxism and structural anthropology, at the very moment of their most strenuous, telling and productive encounter. I propose that we see the conflict of the early 1960s as truncated, as leaving an unfinished legacy, deferred through the decades of deconstruction, and that it's for us now to resume the question—not because the individuals Sartre, Levi-Strauss, have a privilege, but because the struggle of concepts remains significant and deep.

I have cited the brisk assertion in Sartre's *Critique*: 'Everything is to be explained through need.' 'Need' is the striking cardinal term—striking because it has replaced 'desire' in the philosophy of Sartre, and in the tradition behind him. Why does he choose need? Why does he want it, desire it? Most clearly, I propose, because for Sartre, need forces us into struggle with the world. Need preserves us as historical beings with political responsibility, the responsibility to address the mortal threat of scarcity. Need is how we come to the world, one at a time, and then in groups and classes. It incites us to enter history.

Need—this is how Sartre comes to put it—brings labour into being. Experiencing the pain of scarcity, feeling hunger, thirst, cold, we recognize that our inner sensations require outer solution. Labour is this turn from inside to outside, from the feeling of inner lack to the material world that may relieve us. Labour is always to be oriented toward the world to come: beyond the scarcity of nature, beyond the dead hand of our past failures. Labour projects and organizes a world to reduce the pain of need. The meaning of labour, writes Sartre, 'is provided by an end', and therefore need is 'the lived revelation of a goal to aim at' (2004: 90). We will need, and will continue to labour out of need, until we come to full shared consciousness of the meaning of human history: the end of need. Then we can overcome and free ourselves from its cruelty. Until then, until we are free, we will never be satisfied. We will need, and need again, until we solve the problem of history.

Desire carries a different force, precisely the force of yearning that can sometimes be fulfilled, that aches when it cannot, but then glories when it can. If desire disappears from Sartre's work, it's because it fails to bear the promise of history. Desire risks trapping the individual within the repetitive apparatus of wanting and having, having and wanting again, without opening to the world beyond. Desire forgets that we live in a world of scarcity, which is what need always remembers.

Freud cannot be repressed any longer here; Freud as a doctor, not simply of desire, but of how desire lives in time, how it works us and we work it. I turn here to the under-appreciated essay with the shock-effect title: 'A Child is being beaten'. Freud takes that title from a recurrent phantasy reported to him by his patients—a phantasy that resolves into a single pattern of imagery, the beating of a child, an unknown child, usually a boy, beaten by an adult. The paper carries a more clinical sub-title: 'A Contribution to the Study of the Origin of Sexual Perversions'. As such, it attempts to recover the early phantasies that precede and explain the patients' obsessive return to a scene of violence. Freud distinguishes male and female patients and concentrates on the latter, setting out the problem of how the young girl gradually comes under the influence of the scenario. To put it in Freud's terms:

> By what path has the phantasy of strange and unknown boys being beaten (a phantasy which has by this time become sadistic) found its way into the permanent possession of the little girl's libidinal trends? (1919: 186)

A creepy and difficult question, with a surprising bearing on the subjects that concern us here. Freud goes in search of the origin of the beating phantasy which his patients have brought to therapy. Where does it come from? He responds by helping them recover a distant image of the patient's father beating another child, a rival for paternal affection, a brother or sister. The original image is then written in this form:

1. My father is beating the child (whom I hate).

In that first phase of phantasy, according to Freud, the violence satisfies the child's jealousy. The unconscious thought is: 'My father does not love this other child, *he loves only me*' (1919: 187). But *this thought*— which he describes as both sexual and sadistic—suffers the fate of all incestuous desires; it attracts guilt and it must undergo repression.

So, the phantasy changes, because, as Freud puts it, 'the sense of guilt can discover no punishment more severe' (1919: 189) than to reverse the original triumph over the rival. The initial phantasy is then re-scripted. Instead of the picture of the father beating another, now there is a new image:

2. I am being beaten by my father.

Freud notes that this phantasy has been repressed; it has remained unconscious for most of his patients; it only comes to the surface in therapy. Too much is at stake here in the mix of guilt and desire. So, the patient covers it over and turns it into yet another picture, the third:

3. A child is being beaten.

This is the image that gives the title of Freud's essay, and it is in these words that the patient is able to describe the troubling image and in these words that the scenario can become conscious. It's a safe version because the actors have lost their earlier identities. Now, as Freud puts it:

> The person beating is never the father, but is either left undetermined just as in the first phase, or turns in a characteristic way into a representative of the father, such as a teacher. The figure of the child who is producing the beating-phantasy no longer itself appears in it. In reply to pressing enquiries the patients only declare: 'I am probably looking on.' Instead of the one child that is being beaten, there are now a number of children present as a rule. (1919: 186)

Freud's concern in the essay is in getting back to the source, the repressed origins. My own interest lies in the other direction, the movement of desire and phantasy through time—the way desire transforms, showing itself not as static repetition but as continual adjustment and modification. The inner logic of our wishes moves us onward and outward, and as our phantasies evolve, as in this example, they take on a distinctive form that I describe in what follows.

But before I get there, let me remind my reader of the broader arc of the argument. We began with the claims of Sartre for the primacy of need. Need, in his view, as at the base of our subjective lives and as the force that drives us forwards and outwards. Again I quote: 'Everything is explained through need.' Need is what moves us from inner lack to outer labour, from our private lives into shared associations. It drives us into history, where we must struggle to solve the problem of scarcity—this as the mission of history.

Sartre, I said, resists the concept and experience of desire; because for him, desire throws us back on individuality; it takes us out of history. Desire, for Sartre, folds back on itself and lures us away from encounter with the world.

Freud, however, suggests a way to reinterpret the notion of desire on which he depends. 'A Child is being beaten' shows how desire changes, *re-forms*. It is striking in these examples, how the patients keep extending their phantasies into the social world—the world of schools, or hospitals, or teachers, nurses and doctors, and of many children, all being beaten by authorities. The phantasies grow out of all proportion.

We reach a point of approaching the work of art, as such. But before reaching it, we need one last context of inquiry, one that derives from Hegel in the *Phenomenology*, a sequence where he makes the crucial movement—no movement more crucial for Hegel—from desire to work:

> Desire has reserved to itself the pure negating of the object and thereby its unalloyed feeling of self. But that is the reason why this satisfaction is itself only a fleeting one, for it lacks the side of objectivity and permanence. Work, on the other hand, is desire held in check, fleetingness staved off; in other words, work forms and shapes the thing. (1996: 35)

So here, in the Hegelian version, desire negates the object, interested only in its own satisfaction. Desire uses and devours objects in the world, to achieve what Hegel calls the 'unalloyed feeling of self'. But it can't last, this satisfaction: it leaves nothing abiding in the world. Only labour can achieve this. Work checks desire, he says: it 'shapes the thing' and achieves permanence—something desire can never accomplish.

And yet Freud gives us a way to think otherwise. His careful charting of the logic of phantasy suggests that what's at stake is not the Hegelian contrast between work and desire, but rather the work of desire, desire *as never not at work*, as an ongoing making and re-making of the phantasies that populate our lives. This is what his poor patients have shown us. We don't simply have desires; we *re-mold* and re-make them, work them over, labour with our desires, until they change.

And tellingly, as he follows the turns of phantasy and desire, Freud stumbles upon the work of art. 'Art' receives just two passing mentions in the essay on beating. We are told, first, that as the patients left childhood, the effects of reading give new stimulus to their beating fantasies, especially the effect of reading such works as *Uncle Tom's Cabin*. At this point,

> the child began to compete with these works of fiction by producing his own phantasies and by constructing a wealth of situations and institutions, in which children were beaten... (1919: 180)

The second mention occurs when Freud records the elaborate day-dreaming that can take over the lives of his patients. He writes that they build 'an elaborate super-structure of day-dreams', extended stories, which, he writes, 'almost rose to the level of a work of art' (1919: 191).

Because Freud is interested in traveling back toward origins, the question of art is indifferent to him. But for me, it opens an important turn of thought. What I have been describing as the *labour of desire*—the working through and working over of our fantasies—reopens the question of the aesthetic and the artwork.

This is a point I want to press and also to re-frame by placing the art-work in new relation to habit—which I can do by summoning a well-known parable from Kafka:

Leopards break into the temple and drink to the dregs what is in the sacrificial pitchers; this is repeated over and over again; finally, it can be calculated in advance, and it becomes a part of the ceremony. (1969: 93)

This miniature tale is often used to illuminate the exhaustion of novelty—including the exhausted novelty of the Avant-Garde. A recent exhibition of contemporary sculpture went under the heading, 'Leopards in the Temple'. The text of the show's catalogue described Kafka's parable as disclosing the 'rapid sequence of repetition, exhaustion, and eventual incorporation', that became so familiar in the twentieth-century history of art: repetition, exhaustion, incorporation.

This is indeed the accepted way of reading Kafka's few lines and an accepted way of understanding the damage of habit. It aligns with the commentary in Pater with which I began—'Failure is to form habits'—and it appears notably in the work of Samuel Beckett. Here is Watt in Beckett's novel of that name, ruminating on his desire to see Mr. Knott, and his fear of so doing:

But as time, as time will, drew on, and Watt's period of service on the ground floor approached its term, then this wish and this fear, and so this sorrow and this gladness, like so many other wishes and fears, so many other sorrows and gladnesses, grew duller and duller and gradually ceased to be felt, at all. (2009: 124)

This is habit and repetition as the exhaustion of desire, the aging of the wish, the diminishment of feeling as such. The force of the image is clear. But if we think more closely about Kafka's miniature, then it is possible to see that even in its few lines, it suggests more than the absorption and exhaustion of novelty.

The intrusion of the leopards will be 'calculated in advance' and become 'part of the ceremony', but only 'Finally' (*Schliesslich*)—only after being 'repeated over and over again'. There is a span, a duration—who knows how long?—between the first shock and confusion and novelty, and the resettlement of habit. This is the space that the parable opens: not the simple arc from novelty into habit, but the rhythm of uncertainty: how much repetition before the (re)founding of ceremony? How many leopards before they enter the ritual?

What Freud's dark materials subtly disclose is that desire cannot simply work itself into a pure novelty, free from the clutch of habit. Desire unfolds and changes—takes on new objects, spreads into schools and hospitals—but desire also goes back to habit, returns to familiarity, touches the old scenarios, which it elaborates and re-figures. Even as phantasies twist and change in Freud's patients, they revive the old and early wishes, being beaten: one way or another. The going beyond comes out of the going back—which is to say that desire and habit are in perpetual transaction.

This, in fact, is what Beckett sees and says elsewhere, and what Gertrude Stein's career caresses and celebrates: that habit exhausts but also excites desire. Repetition is a dulling and corroding, but it is also a friction and a flaring. It numbs until it excites, and excites until it numbs. This is the rhythm of habit. And it's also a rhythm that lets us see how the art-work can at once summon infantile experience and also social practice. To think of the art-work alongside the experiences of need and desire, labour and habit, is to recognize the suspension and oscillation of art between regressive fantasies of childhood and engagement in the social field. To put it in these terms—the infantile and the social—is again to raise the question of history, personal and public history. It's a question that takes us back to Sartre and Levi-Strauss.

The vivid historical claim of the *Critique of Dialectical Reason* is that we live within the horizon opened by the French Revolution. Our needs have generated our labour, but only now can we understand that our task is to complete the history begun in France in 1789. For Sartre, that is, history in its full sense is only possible within the frame of modernity. A history which understands its basis in freedom must be a product of the self-consciousness achieved through both industry and modern philosophy. We do not begin as historical beings. Our ancestors knew no history. Only since 1789 has the project shown itself to us.

In the last chapter of *The Savage Mind*, Levi-Strauss responds with his strongest repudiation to these Sartrean propositions. He does so by asking what claim history itself has on our thinking, our self-understanding. What is this history that Sartre makes foundational? What does it mean?—and what does it mean, most especially, within the frame that anthropology can enlarge: the frame that includes the so-called Savage Mind, the pre-modern people, 'without history':

> what can one make of peoples "without history" when one has defined man in terms of … history. (1966: 258)

For Sartre, ours is a Modern History that no savage mind could understand or indeed live. What Sartre forgets, insists Levi-Strauss, is

> that each of the tens or hundreds of thousands of societies which have existed side by side in the world or succeeded one another since man's first appearance, has claimed that it contains the essence of all the meaning and dignity of which human life is capable... (1966: 249)

The lesson of anthropology is that even the most committed historical agent must admit

> that what he lives so completely and intensely is a myth—which will appear as such to men of a future century, and perhaps to himself a few years hence, and will no longer appear at all to men of a future millennium. (1966: 255)

The moment of 1961 opened this struggle between a Sartrean history of need-labour-revolution and a structuralist recasting of history as only one myth among countless others. This difference, I've said, belongs to a conflict that has been deferred these fifty years. But twenty-five years before those fifty, Walter Benjamin brought the problem into his own meditation on the work of art, without acknowledging that he was doing so. It's Benjamin who will lead us toward conclusion.

Benjamin, too, is a philosopher of habit. In reflecting on the work of art in the age of mechanical reproduction, he thinks about habit in terms of cinema and the cinema audience. He does so by challenging the polemic against film in the 1930s; namely, the charge that it splinters the attention of its audience: that its *pace*, its shock-effects, its *stimulation*, baffle the concentration, the absorption of the viewer. The cinematic audience is a distracted audience. But Benjamin's counter-polemic is to insist that in its distraction lies its force and promise. Here is the strong utterance:

> The distracted person, too, can form habits. More, the ability to master certain tasks in a state of distraction proves that their solution has become a matter of habit. (1968: 240)

The quick-changing attention in the cinema—the inability to fix the gaze on just one precious object—that is what modern life demands. Watching films teaches us how to live in modernity, how to create new habits for an accelerated world.

Benjamin's essay, it should be said, depends upon its own historical directedness. Like Sartre's, Benjamin's history moves forward—in this case, from the religious to the secular, from the physical to its virtual representation, from what he calls cult value to exhibition value, from the sacred shrine to the picture palace. The arrow of history points strongly in one direction: toward modernity, toward mechanical reproduction, toward the new habits we learn through film.

But one of the extraordinary aspects of the evergreen essay is a change at its very end. After probing thought about film, Benjamin—suddenly and uncannily—turns to architecture, and reflects on how the special power he had located in film—'reception in a state of distraction' (1968: 240)—also belongs to our experience of architecture. 'Architecture', he observes,

> has always represented the prototype of a work of art the reception of which is consummated by a collectivity in a state of distraction. The laws of its reception are most instructive. Buildings have been man's companions since primeval times. Many art forms have developed and perished. Tragedy begins with the Greeks, is extinguished with them, and after centuries its 'rules' only are revived. The epic poem, which had its origin in the youth of nations, expires in Europe at the end of the Renaissance. Panel painting is a creation of the Middle Ages, and nothing guarantees its uninterrupted existence. But the human need for shelter is lasting.

Architecture has never been idle. Its history is more ancient than that of any other art, and its claim to being a living force has significance in every attempt to comprehend the relationship of the masses to art. (1968: 239–240)

In architecture, as in film, we are unable to absorb ourselves in one scene or to gaze with concentration upon one object. We move within and around a building; all senses are in play; we are distracted, but in a productive distraction that can teach new habits. Yet only think what has happened to the course of Benjamin's argument at this point. An essay whose focus had been on the promise of modern culture—*the promise of film to create new habits in distraction*—suddenly breaks the arrow of history. What film has lately achieved has always been present in architecture. Buildings cross time: from the primeval to the present. What can we make of this? How shall we read the sudden disregard of history and the leap across time to encounter the universal truth of architecture?

Notoriously, in the 'Contribution to the Critique of Political Economy', Marx raised the question of what the Greeks can have to do with us, Greek art, Greek epic. The difficulty, he writes:

…lies in understanding why they still constitute with us a source of aesthetic enjoyment and in certain respects prevail as the standard and model beyond attainment. (1986: 20)

To which he promptly gives the brief and notorious answer:

A man cannot become a child again unless he becomes childish. But does he not enjoy the artless ways of the child and must he not strive to reproduce its truth on a higher plane? Is not the character of every epoch revived perfectly true to nature in child nature? Why should the social childhood of mankind, where it had obtained its most beautiful development, not exert an eternal charm as an age that will never return? (1986: 20)

It's no part of my brief to defend the judgment—the aesthetic or the historical judgment—but I am concerned to make something of the insight. What remains striking and suggestive in the passage is just the intersection of individual life history (our lives one at a time) and a shared social history. Marx conjoins the two. The Greeks were children; we have grown; we glance back with sentimental nostalgia to an irrecoverable youth. Brought together here, the Greeks and the moderns—the individual and the world-historical—help us see how our imaginative life will always summon archaic wishes, early fantasies, ancient dreams, even as they *incite us to look outwards* and to work on the stubborn materials of the world.

We may grow past classical Greece, but we never outgrow the need/desire nexus that, like Benjamin's architecture, has been our companion from primeval times. In this respect, we are always the children of our own childhood, and are always leopards breaking into the temple. But also, and from the start, we are the ones calculating the intrusion, preparing to convert it to the habits of ceremony. As we labour over our desires, like Freud's patients we bring them into the social world, where all work is deposited. The work of art occupies the nervous point of convergence—how can we enjoy the Greeks?—where the historical and the trans-historical, the infantile and the social, cannot help but meet. To meet and to show without saying: I have desired thus before. Another has laboured as I labour here. My novelty has become a habit.

Notes

1. This is an entry in Tolstoy's *Diary*, from February 29, 1897.
2. Viktor Shklovsky, 'Art as Technique', in *Russian Formalist Criticism: Four Essays*, trans. Lee T. Lemon and Marion J. Reis, pp. 11–16. University of Nebraska Press, 1965.

References

Beckett, S. 2009. *Watt*. London: Faber and Faber.

Benjamin, W. 1968. The Work of Art in the Age of Mechanical Reproduction. In *Illuminations*, ed. Hannah Arendt, trans. Harry Zohn, 217–252. New York: Schocken Books.

Freud, S. 1919. 'A Child Is Being Beaten' A Contribution to the Study of the Origin of Sexual Perversions. *The Standard Edition of the Complete Psychological Works of Sigmund Freud,* vol. XVII (1917–1919), 175–204.

Hegel, G.W.F. 1996. *Hegel's Dialectic of Desire and Recognition: Texts and Commentary*, ed. John O'Neill. New York: State University of New York Press.

Kafka, F. 1969. *Parables and Paradoxes*. New York: Schocken Books.

Levi-Strauss, C. 1966. *The Savage Mind*. Chicago: University of Chicago Press.

Marx, K. 1986. Contribution to the Critique of Political Economy. In *Karl Marx: A Reader*, ed. John Elster. Cambridge: Cambridge University Press.

Sartre, J.-P. 2004. *Critique of Dialectical Reason*. London and New York: Verso.

Shklovsky, V. 1965. Art as Technique. In *Russian Formalist Criticism: Four Essays*, trans. Lee T. Lemon and Marion J. Reis. Lincoln: University of Nebraska Press.

3

Wittgenstein as Unreliable Narrator/Unreliable Author

Rupert Read

Summary

In Wittgenstein, philosophy comes to know itself. Throughout his career, and especially in his *Tractatus Logico-Philosophicus* and *Philosophical Investigations*, Wittgenstein was profoundly concerned with what we can loosely term[1] the 'conditions of possibility' of what philosophers sought to do—and (thus) of his own writing.

Examining, in particular, the famous section 133 of the *Investigations*, I will seek to elucidate Wittgenstein's extraordinary writing-stratagem. His writing has often been criticised as 'obscure'—this evinces a fundamental failure to understand the way Wittgenstein writes, especially in those works where he laboured for years over how to present them. In his two masterworks, Wittgenstein operates, in broadly Modernist terms, as an unreliable narrator, or rather, perhaps what William Golding (in *The Hot Gates*) calls an "unreliable author". (I will briefly

R. Read (✉)
University of East Anglia, Norwich Research Park, Norwich, UK
e-mail: r.read@uea.ac.uk

© The Author(s) 2018
A. Falcato and A. Cardiello (eds.), *Philosophy in the Condition of Modernism*,
https://doi.org/10.1007/978-3-319-77078-9_3

offer some cases from the cinema, to illustrate further the potentially 'therapeutic' (or, better 'liberatory') nature of such unreliability: *Memento, Persona,* and *Fight Club*.)

Wittgenstein seems to offer a theory to end all philosophical theories, in his early work. In his later work, he seems to offer a discovery to end all philosophical discoveries. Both appearances are subtly, deliberately, seriously delusive. And necessarily so: any strategem that does not involve such 'indirection' will tend to fall back into the very thing it criticises. If one wants to make it possible for philosophy to be written at all, after Kant and Frege, one needs to avoid hoisting oneself on one's own petard: but "...to end all..." style thinking endlessly self-hoists (as is patent in the fate of the Logical Positivists, for instance, who failed to understand Wittgenstein's stratagem).

I examine the well-known invocation of therapies and the discussion of 'the real discovery'—the one that allegedly enables one to stop philosophising—in 133. The translation of 133 is pondered, and a reading proposed wherein this passage certainly does not amount to any crude 'end of philosophy' thesis, and is rather profoundly manifestative of the kind of aspect to Wittgenstein's writing that Cavell has taught: i.e. 133 too turns out not to be a 'statement' of Wittgenstein's 'position', but a set of temptations that need careful work by one to avoid entrapment by.

Wittgenstein writes as he does, not out of a faddish desire to make it new, but out of a profound need to plough over the field of language. His aim is to get the reader to do the kind of work that he himself was painfully doing: to seek to free oneself from the endless pull of philosophical delusion and premature self-satisfaction.

Introduction: A Philosophy of Self-Reflection and Literary Experimentation

There is no philosopher more *self-aware* than Wittgenstein. He takes inspiration from the Delphic-Socratic injunction, "Know thyself", and his philosophy can be well understood as an endeavour to see philosophy *as* self-knowledge, and as knowledge of one's philosophical interlocutor.[2] His *Philosophical Investigations* opens by paying homage to Augustine, whose work Wittgenstein greatly admired, and the book can be well read as a 'confession' of long engagements with what turns out to be a latent desire to speak nonsense, on Wittgenstein's part. Wittgenstein was always first and foremost concerned to think about the *method*(s) of what he was doing (and to ponder how to enable others to understand it).

In this way, we might see Wittgenstein as a Modernist thinker.

Now, in other ways, Wittgenstein was profoundly anti-Modernist. Most notably, perhaps, in his abyssal critique of the narrative of 'progress'. (I have addressed this crucial and brilliant aspect of Wittgenstein's thought elsewhere,[3] and will not dwell on it here.) But in his conception of philosophy itself, and in his highly innovative literary mode(s), a genuine affinity can be discerned with the Modernism that was going on around Wittgenstein in his lifetime. It is this that is my primary concern in the present essay.

Wittgenstein's writing strategem is highly unusual. In one way it is incredibly simple and direct; in another, 'indirect' and peculiar. He seeks truthfully to tell of his own struggles to attain clarity. He expresses this by way principally of dialogues with others and with himself: "Nearly all of my writings are private conversations with myself. Things that I say to myself *tête-à-tête*.", he said, in 1948 (C&V, p. 77. Source: MS 137, p. 134. 26 December 1948). *By means of doing so, he hopes to engage the reader in the undertaking of a similar set of self-reflective and dialogical processes.*

Wittgenstein's writing, because of its highly unusual forms and organisation, is often claimed to be obscure. Many philosophers, including many of Wittgenstein's supposed followers, 'improve' it, extract 'theses' from it, and so forth.

This seems to me a failure. A failure to appreciate the reasons why Wittgenstein wrote as he did. A failure to follow him. Or at least: if these philosophers are right, then *Wittgenstein* was a failure. He wrote obscurely and inefficaciously. I prefer to take seriously the possibility that there were (good) *reasons* that Wittgenstein wrote as he did. The reasons already indicated above: that it was honest; that it could help a reader to avoid being taken in by the sometime-appearance of philosophy as the production of generalisations as if it were a sort of 'super-science' or of essentialisations as if it were 'meta-physics'; that, in short, it guarded against insufficiently reflective philosophy.

In what follows, I will home in on one moment in Wittgenstein's writing, *Philosophical Investigations*, section 133: A famous moment, in which he appears to entertain the drastic idea of ending philosophy altogether. I shall maintain instead that *the wording of 133 deliberately embodied a 'final' temptation: the fantasy of the ending of philosophy via one discovery.* And that it helps one to work through that temptation, to a sounder idea of the nature of philosophy, as Wittgenstein practiced it.

An 'Object of Comparison': Namely, *Objects of Comparison*

Let us look very briefly at the remarks that precede *PI* 133, which introduce a new concept in philosophical method: that of 'objects of comparison':

> 130. Our clear and simple language-games are not preliminary studies
> for a future regimentation of language – as it were, first approximations,
> ignoring friction and air resistance. Rather, the language-games
> stand there as *objects of comparison* which, through similarities
> and dissimilarities, are meant to throw light on features of our language.
> 131. For we can avoid unfairness or vacuity in our assertions only
> by presenting the model as what it is, as an object of comparison – as
> a sort of yardstick; not as a preconception to which reality *must*
> correspond.

With an object of comparison, one gains from the dialectic back and forth between the object and what one is comparing with it, what one is seeing via it, both in terms of dissimiliarities and similarities. (I have shown *how* this works at length elsewhere, for instance, in the Wittgensteinian work on the film *Memento* that Phil Hutchinson and I published in *Film as philosophy: essays on cinema after Wittgenstein and Cavell.* Protagonists/characters in philosophical films often function precisely as something like objects of comparison; one's journey of identification and disidentification with them is frequently a crucial part of the transformative work that such films undertake or facilitatively make available to the (serious) viewer.[4] We will recur to the example of films-as-philosophic 'objects of comparison' at greater length, including *Memento*, later in this chapter.)

In thinking *through* the object of comparison before one, one is, for Wittgenstein, encouraged constantly to be aware that one will likely exaggerate similarities at the expense of differences. Thus, as a corrective, one ought, if anything, to emphasize the differences over the similarities. This is a key way in which the 'object of comparison' object of comparison focuses *our* activity more healthily and effectively than the 'model' object of comparison (or certainly than the 'model' *model*); it underscores the profound difference between the scientific sensibility and 'our' (Wittgensteinian) philosophical sensibility. For modelling is focused primarily on the similarities, typically ignoring the dissimilarities (just in the way that Wittgenstein draws attention to in 130).

As Wittgenstein says in 131, we will be "unfair" if we fall away from the seeking after 'objects of comparison' into a seeking after 'models' in the usual sense of that word.[5] One will fail to be fair—to the phenomena; and in particular (more literally), to those who one might be disagreeing with—one will fail to have integrity, fail to be doing the right thing, if one does not give dissimilarities their due just as much as similarities. And one will almost invariably incline—this is at the root of the deep attraction of scientism—toward over-estimating the power of the similarities that inclined one in the first place toward the object of comparison one picked. As outlined in the *Blue Book*, pp. 18–19, where Wittgenstein suggests that a main source for...

> our craving for generality [is] our preoccupation with the method of science. I mean the method of reducing the explanation of natural phenomena to the smallest possible number of primitive natural laws; and, in mathematics, of unifying the treatment of different topics by using a generalization. Philosophers constantly see the method of science before their eyes, and are irresistibly tempted to ask and answer questions in the way

science does. This tendency is the real source of metaphysics, and leads the philosopher into complete darkness…

This is why we have, above all, to teach/learn/realise *differences*.[6] Philosophy essentially involves seeking to be just to what it is that one is oneself wanting to say and succeeding in saying, when one successfully says things—and to be just to others in just the same way.

This objects of comparison of which Wittgenstein speaks are introduced with the purpose of seeking to make (particular? all?) philosophical problems (completely!) disappear. Or so, at least, Wittgenstein now goes on to (seem to?) suggest.

Wittgenstein and the End of Philosophy?

In *PI* 133, Wittgenstein famously introduces[7] an object of comparison for philosophy itself: that of therapy. (Or rather: that of therapies. This is important: it reminds us that if we speak, as (following later Baker) I do, of "Wittgenstein's method" or of "our method", we must avoid being deluded into thinking that we are talking about one thing.)

Kelly Dean Jolley, a very acute reader of Wittgenstein, wrote an article some years ago offering a 'close reading' of section 133 of Wittgenstein's *Philosophical Investigations* (*PI*).[8] His article performed some useful services. For instance, it highlighted the connection of para. 109 with para. 133, and the precise ambiguity of the former. (Is (ordinary) language what bewitches us or what enables us to escape bewitchment? Surely both.) It also made a provocative and fairly compelling connection between Wittgenstein's remark in 133 that "…series of examples can be broken off…" and his methodology particularly as declared in the Preface to *PI* (viz: that his thoughts had to proceed from one to another *with* some breaks). Jolley's reading amounts to an accenting, in some detail, of how to respond to the widespread, problematic claim that Wittgenstein is an 'end-of-philosophy philosopher' by means of reinterpreting the passage in the *Investigations* that most plausibly may be read so as to make that claim.

Nevertheless, I wish to contend that Jolley missed one part of the heart ('the spirit') of section 133, on what desire or hope we may reasonably have for philosophy, and thus that he missed a signal element of Wittgenstein's conception of philosophy *throughout* his life's work, and failed to touch the heart of how 133 is not an end-of-philosophy proclamation.

In explaining this, I want to follow upon the ground-breaking work of Cora Diamond and James Conant,[9] writers who have most efficaciously shown how the *Tractatus* is best read as not as stating or exposing, or even gesturing, at profound, unutterable truths, but rather as *engaging* our *temptation(s)* to utter nonsense. But then what are we to make of the idea in 133 of "the discovery", and apparently of an end to philosophy. Does this idea suggest that this discovery at least is not itself a temptation to nonsense, but a sensical revealing of such temptations?:

> ...[T]he clarity that we are aiming at is certainly a *complete clarity*. But this just means that the philosophical problems should *completely* disappear.

> The real discovery is the one that makes me capable of breaking off philosophising when I want to.—The one that gives philosophy peace, so that it is no longer tormented by questions which bring *itself* in question.—But now we demonstrate a method by examples, and the series of examples can be broken off.—Problems are solved (difficulties eliminated), not a *single* Problem.

Now, Jolley claims that "Wittgenstein ...seems to have had an idea of what it would be like to have reached philosophy's end. Wittgenstein thought he could accomplish this feat simply by making what he called 'the *real* philosophical discovery.'" However, surprisingly, he leaves entirely open what "the real philosophical discovery" is, or could possibly be, only claiming that "...Wittgenstein did not think he had made the real philosophical discovery" (Jolley, pp. 327–328). But, not having been given an idea of what the *content* of such a discovery would be (as opposed to merely considering in the abstract its *role* in 'ending philosophy'), why ought we think that (according to Wittgenstein) there is, or could be, any such thing, any more than there is one singular philosophical problem?

The possibility opened up for us by Diamond, Cavell et al. is that even here, at what others have called the close of the 'chapter' of *PI* on Philosophy, Wittgenstein is still dealing with a logical temptation. That is: is it at all clear that the implied author of *PI* is counselling us unreservedly to aim at complete clarity (and so forth)? Might it not be rather that one's right aim can best—or even only—be realized by means of appreciating that a third way is possible, one that does not simply buy into the 'correct', 'conceptual clarificatory' mode of proceeding; even as it sees clearly the mythicalistic errors of interlocutorial voices that would counsel scientism (or even counsel deliberate unclarity)? For, after all, most of the preceding 50 sections, or more, clearly engage critically such *temptations* both away from *and toward* clarity, logic. Why not here too? That is to say, if we can agree that the "sublimity" and non-vagueness of logic, the "hidden essence" of language, the ideal of "crystalline purity"; …if we can agree that these conceptions are not allowed to masquerade as well-formed by the implied author of *PI,* even when they seem absolutely to *press* themselves upon one, should we not be similarly willing to entertain the thought that the conceptions of "*complete* clarity", of the complete disappearance of philosophical problems, of "the real discovery", even of "[giving] philosophy peace", may well themselves be similarly—thoroughly—problematic? As it were, the best that one can say for the content of *Jolley's* 133 is then that "we should yield to the temptation to use this picture, but then investigate how the *application* of the picture goes" (*PI* para. 374; and cf. para. 424).

To argue thus is not to be committed to a totalistically dialogical/dialectical model of *PI* in the sense of holding that there are no moments that we can provisionally identify as being closer to Wittgenstein's implied 'view' than any others. But this is *only* because, roughly speaking, the 'correct' voice *would* as it were be correct, would in all probability be Wittgenstein's view, were that all there is to it, were we still able simply to engage in old-fashioned philosophical debate with more or less substantively and definitively misguided interlocutors. (We might, riffing on a well-known turn of phrase of Cavell's, call this the "conditional correctness of the later Wittgenstein's philosophical position".)

The problem of course is, that once we have perhaps 'grasped' the nature of highly unconventional 'Modernist' method that Wittgenstein can best be read as essaying, then we go beyond this 'correct' view, too, and stop seeking for a philosophical position, *of whatever kind*. We must seek to understand 'where we already are': Cf. Wittgenstein, at p.10 of the revised edition of *C&V*:

> I might say: if the place I want to get to could be only reached by way of a ladder, I would give up trying to get there. For the place I really have to get to is a place I must already be at now. // Anything I might reach by climbing a ladder does not interest me.

We seek to understand what is "in plain view"—while appreciating that even terms such as these (can easily) exert a problematic *hold* on us, and at best serve, ultimately, to point up *their own* perniciousness along with that of the philosophical pictures they were seemingly designed directly to combat, or to help us overcome.

The *Real* [Philosophical?] Discovery

Let us back up a little. For it might be objected that there are conceivable candidates for the content of "the real philosophical discovery", which Jolley could have considered had he been so minded. And surely there are: there are the kinds of discoveries made by Russell, Gödel, 'the author of the *Tractatus*'. But these, Wittgenstein repudiated; according to the Diamondian reading (and it is mine too), the possibility of making fundamental philosophic discoveries was actually repudiated by Wittgenstein already *in the* Tractatus *itself*, by 6.53.

Perhaps "the real philosophical discovery" for Wittgenstein, might be something like how everyday language actually is? No. Something like that might be one idea animating classical 'Ordinary Language Philosophy'. But Wittgenstein steers carefully clear of such semi-sociolinguistics, throughout *PI* 1–133.

And even if somehow one *could* be usefully said to discover something like this, in philosophy, this would still not amount to there being such a thing as "the [singular] real philosophical discovery", only lots of little such 'discoveries'. And, in this connection, we should note that it is the dissolution of various particular confusions and problems that Wittgenstein mentions with approval toward the close of para. 133.[10]

Though even this, we should be very careful not to over-read. One of these little discoveries may work, for some people (at least one person),[11] for a while. We shouldn't bank on any more than that.[12]

Are there any candidates for "*the* real philosophical discovery" that Wittgenstein did *not* repudiate? Here is my central contention in a nutshell: that there is *no* indication in Wittgenstein's *oeuvre* that he thought the notion of *the* "real discovery" mentioned in 133 to be even sensical.

An Objection?

An objection might be made at this point: that a reading of *PI* after the fashion of Diamond et al. has not with completeness been given. This may be true. The work of Cavell, Diamond, Conant, Winch, Putnam, Minar, Guetti, Lugg, Hutchinson and my own work (and that of the later Baker; and of many more authors on *PI* who take these thinkers as their inspiration, in turn) is still in this sense 'incomplete'. That is, an interpretation (of) the *Investigations* in earnest, *in toto,* from such an angle, has still not yet been accomplished. (Whereas e.g. (Baker and) Hacker have, at least, given a very complete reading of the 'correct voice' beating down its interlocutor(s) throughout *PI*. They take about as far as one can the project of demonstrating the philosophical correctness and virtuosity of 'Wittgenstein's position'; only, in the process, they necessarily make Wittgenstein sound sometimes much like any other philosopher with theses to support and an over-arching position to argue for. Thus, as Hutchinson and I have set out in some detail elsewhere,[13] they fail to follow Wittgenstein.) The objection would then continue that, until such a reading has been given, we cannot know that the real philosophical discovery is not lurking somewhere in Wittgenstein's text.

But such an objection is unreasonable, by Wittgensteinian lights. I have in mind the repeated reminder (in *PI* and *On Certainty*) that the theoretical possibility of a doubt is not a doubt. The same goes for a hope—or for a problem with a reading. (Compare also Wittgenstein's thinking on the theoretical possibility of a hidden contradiction, in maths.) Just because there might conceivably be some way of reading 133, when a 'complete' reading of *PI* is allegedly available, which would amount to identifying 'the real philosophical discovery', is no reason to assume that such a discovery is in the offing. (This reply is especially so, given that a 'complete' 'reading' probably isn't available even in principle…For Wittgenstein *has* no '*position*'.)

Sure; there is more work to be done to form such an interpretation of ('the later') Wittgenstein; I am contributing a tiny piece of it here, even, and this book on Wittgenstein and modernism constitutes a little more of it. But what I hope *already* to have shown is this: that one of the passages in Wittgenstein's work that might appear most strongly to resist the Diamond/Cavell manner of availing oneself of Wittgenstein's philosophy can be read without difficulty as explicating or, better, exemplifying it. 133, I have suggested, *continues dramatically the dialectic of temptation and correctness* that characterises so much of the text of *PI*. There is nothing dogmatic about 133; it does not violate Wittgenstein's cautions against a would-be philosophical finality, on my reading of it.

Philosophy Bringing Itself into Question

One problem that may remain is this. Consider this moment in 133 again:

> "The real discovery is the one that makes me capable of stopping doing philosophy … [t]he one that gives philosophy peace, so that it is no longer tormented by questions which bring *itself* in question." If "the real discovery" is something we desire but that we should not assume that we *should* (simply) desire, then, despite the importance of Wittgenstein's remarks on the not-necessarily-problematic character of philosophising about philosophy (there being no need for a "second-order philosophy" (121)), there remains a sense in which Wittgenstein's later work must run the same risks as the *Tractatus* evidently ran: philosophy will always periodically be bringing itself in question.

But perhaps that is unavoidable. For note a key way in which Jolley's interpretation of 133 is dogmatic. Jolley speaks of "the real philosophical discovery". But the word "philosophical" here is a leap, an unnecessary—unwarranted—insertion into Wittgenstein's prose. Wittgenstein, in fact, speaks only of "the real discovery". (And a moment's reflection suggests a possible reason why: for if this discovery were *philosophical*, then, by virtue of itself, it arguably wouldn't quite amount to an ending of philosophy! Philosophy would be continued, by virtue of the very 'end of philosophy' move....)

"The real discovery is the one that enables me to break off philosophizing when I want to." This is palpably an image of liberation. One that takes one out of the sphere of philosophy. But we should be careful. We should be careful not to assume that such liberation is available in the way that we want it to be.[14] (Remember what we teach children that "I want!" doesn't get....)

Philosophy may be the subject that from time to time can't help bringing itself into question. And a discovery that isn't philosophical that could enable one to break off philosophising sounds desirable, and may well be possible sometimes. I think it is. (Such a discovery might be something like: being struck by the beauty of a person or a place, and finding peace in contemplation of them.) But the (/our) method(s), its series of examples, don't get broken off voluntaristically. Problems are solved/overcome when they are, if they are—and likely not forever. The price of philosophical freedom, on my understanding of Wittgenstein's authorship, is vigilance whenever needful, including at times when one thinks one is no longer in need. Sometimes, *especially* at those times...

A Healing Philosophy, *a* Philosophy of Healing

Let us return to where 133 then *leaves* us. The new Hacker and Schulte translation of the final sentence of 133 is helpful here[15]: "There is not a single philosophical method, though there are indeed methods, different therapies, as it were." This makes it clear that the comparison with therapies is non-accidental. These different methods of philosophy ARE—*as it were*—different therapies. That is what is being said here.

In its full directness—and qualifiedness. The therapy/medicine[16] object of comparison is worth taking seriously.

Wittgenstein *might* have said: "there are [different] methods [of philosophy], like different kinds of sport, or different ways of gardening". Wittgenstein described himself as a disciple of Freud; I think it hard to imagine himself describing himself as (say) a disciple of Donald Bradman, or of some famous gardener.[17] Evidently, the therapy analogy is chosen because of the deep parallels that can be drawn, for our purposes, between philosophy and therapy/ies. That is why Wittgenstein described himself as "a disciple of Freud" (see the Introduction to *Lectures and Conversations of Aesthetics, Psychology and Religious Belief*); and in that connection we might find another way in which it is intelligible to regard Wittgenstein as a Modernist thinker.[18]

Wittgenstein as Unreliable Author

We have seen, above, an instance of how Wittgenstein's writing works on one, and how one needs to find one's own way through it. I would generalise, roughly, in the following manner, from this: In his two masterworks, Wittgenstein operates as, in broadly Modernist terms, an unreliable narrator—or rather perhaps what William Golding (in *The Hot Gates*) calls an "unreliable author". Or even, in fact, both: for, as I shall briefly explain, Wittgenstein is an 'unreliable' author who writes 'unreliable' voices, including even—specifically—an 'unreliable' narrator.

For Wittgenstein, authorial strategy, as I have already indicated, is no accident, no 'obscurity'; it is a deliberate effort to seek to ensure that whatever the reader can do, one leaves to the reader.[19] It has sometimes been called 'therapeutic' (including by me),[20] and this is a useful object of comparison for it, as *PI* 130–133 indicate; better still, I now believe is the object of comparison of *liberation*: Wittgenstein fundamentally *frees* the reader (and himself) to find their own way, in philosophy. Wittgenstein 'forces' one to be free by imposing upon one a great discipline (this is no freedom of mere license of 'anything goes', no post-modern relativism): the discipline of having to *place* oneself in (relation to) his dialogues. Having to work through the manifold of temptations that are set before one, including 'ultimate' temptations such as the fantasy of an outright end to philosophy.

If Wittgenstein were a 'reliable' author, then all this would be short-circuited. The reader would seek to operate with *Philosophical Investigations* as if it were a textbook[21]; only a very poorly written one. And that is of course how, from Pole and Strawson to Hacker and Horwich, *PI* is most often treated; an absurd fate for the masterwork of a world-historical philosopher.

Thus a useful object of comparison for Wittgenstein that we can draw from Modernism is precisely that of the unreliable author. One who creates further voices, that themselves are not reliable: even the 'voice of correctness', as I discuss above, should not be mistaken for Wittgenstein's own. And even the 'narratorial' voice that Wittgenstein sometimes adds to that, especially in his 'meta-philosophising' (as in much of 133).[22] Rather, he is the totality of the voices; but simply to combine all the voices in which he speaks produces a hopeless mish-mash, a tissue of contradictions. The only way that totality can be properly *realized* is *in you*. Wittgenstein's 'unreliability' is the necessary condition for the reader's autonomy. And such autonomy, that freedom, in a thoroughly social, *post*-transcendental, true sense of it, is precisely what Wittgenstein's philosophising is *for*.

Some Filmic Objects of Comparison

I now briefly offer some cases from the cinema, to illustrate further the potentially 'therapeutic' (or, better 'liberatory') nature of such unreliability as outlined above: *Persona, Fight Club, and Memento*.

For Wittgenstein's concept of 'object of comparison' is, as I have already implied, a thoroughly promiscuous one, hardly a technical term. (This is itself part of Wittgenstein's deliberately non-scientific practice.) One can think of 'language-games' as being objects of comparison; but equally, of 'pictures', of 'perspicuous presentations'; or of Wittgenstein's book as a whole. One can think of (various) characters in films as being objects of comparison ('for example': for oneself); or the films as a whole.

Here are three cases, three films which offer some fruitful objects of comparison at various levels—for shedding light on Wittgenstein's own practice.

Bergman's *Persona* is crucially changed, in one's understanding of it, by thinking its final portion, in which one has to put into question what had seemed reliably narrated to the viewer: that this was the story of two women and their encounter. By the end of the film, another possible reading is demanding attention: that, rather than being a story of the therapy of an actress at the hands of a nurse, this might instead be a story of the therapy of a nurse who has projected a persona of an actress. In other words, *Persona* can be viewed as a drama of integration, of coming to terms with one's own tendency to alienate from oneself a part of oneself, and, in bad faith, to treat that part of oneself as another.

Such a take on *Persona* might be supported by a close look at another film of unreliable narration, *Fight Club*. The two films superficially have little in common, but *Fight Club* serves as an extraordinarily revealing object of comparison for *Persona;* it *reveals* the possible reading of it that I just sketched; it *develops* that possibility. *Fight Club* is, it turns out, a drama of integration. The violence at its centre, like the violence at the centre of *Persona*, may well be a blind route, or at most, merely a route to the coming to terms with the violence one has been doing to oneself. It turns out in *Fight Club* that the narrator has created another persona which is a projection of all he wishes to be. We *see* that projection ((as if) on a screen…); evoking the power of the (bad-faith) experience here. Thus the therapeutic journey to acknowledgement of reality, to *self*-knowledge, is as deep as it is dramatic.[23] The protagonist's reintegration into one self is the denouement of the film.

Finally, consider the Nolans' remarkable philosophical work, *Memento*.[24] Here, there is a still more direct comparison with Wittgenstein available. The narrator of *Memento*, Leonard Shelby, whose memory has been damaged by a traumatic physical injury inflicted on him in an emotionally-traumatic event in which his wife was murdered, is a kind of philosophical detective into his own life. He confesses a kind of anti-empiricist philosophy as he goes along, arguing that memory is unreliable. We experience reality with and through him—and come gradually to see that he is radically confused about his own life. I would argue that we also come to realise that this confusion might even be wilful on his part; for his own knowledge of his own memory-loss condition suggests a contradiction within that condition, and suggests that it must be a condition that in some sense he is imposing on himself. Perhaps because he doesn't want to remember. (Like in Wittgenstein: the deepest problems tend to be problems of will and willpower, not narrowly intellectual problems.)

Our desire to compare ourselves with Leonard, both in terms of similarities and in terms of differences, is thus a desire that the film increasingly interrogates as well as stimulates.

These films (and others like them: I'd make similar cases about *Hiroshima mon amour, Last year in Marienbad*, and other major Modernist film-texts[25]) could be *viewed* as forming a quasi-Wittgensteinian 'argument' against modelling and in favour of objects of comparison, with regard to cases in which modelling will crudify, reduce, and offer a false, cheap illusion of knowledge.

These three (very different but all fundamentally Modernist in style, in narration) films offer *various* kinds of possible objects of comparison with Wittgenstein: with his narratorial style and voices, with his authorship, with his method(s), with his critiques of Cognitivism and Empiricism, with his work as a whole. And there are various elements of these films which work in this way: one can compare the films with each other, with *Philosophical Investigations*; one can compare characters in them with oneself, with Wittgenstein; and so forth. There is a rich vein to mine here, through which to think of the benefits (as well as the burdens) of Modernistic 'unreliable narration' objects of comparison in a distinctively Wittgensteinian vein.

Conclusion: Beyond Modernism

Wittgenstein seems to offer a theory to end all philosophical theories, in his early work. In his later work, he seems to offer—to hold out, tantalisingly, in 133; to seem to place a claim to—a discovery to end all philosophical discoveries. Both appearances are subtly, deliberately, seriously delusive. And necessarily so: any strategem that does not involve such 'indirection' as Wittgenstein does, working *through* one's temptations to 'end it all', will tend to fall back into, or indeed to be consumed by, the very thing it actually seeks to criticise (including: the dangerous, essentialising tendency to make philosophy itself into one simple unified thing). If one wants to make it possible for philosophy to be written at all, after Kant and Nietzsche and Frege, one needs to avoid hoisting oneself on one's own petard: and "...to end all..." style thinking endlessly so self-hoists (as is patent in the self-consuming fate of the Logical Positivists, for instance, who patently failed to understand Wittgenstein's strategem, and were thus destroyed by their own Verification criterion).

Thus I have suggested that 133 involves at its heart a deliberate unreliability, a logical temptation.

It's notable that Wittgenstein in 91 warns against the tempting picture of a complete analysis of language. I think the 'real discovery', insofar as there is might be said to be any such thing at all as something more than a logical temptation, would include realizing that one can sometimes successfully address philosophical problems through the family of methods and approaches demonstrated in the *Investigations*. This vote of confidence might be called the 'real discovery' because it liberates us from the false ideal of (dependence upon) a 'complete analysis'.

133 is itself putting forward a kind of object of comparison with which to reflect on philosophical practice. I want to allow that Wittgenstein's development of his later approach is a real breakthrough that can take us past the see-sawing between dogmatic positions so characteristic of traditional philosophy—while not presenting it as self-satisfiedly leaving behind or allegedly-definitively-overcoming the kinds of questions concerning our practice that we always need to leave room for, if we are not to end up producing a new jargon or a new beam in our eye.

Wittgenstein writes as he does *not* out of a faddish desire to make it new, but out of a profound *need* to plough over the field of language. His aim is to get the reader to do the kind of work that he himself was painfully doing: to seek to free himself from the endless pull of philosophical delusion and of premature self-satisfaction. Including, about philosophy itself and what we can hope for from it.

Thus Wittgenstein might helpfully be said to be, in some respects, a Modernist author. And in other respects, beyond Modernism (or also, as I have noted, in certain respects, anti-Modernist). But, thus understood, what lies beyond Modernism is nothing like Post-Modernism. It is, rather, a call to freedom (from prejudice, from dogmas) and to the intellectual virtues.

It is a much harder call to heed. And a much more weighty one.

Envoi: Beyond Thought?

A last thought. If you are in agreement with my critique of the standard ways of taking *PI* 133, but unconvinced by my own reading of 133, my own way of casting of it as this radical move into and beyond modernism, then there is, it seems to me, one move still left open to you. And it may yet be a productive one.

If we think that there is anything left of the idea in 133 that there is a 'therapeutic' real discovery to be made that would put an end to the tormenting questions that philosophy catches itself in, then perhaps it is this: perhaps there is a sense in which Wittgenstein is inviting us to undertake a liberatory quest with some similarities to Buddhism (and, contemporarily, to that of Eckhart Tolle). Perhaps, that is, he is inviting us to wake up from the dream of thought. Perhaps no longer compulsively having to think at all is what it might yet mean, to be able to stop doing philosophy when one wants to.

Notes

1. Only loosely, because too literal an understanding of this phrase would be likely to pitch us into thinking that Wittgenstein was some kind of Kantian transcendental philosopher, which on my reading (as we shall see) he definitely is not.
2. See, James Conant's work on Kierkegaard on Wittgenstein, and his and Diamond's writings on the task laid down by Wittgenstein in

the *Tractatus*—that of understanding him, not his book (for: there is no such thing as literally understanding his book; for, 'understood' aright, it is *einfach Unsinn*). See also the later Baker's book *Wittgenstein's Method: Neglected Aspects* (henceforth *BWM*).

3. See my paper on Wittgenstein and progress, here: https://www.cambridge.org/core/journals/royal-institute-of-philosophy-supplements/article/wittgenstein-and-the-illusion-of-progress-on-real-politics-and-real-philosophy-in-a-world-of-technocracy/9FE76934F2B0A5071E-7AA7D65CB3D614.

4. See for instance my analysis of this process in Lars Von Trier's *Melancholia*: http://reframe.sussex.ac.uk/sequence/files/2012/12/SEQUENCE-1.2-2014-SEQUENCE-One.pdf.

5. A kind of seeking which, incidentally, is in my view widespread—for instance, one finds it in Ricoeur's influential hermeneutic 'model', (as) in his epochal article "The model of the text".
   Note that Wittgenstein has already prepared the ground for the questioning of this 'model' model, in 120: "In giving explanations I already have to use the language full-blown (not some sort of preparatory, provisional one)…".

6. There are many instances of the centrality of this teaching in *PI*: consider, as a couple of prime examples, 339 and 571.

7. I mean: it is the first time that this analogy is introduced in *PI*.

8. http://onlinelibrary.wiley.com/wol1/doi/10.1111/j.1467-9205.1993.tb00471.x/abstract.

9. See e.g. their articles in *The New Wittgenstein*.

10. Cf. here *Z* 447, which helps dissolve any remaining element of perplexity about *PI* 133, in this regard: "Disquiet in philosophy might be said to arise from looking at philosophy wrongly, seeing it wrong, namely as if it were divided into (infinite) longitudinal strips instead of into (finite) cross strips…So we try as it were to grasp the unlimited strips and complain that it cannot be done piecemeal. To be sure it cannot, if by a piece one means an infinite longitudinal strip. But it may well be done, if one means a cross-strip. – *But in that case we never get to the end of our work!*—*Of course not, for it has no end.*"

11. Cf. p. 37 of *BWM*: "Both the claim that the order [emphasised in 132] is purpose-specific and the acknowledgement of the possibility of different orders indicate that [Wittgenstein's] aim was to produce for each problem an order which would make *it* completely disappear, not to establish a single order which would make every problem disappear."

12. Compare p. 213 of *BWM*: "[Wittgenstein] targets 'philosophical problems', i.e. the particular disquiets of individuals which we call 'philosophical problems' (von Wright 1982, Band XI, p. 35). 'Our method' is *aimed* at getting philosophical problems to disappear completely—*in this sense of 'problem'*."

13. See e.g. www.jstor.org/stable/4619665 & https://www.academia.edu/207731/ Toward_a_perspicuous_presentaton_of_perspicuous_presentation.

14. Contrast J. Genova's reading of 133 (see http://philpapers.org/rec/ JUDAMO), which involves the almost-sophomoric exegesis of that paragraph as philosophically licensing one to stop philosophising when(ever) one pleases.

15. Especially helpful, in that these two scholars are no friends of the 'therapeutic' interpretation of Wittgenstein. Thus their translating this totemic passage of *PI* thus is perhaps doubly-significant.

16. See *PI* 254–255.

17. Perhaps "different martial arts" (suggested by Oskari Kuusela (personal communication)) would have been better; but, if so, then because it might actually have meant something significant for Wittgenstein to have compared his activity positively with that of Muhammed Ali, or Bruce Lee (though it is still hard to imagine him calling himself their 'disciple').

18. For more on this point, see my joint piece with Hutchinson on "Grammar", in Matar (ed.), *Understanding Wittgenstein, Understanding Modernism*.

19. "Whatever the reader can do too, leave to the reader." (*C&V*, p. 77. Source: MS 137, p. 134. 27 December, 1948).

20. See "Therapy", co-authored with Phil Hutchinson, in Jolley (ed.), *Wittgenstein: Key Concepts*. See also "A healing philosophy", immediately above.

21. See the Preface to the *Tractatus*.

22. For a more general justification of the claim that even Wittgenstein's 'narrator' is 'unreliable', and is not to be mistaken for Wittgenstein *simpliciter,* in *propria persona*, see my and Hutchinson's discussion of David Stern's interpretation, in our "Whose Wittgenstein?".

23. Perhaps the culminatory scene of it is quoted here: http://www.quotes. net/mquote/31796.

24. For a full-length reading, see my and Hutchinson's "*Memento*: A Philosophical Investigation".

25. And I *do* make such a case, in my *A Film-Philosophy of Ecology and Enlightenment*, forthcoming with Routledge.

References

Baker, Gordon. 2004. *Wittgenstein's Method: Neglected Aspects*, ed. Katherine Morris. Oxford: Blackwell (Abbreviated to BWM).

Cavell, Stanley. 1999. *The Claim of Reason*. New York: Oxford University Press.

Conant, James. 1995. Putting Two and Two Together: Kierkegaard, Wittgenstein and the Point of View for Their Work as Authors. In *Philosophy and the Grammar of Religious Belief*, ed. T. Tessin. Ipswich, MA: St. Merlans Press.

Diamond, Cora. 1991. *The Realistic Spirit*. Cambridge, MA: The MIT Press.

Genova, Judith. 1978. A Map of the Philosophical Investigations. *Philosophical Investigations* 1 (1): 41–56.

Jolley, Kelly Dean. 1993. Philosophical Investigations 133: Wittgenstein and the End of Philosophy. *Philosophical Investigations* 16 (4): 327–332.

McGilchrist, Iain. 2012. *The Master and His Emissary*. New Haven, CT: Yale University Press.

Read, Rupert. 2000. *The New Wittgenstein*, eds. Alice Crary and Rupert Read. London and New York: Routledge.

———. 2010. "Therapy", Co-Authored with Phil Hutchinson. In *Wittgenstein: Key Concepts*, ed. Jolley. Durham: Taylor & Francis Ltd.

———. 2012. *A Wittgensteinian Way With Paradox*. Plymouth, UK: Lexington Books.

———. 2014. An Allegory of a 'Therapeutic' Reading of a Film: Of Melancholia. *Sequence* 1 (2). Available at: http://reframe.sussex.ac.uk/sequence1/1-2-an-allegory-of-a-therapeutic-reading/.

———. 2016. Wittgenstein and the Illusion of 'Progress': On Real Politics and Real Philosophy in a World of Technocracy. *Royal Institute of Philosophy Supplement* 78: 265–284.

———. 2017. "Grammar", Co-Authored with Phil Hutchinson. In *Understanding Wittgenstein, Understanding Modernism*, ed. Matar. New York: Bloomsbury.

Sharrock, Wes, and Rupert Read. 2002. *Kuhn: Philosopher of Scientific Revolutions*. Cambridge: Polity Press.

von Wright, Georg Henrik. 1982. *Wittgenstein*. Minnesota: University of Minnesota Press.

Wittgenstein, Ludwig. 1969. *The Blue and Brown Books*. Oxford: Basil Blackwell.

———. 1975. *On Certainty*. Oxford: Wiley-Blackwell.

———. 1984. *Culture and Value*, trans. Peter Winch. Chicago: The University of Chicago Press.

———. 2001. *Tractatus Logico-Philosophicus*, trans. D.F. Pears and B.F. McGuinness. London: Routledge Classics.

———. 2009. *Philosophical Investigations*, 4th ed., trans. P.M.S. Hacker and Joachim Schulte. Oxford: Wiley-Blackwell.

———. 2017. *Zettel*, 2nd revised ed. California: University of California Press.

Filmography

Fight Club, dir. David Fincher, 1999.

Hiroshima mon amour, dir. Alain Resnais, 1959.

Memento, dir. Christopher Nolan, 2000.

Persona, dir. Ingmar Bergman, 1966.

4

Embodied Ghosts: Coetzee's Realist Modernism

Ana Falcato

Introduction

What is *ersatz* or substitution ethical thought? Roughly, one can say that it replaces the conveying and assimilation of genuine ethical thought—thought, that is, that promotes or facilitates the living of an ethical life. Jonathan Lear has argued that (genuine) ethical thought "cannot be captured by its subject matter".[1] But perhaps we can begin to identify it more clearly by considering the way in which its actual purpose can be significantly distorted. To see how, consider the following thought experiment, centered on the figure of a philosopher who is trying to put forth an ethical claim. Imagine that our philosopher wishes to convey a certain idea: namely, that the most important truths about human psychology can be neither communicated nor grasped by intellectual activity alone, since powerful emotions play an irreducible cognitive

A. Falcato (✉)
Institute of Philosophy of Nova (IFILNOVA),
New University of Lisbon, Lisbon, Portugal

© The Author(s) 2018
A. Falcato and A. Cardiello (eds.), *Philosophy in the Condition of Modernism*,
https://doi.org/10.1007/978-3-319-77078-9_4

role in self-understanding. If he states this view in a written form that expresses only intellectual activity and addresses itself exclusively to the reader's intellect—as is normally the case in most philosophical essays, the present one possibly included—we seem to face a dilemma: Does the author really believe what his words in fact state? How can he avoid the charge of inconsistency? The philosopher may believe that the psychological thesis itself is not among the truths that must be grasped through emotional activity. Or he may believe that the thesis is among those truths but remain indifferent as to whether or not the reader grasps it. Whatever the case, this example demonstrates how easily and intuitively the paradox arises. By contrast, a novelist aiming to convey the same idea can avoid the charge of inconsistency to the extent that he expresses its (merely) propositional content through the text's formal features—such that the relevant claim about self-knowledge is revealed to the reader precisely via formal devices that allow for emotional engagement. Such a writer can even directly display this conflict to the reader by incorporating philosophical discussion of the relevant paradox into a broader literary work that ultimately illuminates the inconsistencies associated with its purely intellectual expression taken in isolation.

In this paper, I argue that J.M. Coetzee succeeded in superseding this paradox (crucially, by addressing its tensions) in his 2007 novel, *Diary of a Bad Year*. My claim is that Coetzee accomplishes this via the introduction of a pseudonymous writer, JC, who writes a book of political-philosophical chronicles that clearly falls prey to the paradox of the psychological thesis—a trap whose logical tensions Coetzee, in fact, overcomes by moving in a literary space that moves beyond the essayistic and its typically assertoric stance. I will further argue that both the texture and style of Coetzee's literary prose and Coetzee's authority-divesting posture toward his status as celebrated novelist[2] contribute to stimulating genuine ethical thought in his readers. As we shall see, autonomy of thought is equally required when it comes to understanding the meaning and, more pressingly, the practical import of what Bernard Williams, after Plato,[3] called "Socrates' question": the question of how one should live.[4] The paradox of the promotion of ethical thought concerns the fact that, where such a question is thus articulated and answered in traditional philosophical discourse, the resulting ethical "command" in fact undermines the original practical aim. Finally, I shall argue in favour of the employment of Coetzean maneuvers, such as those found in *Diary*, as a means of undermining the conveying of substitution ethical thought when it comes to philosophical interpretation of Coetzee's novels—an approach that incorporates the above concerns as a central element of its own hermeneutic stance.

1

When *Diary of a Bad Year* was reviewed in the *New York Times*, the meaning of its jigsaw positioning of fiction alongside nonfiction, in line with similar devices used in some of Coetzee's previous novels, was explicitly highlighted. Kathryn Harrison assessed the importance of this maneuver along the following lines:

> *Diary of a Bad Year* is not the first among J. M. Coetzee's works of fiction to force readers to consider the friable boundary between fiction and nonfiction. *Elizabeth Costello* reveals its eponymous heroine, a literary celebrity, through a series of lectures given by Costello, their content familiar from essays published previously — by J. M. Coetzee [...]. *Diary of a Bad Year* forgoes the conceit of a perfunctorily named and differentiated alterego by following the late career of Señor C, who, like Coetzee, is a South African writer transplanted to Australia and the author of a novel titled *Waiting for the Barbarians*. "Authority [in fiction]", Señor C reminds his — Coetzee's — readers, is a construct judged by experts in critical theory (Roland Barthes, Michel Foucault) as little more than "a bagful of rhetorical tricks." *Diary of a Bad Year* would tend to support that thesis.[5]

Although it is true that Coetzee had previously introduced literary alter egos, this is the first of his novels where the voice of one such writer-character is distinguished—or indeed staged—*graphically*. In *Diary*, Coetzee employs an unusual formal technique: each page is divided into two or three separate sections, each representing a different character's perspective. This graphic layering of the book's page and its effect on how one actually approaches the act of reading the text works to destabilize the reader.

It is plausible to assume that Coetzee wanted to test his readers' aesthetic resilience, but it can just as well be argued that he had an ethical purpose in mind: to test the limits of our reading ability as a preliminary to assessing our response to what we read. Thus the top section of the page in *Diary* consists of a series of "opinion chronicles" (a collection titled *Strong Opinions*) by an experienced South African writer, JC. The middle layer of the page corresponds to JC's private voice and offers a raw account of his daily encounters with his Filipino typist, the young and beautiful Anya, who is assisting him in the composition of his collection, commissioned by a German publisher. The lower layer of the page corresponds to the private voices of both Anya and Alan (the latter is Anya's misogynistic partner). In the two lower layers of the text, the reader witnesses the extent to which JC is both tormented by his impending death and somehow comforted by daily contact with a beautiful woman. A first encounter with this novel brings the reader into contact with three private narrative voices, along with what initially reads as a fourth public, "technical" voice, represented by JC's ethical and political opinions. This multiple structure provides a modernistic framing for *Strong Opinions*. (I shall return to this idea in what follows.)

But the book's strange structure further matches a possible ethical aim on Coetzee's part: to somehow endorse the ethically and politically loaded views penned by JC in a way that *both* does justice to the importance of allowing readers to respond to stated moral views from a position of autonomous reasoning *and* avoids the self-contradictory move of stating this explicitly. This unusual rhetoric maneuver is all the more striking given the similarities between JC's views in *Strong Opinions* and Coetzee's similar (public) stances on the same range of topics, which those familiar with his work are sure to recognize.

Approaching the page vertically, we encounter in *Diary* various heteronomous views, held by the various narrative voices at play in what Lear called "a spectacle of embedding".[6] Consider, for example, the following:

> '[*On Democracy*] The main problem in the life of the state is the problem of succession: how to ensure that power will be passed from one set of hands to the next without a contest of arms. In comfortable times we

forget how terrible civil war is, how rapidly it descends into mindless slaughter. René Girard's fable of the warring twins is pertinent: the fewer the substantive differences between the two parties, the more bitter their mutual hatred. One recalls Daniel Defoe's comment on religious strife in England: that adherents of the national church would swear to their detestation of Papists and Popery not knowing whether the Pope was a man or a horse. [...]

All the while she was conveying this rather desultory information the air around us positively crackled with a current that could not have come from me, I do not exude currents any more, must therefore have come from her and been aimed at no one in particular, just released into the environment. Hospitality, she repeated, or else perhaps human resources, she had some experience in human resources (whatever those might be) too; and again the shadow of the ache passed over me, the ache I alluded to earlier, of a metaphysical or at least post-physical kind.'[7]

Questions about the relationship between stylistic devices—such as the split page—and the ethical ideas conveyed by a given novel can, of course, be situated within more general philosophical accounts of the impact of literary style (how a given position is articulated) on the statements being expressed.[8]

In this context, we encounter philosophers—many of whom mirror the history of tensions within their own discipline—who struggle theoretically with (what is apparently) the same issue. A classic example of philosophical reflection on the significance of the style-content dichotomy, both in literature and philosophy, is Martha Nussbaum's *Love's Knowledge* (1990), where emphasis is put upon the fact that the "ancient quarrel"[9] between poets and philosophers, formally acknowledged in Plato's *Republic* could only be termed "a quarrel" because it was about a single subject or intellectual territory: the question of how to live a good life and, simultaneously, of how different literary responses to it entailed different ethical priorities.

On deeper analysis, Nussbaum's claim reveals itself as twofold: both in the philosophical text or essay (where literary style, the way content is conveyed, is often sacrificed in favour of substantial theoretical claims) and in the literary piece (where concern with form can reach such heights that content becomes impenetrable—arguably more so when one turns to modernist projects), style is an "assertion of content" in itself. But, as shall be confirmed in what follows, Nussbaum is far from being alone in maintaining this position in the current philosophical landscape.

Because I have chosen to begin with a literary text, I will first concentrate on the second part of Nussbaum's claim and say that *Diary*'s prose, and in particular its formal structure, is a remarkable example of how the successful expression of propositional content is genuinely inseparable from matters of form. Coetzee's text reveals that "[literary] form is itself a statement, a content",[10] such that formal composition is really a means of asserting, of putting forward, propositional claims. But the content conveyed by the literary form of *Diary* isn't merely "rightly-shaped matter", a casually well-accomplished combination of compositional technique and the thought expressed by that literary framing. Rather, Coetzee manages to convey ethical thought by staging a direct simulation of ethical thought, precisely because this simulation is presented in a register very close to his own. The result of the simulation is a collection of opinions (JC's *Strong Opinions*) that is aesthetically maimed, theoretically convincing, and completely sterile, from a practical point of view—notions that will also be developed ahead in this essay.

At this point, two questions present themselves as interrelated: (1) what does it mean to argue that the structure of *Diary* conveys ethical thought? And (2) how does the novel do this without slipping into "*ersatz* ethical thought", precisely by staging a version of this kind of displacement?

Attention to the specific kind of storytelling at work in *Diary of a Bad Year* reveals a strategy for answering questions (1) and (2). If conveying ethical thought via writing involves providing some kind of practical guidance as to how one should live, as well as guidance on how to read the text in question and appreciate its message, then we can say that *Diary* does both by incorporating a vision of how one can fail in both regards, i.e. by calling the reader's attention to how the expression of genuine ethical thought in such a text can slip easily into the communication of *ersatz* ethical thought, and by isolating and thus revealing a layer of interpretation—a way of reading the text—that is both tempting and inadequate. *Ersatz* ethical thought is, as we've seen, the mere simulation of ethical thought—a substitution for genuine ethical thought, which, although intellectually graspable, does not actually make a practical difference in terms of how we shape the world and act upon it. As Coetzee seems to imply, this is the form of thought expressed in *Strong Opinions* and in JC's stance towards his book and its readership.

With this brief sketch of the problem at hand, we can now begin to turn to another question raised by Coetzee's method in *Diary*: how can a text convey genuine ethical thought as opposed to mere *ersatz* ethical thought? Is this at all possible? We shall see more clearly how, in *Diary of a Bad Year*, Coetzee's answer to this question hinges on the triadic structure of the page and our confrontation with the book within the book, i.e. *Strong Opinions*, situated as it is within *Diary*.

2

The rhetorical strategy at work in *Diary*, which allows Coetzee to show, in different ways, the need for an autonomous ethical response by the ethical agent (and, equally important, for an autonomous stance on the part of the reader) is multifarious and thus difficult to systematize. In *Diary*, as in many of his previous novels, the literary maneuver of de-authorizing the commanding voice of the author has been strongly associated[11] with the apathetic character of Coetzee's narrators and the soberness of his realistic prose, both crucially framed by identity-puzzles that occur on various levels within the plot—all of which lends a self-reflecting modernist flavour to the apparently linear flow of the narrative. And these puzzles are, again, multifarious. For instance, it may be tempting to identify the author of *Strong Opinions* with the author of *Diary of a Bad Year*. The ostensibly straightforward identification of JC with John Coetzee is only partially accurate, however, and more must be said on this point. In truth, the connection between JC and John Coetzee has highly elusive—and not merely stylistic—implications; it is no mere curiosity, reducible to self-indulgent vanity on Coetzee's part. Indeed, the temptation to merge their identities is a result of our having succumbed, in part, to *ersatz* ethical thought.

JC is an elderly South African writer, who has recently relocated to Australia. When asked by a German publisher, he agrees to record his opinions on some of the most pressing issues of global society (terrorism, ethnic conflicts, global warming, animal rights, genetic experiments) in a collection of essays. As JC confesses, the prospect is a welcome one: "An opportunity to grumble in public, an opportunity to take magic revenge on the world for declining to conform to my fantasies: how could I refuse?" (Coetzee 2008: 33).

Although it is tempting for readers to conflate JC and John Coetzee, there is something that sets the two apart unmistakably. JC is willing to publish his strong opinions on contemporary social issues just as they stand (parched theoretical fruits from a stage of life of decreasing vitality). John Coetzee is not willing to do so. The latter published his strong opinions alongside "soft opinions": a "Second Diary" of intimate notes on the everyday life of a man sinking steadily toward decrepitude—some erotic, but most representing an almost always dull routine involving a series of nuisances. This "Second Diary", we've seen, is the text that occupies the lower layers of *Diary*'s pages. John Coetzee tells us about JC, and it is only in doing so that he gives us access to his opinion essays.

The formal technique employed by Coetzee in *Diary of a Bad Year* can be interpreted as a rhetorical maneuver that confronts the reader with a challenge (a difficulty, one might say) and thereby manages to convey disparate contents, graspable only by "different parts of the soul". The book *Strong Opinions* is embedded in *Diary of a Bad Year*; were it published in isolation, it would require a different kind of focus from that which the reader brings to the latter. The disparity between the type of content articulated at the top of the page in *Strong Opinions*, on the one hand, and JC's, Anya's and Alan's notes on daily life, on the other, is sufficiently striking to induce a conflict for the reader, particularly when it comes to how she ought to assimilate what she reads.

Were we to read JC's *Strong Opinions* on its own, approaching the broader work in which it is situated only horizontally, as it were, we would encounter a space of argumentation. JC's book, which John Coetzee didn't give us separately, addresses the rational part of the soul almost exclusively. This approach relies on an affinity between sender and receiver, insofar as the rational part of JC's soul addresses the rational part of the reader's soul. (Obviously, this is an oversimplification; it is useful, however, when it comes to the issue of methodology in interpreting *Diary* and Coetzee's therapeutic role as writer and creator of JC.)

If we instead adopt a vertical reading of the pages of *Diary of a Bad Year*, we come across Lear's "spectacle of embedding". Relying on the plasticity of this expression, Lear describes the heart of the connection between the book's page structure and Coetzee's handling of the stories of his main characters: if we read the book vertically, we see how the compilation of JC's "strong opinions" is embedded in the presentation of the fantasies and daily lives of the three main characters. As we read down the page, we also move further into the lower part of the soul (and even to the presentation of lower parts of the body: Anya's body, JC's body and Alan's body). This "inferior" display of aspects of daily life is the separable (because useless) part of a book of "strong opinions" on contemporary social and political issues from an ethical perspective. But it is not separable from the realist modernist book that Coetzee offers us. *Strong Opinions* is thus a realistic (pseudo) book written in the form and under the influence of argument, but this form is only one aspect of the organic unity of form and matter embodied by JC's collection, embedded as it is in the episodes that make up his daily life. JC's authority as a character influences the fundamental structure of *Diary*; Coetzee has us actually read *Strong Opinions* and does not merely tell us about the process of its composition (which, were it so, would detract considerably from the novel's effectiveness).

We must still examine in more detail and finally move beyond the more or less methodological and associative elements discussed until now if we want to make clear how embedding JC's strong moral opinions in descriptions of his private daily life prevents the mere communication of substitute ethical thought and instead promotes authentic ethical thought through the text's destabilizing form. To do so, I will proceed as follows: (a) I will examine how the compositional form of *Diary of a Bad Year* precludes what I have been calling *ersatz* ethical thought by incorporating a simulation of this type of thought; and (b) I will analyze one of the opinions in *Strong Opinions*, as a "case study" of sorts, in order to obtain confirmation of (a).

3

When narrating first-hand experiences of barbaric situations, John Coetzee's tone tends to be unsettlingly apathetic. Yet, as we shall see, it is precisely this narrative style that provides an antidote to any conceivable form of substitute ethical thought. *Diary* portrays something that is itself an ethical issue—the intrusion of forms of *ersatz* ethical thought into a literary work that aims to convey ethical content. Mostly by way of the inclusion of *Strong Opinions*, Coetzee's technique allows him to show how difficult it is for a literary text—one meant to convey ethical thought—to avoid becoming a vehicle for ersatz ethical thought (such as an opinion chronicle, for example). JC falls into this very trap, and he is "a prestigious South African writer". What guarantee do we have that Coetzee will not do the same?

Coetzee's body of work as a whole incorporates a heavily self-referential component, which he has refined in his later books by means of some highly sophisticated rhetorical strategies. In addition to *Diary*, we find a remarkable self-referential strategy in *Summertime* (2009), where the author employs another technique to replace substitution ethical thought. Whereas the technique for preventing *ersatz* ethical thought in *Diary* is mostly based on the triadic narrative voice—with the nuances and degrees of formality I have analysed thus far—the relevant technique in *Summertime* is its *post-mortem* structure. The writer John Coetzee has recently died, and the whole book, whose starting point is this very fact, is a collection of personal accounts of his life, as related by different narrators (including a former lover, a neighbour, and the mother of a former student in Cape Town).

Insofar as the (potentially dangerous) self-referential literary techniques vastly and variously employed in his books are one of Coetzee's assets in defeating *ersatz* ethical thought, and insofar as defeating it matters at least as much to us as finding out how such a defeat might be accomplished, in both literature and philosophy, I shall concentrate on the details of these techniques in Coetzee's novels, later applying the results to my own philosophical inquiries. Having already explored one such maneuver—the complex overlapping of the personal identities of Coetzee and JC—we shall now turn to another: JC's commitment to specific political views that are easily attributable to publicly assumed views of its creator, novelist J.M. Coetzee.

4

In the "spectacle of embedding" that is *Diary of a Bad Year*, a reflection entitled "On National Shame" is included as a section of JC's book, *Strong Opinions*. In this section, JC is credited with having written the following:

> An article in a recent *New Yorker* makes it plain as day that the US administration, with the lead taken by Richard Cheney, not only sanctions the torture of prisoners taken in the so-called war on terror but is active in every way to subvert laws and conventions proscribing torture. [...] Their shamelessness is quite extraordinary. Their denials are less than half-hearted. The distinction their hired lawyers draw between torture and coercion is patently insincere, *pro forma*. In the new dispensation we have created, they implicitly say, the old powers of shame have been abolished. Whatever abhorrence you may feel counts for nothing. You cannot touch us, we are too powerful.
>
> Demosthenes: Whereas the slave fears only pain, what the free man fears most is shame. If we grant the truth of what the *New Yorker* claims, then the issue for individual Americans becomes a moral one: how, in the face of this shame to which I am subjected, do I behave? How do I save my honour? [...] Dishonour is no respecter of fine distinctions. Dishonour descends upon one's shoulders, and once it has descended no amount of clever pleading will dispel it. (Coetzee 2008: 39)

The aim of this reflection (both JC's and my own in this paper) is to inquire into how a relevant "moral issue" can be articulated by means of what I—following Jonathan Lear—have called the "dialectic of responsibility". Within JC's *Strong Opinions* itself, there is a sort of "division of explanatory labour" at work between a broader theoretical position (a view on national shame) and the illustration of that position (examples of torture) in "On National Shame". Furthermore, to the extent that we are familiar with Coetzee's work (his fiction and his essays) and thus acquainted with some of his own public views on international politics, we could easily ascribe this stance on American governmental decrees related to the so-called post-9/11 "war on terror", here apparently held by JC, to Coetzee himself.

In the preceding section of *Strong Opinions*, JC analyses a moral-political position held by Machiavelli in *The Prince*: the *Necessità*:

> Necessity, *Necessità*, is Machiavelli's guiding principle. The old, pre-Machiavellian position was that the moral law was supreme. If it so happened that the moral law was sometimes broken, that was unfortunate, but rulers were merely human, after all. The new, Machiavellian position is that infringing the moral law is justified when it is necessary.
>
> Machiavelli does not deny that the claims morality makes on us are absolute. *At the same time he asserts that in the interest of the state the ruler "is often obliged [necessitato] to act without loyalty, without mercy, without humanity, and without religion".*[12] (Coetzee 2008: 26)

A suitable adaptation of Machiavelli's idea, here, is the notion that there is no such thing as national shame, let alone "shame assimilated by mere citizenship"—contrary to what JC contends, though Coetzee has him writing this from *The Prince* in *Strong Opinions*—because one must do whatever one must in order to protect and preserve the state. Yet an important social group, which JC calls "liberal intellectuals", rejects *both* Machiavelli's *Necessità* and the "assimilation of shame by citizenship" argued for by JC. Here, JC refers specifically to the Bush administration and to the behaviour and political views held by liberal intellectuals in post-9/11 American society, where these intellectuals aimed to distance themselves from both positions by means of rational self-justification. This specific example represents a more generalizable ethical posture, however, in which personal responsibility is denied and blame shifted to another. The dialectic of responsibility, aimed at deconstructing this posture for the reader of both the book and the pseudo-book (*Diary* and *Strong Opinions*), will operate through my own interpretation of JC's argument for national shame in this section of *Strong Opinions*, to which I now turn. This stance is easily attributable to Coetzee himself, and the following analysis aims in part to reveal the role that JC—himself a fictional creation—plays with regard to the author of *Diary*.

JC describes the mechanism of a self-justifying denial of national shame as involving three steps: (1) the ascription of shameful guilt to the political leaders of the relevant country—i.e. US post-9/11 political leaders; (2) a massive distancing from the positions adopted and the actions carried out by these leaders; and (3) a rejection of both moral dualism *and* the divide between theory and practice inherent in Machiavelli's *Necessità*.

Liberal intellectuals actively want to distance themselves from both the central idea of *Necessità* and the attribution of national shame, precisely because such positions implicate *them*. However, there is something the liberal intellectual does not see—mostly because he cannot see it—and this is the fact that shameful guilt descends like a curse and cannot be removed by argument. Liberal intellectuals cannot recognize this phenomenon because they want to deny their involvement in national shame by way of logical justification.

At this point in JC's strong opinion on national shame, the astute reader of *Diary* gradually realizes that JC might be talking about, and to, the reader *herself* whenever he writes about "liberal intellectuals", describing their behaviour and the structure of their stance in view of this specific moral and political issue. And, at the same time that this maneuver is acknowledged, the reader is further reminded that JC is no more than a product of Coetzee's literary imagination. Although Coetzee gives us *more* than *Strong Opinions*, he offers it to us nonetheless, and so must somewhat be held accountable for whatever positions are defended therein—even if he sometimes feels tempted to decry JC's decrepitude and misogyny and never completely identifies with his alter-ego. In spite of the likely frustration, sometimes akin to a certain feeling of complete lack of control over the reading process, caused by this device, the dialectic of responsibility extends to the reader herself, who, after all, chose to take up the novel in the first place.

The dialectic of responsibility can therefore be said to act upon the reader of *Diary of a Bad Year* via a mechanism of identification. At the moment in *Diary* where the above quotation occurs, it is again Coetzee who wants to make us understand that there is something extremely inconsistent about the stance of these "liberal intellectuals". More specifically: how can "they" be opposed to both Machiavelli's *Necessità*, as a positive stance, and the assimilation of shame by citizenship, when both positions represent contradictory yet complementary ideas that "exhaustively cover a domain of intelligible positions"? The problem arises precisely because one must choose between the following options:

a. Either there is no such thing as national shame, because one must do whatever is needed to protect the interests of the state (*Necessità*); or

b. National shame exists and does not pertain exclusively to political leaders, insofar as it spreads via non-rational mechanisms, its removal cannot be effected by rational justification, and these leaders were elected by the public. To accuse political leaders of "shameful behaviour" *is already to experience the curse of this shame.*

This inconsistency, however, belongs also to *me*—an astute, well-informed reader of *Diary of a Bad Year*. I am perfectly capable of understanding the structural paths of this inconsistency, and I can even detect the responsibility-divesting cynicism inherent in it, so long as I am able to rely on the scapegoat of the third person. *It is "them", of whom we speak, so-called "liberal intellectuals".*

Only by means of the formal use of the third person to refer to this social group does Coetzee manage to convey his intended content in an effective way, removing the veil of blindness that risks shielding the eyes of the liberal intellectual reader now busy with the decoding of hidden messages in *Diary of a Bad Year*. The dialectic of responsibility is the reading process by which we achieve the lifting of this veil.

It is more than plausible to suppose that, upon finishing *Diary*, one might come to view this formal strategy as a "formal subterfuge" and thus be left feeling naked and doubly deceived—for we do not like the position held by the liberal intellectuals, which isn't actually "their" position, but rather *ours*, and we do not like the way Coetzee's text pretends to tell us about an abstract group of people who can only stand for strong positions by being blind to their own point of view, when actually it describes us.

The dialectic of responsibility—this whole process—functions as a bridge between the *formal method of writing* and *the act of conveying ethical content* (both as a "material" posture towards human action and as a strategy for reading the book). It is by means of this dialectic that the reader manages not only to understand her place on the plane of reasons embodied by *Diary of a Bad Year*—becoming aware that she is an integral part of this space and not a mere spectator—but also to replace substitute ethical thought (the only kind available to any reader who merely occupies the position of spectator) with a straightforward but difficult ethical attitude: a commitment to decide how she should live and behave, given the shame that is hers ab initio—maybe because she is American, most likely because she is human.

But why would J.M. Coetzee feel compelled to use JC to morally educate *his* readers, while refusing to reveal his precise relation to this character and his views? Isn't this, after all, a sheer abuse of well-known rhetorical devices? In other words, isn't he as shameless as any liberal intellectual?

5

Admittedly, we may not ultimately settle on the interpretation of *Diary* I have been offering here; it is, after all, just one of many possible approaches to Coetzee's work, with its own potential shortcomings. With this said, however, two points in particular have thus far become apparent: both in the sections that Coetzee wants to attribute to JC and in the lower sections of the page that he doesn't mind presenting as his own, Coetzee's writing style is extremely clear, descriptive and neat. Indeed, he must avoid obscurity and linguistic excess if he wants the narrative to progress through the different sections of the book's pages, to preserve the important connections between them, and to hold the reader's attention. On the other hand, the narrative device of a split in the author's voice instantiates a gap with regard to the identity of the novel's author at the very outset. The graphic structure of the book's page is, of course, highly unconventional, and both it and the related identity split between JC and John Coetzee are features that the reader confronts from the moment she takes up the novel.

Indeed, Peter Child's general characterization of the defining features of modernist prose—its "radical aesthetics, technical experimentation, spatial or rhythmic rather than chronological form, self-conscious reflexiveness [...]"[13]—neatly fits a cluster of devices at work in Coetzee's novels besides the overlapping in *Diary* of the writer and the writer's writer—e.g. the creation of (another) fictional Australian novelist, Elizabeth Costello, who shows up, in Coetzee's Tanner Lectures at Princeton in 1997, to deliver the (imaginary) Gates Lecture at Appleton

College; the (semi-) autobiographical report of the writer John's youth in Worcester (South Africa) during the 50s, rendered in the third person in *Boyhood*; or the post-mortem reports in *Summertime*.[14]

Such rhetorical maneuvers, used to reconstruct the author's presence and combined with an overtly minimalist literary style (which extends even to the description of imaginarily "physical" settings as complex as the Paradise *qua* socialist allegory, which we may imagine to be the place where *The Childhood of Jesus* is set), have led philosophers currently working on Coetzee to categorize its aesthetic features as "realist-modernist".

Alongside Lear's reading, Stephen Mulhall has been working out the implications of this dialectical aesthetics for a philosophical assessment of Coetzee's prose (in a way that doesn't lose touch with the novels' concreteness). Mulhall argues that Coetzee's work can be helpfully described as "realist-modernist" in light of a cluster of features, including the stylistic intertwinement at work in what is otherwise an essentially linear narrative mode; Coetzee's self-restrained prose; the above-mentioned author/narrator identity-puzzles; and, importantly, the meta-reflective dimension of the text—in particular, reflection on elements of formal realism present in Coetzee's own prose.[15] Besides the dialectic character of his writing, Coetzee sometimes indulges himself on some reflections upon the historical evolution of formal realism. A key passage from *Elizabeth Costello* reveals this second-order theoretical mirroring:

> The blue costume, the greasy hair are details, signs of moderate realism. Supply the particulars, allow the significations to emerge of themselves. A procedure pioneered by Daniel Defoe. Robinson Crusoe, cast up on the beach, looks around for his shipmates. But there are none. "I never saw them afterwards, or any sign of them", says he, "except three of their hats, one cap, and two shoes that were not fellows". Two shoes, not fellows: by not being fellows, the shoes have ceased to be footwear and become proofs of death, torn by the foaming seas off the feet of drowning men and tossed ashore. No large words, no despair, just hats and caps and shoes.[16]

This passage, whilst ostensibly a comment on Defoe's prose, self-reflectively expresses something about the aesthetic significance of its own naked expression. And Mulhall takes this reflection on the dialectic playfulness between realism and modernism one step further when he argues that a similar struggle, in terms of stylistic innovation and the corresponding impact on the material topics expressed, is intrinsic to both the imaginatively mimetic design of the modern novel since its inception (be it the nostalgic parable of *Don Quixote* or the pioneering realistic reportage of Daniel Defoe) and the realistic efforts of modern philosophical projects that historically coincide with the emergence of the new literary genre. Here, he refers specifically to the anti-authoritarian arguments of modern philosophers and scientists such as Bacon, Descartes, Locke and Hume, who systematically rebelled against the inheritance of Aristotelianism and religious restrictions on the announcement of scientific breakthroughs. In *The Wounded Animal*, we find the following comments on both traditions:

> The history of the novel since Defoe, Richardson and Sterne might therefore be written entirely in terms of the ways in which novelists repeatedly subject their inheritance of realistic conventions to critical questioning in order to recreate the impression of reality in their readers (in large part by encouraging those readers to see prior uses of convention to represent the real as merely conventional in contrast with their own, far more convincing ones). [...] It is not simply that the novel has a cannibalistic relation to other literary genres; from the outset, its practitioners had a similarly Oedipal relation to prior examples within the genre of the novel, and so to the prior conventions within which they necessarily operated.[17]

On a similar struggle within modern philosophy at the turn of the twentieth century (echoing Wittgenstein's famous claim: "not empiricism and yet realism in philosophy, that is the hardest thing"[18]), Mulhall writes the following:

> [...]Realism is both a recognized category of philosophical thought and a contested one. Aiming to be realistic is a central, perhaps even a defining, motivation in philosophy, insofar as it amounts to grasping the truth of things, the way things really are; but no sooner does one philosophical position or approach claim to have achieved that aim than its successors criticize it precisely for failing to have done so, and substitute what they take to be a more authentic form of realism.[19]

The cannibalistic threat to former projects of both traditions extends itself further as the fundamental hermeneutic principle of the dialectical reading I will be developing here—a reading which, as we shall see, also incorporates a self-overcoming element regarding its own methodological inheritance.

The crucial issue at this point may be put thus: recent philosophical projects—such as Mulhall's reading of *Elizabeth Costello* or Lear's interpretation of *Diary of a Bad Year*—have turned to the work of a great contemporary novelist and found that they have such-and-such to say about it, showing an openness to literature and literary criticism that surpasses the Socratic prejudices against artists and thus allows for the reintegration of writers into the philosophical citadel. But who, in turn, examines these philosophical commentaries on literary projects? Coetzee himself tends to be extremely critical when engaging in reflection of this sort—as occurs, for instance, in his dismissal of the single-minded philosophical voice of JC within the overall framework of *Diary*, which leads him to write a book that is utterly different from JC's realistic set of chronicles on contemporary ethical and political issues.[20] Is there perhaps a more genial approach available to us?

6

More systematically in *The Wounded Animal*, but also in two of the essays that comprise *The Self and Its Shadows*[21] (2013), Mulhall has developed an interpretative account of the tensions between realism and modernism in Coetzee's prose, which detects in the stylistic features underlined above what I will term a "conventionalist" pattern of self-overcoming with regard to inherited literary styles. At the risk of oversimplifying Mulhall's very dense account of realist modernism in the contemporary novel (which I will put to my own purposes below), we can describe his proposal as follows. Mulhall insists on the presence of an inner and inevitably doomed struggle within literary prose itself, in place since the very inception of the genre, and argues that the novel has been dialectically fighting its own conventional status as an artistic genre in the name of fidelity to the facts. However, since these supposed facts are themselves a product of the literary imagination (and since, as linguistic creations, they are particularly "conventional"), the realistic novel is logically doomed to inflict on its descendants the same Oedipal tension it inherited from its ancestors (this is the material point of the reference to intra-genre "cannibalism" alluded to in the quotation above).

This dialectic of self-overcoming is made all the more acute by a progressive awareness within the modernist tradition of the fact that the methodological aims of formal realism can only be accomplished via a means of expression that is highly conventional or non-natural—*a means that must be acknowledged as such.* Applying this dialectical model to a literary project like Coetzee's therefore involves assessing his literary-critical reflection on this arguably historical aim and its relation to his work.

The realist-modernist dynamic, so the argument goes, has historically prompted reflection on the insurmountable barrier separating the realistic writer from the factual world that his prose intends to represent, thereby offering literary prose a path to awareness of its facticity *qua* prose and for further self-criticism regarding both its representative potential and its representative limits. This, in turn, calls for a reflective turn within the prose itself in terms of the conditions of its own possibility as a (conventional) representative device—something we've seen exemplified in Coetzee's modernistic approach to his own literary project (in particular, in his inclusion of reflection on the conditions of the production of *Strong Opinions* in *Diary*).

In *Diary of a Bad Year*, Coetzee directs ancient philosophical worries about the idolatric character of poetry—which would allegedly lead us away from virtue—against the philosopher himself (that is, the philosopher at work in the book, JC, who is curiously enough a literary creation) and works his way out of a rationalistic trap by paying close attention to the work's form. In addition, he both creates an alter ego, who more or less succumbs to the trap, and attaches his name to a larger book, a move that finally frees him from the bonds of mere argument by incorporating argument into the larger whole of his text and presenting it as essentially defective.

And yet one question still remains: *who* reads J.M.Coetzee and tackles his therapeutic aims, in part by showing that she has been cured of the argumentative blindness he diagnoses? In other words, is it possible for Coetzee's charges against philosophy to be not only answered but even incorporated into a new way of *writing* philosophy? I have implied that the answer is yes, but I have yet to say *how* this might be achieved.

One of the things that ought to be highlighted once more is that Coetzee himself writes his novels (and voices his charges) *in a specific way*: his style is sober, compact and self-conscious, all at once. Furthermore, he reflects on the peculiarities of (his own and others') literary outlooks, and, partially because of this incorporated self-reflection, his novels belong to what philosophers like Mulhall have termed "realist modernism". How can we account for *that*—that is, for our claim, as philosophers, that Coetzee is a "realist-modernist" writer?

To my analysis of the split page, we should also add a consideration of the remarkable methodological differences between the voices of JC and John Coetzee in *Diary*, played out by the latter as part of his therapeutic induction of readers of *his* book. The passages from both *Strong Opinions* and the lower sections, cited above, which Anya encourages JC to call "soft opinions", attest to a genuine difference of tone with regard to each voice. JC's monograph is as informative and opinionated as a thematic essay can be, and he never allows his reasoning to deviate from a clear argumentative pattern. *Strong Opinions* is rightly described as a *realistic report* on contemporary ethical and political issues. In the lower sections of the page—where we also read how the upper ones were produced—Coetzee departs from straightforward reasoning, allowing for suspensions, onomatopoeia and markedly emotive language. It seems likely that Coetzee wants his readers to realize *that and how* a maximally comprehensive literary achievement cannot rely merely on the politically realistic prose characteristic of JC's voice. The way Coetzee shows us this, as we've seen, is via a modernistic embedding of *Strong Opinions* within his own book.

This embedding is one of the key features of Coetzee's realist-modernist literary project at this stage of its evolution. One of the practical outcomes of this maneuver is the achievement of a morally autonomous response on the part of the reader, both to the ethical and political issues dealt with in *Strong Opinions* and to the way they are deployed within the larger book. This response is accomplished via a refusal to feed the reader a straightforward argumentative treatise (such as *Strong Opinions*) alone—precisely because, as an instance of *ersatz* ethical thought, it cannot perform the job JC intends it to. But once this is acknowledged, we would seem to be compelled to acknowledge the relevance of this problem for the present examination: for how can an explanatory essay on *Diary of a Bad Year* possibly escape the fate of communicating merely *ersatz* thought itself? What I want to say is: how can a plausible theory on *ersatz* ethical thought avoid collapsing into mere substitution ethical thought, given that such a failure is attributable, in part, to its very plausibility and persuasiveness? After all, the discovery of an adequate explanatory model usually provides us with a grounded excuse to stop thinking about the topic thus explained. We assume that we know, and we proceed from there.

Thus we might suspect that this paper should itself have been written in three layers, to the degree that its aim was still to dispel *ersatz* ethical thought. But then, what would have been the point of writing it, other than to rephrase *Diary of a Bad Year*, re-composing it in other words and perhaps damaging the original's reputation? Is there anything left for us to do when the target of our inquiry, with which we are directly confronted, throws itself back upon us? We should pay close attention to how philosophers have been dealing with the traps left by a novelist they do not want to expel from their citadel again—such as Coetzee.

Mulhall is a case in point. In *The Wounded Animal*, he explores various possibilities for *staging* or *performing* the literary encounter between realism and modernism in the story of Elizabeth Costello, displayed in the novel of the same name (as we have seen, the same can be achieved with regard to *Diary of a Bad Year*). This staging isn't merely theoretical, however; Mulhall's philosophical prose embodies what it argues for, thus undermining *ersatz* ethical thought and avoiding the paradox of the psychological thesis mentioned at the beginning of this essay. (Because his approach doesn't duplicate Coetzee's ways, it can, at least on the face of it, avoid the charge of being involved in an inconsistent—or desperate—appeal to the authority of the writer, which would otherwise entail a certain irresponsibility on Mulhall's part along precisely the same lines as JC's irresponsibility within the dynamics of Coetzee's novel.)

Mulhall chooses to focus on *Elizabeth Costello*. Readers of this book, he claims, are introduced to events that take place in the protagonist's academic and family life—both of which happen to be products of Coetzee's literary imagination, as are *Diary*, *Strong Opinions* and JC. Reading *Elizabeth Costello*, we learn about the protagonist's physical decay, which contrasts sharply with the prodigiousness of her literary imagination and the playful recreation of the history of the novel she provides in *The House on Eccles Street* (a novel supposedly written by Costello, to which we have no access whatever), in the Gates Lecture at Appleton College, and in private conversations with John, her son.

The set of episodes in Costello's life brought together by Coetzee in a novel published several years after their individual presentation as lectures[22] does not present us with a theory about the (realistic) evolution of formal realism up to the modernistic turn (just as the modernistic performance of embedding one realistic book—*Strong Opinions*—within a larger one and toying with the names of their respective authors does not constitute a theory about the evolution of these formal techniques, or even about the evolution of both books as instances of each). Rather, the novel stages or performs this evolution, in part by including reports on unexpected events during Costello's visit to Appleton College and to John's family. What happens during this visit (both the lectures and the meetings they occasion), provides the raw material for a realistic novel which, in modernistic fashion, reflects both upon its own conditions of possibility and development as a specimen of the genre and upon the historical evolution of the latter. *Elizabeth Costello* is precisely this work, and Mulhall, in his reading of it and the modernistic turn it instantiates, chose not to bring either its story or the puzzle of the identity of its author and narrator into a scholarly frame.

Instead, and battling against the standards relied upon by his own analytic-philosophical inheritance, he does justice to the literary and philosophical aspects of both (story and puzzle) by giving them a voice in his own reading—itself an example of the interdisciplinary conversation between philosophy and literature I have been tracing, which becomes possible when traditional, discipline-specific strictures are loosened. In precisely this way, and much like Coetzee's, his own work represents a critical response to traditional philosophical modes of investigation, and thus also an Oedipal overcoming of a widely accepted methodological practice. Contrary to what occurs with Coetzee-the-writer, however, this way of doing philosophy is polemic and faces several kinds of Platonic criticism. It does reply to Coetzee's challenge, though, and without replicating its form—which is crucial to its avoiding the descent into *ersatz* ethical thought. With this important development noted, what this open-ended inquiry would still seem to require is a similarly Oedipal critique of the tentative reflections offered here.

Notes

1. See Lear, J. "Ethics and the Problem of Communication", in *John Coetzee and Ethics: Philosophical Perspectives on Literature*, ed. by Anton Leist and Peter Singer, Columbia University Press, 2010, 65.
2. Lear insists on the indispensability of this move by comparing it with the dialectic of the voices of different characters in Plato's dialogues and parodying the inconsistency of an ethical command. He writes: "There are, of course, many other characters, some with worked-out ethical views, but the dialogues are set up so that there is always some question about how those views should be received. This is not simply a literary device to sustain the reader's interest; it is an ethical strategy: an attempt to defeat any easy attempt to defer to the author or to any surrogate for the author in the text. Even the figures within the text need to be handled with care. If a respected character were to say, 'When it comes to ethics, you really need to think for yourself', one can imagine the response, 'Anything you say: I really must think for myself!'" (Lear 2010: 68). Thus Coetzee systematically creates authority-divesting strategies in both his novels and his critical essays. To list but a few examples: In 1991 he delivered a lecture in Graz, Austria, under the title "What Is a Classic?", which title is borrowed from T.S. Eliot's 1944 presidential address to the Virgil Society in London (see J.M. Coetzee, *Stranger Shores: Essays 1986–1999*, 2001); when invited to deliver the Tanner Lectures in Princeton in 1997, he presented his audience with what Amy Gutmann called "two lectures within two lectures" by reading out Elizabeth Costello's speech at

Appleton College on a topic akin to his own—the abuse of animals (see *The Lives of Animals*, 1999); his Nobel Lecture from 2003 consisted of a supposed correspondence exchange between Robinson Crusoe and his creator, Daniel Defoe, which was titled "He and His Man", and Coetzee even adds to the reading of the piece a further taint of uncertainty by claiming he is not sure ('I cannot remember which comes first', he claims) whether its title is 'He and His Man' or 'His Man and He' (see the Nobel website: http://www.nobelprize.org/ nobel_prizes/literature/laureates/2003/coetzee-lecture-e.html).

3. See Plato's *Republic* 352d: "But whether the just also live better than the unjust and are happier, which is what we afterwards proposed for consideration, must be considered. And now, in my opinion, they do also look as though they are, on the basis of what we have said. Nevertheless, this must still be considered better: for the argument is not just any question, but about the way one should live" (Trans. Allan Bloom; Bloom 1991).

4. See Williams (2011), Chap. 1. "It is not a trivial question, Socrates said, what we are talking about is how one should live. Or so Plato reports him, in one of the first books written about this subject. Plato thought that philosophy could answer the question. Like Socrates, he hoped that one could direct one's life, if necessary redirect it, through an understanding that was distinctively philosophical – that is to say, general and abstract, rationally reflective, and concerned with what can be known through different kinds of inquiry" (Williams 2011: 1).

5. K. Harrison, *New York Times Book Review*, December 31, 2007.

6. See, Lear, "Ethics" (2010): 70.

7. J.M. Coetzee, *Diary of Bad Year*. London: Vintage, 2008, 13.

8. This issue has also been vindicated by Coetzee scholars as almost an obsession in his later novels (especially those published after his move to Adelaide, Australia, in 2002). Jane Poyner has forcefully argued for the relevance of this topic in Coetzee's later works, particularly in connection with the problem of truth-telling in autobiography, in the following lines: "That Coetzee is concerned with 'how to tell the truth in autobiography' therefore does not mean he is concerned with truth per se, but with its telling. In other words, Coetzee is less interested in the truth value of narrative than in *the mechanisms by which 'truth'*—always a category to be questioned in Coetzee—*is brought to light*. In the later works that foreground intellectual practice, Coetzee focuses not on the

truth-value of the public interventions his writer-intellectuals circulate but on the manner and mode by which these interventions are disseminated" (Poyner, J. *J.M. Coetzee and the Paradox of Postcolonial Authorship*. Ashgate, 2009, p. 168).

9. See Nussbaum, M. (1990). *Love's Knowledge*. Introduction, p. 15. Oxford: Oxford University Press.

10. Idem, ibidem.

11. See Poyner (2009) (especially *Introduction: Positioning the Writer*) and Attwell (1993).

12. The passage in quotes is from Machiavelli's *The Prince*, Chap. XVIII.

13. See Peter Childs' *Modernism* (Routledge 2008, 19).

14. Amongst Coetzee scholars there has been a certain uniformity in describing his oeuvre as a whole as an instance of "late modernism" (see, e.g., Attwell 1993; Attridge 2004; Bradshaw and Neill 2010; Poyner 2009).

15. A striking example of this is the following passage from Elizabeth Costello: "It is not a good idea to interrupt the narrative too often, since storytelling works by lulling the reader or listener into a dreamlike state in which the time and space of the real world fade away, superseded by the time and space of the fiction. Breaking into the dream draws attention to the constructedness of the story, and plays havoc with the realist illusion. However, unless certain scenes are skipped over, we will be here all afternoon. The skips are not part of the text, they are part of the performance". J.M. Coetzee, *Elizabeth Costello: Eight Lessons*. London: Secker and Warburg, 2003, 16.

16. J.M. Coetzee, *Elizabeth Costello: Eight Lessons*. London: Secker and Warburg, 2003, 4.

17. Stephen Mulhall, *The Wounded Animal*. Princeton University Press, 2009: 145.

18. Wittgenstein, L. *Remarks on the Foundations of Mathematics*. Oxford: Blackwell, 1978, VI-23.

19. Ibid. 146.

20. Other examples of staged dialogues with philosophers, extracted from Coetzee's novelistic project, include Elizabeth Costello's acrid reactions to both her professional (and unemployed) philosopher daughter-in-law, Norma Bernard, and the philosophical community at Appleton College; her alternative accounts of animal ethics; the strong opposition faced by David, the main character of both *The Childhood of Jesus* and *The Schooldays of Jesus*, when he attempts to "play Socrates" and

lead abstract discussions on virtues and vices with his co-workers at the grain warehouse, or the acrid response Lucy Lurie gives her father, when David comments on her alternative life-style: 'Yes, when all fails, philosophise.' (*Disgrace* 2000: 60).

21. Mulhall, S. *The Self and Its Shadows: A Book of Essays on Individuality as Negation in Philosophy and the Arts.* Oxford: Oxford University Press, 2013 (see esp.: "The Melodramatic Reality of Film and Literature" and "Countering the Ballad of Co-Dependency").

22. The Tanner Lectures on Human Values, delivered at Princeton University in 1997, under the title "The Lives of Animals" and published in 1999 (Coetzee, J.M. *The Lives of Animals*, Princeton: Princeton University Press, 1999).

References

Attridge, D. 2004. *J.M. Coetzee and the Ethics of Reading.* Chicago and London: The University of Chicago Press.

Attwell, D. 1993. *J.M. Coetzee: South Africa and the Politics of Writing.* Berkeley and Los Angeles: University of California Press; Cape Town: David Philip.

Bradshaw, G., and M. Neill. 2010. *J.M. Coetzee's Austerities.* Aldershot: Ashgate.

Childs, P. 2008. *Modernism*, 2nd ed. London and New York: Routledge.

Coetzee, J.M. 1999. *The Lives of Animals.* Princeton: Princeton University Press.

———. 2000. *Disgrace.* London: Vintage.

———. 2001. *Stranger Shores: Essays 1986–1999.* London: Vintage.

———. 2003a. *Elizabeth Costello: Eight Lessons.* London: Secker and Warburg.

———. 2003b. He and His Man. *The Official Website of the Nobel Prize.* http://www.nobelprize.org/nobel_prizes/literature/laureates/2003/coetzee-lecture-e.html.

———. 2008. *Diary of Bad Year.* London: Vintage.

———. 2009. *Summertime: Scenes from Provincial Life 3.* London: Harvill Secker.

Harrison, K. 2007. Strong Opinions, *New York Times Book Review*, December 31.

Lear, J. 2010. Ethics and the Problem of Communication. In *John Coetzee and Ethics: Philosophical Perspectives on Literature*, ed. Anton Leist and Peter Singer. New York: Columbia University Press.

Mulhall, S. 2009. *The Wounded Animal*. Princeton, NJ: Princeton University Press.

———. 2013. *The Self and Its Shadows: A Book of Essays on Individuality as Negation in Philosophy and the Arts*. Oxford: Oxford University Press.

Nussbaum, M. 1990. *Love's Knowledge*. Oxford: Oxford University Press.

Plato. 1991. *The Republic*, trans. Allan Bloom. New York: HarperCollins.

Poyner, J. 2009. *J.M. Coetzee and the Paradox of Postcolonial Authorship*. Aldershot: Ashgate.

Williams, B. 2011. *Ethics and the Limits of Philosophy*. Foreword by Jonathan Lear. London: Routledge.

Wittgenstein, L. 1978. *Remarks on the Foundations of Mathematics*, ed. G.H. von Wright, Rush Rhees, and G.E.M. Anscombe, 3rd ed. Oxford: Blackwell.

Part II

Language and Contents

5

The Medium Itself: Modernism in Art and Philosophy's Linguistic Self-Analysis

Garry L. Hagberg

Multiple definitions of Modernism have been put forward, often focusing on the character or features of the works of art and literature produced within this cultural movement. Here, I want to change the focus somewhat, looking into the sensibility of Modernism as this has manifested itself in a special concern not with the content of representation, but with the materials out of which a representation is made. In eighteenth-century English portraiture, for example, the concern is with the features of the person portrayed, the social position of that person, and the networks of relations within which that person moves and exercises agency. The materials of those representations—oil and canvas, and the techniques of producing those representations—brushstroke, palette, are meant in a sense to disappear: one is intended to see the represented person *through* them, where one measure of success is the extent to which those materials and techniques have become invisible. In nineteenth-century French political painting, one

G. L. Hagberg (✉)
Bard College, Annandale-on-Hudson, NY, USA
e-mail: hagberg@bard.edu

© The Author(s) 2018
A. Falcato and A. Cardiello (eds.), *Philosophy in the Condition of Modernism*,
https://doi.org/10.1007/978-3-319-77078-9_5

101

similarly is meant to see the symbolic figure transparently—the political significance is seen within the figure and her action, but again the brute reality of the materials, and the artifactual technical manipulation of them, is, if successful, concealed beneath representational and symbolic content. But in Modernist painting and its immediate predecessors, the materials themselves are brought both to the surface of the painting and to the surface of the viewer's awareness. One sees representational content not *through* the materials and technique, but rather—in what I will suggest is a stylistically definitional feature—*in* them. And as Modernism reaches its fulfillment by making this aspect central, it submerges representational content beneath the material and technique, leaving abstract content in its place. The medium, as McLuhan said in too-concise form, is (or I would say has become through a Modernist inversion of previous content-material relations) the message. One sees this in painting, in architecture (where Modernism leaves exposed materials as the non-disguised skin of buildings), in music (where, in serialism, pitches themselves are ordered and presented to the ear without being hidden within, or contained within, a recognizable harmonized melody that, in a sense parallel to the eighteenth- and nineteenth-century painting mentioned above, displaces our attention away from *them*), in "language poetry", where the words themselves are set before the eye and ear of the reader independent of narrative flow or thematically-introduced expectation. And one finds this approach, this way of seeing, in philosophy—particularly in the work and influence of Wittgenstein.

In Wittgenstein's work, unlike that of, say, John Locke, language is no longer regarded as a transparent medium, as the ideally invisible technique that only serves to deliver content beyond it—the exact philosophical analogue of the English portrait sitter or the French figure leading the people. The philosophical interest and focus of attention—like the inversion of the relations between represented content and artifactual medium—is now on the language *itself*, on how it works, how it functions interactively, how its meaning is derived, and—rather complexly, as we shall see in connection with Wittgenstein's private language argument—what our relation is as speakers and writers to it. And that distinctive attention, that sustained focus, is the philosophical version or manifestation of what was, in the last decades of the nineteenth century into the early to middle decades of the twentieth century, the new Modernist sensibility. Indeed, the triumph of the philosophy of language in the twentieth century (as motivated centrally by Wittgenstein's achievement and methods of working in philosophy) as we shall see, is deeply analogous to the aesthetic achievements in painting, architecture, and music in the same decades.

So in this paper, I will consider the part of Wittgenstein's philosophical work that I think most captures the spirit of Modernism in the arts, and then consider some selected parallel movements and analogues in the arts themselves. Each side of the larger analogy I am suggesting—language seen one way, and art developed one way—casts light on the other, and in the end what I am suggesting is essential to the Modernist achievement may emerge in high relief: artistic thinking takes place within (and not behind, before, or beneath) paint and visible, attention-capturing brushstrokes, it takes place within a striving for the purity of visible and exposed architectural design, and it takes place within the unfolding of modern musical logic, music sense. All of this, as I will suggest, is profoundly like language as Wittgenstein investigated it. As he wrote, language *itself* is the vehicle of thought.

I

But how might one understand this encapsulated remark of Wittgenstein's? The answer to it, I want to suggest, captures, if in its distinctive way, the soul of Modernism. Or if that sounds more suggestive than explanatory, one could say: the answer to this question provides a conception of language that is a model for the Modernist conception of the materials of art within culture and the artist's relation to those materials.

In *Philosophical Investigations*, Sec. 243, he writes:

A human being can encourage himself, give himself orders, obey, blame and punish himself; he can ask himself a question and answer it. So one could imagine human beings who spoke only in monologue, who accompanied their activities by talking to themselves – An explorer who watched them and listened to their talk might succeed in translating their language into ours. (This would enable him to predict these people's actions correctly, for he also hears them making resolutions and decisions.)

But is it also conceivable that there be a language in which a person could write down or give voice to his inner experiences – his feelings, moods, and so on – for his own use? – Well, can't we do so in our ordinary language? – But that is not what I mean. The words of this language are to refer to what only the speaker can know – to his immediate private sensations. So another person cannot understand the language.[1]

Because we can self-encourage, self-order, self-ask and answer, it is an easy matter to intuitively accept without further reflection that we could have—and we alone could have autonomously invented—a private language. This intuition is further reinforced by imagining, as does Wittgenstein, a monologue society. But the strongest initial intuitive support for the possibility of a private language comes from Wittgenstein's next observation in the foregoing passage: if we can within our ordinary language, within the language we already speak, write down or give voice to our inner feelings, experiences, and moods, then we take it as obvious that we could do this privately. So the thought here is: we use the concept of privacy all the time, and we know how to make the distinction between the public and the private (we might, for example, do this in speaking to a reporter on or off the record). A private language would thus be the language, or really the subset of our larger language, with which we name and record our inner personal content. And with that, we would say that the private language Wittgenstein is asking about is flatly and plainly conceivable. And moreover, to the extent that we do name and record our interior life, this private language is actualized—it already exists within the world of our linguistic practices. So there is, one thinks, no philosophical or conceptual problem on this point. But Wittgenstein says here—opening the way into one of the most profound reflections on the nature of language and our relation to it in philosophical history—"that is not what I mean".

What does Wittgenstein then mean? A private language, as described, is not only readily conceivable but indeed actual: we could if we wanted all make secret diaries of the thoughts and images that go through our minds between the time we place our heads on the pillow and the time we fall asleep. But the point of Wittgenstein's remark is: this is not the sense of "private" that he is herein considering. As we will see more fully in a moment, this is the kind of privacy that is already resident within a public shared language of a community, of a culture. We all know, together, what the intuitive sense of "private" is; we readily and unproblematically recognize usages of it; we readily distinguish between correct and incorrect usages of it. Consider the analogy to private property: one can post "Private Property" signs along the border of one's land, and this means that one should not enter or trespass here. One should not—but one *could*. Just as one should not read the secret diary—but reading it is, however intrusive or disrespectful, readily possible. Wittgenstein is asking about the case, unlike our uses of "private" in the diary or property cases, where one cannot, as a kind of logical impossibility, trespass or read. He is asking about a border that is drawn not legally or ethically, but rather about a border drawn by metaphysics. "The words of this language are to refer to what only the speaker can know—to his immediate private sensations". The words with this kind of privacy (necessary, not contingent privacy, but I will come to that shortly) are not words that another happens not to know (you know the meaning of "astringent" and I do not), but words that another cannot know. Hence: "So another person cannot understand the language".

One can already see some important connections here: it was assumed (on what we might here abbreviate as) the Romantic model of artistic expression that the arts constituted a kind of private language on the part of the Great-Souled Artist (Wagner et al.). That is, the arts, in M.H. Abrams' famous contrasting terms, functioned (until the cultural-conceptual transition from late Romanticism to early Modernism) as lamp, not as mirror[2]; rather than mimetically representing reality so that the aesthetic content came from the appearances of the outside world, aesthetic content became personally expressive content, with the "lamp" radiating from within. But if it turns out—as it will, as we follow more of Wittgenstein's reflections—that the expression of inner content in language does not work in the way we thought or presumed, then to the extent that we model our understanding of artistic expression on linguistic expression, the arts do not work the way we thought or presumed either. We will come to this, but we must first consider the work Wittgenstein undertakes to clarify this issue.

Having asked, "In what sense are my sensations *private* (*PI* 246), Wittgenstein works through a discussion of when it does, and when it does not, make sense to speak of the knowledge of pain, writing "it makes sense to say about other people that they doubt whether I am in pain; but not to say it about myself" (*PI* 246). This observation already shows that there is a requirement for intelligibility, for sense, that is public, social, cultural, in nature, and that we cannot simply use words as we like from a hermetically bounded or solipsistic interior—the sense of our speech is not determined from an inner self-contained authority, from an autocratic interior. And this too, as will emerge below, is of direct significance for the Modernist conception of the arts in culture.

Imagining (or trying to imagine) a child genius who invents his own language, Wittgenstein writes:

> Well, let's assume that the child is a genius and invents a name for the sensation by himself! – But then, of course, he couldn't make himself understood when he used the word. – So does he understand the name, without being able to explain its meaning to anyone? – But what does it mean to say that he has 'named his pain'? – How has he managed this naming of pain? And whatever he did, what was its purpose? – When one says "He gave a name to his sensation", one forgets that much must be prepared in the language for mere naming to make sense. And if we speak of someone's giving a name to a pain, the grammar of the word "pain" is what has been prepared here; it indicates the post where the new word is stationed. (*PI* 257)

Writing the secret diary or speaking off the record, trespassing the property line or reading another's diary; these are creations and transgressions of privacy, but they are not analogous to the imagined linguistic work of the child genius or those to whom he would make himself understood. In all those cases, we know in advance where the new word is stationed, we have in place a large and indeterminately-bounded conceptual web or structure within which these activities are made possible and are thus intelligible or conceptually coherent. Indeed, what does it mean to say that he has named his sensation, but without first establishing, or without (as we so easily do) unquestioningly presuming, the concept of a language, within which the act of naming takes place? So two problems exist here side-by-side: (1) the private-namer could never make himself understood because of the metaphysical inaccessibility of the referent, and (2) we cannot so much as make sense of the act of naming without having so very much "prepared" in Wittgenstein's sense, without first contradictorily importing the concept "naming" from our established public language (in fact we should just say "language"—we use the term "public" to stand in contrast to what we will see below is an incoherent concept in a category with "round square", "bounded infinity", and as we shall see, "wholly privately determined artistic expressive content", where the "grammar" of the word "artwork" requires the same preparations as Wittgenstein's word "pain" here—a truth profoundly acknowledged within the practices and the ethos of Modernist culture).

But what, more precisely, is the problem of the referent and its naming, and why shouldn't this conception of a first act of naming account for both the origin and essence of language? Wittgenstein writes (as usual, dialogically, that is, with imagined voices presenting various views as separated by dashes), in what is surely among the most famous and most debated sections of *Philosophical Investigations*:

> Let's imagine the following case. I want to keep a diary about the recurrence of a certain sensation. To this end I associate it with the sign "S" and write this sign in a calendar for every day on which I have the sensation. – I first want to observe that a definition of the sign cannot be formulated. – But all the same, I can give one to myself as a kind of ostensive definition! – How? Can I point to the sensation? – Not in the ordinary sense. But I speak, or write the sign down, and at the same time I concentrate my attention on the sensation – and so, as it were, point to it inwardly. – But what is this ceremony for? For that is all it seems to be! A definition serves to lay down the meaning of a sign, doesn't it? – Well,

that is done precisely by concentrating my attention; for in this way I commit to memory the connection between the sign and the sensation. – But "I commit it to memory" can only mean: this process brings it about that I remember the connection *correctly* in the future. But in the present case, I have no criterion of correctness. One would like to say: whatever is going to seem correct to me is correct. And that only means that here we can't talk about "correct". (*PI* 258)

Let us consider what these observations mean both for the immediate problems of inward naming and for our larger understanding of language and our relation to it.

If we restrict ourselves to what is actually available in the scenario as described, we have *only* the sensation, and the sign "S". So of course, no definition of the sign could be formulated because there are as yet no further words in which to formulate that definition. Worse, there is as yet no such thing as a definition—the very idea would be again inconsistently introduced prior to its invention within this minimal sensation "language". And if we then think that we can obviate this problem by giving ourselves an internal ostensive definition, we are then still using the concept of the relation between a name and an object; that is, we are still using more than this origination of a private language could allow at this first stage of a posited link between sign and sensation. If we claim we can concentrate our attention on the sensation and then record it with the sign, and we insist that is all that is required, this still is relying on far more than we actually have in play at this point—this very thought is still dependent upon a host of features of our spoken language to which we do not on this scenario yet have access. Thus, when Wittgenstein's imaginary interlocutor attempts to defend the idea of a private language by insisting that the link between sensation and sign is committed to memory, Wittgenstein's answer is that there would be, in such a case, no distinction between believing oneself right about the connection in the future and being right in the future. This point has been sometimes understood as a "memory-skepticism" argument, where the problem is only that we cannot find an external standard of correctness (so that if we could solve that problem, everything else would be fine). But Wittgenstein's point is more profound: the problem is that the very concept of memory, the appeal to memory, is out of place to the point of unintelligibility—the inability to talk about "correct" is an inability to make the use of the word "memory" here coherent. Although disguised by the ready familiarity of the concept memory as we ordinarily use it in "public" language, "memory" here is no better than "round square". That is to say, the idea of originating a private language from this internal linkage between sensation and sign is irremediably hopeless, because (1) the very idea of a name, of a connection, of a link, requires far more in terms of linguistic context and understanding than it should if we are to think of a first step of a metaphysically private language in this way. And (2), it depends on an external or independent measure of consistency that not only cannot be relied upon (the memory-skepticism problem), but far deeper cannot be articulated so that even the ideas of memory and of consistency are made coherent. Before considering the connection of this failed attempt to the way Romanticism saw the nature of artistic expression and aesthetic content, and the way Modernist artists put into aesthetic practice and their relation to materials what Wittgenstein sees here about our connection to language, let us consider Wittgenstein's vision of language more fully.

Extending and sharpening his investigation, Wittgenstein writes:

> What reason have we for calling "S" the sign for a *sensation*? For "sensation" is a word of our common language, which is not a language intelligible only to me. So the use of this word stands in need of a justification which everybody understands. – And it would not help either to say that it need not be a *sensation*; that when he writes "S" he has *Something* – and that is all that can be said. But "has" and "something" also belong to our common language. – So in the end, when one is doing philosophy, one gets to the point where one would like just to emit an inarticulate sound.

And then he adds, of great significance for our discussion of the Modernist conception of artistic meaning and materials to follow:

> –But such a sound is an expression only in a particular language-game, which now has to be described. (*PI* 261)[3]

"Sensation" is a word in *our* language, as are "something" and "has". "Has" is of particular importance here, because a close focus on this word as it is used shows precisely what Wittgenstein meant above by "preparations"—we initially think we can easily describe the scenario of a privately-initiated language that only the child genius or private diarist can understand. But on every effort to think that through, we either lapse back into the "public" conception of privacy and illegitimately borrow meaning from it, or we lapse into incoherence or unintelligibility. And being reduced to emitting an inarticulate sound is interesting here: one is backed into that corner by these considerations—but even here, the ideas "inarticulate" and "making a sound" are already within, and drawn from, the contexts of discourse that give our words and sentences meaning. Meaning is not in the first instance contained within, radiating out from those who find the external materials to carry the inner private content that this expressive individual (child genius; private diarist; Romantic artist) attaches to those external materials. And that last line? The very idea of emitting a sound *as an expressive utterance* (here one of philosophical exhaustion or futility) requires that it be uttered as a move in a particular language-game, in a circumscribed context of interactive discourse in which such an utterance, such a gesture, has a natural home and within which it has a force and a resonance with other words, sentences, gestures, interactions within that game. The sign "S", the inarticulate sigh, Franz Kline's broad brushstroke on canvas, Stravinsky's ascending minor sixth, T.S. Eliot's phrase "a raid on the inarticulate", Mies van der Rohe's presentation of steel, Antonioni's composition of light and shadow within a frame, and Giacometti's elongated figures walking; all do not derive meaning, do not gain cultural significance, by carrying as initially lifeless signs the life-giving content of attached inward "Somethings". Just as Wittgenstein shattered that conceptual illusion about language, Modernism shattered that Romantic myth about art.

If the "S" theory were true, then the criterion for determining whether a person understood the meaning of a word—on this model a sign (and that itself is a problem: words are not in usual contexts signs)—would be straightforward and uniform across all cases. If the person knew (despite the problems already discussed) the content attached to the sign, the person would know the meaning. For reasons we have seen, this entire picture or conceptual model is far beyond repair, but if we for a moment assume far too much and think this way, another significant truth emerges. Wittgenstein writes:

> Let us remember that there are certain criteria in a man's behaviour for his not understanding a word: that it means nothing to him, that he can do nothing with it. And criteria for his 'thinking he understands', attaching some meaning to the word, but not the right one. And lastly, criteria for his understanding the word correctly. (*PI* 269)

The point (and a powerful one): to the extent that we can speak of so much as attaching a meaning to a word, the criteria we use for judging whether there is no understanding, wrong understanding, or correct understanding are themselves external, public, and varying across cases and suited to, or emergent within, those cases. Such criteria are nothing like what the "S" theory of meaning would imply. Nor is any artist's understanding of the possible usages and meanings of specific materials in particular circumscribed cases anything like parallel to the "S" theory. Meaning in the arts as they function within a culture does not, because it could not, conform to that conceptual template. Art could not work like that. One could come to see this by working through Wittgenstein's conceptually clarifying investigation of language and, as we are doing presently, considering parallel significance for the arts; or one could come to see this by working within the arts independently and—as most of the Modernists did—both implicitly realizing and showing within their practices the vision of materials analogous to Wittgenstein's vision of language; or one could (as a philosopher-artist) do both. We will consider aspects of these three possibilities below, but before moving to that there is a bit more that must be taken on board from Wittgenstein.

There is a deep respect for our human practices that is woven throughout Wittgenstein's philosophical work, and time and again, he returns to particular cases in which we use the words that are now at the center of our philosophical attention. Such returns to actuality often dissipate the mist of philosophical confusion, and they remind us of how our words mean as they are used *by persons* in particular contexts of discourse, in particular language-games, and inside the intricate web of a living culture.

> Look at the blue of the sky and say to yourself, "How blue the sky is!" – when you do it spontaneously – without philosophical purposes – the idea never crosses your mind that this impression of colour belongs only to *you*. And you have no qualms about exclaiming thus to another. And if you point at anything as you say the words, it is at the sky. I mean: you don't have the pointing-into-yourself feeling that often accompanies 'naming sensations' when one is thinking about the 'private language'. Nor do you think that really you ought to point at the colour not with your hand, but with your attention. (Consider what "to point at something with one's attention" means.) (*PI* 275)

The sense that the color is privately "owned" exclusively by oneself, that it is thus ultimately unsharable, and that this unsharable content is the origin of meaning; the sensed resistance about pointing out the special blueness to another; the pointing inwardly with attention to a metaphysically hidden experiential content and the sense that the hand is not the right thing with which to point—all of these are strangely alien to our life in the world and with others, and they can only come into play (and very oddly at that) under the influence of the philosophical picture, the misdirecting conceptual template, of a private language. Despite the initial intuitive power and intellectual attractiveness of the private-language model, this model severely miscasts our life in language, our relation to language. And this model's parallel in the arts, its parallel when thinking about cultural expression, miscasts an artist's life within the materials of art, within the web of possibilities of cultural expression for that artist. It is as remote—instructively, precisely as remote—from actual practice as is the private conception of seeing and remarking on the special blueness of the sky from actually seeing and remarking on the special blueness of the sky. Our life in language is real; the philosophical warping of that is illusion. And an artist's life in paint, in notes, in words, in film, in buildings, in sculptural composition, are all real in the same way. Modernism, always in practice and not infrequently in theory, knew this, and it treated the materials of the arts accordingly.

With all of the foregoing in mind, one could say that Wittgenstein, in another famous and much-discussed passage—although he is of course writing in the philosophy of language—captured the essential difference between the Romantic and the Modernist conceptions of the materials of art and the way artists interact with them:

> If I could say of myself that it is only from my own case that I know what the word "pain" means – must I not say *that* of other people too? And how can I generalize the *one* case so irresponsibly?

> Well, everyone tells me that he knows what pain is only from his own case! – Suppose that everyone had a box with something in it which we call a "beetle". No one can ever look into anyone else's box, and everyone says he knows what a beetle is only by looking at *his* beetle. – Here it would be quite possible for everyone to have something different in his box. One might even imagine such a thing constantly changing. – But what if these people's word "beetle" had a use nonetheless? – If so, it would not be as the name of a thing. The thing in the box doesn't belong to the language-game at all; not even as a *Something*: for the box might even be empty. – No, one can 'divide through' by the thing in the box; it cancels out, whatever it is.

> That is to say, if we construe the grammar of the expression of sensation on the model of 'object and name', the object drops out of consideration as irrelevant. (*PI* 293)

The object drops out of consideration as irrelevant. The meaning of the word "pain" would seem at first philosophical glance to be among the most private words in the language, and the image we make of it is: we have the inner sensation, we attach the word—what we think of as the external sound—to it, and as the only person who truly knows to what it refers, have the first word in a private language. And we then generalize that to all persons, all speakers who use the word "pain". This picture of language is the linguistic model for a pre-Modernist conception of artistic expression and the relation of the artist to her materials, and this picture is herein demolished. We can all have our "beetle", they can be the same, they can differ, they can change into other things, they can be absent: the word in its use is not dependent on a tight and invariant referential connection to the object, whatever it is, of the "beetle". Against the inner-referent picture, we can divide through and cancel out. The grammar, the philosophical logic of the term, does not conform to a misleading picture or conceptual model of "object and name". The "material" of language does not derive its meaning, does not function on the level of usage, in this way. The language, one might say, has a kind of life of its own.

II

When Matisse painted *The Green Stripe (Portrait of Madame Matisse)*, completed in 1905 and exhibited in Paris in 1906, the extremely strong use of green dividing the face from forehead to chin and neck caused the critics to deride the work as one of *Les Fauves*, the wild beasts, objecting strenuously to this use of color and what they regarded as the deliberate ruin, or indeed demolishing, of the portrait. What Matisse along with his colleagues did (they were not alone, but this is a striking case) was in a sense to declare the independence of color, and to let that color interact with and stand against the three major background colors behind the face, but still more importantly to put viewers in a position to see the face in, or behind, the green stripe. The effect is that the stripe, the powerful gesture made within paint, initiates a process of "dividing through" by the representational content. Or given the strength of this aesthetic gesture, one could say that if the "object" is the person depicted and the "name" is the painting, the oil on canvas delivered by a human gesture, the "object" is subordinated to a point where it drops out as irrelevant. Or it is on its way to doing so. The sheer width of the brushstrokes in this work as seen in the comparison of the sitter's right cheek (the greenish side) with the left cheek also works toward this independence. The greenish side is far more consistent with the tradition of portraiture to that point, where paint is subordinated to, and serving, representation—the "object" remains primary. But the flesh-toned side shows brushwork so heavy, and oil so thick, that if we look closely, the representational content recedes so much that we have to exert imaginative effort to see the face within it. Similarly, if we look closely at the darkening of the eyes to the sides of the bridge of the nose, and we focus on those darkenings, we can suddenly react with the thought that they do not belong in this portrait, they cannot be true of the face. But then we think: why are we, like those early pre-Modernist critics, judging what does and does not belong, independently of the interaction of the paint in use here, the interaction of the paint within this visual language-game? A close look at the nostrils can stimulate the same experience: at first we see that they are nostrils within the larger look of the canvas, then we look closely and see that they are blotches, gestural dabs, that are not in the shape of nostrils at all, and then we back away again and see those gestural blotches as nostrils. The lines demarcating the tops of the shoulders participate in the same work.

If we keep what Matisse achieved here in mind and then turn to his Fauvist colleague Andre Derain's painting *La jetee a L'Estaque* of 1906, we see the independence of color further strengthened and joined by the independence of line: the boats, the jetty itself, and even the human figures at the end of the jetty are all depicted behind, or beneath, or within, the oil paint, so that, to again use Wittgenstein's terms, the "objects" are now entirely subservient to the "name". Jetties, of course, are not composed in reality—that is, in the external thing to which the painting, like the word, would refer and from which it would derive its meaning—of red-orange stripes, nor are boat masts tan on the lower half and orange on the upper half. Coastal hills are not orange and light blue. And from an overall perspective we see the boats, but if we narrow the focus to the area of the painting depicting the boats; if we restrict ourselves to what we see exclusive of what we know, we cannot see them in the brushstrokes. We have to stand back, and view generally, allowing cognitive content to visually saturate the oil and transform gestural strokes into represented content. The picture with which Wittgenstein began his discussion of the possibility of a private language is being analyzed, subjected to scrutiny, and dismantled (just as did Wittgenstein on language) step-by-step.

It was in a lecture delivered in Vienna, in 1908, that Adolf Loos famously proclaimed, "Ornament is crime". For Loos, this was a moral as well as aesthetic matter, and he regarded the covering of the materials of architecture ("real" materials, in the sense discussed above) with decoration and ornamentation as a sign of spiritual weakness and a form of dishonesty: "Freedom from ornament is a sign of spiritual strength". A degenerate culture, he claimed, will fail to acknowledge the clarity, strength, and power of materials themselves, covering them over with false appearances that make them conform to a misleading conceptual model. This, for Loos and his colleagues, is an issue of respect, and it is to see architectural materials as working together to create a kind of meaning that is internal to them, that is a function of their "conversational" interaction, and that acknowledges that such materials are themselves the vehicles of architectural thought—they are not used for a purpose external to themselves. For him, the progress of culture—for him, Modernist culture—was inversely proportional to the presence of ornament, and he saw this as true from grand public buildings all the way down to ordinary household utilitarian objects. For him, leather goods of very high finish and quality, along with fine silverwork when plain, were particularly attractive because the beauty of the materials themselves spoke for themselves. And those artifacts allow us to say, in a shared cultural world of aesthetic sensibility, sentence-analogues of Wittgenstein's "How blue the sky is!" above. And like Wittgenstein's criteria for understanding discussed above, Loos regarded the intelligent perception of composition employing respected materials honestly without any call for decoration as the criterion of cultural-architectural understanding. All of his architectural work showed this philosophical position; that is, it showed his conceptual work *inside* this form of art.

Loos received the contract for a major business building in central Vienna in 1909, known as the Looshaus. On its completion, it was immediately severely criticized for insufficient decoration. It presents a marble colonnade of Tuscan (unadorned, unfluted, simplified) columns at the ground floor entry, with the top stories in plain plaster with strong and clear geometric fenestration where each window is itself geometrically subdivided in a formally clear language. The copper Mansard roof is also completely unadorned and so structurally eminently clear, unlike its neighboring buildings. The building was noted for the very high cost of the materials, particularly in a building that was unadorned, again unlike its Beaux-arts neighbors. The Emperor

Franz Joseph, despising the structure, henceforth avoided passing by the building and is said to have left the window shades closed on the side of the Hofburg Palace looking toward the Looshaus. This was moral war in architectural form, just as it was an aesthetic war about meaning. Franz Joseph thought his city's buildings should serve as an "S" for his private sensibility; Loos wanted to divide through and let the materials speak. Loos was forced, after an appeal to obscure city regulations, to add flower boxes under the windows, minimally but significantly marring what is otherwise the relentless honesty of the building. Evening the score later, Loos' *Villa Muller* of 1930 takes the point as much further as did Derain's work following Matisse. It is a house in which, to summarize his Modernist conception, walls are definitely walls. That this has become an aesthetic desideratum constitutive of Modernism is evident, but if we consider a work that became iconic of this style, Le Corbusier's *Villa Savoye* of 1931 with all the foregoing in mind, we can see the striking fact that the ground-level colonnade is made of steel poles and nothing but—no bases, no capitals, no added texture of any kind, and what they support is a rectangular second story containing horizontally elongated rectangular windows with partial balconies inwardly contained so as not to disturb the clarity of the second-story geometry. It is coherent unto itself.

The early deeply negative reactions to these works (works all richly celebrated later) constitute a debate about the proper role of the materials of the arts, about the meaning of the "words" in the language of art and the origin of that meaning. It is about whether the materials of the arts as established and evolved within a culture serve something outside of themselves. Should they be made to answer to some external demand? Or is artistic meaning, like the sound or the sigh from Wittgenstein's remark above, meaningful because they have a home within the life-giving context of a culturally enmeshed language-game?[4]

Arnold Schoenberg faced this problem, and he thought deeply about the nature of meaning in music and the kind of declaration of materials-independence that we saw in Matisse, Derain, and his Viennese colleague Loos. Of course, if music is composed to a text, and particularly if this involves "word painting", the composing of a passage that "paints" in sound the content of the text being set, then music is answering to something outside itself.[5] But the question here, the question Schoenberg faced, is a different one. Tonal harmony *itself* can be considered a demand, an external requirement superadded to musical sound, to which composition must answer. That is, any given employment of a pitch would in conventional harmony be required to satisfy demands external to that pitch and accord with rules of harmonic sense. In conventional or tonal harmony, melodic coherence is always at the same time harmonically coherent. Melodic pitches brought together do form a coherent "sentence", but at the same time they are working for "someone else", working as representatives or instantiations of another thing. Schoenberg thus thought deeply about the musical analogue to the freedom of the brushstroke—a declaration of independence for pitches. They could be brought together in a way that made internal sense within the confines of their circumscribed language-game, but they might not need to accede to the demands of vertical harmonic necessities. That, Schoenberg saw (although he did not put the matter in Wittgensteinian terms—his philosophical thinking was undertaken within music just as Matisse's was undertaken in painting and Loos' in architecture), would be to divide through by the beetle in the box and to see pitch-usage as free of that conceptual picture. Rather like Wittgenstein on language, Schoenberg realized that the demands on composition generated by that picture might be illusory and that musical sense might in truth be independent of that conceptual model.

His philosophical investigation was thus initiated in his move beyond tonal harmony into atonality. Schoenberg's musical language originated in the musical worlds of Brahms on one hand and Wagner on the other, so like the artists we have considered above, he too is positioned at a moment of transition from late Romantic to early Modernist culture. Schoenberg's *Chamber Symphony No. 1*, Opus 9, of 1906 is particularly important in the terms being discussed presently. In it, one sees the point of emergence from earlier presuppositions; instead of fully acknowledging the dictates of conventional harmony, we see the production of musical sense generated by the stacking of fourths (traditional harmony of course stacks thirds), so there is the sense that the work both stays within, and yet moves beyond, harmonic rules. It is still stacked harmony—but it does not generate the world of diatonic harmony so familiar to western ears. A step of creative evolution, it is from it, but not like it. And the piece also utilizes whole-tone structures extensively: these are particularly interesting in the present context because the whole-tone scale is, after all, a scale (like the major scale that, stacked on itself in thirds, generates diatonic harmony), but it is one that misses the dominant-tonic relation because the whole tone steps of the scale land on an augmented fourth and augmented fifth, not the perfect fourth and, more importantly to diatonic harmony, not the perfect fifth. And the whole-tone scale does not have a leading tone, a half step, from the seventh to the eighth scale degree, but rather a whole step. This scale, as a generator of harmonic relations, seems to simultaneously stabilize and destabilize harmony. It is in the process of breaking free, like the green stripe.

That emancipation—in Wittgenstein's phrase from above, "the language itself"—is fully realized in the second decade of the twentieth century, when Schoenberg develops his serial or twelve-tone compositional method. But one should say: "Method" can be a misleading word here. Like Wittgenstein's conception of a language-game, in which there is great latitude for creative development rather than being locked into formulaic rules, Schoenberg's serial compositional technique—serial language—is not (and this has been a point of widespread misunderstanding) formulaic, not narrowly prescriptive. What it does do, in first identifying a twelve-tone "row"—an ordering of the twelve pitches of the chromatic scale that tend to avoid conventionally strong dominant-tonic intervals or thirds that are strongly suggestive of diatonic harmony—is to set out the basic structure out of which the piece will organically grow, but, as Schoenberg insisted (and this too is particularly important for the present discussion), where each pitch is as important, as central, as every other. He called this "a method of composing with twelve tones which are related only with one another".[6] "Pain" is a word in our public language, and it gets its sense by standing in relation to the other words as used within its language-games. The pitches (in this idiom called pitch-classes rather than scales) in one of his masterpieces in this language, his *Variations for Orchestra*, Opus 31 of 1928, work with robust energy in precisely this way.

III

I mentioned above that the investigation into meaning of the kind that Wittgenstein undertook could take place in philosophy (as we followed parts of that investigation as the foundation of this discussion), in the arts themselves (as we have followed some of those with Matisse, Derain, Loos, Corbusier, and Schoenberg), and in both, that is, in the work of philosopher-artists, or philosophically engaged artists. Here I will touch briefly on this third category.

Speaking of the need to move beyond the presumption that artistic meaning can be fully captured in language or translated into it, but still that the arts do constitute a form of meaning and are an evolving language of their own, Robert Motherwell wrote, "I do deem it likely that music, when it gave up *words*, whether a chorus or a mass or lyrics, already had made a parallel leap, on occasion. No one knows how to describe adequately in words the content of a late Beethoven quartet, a Bach fugue, or Bartok's "Concerto for Two Pianos and Drums".... But no one questions that they are all charged with content of the highest order. Wittgenstein...spent a large part of his time at Cambridge in England demonstrating that, at the point where things become most 'interesting', logical description fails us".[7] (He says "logical description", but it is clear from the context that he means the verbal articulation of artistic content.) Motherwell had been speaking in those passages of "moving toward *a new pictorial language*" (p. 328), working on the idea that art could arrive at a place where (a) richness of meaning or "content of the highest order", (b) irreducibility to our spoken and written language, (c) visual and compositional coherence on its own terms in a way internal to the work, (d) a respect for and full exploitation of the power of materials taken as themselves, and (e) formal-compositional power, would all come together. Motherwell graduated college in philosophy, and he studied it in graduate school as well, and one can easily see the themes discussed above at work in his canvases. (Given what Wittgenstein said about the experience of remarking on the deep blueness of the sky, it is fitting that Motherwell so publicly expressed his love of the special blueness of the California sky in his frequent use of ultramarine blue in his abstract paintings, where his "remarks" are of course visual; see his *Blueness of Blue* of 1974.)

Motherwell is thus not interested in, nor a believer in the very possibility of, any equivalence of language and art; again, he insists that the former cannot in any case sufficiently capture the content of the latter. But he is profoundly interested in a deep analogy between language and art, and the ways in which he works toward the combination of the attributes mentioned above in a new pictorial language constitutes a philosophically-informed investigation into meaning in a way that extends into more recent Modernist painting all of the foregoing. The formal power, and the language of developing variations in his *Elegies to the Spanish Republic*, show this, and *The Poet* of 1947 displays a combination of visual coherence with an internal dynamism: dynamism generated from the interaction of elements within the piece. If one looks at his early *Le Belle Mexicaine* (Maria) of 1941, a closer look at the sitter's lower lip, eye, and left arm shows that the Modernist theme of material and brushstroke and color perhaps yielding but not serving representation has been extensively developed within this visual language-game. Motherwell's most famous remark is: "Whenever art appears, life disappears". He has said, above, that the highest content in art is unmistakable; with this remark, it is plain that the content to which he refers, the artistic meaning, does not necessarily stand in a dependency relation to the world outside it. It is not modeled on a conceptually pictured relation between sign and sensation, and the sense of the work is not given through a meaning-giving relation between the "S" and a "Something". The Modernist project sees meaning differently.

The foregoing themes taken together opened the space in which Joseph Kosuth's most discussed piece of conceptual art, his *One and Three Chairs* of 1965, could occur.[8] Throughout his work, Kosuth has frequently referred to Wittgenstein's philosophical writings, and his *One and Three Chairs* is an invitation to think within the range of implications (itself a Wittgensteinian idea concerning the nature of meaning)[9] opened by this work. We see, here, a chair on the floor of the gallery standing in front of the wall behind it; to the viewer's left of the chair on the wall, we see a life-size photograph of that chair in that exact location, and to the right of the chair, we see on the wall an enlarged dictionary definition of the word "chair".

Platonically speaking, we have the material object, the mimetic representation of the object, and the definition of the class into which the object falls. In terms of nominalism, we have the linguistic definition of the chair that makes the physical object what it is, and the representation of that chair is subsequently called a "picture of a chair" only because of that definition. In terms of realism, we have an existent material chair first, and then the representation of it has content because it follows that existent particular, and the definition is a verbal description that answers to that material entity, which is on the realist view primary. But in terms of Wittgenstein's philosophy, we see still more.

Could we name that object in a way idiosyncratic to us? The answer is certainly yes—we could give it a proper name for example. But Wittgenstein said: "That is not what I mean". Could we internally and in isolation from any prior language, name it with the sound "chair"? We could not, of course, produce the definition in the first instance of naming privately—all those words in the definition are already in a public language. When we view the chair, do we then have an internal, private, mental version of the photograph of the chair? Could that serve as the referent of the word "chair"? If we think of a private language in which we would call the object by a name, are we actually presupposing far too much about what a word is, what naming is, what giving a thing a name is—are we merely thinking of "the post where the new word is stationed" and thinking of that? Or if we focus on the sensory experience of encountering the chair, is it that sensation by virtue of which we in the first instance and autonomously or privately know that it is a chair? But recall Wittgenstein: "sensation" is a word of our common language, which is not a language intelligible only to me". Are the word and the definition only intelligible within a language, within an evolved language-game? What are the criteria for understanding, misunderstanding, or not understanding the word and its definition as presented to us here? And perhaps most important, could we see this one object for the work of art it is independently of the culture within which its creation and its content are made possible? Or like a word, does that recognition of an artwork depend on much more than what a private model could capture or accommodate? Or does this very question rather direct our attention toward the persons, the situated gestures, the practices, and the intricate web of conceptual connections upon which the identity of this work depends? Do we see the materials as presented before us functioning in the way Wittgenstein's investigation led us to see language? And when we exclaim to our fellow viewer about the conceptual content of this work, are we in truth speaking about a metaphysically hidden inner sense? When you point to any of its three parts, should you really be pointing with your attention to an inner object? Or rather: can one "divide through", with the "object dropping out as irrelevant"? When we think through those issues, we think through the content of this work in a way informed by a deep analogy between language and art, and we do so within the culture that this work is positioned. And we see in a way deeply consonant with the Modernist conception considered in all the foregoing, that the materials have an interactive and meaning-generating life of their own, that artistic composition cannot fit into the "S" theory, and we see much more of what it means to claim that—to adapt what we saw Wittgenstein say of language at the outset—material itself is the vehicle of artistic thought.

Notes

1. Ludwig Wittgenstein, *Philosophical Investigations*, Revised 4th ed., ed. P.M.S. Hacker and Joachim Schulte, trans. G.E.M. Anscombe, P.M.S. Hacker, and Joachim Schulte (Malden: Wiley-Blackwell, 2009).
2. M. H. Abrams, *The Mirror and the Lamp* (Oxford: Oxford University Press, 1971).
3. See in this connection Rush Rhees, "Can There Be a Private Language", in his *Discussions of Wittgenstein* (London: Routledge & Kegan Paul, 1970). He begins the essay with, "The problem about private languages is the problem of how words mean. This is much the same as what a rule of language is. When we talk about something, our language does not point to it, or mirror it. Pointing and mirroring could refer to things only within a conversation, anyway: only when there is a way in which

pointing is understood and a way in which mirroring is understood. I point for the sake of someone who understands it. Apart from that it were an idle ceremony; as idle as making sounds in front of things" (p. 55).

Also, in addition to the significance of the private language considerations for capturing something at the heart of Modernism, there is the style of Wittgenstein's philosophical work, which is itself an exemplification of Modernism's working with and inside materials themselves. Stanley Cavell, in "The Availability of Wittgenstein's Later Philosophy", in his collection *Must We Mean What We Say?* (Cambridge: Cambridge University Press, 1976), writes: "The first thing to be said in accounting for his style is that he *writes*: he does not report, he does not write up results. Nobody would forge a style so personal who had not wanted and needed to find the right expression for his thought. The German dissertation and the British essay—our most common options for writing philosophy—would not work; his is not a system and he is not a spectator. My suggestion is that the problem of style is set for him by the two aspects of his work which I have primarily emphasized: the lack of existing terms of criticism, and the method of self-knowledge" (p. 70). *Not a spectator*: Modernist work is not work at a distance from its materials. "The Method of Self-Knowledge" is what I had in mind in the phrase "Philosophy's Linguistic Self-Analysis" in my title.

Closely connected, yet beyond the reach of the present discussion, is Cavell's observation that philosophical work, as practiced by Wittgenstein and in a Wittgensteinian vein, is actually "a spiritual struggle, specifically as a struggle with the contrary depths of oneself", in his *This New Yet Unapproachable America* (Chicago: University of Chicago Press, 1989), p. 37. This is a conception of philosophical engagement particularly fitting with the entire Modernist ethos. That struggle— that distinctive *kind* of struggle—can easily be seen as the motivating drive behind the work of a number of the greatest Modernist painters: Rothko (think of the chapel); Barnett Newman; Gauguin (at the point of Modernism's prototypical emergence); Brancusi (if in an interestingly different way); Malevich; a phase of Pollock (around 1947); and Robert Motherwell, among others. What Cavell sees in Wittgenstein's *personal* work of this distinctive kind in philosophy (and I think this has been nearly universally missed in the literature on the relations between Modernism and philosophy) is strikingly discernible within the work of these Modernist artists. In this way too, and revealingly, Wittgenstein works on and in language in the way that they work on and in the materials of their art (as I will discuss more fully below). There is a particularly interesting discussion of the private language idea relating Wittgenstein and Saul Bellow's work in Michael Lemahieu, "Bellow's Private Language", in *Wittgenstein and Modernism*, ed. Michael Lemahieu and Karen Zumhagen-Yekple (Chicago: University of Chicago Press, 2017), pp. 231–253. See particularly his discussion of the Cavell remark concerning struggle, pp. 252–253.

4. For a richly informed study of the broad cultural context of Modernism and its manifestations, see Michael Levenson, *Modernism* (New Haven: Yale University Press, 2011). Also see, for another rich study that interweaves the striking developments in politics, science and technology, art, literature, and psychology between 1880 and World War I (that is, that describes the intellectual and cultural context within which Modernism emerged), see Stephen Kern, *The Culture of Time and Space: 1880–1918* (Cambridge, MA: Harvard University Press, 2003).

5. The libretto in an opera, or the poem being set to music, is of course essential to, and constitutive of, the work in question, but the issue here concerns the role the notes themselves are playing, and are the pitches independent or subordinate, and is the meaning autonomous inside instrumental sound itself or is it externally derived?

6. Arnold Schoenberg, *Style and Idea: Selected Writings of Arnold Schoenberg*, ed. Leonard Stein, trans. Leo Black (Berkeley: University of California Press, 1984), p. 218. It is of interest to consider Schoenberg's atonal and serial works against the background of the tonal works from which Schoenberg's later styles emerged. For a helpful discussion, see Oliver Neighbor's insightful analysis in Oliver Neighbor, Paul Griffiths, and George Perle, *The New Grove Second Viennese School* (New York: Norton, 1983), pp. 27–68. As with richness in a Modernist novel or painting or architectural work, he writes "The interplay of melodic and rhythmic motifs is responsible to a very large extent for the extraordinary richness of the music, bringing about in the course of a work the gradual accumulation of a mass of affinities between disparate elements" (p. 53).

7. Robert Motherwell, *The Writings of Robert Motherwell* (Berkeley: University of California Press, 2007), p. 329.

8. I am indebted to Tobias Servaas for helpful conversations about Kosuth's work and about this piece and its philosophical significance in particular.

9. I pursue this issue in "Implication in Interpretation: Wittgenstein, Artistic Content, and 'The Field of a Word'", *Mind, Language, and Action: Proceedings of the 36th International Wittgenstein Symposium*, ed. Daniele Moyal-Sharrock, Volker Munz, and Annalisa Coliva (Berlin: De Gruyter, 2015), pp. 45–63.

References

Adams, M.H. 1971. *The Mirror and the Lamp*. Oxford: Oxford University Press.

Cavell, S. 1976. The Availability of Wittgenstein's Later Philosophy. In *Must We Mean What We Say?* Cambridge: Cambridge University Press.

———. 1989. *This New Yet Unapproachable America*. Chicago: University of Chicago Press.

Hagberg, G. 2015. Implication in Interpretation: Wittgenstein, Artistic Content, and 'The Field of a Word'. In *Mind, Language, and Action: Proceedings of the 36th International Wittgenstein Symposium*, ed. Daniel Moyal-Sharrock, Volker Munz, and Annalisa Coliva. Berlin: De Gruyter.

Kern, S. 2003. *The Culture of Time and Space: 1880–1918*. Cambridge, MA: Harvard University Press.

Lemahieu, M. 2017. Below's Private Language. In *Wittgenstein and Modernism*, ed. Michael Lemahieu and Karen Zumhagen-Yekple. Chicago: University of Chicago Press.

Levenson, M. 2011. *Modernism*. New Haven: Yale University Press.

Motherwell, R. 2007. *The Writings of Robert Motherwell*. Berkeley: University of California Press.

Neighbor, O., P. Griffiths, and George Perle. 1983. *The New Grove Second Viennese School*. New York: Norton.

Rhees, R. 1970. Can There Be a Private Language? In *Discussions of Wittgenstein*. London: Routledge and Kegan Pau.

Wittgenstein, L. 2009. *Philosophical Investigations,* trans. G.E.M. Anscombe and ed. P.M.S. Hacker and Joachim Schulte, revised 4th ed. Malden: Wiley-Blackwell.

6

Encountering the Alien: Paul Bowles on Death and Madness at the Edge of the World

Tanja Staehler and Alexander Kozin

I

The subject of this essay is Paul Bowles' 1949 novel, *The Sheltering Sky*. At the same time, the term 'novel' is perhaps the least apt definition for a work that resists any formal typology of genre, just as it resists any interpretation that leans in on the manner of emplotment which is featured by this work. All the formal literary criteria are nonetheless present: narrative action, development of characters, descriptions of inner states, relational conflicts, and unusual locations, all pointing strongly to the dramatic incline. Indeed, in his first written autobiography, Bowles chose to describe his work as a classical triangle, a joint venture of life, love, and death. When the novel took off from the page, in 1990, in a cinematographic version shot by Bernardo Bertolucci,

T. Staehler (✉) · A. Kozin
Centre for Literature and Philosophy, University of Sussex, Brighton, UK
e-mail: T.Staehler@sussex.ac.uk

A. Kozin
e-mail: alex.kozin@gmx.net

© The Author(s) 2018
A. Falcato and A. Cardiello (eds.), *Philosophy in the Condition of Modernism*,
https://doi.org/10.1007/978-3-319-77078-9_6

127

The Sheltering Sky appeared precisely that, a psychological drama with the elements of exotic adventure that ends in a tragic loss of life. Despite the fact that the theme of adventure runs strongly throughout the novel, the action of *The Sheltering Sky*, no matter how intense and convoluted, does not create a straightforward accumulative storyline, nor does it offer an explosive conclusion; on the contrary, its telling tends to spiral down or go aside, sometimes bringing the interpersonal component to the fore and sometimes downplaying it to the point of non-existence, depriving the reader of the illusion that *The Sheltering Sky* is a drama in disguise. The, thus created, ambivalence is reflected in a unique style that presents the novel's plot as if it develops entirely by itself without any intervention on the part of the writer. In fact, the life of Paul Bowles and his creation have much in common; however, this commonality is also less than straightforward.

When speaking about himself as an American ex-patriot, who left the United States at the age of 33 for an unknown destination, Paul Bowles hints at the possible autobiographical origin of the novel by linking it to his own desire to leave the United States, going for something other, something else. Even the title of his 1972 autobiography, *Without Stopping* speaks of the relief after that very desire became fulfilled. "Each day spent on the other side of the Atlantic was a day out of prison" (1972: 165). It is hardly a coincidence that the first port of arrival for the novel's characters, who are also on the run from the oppressive landscape of New York City, is Tangiere. This place is significant, already, because it gave the ultimate refuge to the writer, who spent the rest of his life there after refusing to settle in Europe. However, to link Paul Bowles' life to the novel would be inappropriate due to the writer's reference—in the same autobiography—to his disinterest in both cultural explorations and personal exploits. Despite his multiple talents: he was not only a writer, but an accomplished composer and a sketch artist, all which presuppose unbridled creativity, Paul Bowles was remembered by his contemporaries as a quiet and introspective man, whose strong opinions never stole from his most favorite pastime: observing life as it unfolded before him in local cafes, or on his regular evening walks along familiar streets of the African Port. It was there, and not in Paris, his first out-of-home 'shelter', that the writer's attention was drawn to those 'tiny little things' that were so ordinary that they would be barely remembered by the actors themselves.

Bowles's intense observations turned people into characters and placed them, naturally, in a book. In his film *The Sheltering Sky* Bernardo Bertolucci captured this kind of attentiveness in the figure of the narrator, whose character and voice were designed to provide an introduction to the film and to appear now and then in the novel with some comments and observations. The narrator is Paul Bowles himself. One can trace melancholy in his voice, but this sentiment belongs to the novel and not Paul Bowles, who loved living just so; his life was neither a romance, nor an adventure, nor a drama, but it was a life filled with the everyday existence to the utmost. Still, *The Sheltering Sky*, the novel, does not seek to replicate the life of the writer, but it does enhance its sense, no matter how spontaneously, by bringing its action to the level of the extreme, revealing to the reader the end of the path the writer never happened to tread himself.

Considering the encounter with the alien under the extreme circumstances imposed on the travelers by the alien-land to be the main theme of the novel, we would like to suggest phenomenology ('xenology') as a method for the analysis of *The Sheltering Sky*. In order to give some credence to our methodological choice, in the next section, we present a brief elaboration on what we consider to be a mutually enriching relationship between phenomenology and literature.

II

It is largely to Martin Heidegger that we owe the, by now common, association of Plato with phenomenology.[1] Standing in agreement with Heidegger, Jacques Derrida pointed out that Plato's philosophy is phenomenological not only because it is given in the literary form of 'play,' which creates the essential—for phenomenology—ambiguity of sense. In fact, his dialogues can be considered as "small fictions."[2] With the help of the literary form that coincided with a particular way of thinking, Plato chose to use the aesthetic rather than logical or analytical discourse to achieve his argument. In addition to obvious philosophical contributions, his analyses of myths indicate the beginnings of literary criticism, as Plato is already sufficiently detached from the sacred literal meaning of myths. Therefore, for phenomenology, literature, together with other arts, is a mode of discovery in its own right. The name of this mode, according to Heidegger, is 'disclosure.' Disclosure is characterized by the discovery of poetic modalities which condition the appearance and existence of aesthetic phenomena. In the "Origin of the Work of Art," Heidegger writes: "Art is the disclosure of being by which alone Being can be defined" (1971a: 85). In contrast to 'manifestation,' which is a mode that gives us a 'common,' that is, habitualized appearance, in the manner in which we usually 'take' objects in the natural attitude, as they immediately appear to us, and 'revelation,' which characterizes mystical phenomena, disclosure is a mode which helps us "open up a world and keep it abindingly in force" (ibid.: 43).

In his discussions of Hölderlin, Heidegger endowed literature with an even greater role by claiming that the relationship between literature and phenomenology was that of a method that informs very basic phenomenological premises and which is informed by them through a continuous rejuvenation of the same theme (1971b: 111–139).[3] In comparison to traditional phenomenological approaches to literature, for Heidegger, imaginary shadows precede illuminated perception, tainting seemingly indubitable facts with the non-enunciative ambiguity, putting a challenge to truth and objectivity of any kind. As for truth itself, "it is inseparable from the expressive operation that says it; it does not precede reflection but is a result of it" (Danto 1985: 7). In other words, truth-fullness, when it is understood not as certainty but as epiphany, is always given at the limit of experience, on the periphery of the imaginary and the unconscious, in other words, "*au bout*, at the edge" (Derrida 1979: 67). The main function of the edge is not to connect the ordinary to the extraordinary, however, but to make their encounter edge out of the world, as it were; hence, the capacity of literature to disclose this world by crossing over their limit and by recounting that experience: "It is by the voice of the imaginary witness that the inaccessible other is told" (Levinas 1998: 146). This is to say that the world, inaccessible in principle, can only be shown by literature, letting us assume that there are possibilities of being that only literature can reveal.

On the level of consciousness, phenomenology can also take credit for showing how literary disclosure utilizes active imagination. For example, for Husserl, the activity of imagination is radically different from the movement of memory, or immediate perception, in that it points neither back nor forward, but configures time exclusively on the basis of the quasi-now, which is not a substitute for being, but a form of suspended being, where consciousness does not produce intentionalities imbedded in immediate perception, but has them imbedded in fanciful worlds, or the worlds of probable essences. This emphasis is preserved in another traditional approach used by Roman Ingarden, who follows Husserl by suggesting that we can enter a literary work through the structure of its object, returning us to the objective world which literature appropriates for reconstruction: "when I understand a text, I think the meaning of the text. When I think the meaning of the text, it appears as a symbolic whole, essentially a totality" (Ingarden 1973: 73). This totality is a world that enters the cognitive processes as specific literary acts of consciousness. In all of the discussed cases, literature appears as the creator of a symbolic, or estranged world. In other words, this world functions as an allegory for the actual world. Even the most realistic works possess that ability; yet, the structure of each literary world is going to be different in any given case.

The effects of phenomenology on literature appear much less explicit or rather more difficult to trace. Traditionally, we perceive as phenomenological those works that invite phenomenology as a tool for examining their structure and meaning, or sense. Here, the so-called 'existential' literature appears to be particularly appropriate. This category draws consistent attention from phenomenologists and includes: Homer, Dante, Cervantes, but also: Marcel Proust, Fyodor Dostoyevsky, Franz Kafka and, more recently: Italo Calvino, Don DeLillo, and David Foster Wallace, among many others. Not all this literature has the same existential force, but all of it pursues the same objective: to lead the reader to some discovery of the world, its structure and its meaning. This list is far from exhaustive, for every period of human history created the kind of works that proffered specific phenomenological themes, for example, the role of soul in the formation of moral responsibility; time, space, and the other as the prerequisites for developing one's self-identity; the uncanny, the surreal, the divine; aesthetics and ethics; humanity and animality; language and expression; simulacrum; action; multiplicity, diversity, number; history, life, and death. Literary variations of these themes enrich our understanding of the world, and at the same time, they provide phenomenology with exemplars that do not just illustrate the objective world, but literally open it from the inside, throw us from the natural into the phenomenological attitude.

Likewise, *The Sheltering Sky*, where maps are fused with territories and the ordinary blends with the extraordinary, takes the master theme for its own: "Literature as a whole may be globally characterized as a quest" (Ricoeur 1985: 19). In other words, we can pre-define the novel's objective to be the creation of a terrain (world), which discloses the sense of the extreme by draining the main characters of their fragile existence, depriving them of their bodies, their voices, their own selves, 'undoing them,' as it were. The unknown they seek and find at the edge of the world becomes the sufficient and necessary condition for what otherwise cannot be expressed; hence, the significance of the novel for contemporary times, which insist on harbouring the belief in the sameness of human life and foundational values of the human world. We know about the fragility of this world, but this knowledge does not prevent us from commonly associating assaults on the world's integrity with either ill intention or arbitrary malice. *The Sheltering Sky* refuses such pretences by showing that mortal danger is always lurking where one expects it the least and that the traveller who goes too far into the land which is not his own is particularly vulnerable, for he or she imagines the alien-world to be an extension of home, where even the most extreme experiences come as familiar shapes and foreseen occurrences. In fact, by itself, the alien-world is always already out of reach; only its limits can be accessible to a stranger.

Following the postulate of the partial accessibility of the other, in this article, we would like to examine this postulate with the help of the phenomenological concepts of the 'alien,' the 'encounter with the alien' and the 'becoming-alien' as the leitmotif for *The Sheltering Sky* that depicts Port and Kit Moresby, two wealthy American travellers, who leave New York City in search of a place as far away from their home as possible. The remote places they intend to visit are chosen at random; the Americans are not searching for a different kind of culture. They are simply looking for whatever may happen, and they happen to find this in Morocco, although the place itself is also hardly essential for what is awaiting them in Africa. Seasoned travellers, the Moresbys had already explored many other close-by locations in South America and Asia, and now, still driven toward some place else, they chose Northern Africa for its convenient proximity to Europe, in case they had to escape to Italy or France, and also because they considered it to be the least touched by the devastations of the Great War. On this journey, they are accompanied by some sort of family friend, Mr. Tunner, who is tagging along more out of boredom than curiosity or interest in local exotics. He is distinctly other in the company of the Moresbys. His unreflective attachment to his home makes him a quintessential tourist. He has no inclination to stay away in Africa for long and is ready to return home any time. Unlike Kit and Port, who come to Africa without such expectations and subsequently are going to be swept away by the alien, Tunner will be barely touched by it.

It is at this juncture that we would like to ask, How shall we understand the meaning of *The Sheltering Sky* phenomenologically? Given that the prevailing theme of the novel is the encounter with the alienworld, we suggest consulting *xenology*, or the phenomenological science of the alien. We present the main tenets of xenology in the next section.

III

As a phenomenological concept, the alien [*das Fremde*] entered Husserl's thought in the late period of his work, when he turned to the problem of community and its constitution. He set up this problem under the question of 'one world' versus 'many worlds' and the conditions of their limits. He thus recognized the life-world as not what allowed for experience, in general, but as what instigated particular kinds of experience that generated constitutive unities within communal worlds. Delimited from each other by an unsurpassable divide (on the level of constitutive genesis), these worlds defied comparison no matter how close they would appear to each other. On the Husserlian account, there is always a limit that separates one communal world from another, making it alien to the home and, when focusing on the constitutive outcomes of the opposite direction, making the alien. This realization leads Husserl to switching from treating the Other as the opposite of the Self to posing the Other as the limit to one's Self. With this shift of focus, Husserl endows the Other with a new epistemological status, and with it, a claim to the transcendental problematic: "at issue here is to somehow accomplish a making home of the alien, as if it were home [...] there is also the question of the limits of such knowledge and the question of justifying the idea of complete understanding" (Husserl 2005: 625).

Husserl's problematization of full understanding and full knowledge of radical difference is hardly a trivial matter, for it needs a justification which, if placed in the contemporary context, would point to the doubt that globalization of human values is not only possible but is accompanied by complete understanding. In addition to the issue of sameness within multiplicity, there hides an implicit assumption that substitutability of worlds could be possible. A whole number of questions arise at this point. First, there comes the question about the extent of separation between the home and the alien. Is it possible to breach this separation? Second, there is the question about the separation itself. Can it count as a separate realm of experience with a clear epistemological significance? Finally, admitting of the relative status of alien-worlds vis-à-vis each other makes Husserl wonder about their role in the constitution of the life-world itself. Importantly, from the phenomenological standpoint, alien-worlds should not be conceived in sociological or anthropological terms, let it be a remotely placed tribe, or a highly industrialized power. The alien-world is not founded on nationality or territory. For Husserl, an alien-world qualifies as such only if it is experienced as abnormal, discordant, non-optimal, atypical, and unfamiliar, but also as a-historical.

The significance of the alien for literature should be obvious if we recollect other literary works that focus on the alien, especially those written in a particular period of human history: the era of great discoveries in the eighteen–nineteenth-centuries brought about both fantastic and extreme descriptions of unsurpassable encounters with the strangeness that never becomes familiar. Although Robinson Crusoe's best friend, native Friday, at the end of his enculturation by his savior refuses to eat human flesh and accepts Christianity, he does not become less accessible. Nor does Kurtz from Joseph Conrad's *Heart of Darkness* manage to become the alien, but his coming too close to the native results in madness: "[..] all the wisdom, and all the truth, and all sincerity, are just compressed into that inappreciable moment of time in which we step over the threshold of the invisible" (1994: 101). Finally, there is colonial and post-colonial literature, which focuses almost exclusively on the encounter with different asymmetrical worlds. As far as the English literature is concerned, Indian stories by Rudyard Kipling, South Pacific stories by W. Somerset Maugham, and others can be taken as examples of the clash between the largely Anglo-Saxon home-world and many indeterminate 'native' worlds, which could not be understood, only conquered. The encounter with these worlds is described not as a journey or adventure, but precisely as the encounter with 'farness' and the subsequent quest to understand it. Here, the rule is that the closer the home dweller comes to the alien, the stronger are the destructive effects of the alien until they completely absorb the foreigner, just like they absorbed Conrad's Kurtz.

In both contexts, literary and phenomenological, the experience of the alien and alien-worlds is commonly accompanied by an encounter with an Alien being. Phenomenologically speaking, the typology of the Alien exceeds the character of the stranger. Coming from, and with, a world of their own that is delimited from our own world, the Alien types who populate respective alien-worlds are considered as shadowy or liminal phenomena. For that reason, Husserl calls them *Limes-Subjekte*. Their typology is limited to animals, children, the insane and the foreigners. Unlike other normal subjects, limit-subjects are intersubjective from the beginning because they already possess or 'own' their worlds exclusively, without the possibility of sharing them with the 'non-members.' Their worlds differ from normative worlds precisely to the extent to which their communities act in accordance with the modified rationality. The work of modification depends on the manner of modalization. The way each different alien modality is given signifies its positionality vis-à-vis the home-world. The difference between the two lies in the affect produced by a specific alien-world.

When describing different alien-worlds, Ludwig Landgrebe, following Husserl, establishes the continuum for their inaccessibility by distinguishing between "far-worlds" and "near-worlds" (Landgrebe 1981: 132). Both extremes are affective, albeit to a different degree. Close alien-worlds often evolve from within one's home, while far alien-worlds dwell on its margins. In other words, the farthest world is the world most removed from our familiar experience, thus posing the greatest challenge to its understanding, while the nearest world implies some degree of comprehensibility. The farthest of the alien-worlds known to humans is owned by the animal. This might explain why Husserl consistently refers to the animal as being 'dark.' The next closest alien-world belongs to the child who is characterized by "the non-recognition of temporality and spatiality and [exhibits] a unique mode of connecting to the others through self-fulfillment" (Husserl 1973: 605). In relation to the figure of madman, Husserl writes: "Isn't it possible that we all become insane and that many subjects live without relying on a life-world, without any communal experience?" (Husserl 1970: 32). As the quote indicates, for Husserl, madness is the last frontier of sociality; yet, it is a form of sociality nonetheless because madness too has a rationality of its own.

As for the foreigner, Husserl singles out this Alien modality because he or she epitomizes community as the primary type of human sociality in possession of the highest form of rationality. Only by way of communal living, does a human become a human and a spatio-temporal being in the cultural linguistic sense. Husserl often models his Alien foreigner on the exotic Alien, the savage [*das Wilde*]. The coincident use of the two terms [*das Fremde* and *das Wilde*] is significant as it points to the extreme end of the position that Husserl assumes toward the foreigner. The foreigner is someone whose home is founded on myths and rituals, in other words, special social activities that engage an entire community of people identifying it not just as a form of sociality, but as a culture, meaning that this community is homogenous, coexisting with other similar communities in the manner of multiple parallel worlds segmented by horizontal relations in the contemporary and vertical in the historical perspectives. In comparison to the animal and the child, the Alien foreigner designates multiplicity within the species. An Alien community is clearly separated from another Alien community by language, territory, traditions and customs, all of which comprise a constitutive terrain, which can be crossed but only at the limit.

This liminal in-between belongs to a realm of experience which is uniquely given only on the basis of limits, borders, and boundaries. This realm is constituted by alienness throughout. Alienness is what delimits us from the outside and therefore fulfils the inside; it never leaves the divide which formulates new and different forms of rationality that belong only to the alien: "Alienness then does not proceed from a division but consists in a division" (Waldenfels 1996: 21). This extraordinary order resides in the twilight and is predicated on ambiguity. This is the reason why limit-phenomena cannot be appropriated, assimilated, brought home, made whole. Regular communication between the home and the alien is conducted over the liminal realm on the outer side of its terrain. This kind of communication is characterized by the minimal effect on both sides. It is possible, however, for the encounter with the alien-world to take place inside the liminal in-between. In that case, alienness may take a grip on the home, capture its subject, for liminality does not feature any mediating structures that could secure a safe passage outside back to the home-land. The resultant affect would be akin to being lost in the fog, where all formerly familiar phenomena have their recognizable shapes dissolved, becoming formless, two-dimensional and free of any specific direction: "We encounter the alien as something that cannot be said or done within our order. The extraordinary makes its appearance as an order existing elsewhere" (Waldenfels 1996: 115). We should ask then, what kind or order is it? What basic structures is it based on?

In fact, the structures of the liminal world are not, properly speaking, structures, but figures. For example, in his lecture course *Parmenides*, Heidegger identifies truth as a goddess or *aletheia* (Αλη θεια). She cannot assume a human form, but she can issue a divine sign. *Aletheia* is thus both a symbolic figure and pure transcendence. However, *aletheia* is most significant for the ordinary world; her presence in this world is continuous and unabiding. For the liminal world, the most significant divinities are daemons. In Ancient Greek, *daimôn* meant the divine sign itself; unlike *aletheia*, which does not stand for truth, but is truth, daemons may warn the person of an impending disaster and/or to lead one to it. In Plato's dialogue *Apology of Socrates*, Socrates referred to listening to the divine voice of a *daimonion* who would function as simultaneously a guardian angel and a punishing force. The etymology of the Greek word also points to division and separation, prediction and divination (δαίω: to divide, to prophesize), as well as leading a person to a particular destiny. Two such daemons figure in the experience of the protagonists of *The Sheltering Sky*. In Plato's dialogue *Symposium*, high priestess Diotima tells Socrates that love (*eros*) brings nothing better than catastrophe, but, at the same time, there is no great healer than love. Because of this duality, she calls Eros a "great daemon" (Plato 1997: 202d). In her story of two realms of being: life and death, "everything daemonic is positioned between divine and mortal" (ibid.: 202d–e). Plato saw the main purpose of *daimonia* and *daimons* as providing "interpreting and transporting human things to the gods and divine things to men; entreaties and sacrifices from below, and ordinances and requitals from above…" (ibid.: 202e).

In *Parmenides*, Heidegger presents *Eros* as a primordial divinity; in comparison to other divinities, he was the first one to appear; however, his parents and origin remain unknown. A messenger of Greek Gods to people, demi-god Eros could acquire a human shape, for the humans were too weak to bear the divine voice without a body. Shuttling between Gods and humans makes Eros a resident of the liminal sphere and thus one of the two most significant figures for our study. The other figure is *Thanatos*, also a divinity, but without the 'privileges' of Eros. Thanatos is the Greek God of darkness, sickness, and death. He also resides in the liminal sphere, maintaining its order by providing the ultimate delimitation for the humans. Georges Bataille put the two *daimons* together when he wrote about the beginning of being human (Bataille 1962: 55–62). Earlier, the Presocratics insisted that death was the ultimate problem of philosophy and used the figure of Thanatos to help them find an explanation for its existence. In contrast, Eros is not only the primordial personification of everything original and, for that reason, already alien; he is also a guide and an affect. The discourse of Eros is desire in its most pure form, as love, the strongest of all human drives. In contrast, Thanatos has no voice and no specific shape. He defies both movement and change. He too is a *daemon,* but his significance is the opposite of moving on, going through or running after. He evokes no need or desire; yet, we should not reduce him to being just a caretaker of departed souls, because he is also the host for all those who reached the end of their destiny. The complementarity and opposition between Eros and Thanatos reveals the synthesis of ambiguity specific to Eros and the finitude immanent to Thanatos. Despite his high profile, Eros, the playful one, is also the most elusive of the two. When he is out there in the human world, he constantly changes shape; he shifts and dodges, one time he is in pursuit, the other time—in flight. In the myth of Eros described by Plato in his dialogue *Phaedrus,* Eros signifies a desire that is evoked in the realm of the sensible and yet transcends all sensibility. As our incarnated souls dwell on this earth, Eros, the *mania* instantiated by the gods, overcomes us when we see something beautiful which reminds us of beauty itself (Plato 1997: 51b). When the loved one is taken away from us, our soul's wings dry out and cause us pain. Hence our desire to be around the loved one at all times—a desire that cannot be accounted for by reason: we cannot explain why the loved one's presence exerts such a strong pull.

The Platonic myth explains that Eros is neither merely spiritual, nor is it merely physical (Staehler 2010: 79–94). Its duality is a reminder that we, as human beings, are being constantly weighed down by the heaviness of earthly existence, and, at the same time it is a reminder of who we can be if we allow our wings to sprawl. Earthly beauty inspires Eros. Prompted by the Platonic myth of Eros and the wings of desire, Emmanuel Levinas endows Eros with the ambiguity of a being that is not only neither here nor there, but that suffers from oblivion which, on the material level, replicates the oblivion of death. Thus, Eros is oblivious to the person as a person; but he is also oblivious of the time when enjoyment withers to anxiety before the inevitable demise. All that concerns death, finitude or mortality is alien to Eros. It belongs to the 'other' domain. In that sense, Eros is carefree: he will never know the burden of Thanatos, but his duality, his immaterial materiality makes Eros "vulnerable and mortal" (Levinas 1997: 230). This tension is a reflection of the original ambiguity involved in Eros, namely, the ambiguity of need and desire. On the level of need, I enjoy the beloved in the oblivion of death. On the level of desire, I encounter the alien Other as a mortal and vulnerable being. Ultimately, the intensity of my enjoyment stems from the combination of these elements that, at their intersection, make me realize that I am a human being.

It is for this reason that we find the greatest benefit in employing a work of literature which does not only focus on the encounter between representatives of two radically different socio-cultural worlds, but poses the encounter itself as an intermittent release of alienness, which constantly shifts the perspective to move the reader through the alien-world with specific, albeit concealed forms of daemonic possession by Eros and Thanatos, which keeps affecting the other until the alien-world and the home-world cross their paths some place in-between, colliding together, thereby leading to the disintegration of the own and the institution of a foundationless state of being for the self that gets swallowed by the liminality of indeterminate existence. In what follows, we would like to demonstrate this very affect as it transpires in Paul Bowles' *The Sheltering Sky*.

IV

The first part of the novel is set up against the sedentary culture of the Moroccan port. More or less decent hotels; safe, albeit brief, encounters with the locals and late afternoon strolls along narrow streets formulate the surroundings, which although undoubtedly exotic are of no interest to traveler Port and only of mild interest to Kit, who finds herself more often in the company of tourist Tunner, whom she despises, but continues to tolerate as a familiar and handsome face. She is often bored in his presence, complaining to Tunner that boredom is the melancholia of modernity: "The people of every country become like the people of any other country" (Bowles 1947: 12). Here, we can read a yearning for the wings of desire, for Eros. In comparison, Port has a somewhat different approach to encountering other civilizations and their inhabitants. In the beginning of his journey to the out-land, he explains why he designates himself as a 'traveler' and Tunner as a 'tourist:' "the traveler goes to other countries and he may never return from his travels; a tourist always returns home, he cannot be lost" (ibid.: 11). This is to say that Port understands that in the alien-land, destinies are not protected by the familiar, especially at the point of movement.

Yet, it will take time for the group to cross over to the other; it has not reached the momentum needed to enter the liminal domain. Their port of arrival is paradigmatic in that regard. The atmosphere of the postwar North African city is described as drab and solemn; there is little wonder to be found there. Moreover, it lacks the energy of movement, the very concern of Port, whose plans to go down South are founded on the ongoing obsession with movement. Moving some place else, any place else, as far away from the home as possible designates his most basic desire. He is oblivious to the complaints by his fellow travelers about inadequate food and service. For him, communications with the hotel staff are difficult but tolerable; the sense of apathy that permeates the city seems to neutralize all the relations between the hosts and the guests. Contacts with the natives are reduced to the minimum. In fact, paradoxically, the Alien has not been seen because the limits of the alien-world have not been breached yet. At this point, Port has no interest to learn about the native or the home comrade, to that matter. Running from the home-land has to imply traveling to the alien-land. As for the Alien beings, they are a part of the alien landscape; for that reason, Port thinks that they do not have any distinct faces. For Port, they are merely human props. If he had an interest in a world, it would not be any specific cultural-historical world, but the other world, the alien-world in the broadest sense.

Yet, in an alien-land one inevitably meets the Alien. And it will be Eros who opens the liminal in-between for Port. Eros will become the messenger of desire. During a late night walk, Port finds himself followed by an Arab man, Smaïl, who talks him into visiting a camp of the nomads down below at the bottom of the city where in one of the tents young and beautiful girls from the Sahara dance for men. After many attempts to shed off the unwelcome other, Port agrees to follow him when he notices that "the presence of the Arab beside him made him feel somehow invisible" (Bowles 1947: 21). Smaïl brings Port to an empty tent where he asks Port to wait until he finally returns with a beautiful young girl. A liminal creature, the guide disappears soon after. In the meantime, the girl, Marhnia, makes tea and then 'dances' for Port, making him feel as if he indeed met a goddess and tasted her flesh. In fact, he meets a particular liminal creature—Eros. He does not understand Marhnia's speech, but the goddess could somehow communicate that she fell down to the earth to dance for the local 'ugly men,' while far out there in the Sahara, there are beautiful men, and they are waiting for her there. Having to make them wait saddens her. The story stayed with Port despite the fact that the dancer tries to rob him, making him run for his life to the safety of the hotel. Only there, he realized that he barely escaped Thanatos, whose grip was represented by the unforgiving 'lawless' crowd.

Later, Port will forget this flight, although the face of the woman who danced for him will come up again and again, reviving her story about the desire for her own celestial home and her own people, fuelling his erotic desire even if it only signified his own home, the very place from which Port is so desperately trying to escape. Coming closer to his own makes the effects of this proximity push Port deeper into the alien-land. An addict of the extreme, he creates improbable possibilities for being, as if this kind of planning is going to save him one day from the non-being. As time passes by, the call of the unknown intensifies, and the plans to leave Tangiere are expedited. Due to the circumstances, which appear superfluous at this point, on the second leg of their journey to Boussif, Port and Kit go different ways: Kit goes by a slow train with Tunner, while Port chooses the company of the Lyles, the mother and the son, who travel in their own automobile, making photographs and collecting information for travel agencies, or so they say.

The two ways of getting to Boussif produce contrary effects. While Port is only annoyed by the English couple and even enjoys the monotony of the sandy hills along the way, the train ride shocks Kit. Overrun by boredom, guilt, and anxiety, Kit walks away on Tunner during her train ride only to encounter horrific images of raw and unpretentious humanity: a zombie-like human mass of the natives in the third-class carriage where men were looking at her without sympathy or antipathy, not even curiosity: "they had the vacant expression on their faces as a man who has just simply blown their nose" (Bowles 65). Apparently, for the Alien, she did not exist. They perceived her not as a creature from some other world, but as a non-entity. In the meantime, she encounters Thanatos: at the door of the general compartment, she sees a severed head of a sheep with glassy eyes and a blue protruding tongue. Kit's squeezing through by the head leaves several stains of blood on her white satin dress. Then, when she has barely recovered from the initial shock, on the platform, she meets the statuette-like leper, who keeps her immobilized until the ice rain chases her back into the first-class-carriage and into the arms of Tunner, her temporary shelter, who 'saves' her from the alien horror by first getting her drunk on champagne and then by taking advantage of her. Their coitus was entirely sexual, however, and thus inconsequential for the encounter with the alien. Eros did not appear there to forge a new alliance. Sex with Tunner was an embarrassment for Kit, a poignant reminder of her home.

After the train ride, Kit, who was extremely sensitive to 'signs,' felt that the alien came closer, brushing against her now and then, but without securing any firm grasp on her being. The horror and the premonitions in its wake were the doings of Thanatos, except that he did not come for her, but Eros did send her a warning about the impending loss, the workings of which began in Boussif, where Port's consciousness starts taking a strange turn toward a sort of disintegration that one mundanely associates with utter loneliness and diagnoses as depression. He feels like he is falling into a dark well a thousand miles deep; with a great difficulty he rises from the lower regions of his consciousness, and when he does, it is always with a sense of infinite sadness and repose. "The soul is the weariest part of the body," he says to himself and makes another attempt to recapture Eros; in a local brothel, he sees a dancing and singing girl of uncanny grace: "The movements of the girl appeared graceful but of the impudence that verged on the comic" (Bowles 1947: 108); yet, her dance was a perfect translation into the visual terms made by the strident and wily sounds of the music. Her face was a mask of perfect proportions whose beauty accrued less from the configuration of features than from the meaning that was implicit in their expression— meaning or the withholding of it. After having realized that the girl is blind, with the unyielding obsession that verges on mania, Port tried to obtain the company of the girl but was unable to reach her, or prevented from it. Eros, as Plato teaches us, cannot be bought or coerced; it can only surprise us. The significance of the failed encounter emphasizes the inaccessibility of the alien in any other way but from within.

V

The second chapter of the book, "The Earth's Sharp Edge," enhances the impact of encountering the alien by moving the action, or rather the journey undertaken by the characters, deeper inside the Sahara. It is there that Port, who no longer travels with Tunner, discovers the loss of his passport. The material loss of his national identity coincides with the sense of self-loss he began to experience back in Aïn Krorfa. His initial suspicion falls on the proprietor of the hotel where Kit and he were staying the night before, but the newly appointed French garrison commander refuses to accept Port's complaint and, in general, considers the whole matter an utmost nuisance. As it goes, Port and Kit were more alien to him than the proprietor, and not because they were Americans but because they were without a home. Port's continuous drive to flee from his home was not understood by him either. In the meantime, his pursuit of complete isolation made him focus almost completely on the landscape which itself changed its meaning from somewhat romantic and exotic to senselessly alien, moving beyond the horizon without an opportunity of ever reaching it.

At the same time, an impelling centrifugal force continued to drive Port to other ways of non-being. Breathing the dust and feeling sharp stones underneath his feet, the chilling wind at night and the blazing sun in the morning were sufficient reminders to him of the destiny that lied ahead. His desire was for that very kind of alienness; it was meant to reduce his isolation. Trying to overcome liminality on his own, Port made his journey even more fragmented; being supremely overwhelmed by the force of being that was not his, he was looking for the repetition that was not and could not be there: "One said: another day, but always with the hidden knowledge that each day was unique and final, that there never would be a return, another time" (Bowles 1947: 104).

But the pressing need to find 'another time' grew stronger as his emotions grew wilder, which coincided with the onset of typhoid that began to weaken his body. The sky, so welcoming in the beginning of the journey now made him avert his eyes. The sound of the wind replaced the sound of human voices. The voices of the locals, discordant and abject, seemed to have only one purpose: to imitate the wind. Port's sight began to give way to hearing, while his hearing began to acquire the ambiguity of an altered state caused by his fast developing illness.

The onset of the delirium made him fall into long dream-like sequences that brought him into the realm of touch, that exquisite refined sense that he himself used to cherish the most, except that this time all that was available to touch was chill. The presence of Thanatos was undeniable, as undeniable as the fact that both Port and Kit crossed over into the liminal world. Another trip and Port finds himself incapacitated and at the mercy of Kit, who becomes more together as his own humanity is being slowly swallowed by typhoid, which can be considered as another name for Thanatos that appeared to Port through the liminal fusion of the wind and of the night. The chill and the moon were all that stood between him and the alien now. His death, which pushed him over the edge gave him the final image: "the spots of raw bright blood on the earth. Blood on excrement. The supreme moment, high above the desert, when the two elements, blood and excrement, long kept apart, merge. A black star appears. Reach out, pierce the final fabric of the sheltering sky, take repose" (Bowles 1947: 188). Port's death was his last possession. Possessed by the liminal underworld of the unformed matter meant to become alien.

VI

The last chapter of the novel is the most important one regarding both the character and the plot. Like the previous chapter, "The Sky" also speaks about possession, but this time it is Kit's story, a story about her possession by the alien. Despite her inner intensity and anxiety before living, Kit comes to Africa not by herself but in Port's possession, physically, materially, and symbolically, and not only as a body but also as an inalienable part of his plan to run away. Without Port and his impossible maps, his obsession with moving, her sense of herself involved only short intervals of time that had no history and no story, only images. After her husband's death, Kit became the only figure in the dual relationship that she could not maintain on her own. Fleeing from the remains of his home-world, Port brought her to the edge of the liminal world and left her there when he died, transferring thereby his sense of self-alienation onto her. In the alien-land, edge is the essence. Yet, without Port's drive to reach the heart of the alien, her encounter with the alien turns into "a new horror, connected with sunlight, dust" (Bowles 1947: 156). The alien elementals become the background of her transformation. She felt as if she could finally live by her omens and by them only, but she did not need to: she became an omen of herself to herself. This mystical auto-affection erased the former edge of her being. Her elation about being absolutely free without Port was, in fact, the symptom of madness that made her become alien in the erotic mode. Her current state of being dispossessed pointed to Eros as a way the alien was given to her. Longing for that essence made Kit discover her new self in the face of the alien who, as the novel goes on, would gain the materiality of the Alien male.

After Kit escaped from the French barracks into the desert night with a valise filled with Port's money and her most precious essentials, leaving the dead body of her husband to the French authorities, she was not the Kit she knew of herself. She refused to look at the past. The past itself became a distant blur, not even a dream. The death of Port too became indistinct, indefinable. She felt renewed. She would not be hysterical any more. She would not be afraid of anything else anymore. Turning off her self-reflection allowed Kit to assume a different and new sense of being. Appropriately, her new Self emerged in the liminality of dusk. It is at that time that the desert appears most mysterious; it alters perception: the sense of distance lapses, each small detail acquires an immense significance. Things come into focus as if on their own, without the assistance of the background or an interpretation. Existence is brought out. Capturing this state makes her feel absolutely free and absolutely determined: "The journey must continue," she says to herself as if the sense of movement symbolized her new freedom and with it came the authority of the traveler (Bowles 1947: 212). When, several hours later, Kit stopped a caravan moving to an unknown destination, she was sure of only one thing—she was not dead. The motions of the camels reminded her of being alive. All else appeared secondary. Only movement mattered. Even when the caravan made the first stop for the night, and master Belquassim and his older friend took her by force one by one, as they continued to do throughout the journey, she did not put up a fight; her screams were directed only at Belquassim, who became her daemon to whom she decided to attach herself and whom she followed to the end of the journey.

She was deeply enthralled by the tenderness of the young master which was mixed with his self-assured power. All this was alien to her, but it was a form of possession that allowed her to hold on. From a spoiled and moody child, she was becoming a different limit subject. The alien within herself stirred like an animal; she was the herdsman's favorite sheep, as she liked to think about herself. She was his property. Her earlier celebration of freedom reached its pinnacle in a celebration of its abnegation. The erotic state of animality was taking a hold on her stronger and stronger, letting her transcend her own being and getting absorbed into his. Her only sense of herself at this point was wholly irrational sensuality, without purpose, determination, or will. The elements around her changed as well. No longer ominous, fragmented, they did not require a separation of the sun from the sky. The entire sky appeared to her as a white metal dome, the symbol of heaven full of beautiful men. She became fully erotic and knew of no other way any longer.

After countless days in the house of Belquassim, Kit's heightened sense of danger told her that she was not safe. A confrontation with the servants and the ensuing fight with the wives one day made her realize that she was discovered and that it was only a matter of time that she was to be killed as an Alien amidst the own. Even after her master takes her as his new wife in an official ceremony, she feels the enclosing presence of some mortal danger. One day, when the endless monotony of the world gets broken by the incessant beating of the drums, she escapes. Her wiles lead her out into the cold moonlight night. After being taken into care by several local men, she manages to become known as the French lady. Her new identity returns her to the appropriate means for that identity. For a brief moment, she crosses the border from the alien-land back home. She remembers that she has to send a telegram. But, unable to articulate the addressor, all she writes is: 'cannot get back.' Even as she utters these words, she realizes that she betrayed her new self and that she could be discovered, and because of that, she needs to run again. The journey must continue.

Although the old identity persists—her home catches up with her in the form of her American passport, the last of her material possessions—she openly denies it. She does not care that the authorities in Algiers have been notified, and the plane was sent to pick her up, with Miss Ferry from the US consulate waiting for her in Tangiers. The last memory of Kit when she boards the plane is the violent blue sky. Like a great overpowering light, it destroyed everything in her mind, paralyzed her. Liberation, relief, an opportunity of coming home, all that passes right by her. Someone else said once that the sky hides the night behind it, shelters the person beneath from the horror that lies above. Now that she is getting back, her anxiety returns: "At any moment the rip in the sky would occur, the edges would fly back, and the giant maw will be revealed" (Bowles 1947: 231). To her, this means the danger of crossing back to normality. She escapes by putting herself on the crowded street train and runs with it through the city until it reaches the last stop.

VII

At the end of the novel, we can obtain a number of different senses of the alien. Some are given traditionally in the natural attitude as stereotypes created by unreflective impositions of the home frame on the alien, its domestication so to speak. Tunner, who never leaves his symbolic home, may count as an example of that attitude. The Lyles, who belong to another type of a Westerner, go a similar yet more bitter route, foreignizing the alien as 'lazy,' 'sneaky,' and 'weak,' evaluating its existential justification only in terms of its usefulness, and doing so with open prejudice. The ethics exercised in both of these approaches is mundane, for it never leaves the a priori system of cultural values which are exercised against immediate, if not divergent, appearances. The phenomenological sense of the alien that exceeds the realm of manifestations belongs only to both Port and Kit. It is noteworthy that while Bowels chooses to grant Port extreme experiences at the margins of the alien-worlds, he places Kit fully inside, allowing her to experience the inaccessibility of the alien from within, so to speak, and to the full effect. The significance of her character lies in that it helps us refine the phenomenological description of the alien, where a home dweller completes her passage to the alien by becoming-alien to the point of self-abnegation, including the loss of the home. In the alien-land, she was true *liminalis,* or obscure materiality.

The ability of the alien-world, upon an encounter with it, to absorb another kind of other consciousness, without reversing the home-world/alien-world relationship, but having done its work in-between, so to say, calls for an ethical reconsideration of the relationships one conducts with the alien other, and not just by separating tourist experiences of the alien from those of a traveler, but acknowledging the inaccessibility of the alien as the ultimate limit of knowing the alien other and therefore oneself. The erotic and the deadly alien, the daemonic Eros and Thanatos are only two possible liminal figures; there are many more such divinities who dwell there, and although their effects on the traveler in the liminal in-between may not necessarily result in intense eroticism or premature death, they may still affect the home-dweller in the sense that coming too close with them could bring about the becoming-alien. Striving to understand liminality, as well as the impossibility of crossing into it without impunity, is particularly pertinent today when translating the alien into home concepts and forms appears to be just a technicality.

The question with the opposite vector shall also be raised: what do we know of the home, or of those very ways that either guard us from the alien or that the alien creates to guard itself from us? These questions have much significance for the modern world because, as Paul Bowles put it, it appears to be more and more homogenous, prompting us to believe that we, people, are the same species and the only ones in the world which we know and control. In turn, taking a purely literary perspective, we would like to conclude by claiming the existence of 'xenological' literature which invites phenomenology for its analysis, on the one hand and, on the other hand, is inspired by phenomenological insights, and therefore ready to expand and deepen the philosophical connection.

In our everyday life, we are not aware of the surrounding context that is so crucial to our existence. Worlds, whether near or distant, homey or alien, are not revealed as such. The experience of literature, however, ruptures the normality of everyday life, and such a rupture is the critical move to philosophy: "In the nearness of the work we were suddenly somewhere else than we usually tend to be" (Heidegger 1971a: 29), Heidegger says. This "somewhere else," this encounter with the alien, is where philosophy and literature touch in the wonder that inspires reflection.

Notes

1. For an argument for this claim, see Kuspit (1968).
2. As Paul Davies characterized them in a public lecture (2014).
3. For Heidegger, unequivocally, the highest form of linguistic expression is poetry; hence, his fascination with Hölderlin.

References

Bataille, Georges. 1962. *Eroticism*. London: Penguin.

Bertolucci, Bernardo. 1990. *The Sheltering Sky*. Film. 138 min. Italy.

Bowles, Paul. 1947. *The Sheltering Sky*. London: Penguin.

———. 1972. *Without Stopping. An Autobiography*. New York: Putnam.

Conrad, Joseph. 1994. *Heart of Darkness*. London: Penguin Classics.

Danto, Arthur. 1985. *Narration and Knowledge*. New York: Columbia University Press.

Davies, Paul. 2014. Useful Fiction. Public Lecture, University of Sussex, November 11, 2014.

Derrida, Jacques. 1979. *Deconstruction and Criticism*, trans. J. Hulbert. London: Continuum.

Heidegger, Martin. 1971a. The Origin of the Work of Art. In *Poetry, Language, Thought*, trans. A. Hofstadter, 15–86. New York: Harper Collins.

———. 1971b. The Way to Language. In *On the Way to Language*, trans. M. Fromt, 111–139. New York: HarperCollins.

Husserl, Edmund. 1970. *The Crisis of European Sciences and Transcendental Phenomenology*, trans. D. Carr. Evanston: Northwestern University Press.

———. 1973. *Zur Phänomenologie der Intersubjektivität: Texte aus dem Nachlass, Dritter Teil, 1929–35*, ed. I. Kern. The Hague, The Netherlands: Martinus Nijhoff.

———. 2005. *Phantasy, Image, Consciousness, and Memory (1898–1925)*, trans. J. Brough. Dordrecht: Springer.

Ingarden, Roman. 1973. *The Cognition of the Literary Work of Art*, trans. R.A. Crowley and K.R. Olson. Evanston: Northwestern University Press.

Kuspit, Donald. 1968. Fiction and Phenomenology. *Philosophy and Phenomenology Research* 29: 16–33.

Landgrebe, Ludwig. 1981. *The Phenomenology of Edmund Husserl: Six Essays*. Ithaca: Cornell University Press.

Levinas, Emmanuel. 1997. *Totality and Infinity*, trans. A. Lingis. Pittsburgh: Duquesne University Press.

———. 1998. *Otherwise Than Being or Beyond Essence*, trans. A. Lingis. Pittsburgh: Duquesne University Press.

Plato. 1997. *Complete Works*, ed. J. Cooper. Indianapolis: Hackett Publishing Company.

Ricoeur, Paul. 1985. *Time and Narrative*, trans. K. McLaughlin and D. Pellauer, vol. 2. Evanston: Northwestern University Press.

Staehler, Tanja. 2010. *Plato and Levinas: The Ambiguous Out-Side of Ethics*. London: Routledge.

Waldenfels, Bernhard. 1996. *Order in the Twilight*, trans. D. Parent. Athens: Ohio University Press.

7

"Stories to Meditate On": Animals in Gaita's Narrative Philosophy

Alice Crary

Among the most provocative and appealing gestures of Raimond Gaita's philosophical oeuvre is a call to transform our approach to philosophy. Gaita urges us to question the view, encoded in the structure of our universities, that the pursuit of philosophy is something that can appropriately be conceived as a profession, as the kind of thing that we may or may not elect to look into in the course of a lifetime, and to exchange this view for an alternative on which philosophizing is a *vocation* or, as Gaita puts it, an activity that "non-accidentally fills a life and worthily fills it."[1] Part of what motivates Gaita's push to alter the way we philosophize is the conviction that bringing the world into focus in a manner relevant to grappling with the core philosophical question of 'how to live' involves a distinctive—not merely theoretical—type of difficulty.

This chapter is the text of a lecture delivered at a public symposium in honor of Raimond Gaita, in Adelaide, Australia, in July of 2015.

A. Crary (✉)
New School for Social Research, New York, USA
e-mail: crarya@newschool.edu

© The Author(s) 2018
A. Falcato and A. Cardiello (eds.), *Philosophy in the Condition of Modernism*,
https://doi.org/10.1007/978-3-319-77078-9_7

153

Gaita holds that getting the world in view here requires a willingness to work on ourselves; to question and perhaps reshape our sense of what matters. He discusses the possibility of philosophical prose that fosters such work, and in some of his writing he himself sets out to realize this possibility. Notable in this connection is Gaita's thought about questions of ethics and animals.

To appreciate the value of Gaita's contribution in this area it is helpful to have a sense of what conversations about the ethical treatment of animals are like. A central ambition of animal advocates today is establishing that, far from being mere instruments or means, animals are proper objects of moral concern. This project is urgent because classical ethical traditions represent animals as mere morally indifferent objects that in themselves fail to impose moral claims on us,[2] and also because the view that animals lack moral standing is reflected in the utterly callous treatment that animals receive in industrial settings such as industrial slaughterhouses, confined feeding operations (or CAFOs), aquafarms, hunting grounds on land or in the oceans and laboratories. Horrified at these practices with animals, animal advocates often start their interventions in public debates by contesting the assumption, embedded in these practices, that animals are morally neutral things. There is substantial variety in the strategies that animal advocates adopt for carrying out this task. If we abstract from this variety, we can say that a large portion of the most widely discussed strategies are informed, if sometimes only implicitly, by the following assumption, namely, that any consideration that a human or non-human creature merits is a reflection of its individual qualities. Members of the group of animal advocates who make this assumption disagree about which individual capacities are 'morally significant', with some mentioning, e.g., our capacities for pleasure and pain[3] and others mentioning capacities such as subjecthood.[4] Setting aside these disagreements, it is fair to say that many animal protectionists treat an assumption about how moral standing is a function of individual capacities—when combined with theoretical assertions about how particular capacities are 'morally relevant' as well as with empirical claims about the capacities possessed by particular human beings and animals—as the source of their conviction that some animals are fit objects of moral concern.

At one juncture in his work, Gaita distills the operative thought like this:

> Take anything whatsoever—an animal, a machine, an angel, an alien—if it has the features and capacities that we regard as morally relevant in our treatment of human beings, then we should treat that thing as we treat human beings with those features and capacities.[5]

This bit of theorizing depends for its apparent practical bite on observations to the effect that some animals possess the same 'morally relevant capacities' as some human beings, and it is not uncommon for animal advocates to make such observations. These advocates frequently insist that some human beings are no better endowed with 'morally relevant capacities' than, say, chimpanzees or pigs are. The human beings who most often get mentioned are those who, as a result of illness, injury, age or some congenital condition, are intellectually severely disabled. Against the backdrop of a theoretical position that grounds moral standing in individual capacities, an observation about human beings whose 'morally relevant capacities' are supposedly no greater than those of certain animals appears to support one of the main ethical conclusions that animal advocates seek to defend, namely, that some animals are morally significant beings with significant claims to moral solicitude.[6]

The bit of theorizing that seems to underwrite this conclusion has a bearing on how we think about the treatment of humans as well as animals, and, in many parts of his writing, Gaita is preoccupied with the human side of things. Animal advocates who trace out versions of the argument just sketched typically wind up making claims that commit them—shockingly—to downgrading the moral standing of those vulnerable human beings who have severe cognitive disabilities. For, as these advocates see it, seriously intellectually impaired human beings are, to some extent, lacking in moral status-grounding, 'morally significant capacities'. Gaita, in contrast, writes eloquently and at length about what he sees as the undiminished moral significance of people with severe intellectual impairments.[7] Interestingly, the animal advocates whom Gaita thus, in effect, challenges often present themselves as moral radicals who courageously contest entrenched beliefs about the kind of consideration merited by cognitively disabled human beings, because they want to contest equally entrenched beliefs about the moral status of animals. These thinkers present themselves as bravely facing up to what they regard as an unavoidable tension between the moral standing of cognitively disabled human beings and the moral standing of animals.

This last comment makes it possible to offer an initial formulation of what is special about Gaita's intervention in conversations about animals and ethics. Part of the appeal of his work has to do with the fact that it shows there is no question of a human-animal tradeoff of the sort that many animal advocates envision. Gaita effectively shows that, however friendly they aspire to be to animals, animal protectionists who ground human and animal claims to moral attention in individual capacities—and who thus wind up undermining the moral standing of severely cognitively disabled human beings—bequeath to us an image of animal life that is not only just as morally problematic as their preferred image of human life but, moreover, morally problematic in an exactly analogous way.

One of the cornerstones of Gaita's work in ethics is an approach to mental phenomena that falls so far outside the framework of mainstream philosophy of mind that it seems fair to describe it as heretical. Debates in philosophy of mind, by and large, take the form of a quarrel between, on the one hand, materialists of different—reductive and non-reductive—sorts (i.e., thinkers who, while disagreeing about a wide range of topics, agree in holding that all real aspects of the world, mental qualities included, are at bottom made up of physical ingredients) and, on the other hand, dualists of different sorts (i.e., thinkers who hold that, in order to do justice to mental phenomena, we need a two-fold metaphysic that includes a non-physical, subjective realm as well as a physical realm). For all of the differences between them, materialists and dualists generally agree in holding that the observable world is exhaustively physical in a sense that entails being available to thought in a morally neutral or indifferent manner. Gaita unequivocally rejects this view. He traces insistence on neutrality as a regulative ideal for all world-guided thought to the idea of a transcendent standpoint from which to discern that any input from human subjectivity cannot help but serve as a cognitive contaminant, and he argues that this idea is incoherent and should not be allowed to structure our image of what cognitive access to the world is like.[8] He, in this way, makes room for the possibility—alien to the debate between materialism and dualism in its familiar guise—that there are forms of judgment that, despite being "undistorted by feeling," are nevertheless not "uninformed by feeling."[9] Moreover, he maintains that this possibility is actualized in thought about mental phenomena. He attempts to get us to see that, when we are trying to do justice to a creature's qualities of mind, we are necessarily concerned with what he at one point calls "understanding of the heart."[10]

Gaita's strategy for defending this view involves following up on strands of Wittgenstein's later philosophy of psychology. Drawing partly on Peter Winch's interpretative work, Gaita argues that we should credit Wittgenstein with demonstrating that our most primitive attitudes or affective reactions to others are "a condition rather than a consequence of ascribing states of consciousness."[11] Gaita notes that it is an implication of this posture that there can be no question of accounting for the authority of our psychological attributions by pointing to *evidence*, if by 'evidence' we mean—psychological, behavioral, etc.—circumstances that are indifferently available.[12] To capture the psychological character of a stretch of conduct, we have to bring to bear on our observations of it a feel for what matters or, alternately, a certain attitude. That, according to Gaita, is what Wittgenstein is saying when, in a well-known passage from the *Investigations*, he declares:

My attitude toward him is an attitude toward a soul. I am not of the *opinion* that he has a soul.[13]

The project of defending the Wittgensteinian approach to mind at issue is by itself a philosophically ambitious one,[14] but this is not the only philosophically challenging step that Gaita takes in this region of his work. Gaita argues that the approach is just as pertinent to our understanding of animal minds as it is to our understanding of the minds of human beings. His thought is that our primitive reactions to animals are internal to "our *very concepts* of thought, feeling, intention, belief, doubt and so on,"[15] and he takes pains to distance himself from the idea that animals represent merely secondary applications of these concepts. He denies that "our ways of speaking about knowledge and belief have… been first and fully formed just in our lives with human beings and then applied conjecturally to animals," insisting instead that "they have been formed at the same time in our lives with animals."[16]

This reorientation in how we conceive animal as well as human minds has significant ramifications for our understanding of the methods of ethics. Insofar as it is a consequence of the envisioned reorientation that we require resources of feeling in order to grasp human beings' and animals' psychological qualities, it follows from it that we need these resources in order to get human beings and animals empirically into view in a manner germane to ethics. We could reformulate this observation by saying that, when in ethics we are trying to bring human beings and animals empirically into focus, we are operating in a conceptual realm—what Gaita calls "the realm of meaning"[17]—in which "understanding is given only when head and heart are inseparably combined."[18] Notice that this means that, in any particular ethically charged situation involving human beings or animals, genuine insight may require the further cultivation of our emotional responses or sensibilities.[19] By the same token, it means that an utterance or inscription that appeals to our hearts may, in doing so, internally inform the kind of understanding we seek in ethics. If we think of literary discourse as discourse that is, as such, in the business of engaging us emotionally, we can gloss this point by saying that it follows from Gaita's views about human and animal minds that speech with literary qualities may, as such, directly contribute to genuine moral understanding.

Gaita is preoccupied with this methodological shift in ethics throughout his work. In *The Philosopher's Dog*, he places special emphasis on its implications for how we approach questions about the ethical treatment of animals. One prominent theme of the book is that literary modes of thought have a much bigger role to play in ethical thought about animals than many animal advocates believe. In the course of developing this theme, Gaita underscores its elusiveness. He notes that some thinkers who set out to take seriously a congenial lesson about the moral significance of literary discourse wind up obscuring the point. Here he considers the writings of a couple of popular authors—Eugene Linden and Jeffrey Moussaieff Masson—who are concerned with the moral standing of animals and who, insofar as they proceed by assembling anecdotes about animals' capacities, appear to allow, as Gaita himself does, that the literary qualities of writing may be internal to its ability to directly inform genuine—objective—understanding. Yet, although both authors do indeed start from what Gaita regards as the reasonable "belief that the assumptions of behavioral science about objectivity and evidence actually distort our understanding of animal life," they nevertheless remain "in the grip of these very assumptions."[20] The trouble is that, in collecting vignette after vignette about animals, they presuppose that "the factual is our best prototype of the cognitive," and they accordingly treat story-telling as at bottom a method for collecting what Gaita calls 'evidence'.[21] There is a sharp contrast between this practice and the practice with animal stories that Gaita recommends. He sees these stories, not as vehicles for conveying evidence, but as occasions for emotionally demanding *meditations* that hold forth the promise of cognitive growth.[22] In addition to insisting on the moral importance of animal stories thus conceived, Gaita recounts a number of stories of his own.

One of his tales is about his "first animal friend," a black greyhound mix named Orloff who, when Gaita was very young, lived with him and his father. Orloff was taller and broader than most greyhounds, and a good portion of Gaita's brief narrative about life with him is devoted to appreciative descriptions of his athletic prowess. Gaita writes about the "strength of [Orloff's] muscular body" and "the speed with which he ran after rabbits," noting that, "if he came across a fence while chasing rabbits, he would angle his body to the side so that he could pass between two strands of wire without noticeably slowing down."[23] Alongside these reflections on Orloff's physical virtuosity, Gaita includes an account of his own youthful love for Orloff as well as of Orloff's love for him. He writes:

> Orloff often accompanied me part of the way [to school] and he would be there, the same distance from the house, when I returned...As I walked from the junction of the road and the rough track to our house

Orloff would bound up to greet me with such enthusiasm that he would knock me over. Lying there in the long grass with him standing over me, legs astride my chest, licking me and making affectionate noises and wagging his tail so furiously that his entire body swayed with it, I felt he was my closest and truest friend and I loved him.[24]

Gaita's reminiscences about Orloff close with the circumstances of the dog's death. Orloff was accustomed to run off on his own during the day, and local farmers suspected him of preying on their sheep. Eventually one of them killed him by tempting him with meat that had been spiked with glass. Bleeding internally, Orloff almost made it back to the Gaita home before he died, but didn't make it over the fence around the property. Gaita tells us that his father tenderly lifted Orloff's body over the fence, bringing the dog home, and that he and his father buried Orloff in the yard and mourned him.

Consider what it might be to treat this brief narrative as something to meditate on. To the extent that we sympathetically identify with Gaita as he presents his fond, non-neutral remembrances about Orloff's athleticism and affectionate nature, we ourselves come to regard the dog as a creature who merits compassionate interest. We find ourselves in a position in which it seems obligatory to ask whether or not this way of looking at Orloff is legitimate. Given that this is a question that crops up in what Gaita calls 'the realm of meaning', it is worth recalling that Gaita maintains that the task of answering questions that arise in this realm is a cognitive one. When we try to determine whether a given attitude is essentially distorting, or whether instead it enables us to see real features of the world that are otherwise hidden from view, we are— Gaita maintains—undertaking an intellectual project that is subject to objective standards. Gaita wants us to pursue this kind of project, specifically in reference to the non-neutral way of looking at Orloff that his story cultivates, because he hopes to lead us to recognize that this way of looking is legitimate and that it brings into view things that aren't neutrally available. Among the things that Gaita thinks it enables us to see is that, in burying Orloff and mourning him, Gaita and his father are responding appropriately and in a manner that it would be wrong to disparage as merely sentimental.

Use of the sorts of literary methods that Gaita favors represents a strategy for intervening in debates about animals and ethics that is very different from the strategies of theorists who tie animal moral standing to individual capacities of mind. Admittedly, in his efforts to motivate his preferred methods, Gaita takes his bearing from the distinctive conception of mind that he attributes to Wittgenstein. But it would be wrong to conclude from this that he is doing something fundamentally similar to thinkers who ground moral standing in individual mental qualities. Gaita does not turn to Wittgenstein's philosophy of mind because he thinks it shows that human beings and animals merit loving attention insofar as they possess status-granting individual mental capacities. Gaita harbors no such thought, and there is for him no question of following in the footsteps of animal advocates who call for leveling down the moral status of human beings with limited mental capacities and who compare these individuals' allegedly diminished status to the moral status of animals with what they regard as similar capacities. Gaita turns to Wittgenstein's philosophy of mind not because he believes it suggests the need for these kinds of human-animal comparisons—Gaita does not believe this—but because he believes Wittgenstein equips us to understand how loving attention can uncover otherwise inaccessible features of human and animal existence. Moreover, although Gaita discusses cases in which such attention illuminates the lives of human beings and animals who possess significant qualities of mind, these are not his only cases. He holds that attention of this kind is equally illuminating of characteristics of those—human and animal—creatures who have no sophisticated mental attributes.

Along these lines, in various parts of his work, Gaita offers illustrations of how loving attention can shed light on the lives not only of cognitively well-endowed human beings but also on the lives of the cognitively disabled.[25] In *The Philosopher's Dog*, he attempts a similar task with regard to animals as well as human beings. He tries to show that loving attention can shed light on features of the lives not only of sophisticated animals such as dogs and birds, but also of more primitive animals such as butterflies, spiders, bees and flies.[26] He also tries to show that a sympathetic eye can illuminate the bodies of dead human beings and animals. Particularly arresting in this last connection is a passage in which he discusses a scene from J.M. Coetzee's novel *Disgrace* having to do with the bodies of dead dogs. Here Gaita brings out vividly how animal as well as human corpses can be said to merit concern and solicitude.[27]

Gaita's reflections on animals are integral to his efforts to get us to see philosophical endeavor not as a profession but rather as a vocation. When in philosophy we grapple with the question of 'how to live', we are after insights that will equip us to appreciate the significance not only of situations involving other human beings but also of situations in which our paths cross those of animals. A key lesson of Gaita's work on animals is that, far from being accessible wholly through maximally neutral ethical reflections, the kinds of insights at issue only surrender themselves to an understanding heart. It is a corollary of this lesson that particular insights may only be available to us insofar as we are open to growing emotionally or, in other words, insofar as we are open to the sort of emotional growth that Gaita's distinctive—philosophically iconoclastic and admirably disciplined—"narrative philosophy" aims to foster.[28]

Notes

1. Raimond Gaita, *A Common Humanity: Thinking About Love and Truth and Justice*, London, Routledge, 1998, p. 196; see also p. 231.
2. For excerpts from the most prominent of these traditions, see Part I of Tom Regan and Peter Singer, *Animal Rights and Human Obligations*, New Jersey: Prentice Hall, 1989.
3. See, Peter Singer, *Animal Liberation*, New York, NY: Harper Collins, 2009.
4. See, Tom Regan, *The Case for Animal Rights*. Berkeley, CA, University of California Press, 1983.
5. Raimond Gaita, *The Philosopher's Dog*, Melbourne, Text Publishing Company, 2002, p. 29.
6. They also often add that any tendency to place value on the sheer fact of being human is therefore unjustified or—to employ a now familiar bit of jargon that was originally introduced by Richard Ryder and popularized by Peter Singer—that any such tendency is a sign of an unwarranted *speciesism*.

7. Here I have in mind, above all, the essay "Goodness Beyond Virtue," in Gaita, *A Common Humanity*, op. cit., 17–28. This essay brings to bear on the lives of mentally ill people the idea, pivotal for Gaita's thought, of the "preciousness" of each human life. For further passages in which Gaita is specifically concerned with human beings who are mentally ill, see *The Philosopher's Dog*, op. cit., 15–17 and *Romulus, My Father*, London, Headline Book Publishing, 1999, esp. 66–67.

8. See, e.g., Gaita, *A Common Humanity*, op. cit., 257–258.

9. Ibid., 89.

10. Gaita, *The Philosopher's Dog*, op. cit., 97.

11. Ibid., 59. In the passage from which the quote in the text is taken, Gaita is discussing what he sees as central themes in Winch's account of Wittgenstein's philosophy of mind, and he is concerned, above all, with Winch's article "Eine Einstellung zur Seele," in *Trying to Make Sense*, Oxford, Blackwell, 1987.

12. See, Gaita, *The Philosopher's Dog*, op. cit., 44–47, 61 and 110. See also *A Common Humanity*, op. cit., 64–65 for a discussion of related themes in relation to certain forms of racism.

13. Cited in Gaita, *The Philosopher's Dog*, op. cit., 58, stress in the original. Gaita discusses this passage—and Peter Winch's reading of it—at greater length in *Good and Evil: An Absolute Conception*, Abingdon, Routledge, 2004, Chapter 10.

14. For a thoroughgoing discussion of the relevant difficulties, see Alice Crary, *Inside Ethics: On the Demands of Moral Thought*, Cambridge, MA, Harvard University Press, 2016, Chapter 2.

15. Gaita, *The Philosopher's Dog*, op. cit., 61.

16. Ibid., 69–70. For a congenial reading of Wittgenstein's later reflections on the mind that likewise represents them as pertinent to animal as well as human minds, see Crary, *Inside Ethics*, op. cit., Chapters 2 and 3.

17. This is the title of a chapter of *The Philosopher's Dog*, op. cit. See esp. 102.

18. Ibid., 83.

19. See, e.g., ibid., 81–82 and 168.

20. Ibid., 108.

21. The inset phrase is from ibid., 109.

22. Gaita talks about animal stories as things to meditate on at ibid., 108.

23. Ibid., 11.

24. Ibid., 12.

25. See the references in note 8.
26. Gaita, *The Philosopher's Dog*, op. cit., 118–119, 122 and 131–132.
27. See, Gaita's remarks on a passage of J.M. Coetzee's *Disgrace* that involves dogs' corpses at ibid., 89–90. For an expansive discussion of forms of respect owed to human and animal corpses, see Crary, *Inside Ethics*, op. cit., Chapter 4.
28. For the phrase "narrative philosophy," which Gaita credits to Roger Scruton, see the introduction to *After Romulus*, Melbourne, Text Publishing Company, 2014.

References

Coetzee, J.M. 1999. *Disgrace*. London: Secker and Warburg.
Gaita, R. 1998. *A Common Humanity: Thinking About Love and Truth and Justice*. London: Routledge.
———. 1999. *Romulus, My Father*. London: Headline Book Publishing.
———. 2002. *The Philosopher's Dog*. Melbourne: Text Publishing Company.
———. 2014. *After Romulus*. Melbourne: Text Publishing Company.
Winch, P. 1987. *Trying to Make Sense*. Oxford: Blackwell.
———. 2004. *Good and Evil: An Absolute Conception*. Abington: Routledge.

Part III

Modern Topics

8

'"Thought in American and for the Americans": Victoria Ocampo, *Sur* and European Modernism'

Laura María Lojo Rodríguez

Introduction

This essay examines the seminal role of Argentine writer Victoria Ocampo (1890–1979) in the reception of the so-called High Modernism—and, most notably, of Virginia Woolf's *oeuvre*—in Spanish-speaking countries through her professional activity as a literary critic and as a publisher under the auspices of the intellectual circle "Sur" ["South"]. In her project of running a literary journal, Ocampo partly emulated the spirit of Sylvia Beach's monthly publication *Navire D'Argent*, but was most positively encouraged by Waldo Frank and José Ortega y Gasset—editors of *Seven Arts* (1916–1917) and *Revista de Occidente* [*Journal of the Western World*],

This essay benefits from the collaboration of the research group *Discourse and Identity* (GRC2015/002; GI-1924, Xunta de Galicia) and the research projects *Women's Tales: The Short Fiction of Contemporary British Writers, 1974–2013* (FEM2013-41977-P, Ministry of Economy and Competitiveness, Government of Spain) and *Intersections: Gender and Identity in the Short Fiction of Contemporary British Women Writers* (FEM2017-83084-P, AEI, FEDER).

L. M. Lojo Rodríguez (✉)
Universidade de Santiago de Compostela, Santiago de Compostela, Spain
e-mail: laura.lojo@usc.es

© The Author(s) 2018
A. Falcato and A. Cardiello (eds.), *Philosophy in the Condition of Modernism*,
https://doi.org/10.1007/978-3-319-77078-9_8

respectively. As Gayle Rogers has explained (2012a: 461), some modernist writers during the interwar period in diverse places of the world considered that Europe could be revitalized from its moral and cultural degeneration in different corners of the world which had remained safe from the war's devastation. Such a collaborative, transnational space would serve the purpose of transmitting aesthetics and varied cultural agendas, which often pivoted around avant-garde journals and periodical publications, such as those run by Ortega y Gasset, Waldo Frank and Victoria Ocampo herself in such a way that their "dialogues with their more familiar Euro-American modernist contemporaries also help to reorient our map of interwar literature and aesthetics" (Rogers 2012a: 462).

As will be argued, both Frank and Ortega were extremely influential in Ocampo's aim to establish an inspiring cultural network connecting Europe and the American continent. Ocampo, Frank and Ortega joined in an effort to counterbalance what they saw as a decadent European aesthetics via Hispanic routes of inspiring connections among cultural capitals in the interwar period; namely Buenos Aires, Madrid and New York: "Europe decays—yet America flourishes", affirmed Ortega (Ocampo 1967: 140).

Paris and *Navire D'Argent*

Victoria Ocampo's visit to Paris during the winter of 1928–1929—at the time a haven for artists and intellectuals of varied nationalities—had been prompted by her profound conviction that only the French capital could satisfy what she defined as her intellectual "hunger" (Ocampo 1934: 171). The temporary visits to her Buenos Aires home of prominent European intellectuals such as José Ortega y Gasset and Hermann Keyserling—also an assiduous collaborator of *Revista de Occidente*, whose ground-breaking views on Spanish history and ethnicity puzzled many readers—had been profitable and inspiring, but she was eager to meet women writers and share with them her intellectual concerns. Ocampo wished to witness the achievements of what Jorge Luis Borges,

Guillermo de Torre and Ricardo Güiraldes termed as the European vanguard taking place in Paris, and which Ortega had defined as an example of *traité de Logique* (Ortega 1974: 146). As many well-to-do Argentine women, Ocampo had previously travelled to Europe, yet this third visit was to mark a turning point in her own development as both writer and editor.

In the conservative Argentine society where Ocampo had been born, she had been prevented from accessing a college education or from dissolving the vows of an unhappy marriage. Literary aspirations were at the time most often regarded as dangerous to the inherent docility expected of a woman, and even the act of reading was itself usually subject to family control and censorship, as Ocampo herself explains:

> I was an easy, voracious and omnivorous reader. The worst thing was that I could not go to a bookshop and buy any book I was interested in [...] An example of this apparently incomprehensible censorship was the confiscation of my copy of *De profundis* (Oscar Wilde), found by my mother under my mattress at the Majestic Hotel (Paris). I was nineteen. (1980: 61)[1]

Ocampo's first steps in the literary scene had not been entirely successful: her first essay, "Babel"—published in *La nación* [*The Nation*], one of the most respected newspapers of Buenos Aires—was coldly received by critics and family alike, as Ocampo herself recalls:

> In those years, the attitude of Argentine society towards a woman writer was not indulgent. What Jane Austen had said in the nineteenth century was still true: 'A woman, if unfortunate enough to know something, should hide it as carefully as she can' [...] For this I received a shower of insults. (1981: 105)[2]

In a similar vein, Paul Groussac, a family friend and director of the Buenos Aires National Library, discouraged young Ocampo from publishing her guide for "common readers" of Dante's *Divina Commedia* entitled *De Francesca a Beátrice* [*From Francesca to Beatrice*]. Ortega y Gasset, however, was interested in the manuscript, which was eventually published in 1924 in *Revista de Occidente* [*Journal of the Western World*], followed by his own epilogue. The essay, originally written in French and translated into Spanish by Ricardo Baeza (Rogers 2012b: 133), already signals Ocampo's daring literary enterprise in a predominantly male-dominated world, and advocates for a democratic reading of Dante's *Divine Comedy* seen from the eyes of the "common reader", as Woolf would have it. Ocampo's insightful criticism, as well as her feminist concerns, are evinced in her approach to Dante's work through the lens of female characters, whose apparent opposition in terms of the virgin/whore Ocampo seeks to undo.[3]

Ortega was, for Ocampo, one of her most profound, long-lasting literary influences, and the two were bonded by "an unconditional friendship", as Ocampo would explain in 1971 after more than forty years of mutual collaboration (1971: 4). Ocampo discovered through Ortega a "dazzling Spain", which made her reconsider her own relationship with Spanish language and literature, which had been neglected in favour of French and English culture, causing her to be "unjustly biased against the language of her own country" (Meyer 1979: 51). Ortega encouraged Ocampo to live fully, to develop her artistic vocation, and to be a witness to the large-scale social changes taking place at the time. Such experiences would be the germ of Ocampo's editorial project, *Sur* [South], and of her own writing practice, largely constituted by a large number of essays compiled in the *Testimonios* [*Testimonies*] series: "It is useless to be admirable if you do not live the *substantiality* of your time [...] Victoria, the change which the world's appearance is yet to experience in four or five years will be fantastic" (Ortega 1974: 150–151).[4]

Ortega's words become somehow a foreshadowing of Ocampo's influence in the literary panorama of her time. Ocampo herself recalls how reassuring Ortega's words had been (*Espectador* [*Spectator*] 1917) after his reading of *De Francesca a Beátrice*, which fuelled her confidence as a writer, so seriously damaged after Groussac's dismissing comments: "Señora, the way you read is by no means unfair or improper. It would be necessary to reassure you of this. In the first place, *because a woman able to write and think with such gentleness shall not be disturbed by injustice*" (Ocampo 1991: 207; emphasis in the original).[5] Ocampo would reply to Ortega in a similar manner in the second number of her literary journal *Sur* [South], acknowledging the philosopher's encouragement: "Seven years ago you were as kind as to write an epilogue to my brief comment on the *Divina Commedia* […] I keep your gesture as a moving and grateful memory" (Ocampo 1931b: 17).[6]

Through Ortega, Keyserling and Drieu de la Rochelle, Ocampo was introduced to a number of active characters in the cultural life of France, such as Paul Valéry, Benjamin Fondane, Maurice Ravel and Anna de Noailles, the poet whom Ocampo had so passionately read in her adolescence (Owen Steiner 1999: 78). Thanks to a letter of introduction by Keyserling, Ocampo was received by Noailles, who soon engaged her in a "loquacious, voluble chatter […] almost without giving you time to reply", as Ocampo recalls in her essay "Anna de Noailles" (1933 [1999]: 13–14). Despite her charm and intelligence, Ocampo was soon put off by Noailles's antifeminism and by her ruthless criticism of other women writers.[7]

From her earlier years, Ocampo's feminist agenda fuelled both her critical writings and her editorial concerns. Ortega's daughter, Soledad, recalls in 1984 how Ocampo has "contributed to social transformation" through her pioneering editorial efforts and her struggle for gender equality (1984: 21). In an essay entitled "Woman, Her Rights, and Her Responsibilities" (1936)—significantly written during the months which followed Borges's commissioned translation into Spanish of Woolf's *A Room of One's Own* published in 1936 in *Sur*—Ocampo compares the repercussions of women's emancipation to those of the advent of the machine age in terms of social transformation: "I believe that the great role of the woman in history, played up to now in a rather subterranean way, is beginning to crop out at the surface. It is *she* today that can contribute powerfully to creating a new state of things" (1936: 231). Ocampo subtly adapts Woolf's arguments in *A Room of One's Own* to the particularities of Argentine society, and appeals to a reduced community of educated women to take the lead in the emancipation movement in order to "acquire a consciousness of their duties which are rights, and rights which are responsibilities", thus voicing the concerns of "innumerable women" who remain silent (1936: 234).

Like Woolf had done in *A Room of One's Own*, Ocampo considers women's inferiority in public achievement as the outcome of poverty, deprivation, unequal opportunities and patriarchal oppression, thus departing from widespread naturalisations of women's intellectual disabilities: "The same capacities of invention or initiative that can assert themselves powerfully in favourable circumstances can be reduced to nothingness in equally unfavourable circumstances" (1936: 230). Ocampo here emphasises the relevance of education in granting women's "spiritual level" and the "development of all her faculties" (232) and appeals to both man and woman for mutual understanding and cooperation, requiring "on man's part, his coercive and patriarchal morality disappear" and "on the woman's part, the false point of view that has been able to create in her the antagonism of her sex, the rebellion against the oppressor" (1936: 233).

The disappointment that meeting Noailles had been for Ocampo did not deter her from seeking other women models: she was determined to follow Ortega's advice to "be soaked by the world" ["hincharse del mundo"] (1974: 150), which certainly led to her visit to "La Maison des Amis des Livres" and "Shakespeare and Company" in Paris, run by Adrienne Monnier and Sylvia Beach, respectively. At Ricardo Güiraldes's suggestion, Ocampo met Adrienne Monnier, since "if someone wanted to find out what was happening in the literary world of that European capital, [...] he only had to stop by that small bookshop on the Left Bank" (Ocampo 1956: 223).

Ocampo was deeply impressed by Beach and Monnier's generous dedication to the intellectual community in Paris (Owen Steiner 1999: 78): Monnier had created a welcoming place for writers and intellectuals to meet, and performed a leading role in running her lending library by holding readings, writing essays and founding a monthly literary journal, *Navire D'Argent*, which would certainly inspire Ocampo in its capacity to simultaneously swim "against the current and keeping afloat" (Ocampo 1956: 223). Sylvia Beach gave Ocampo a copy of Woolf's *A Room of One's Own*, which would immediately trigger Ocampo's imagination, as well as her determination to meet the author.

"Thought in America and for the Americans": *Sur*

Back in Argentina late that same year, Ocampo was to meet Waldo Frank—a decisive figure in her determination to found a literary journal in Buenos Aires—who had come to Buenos Aires on a lecture tour. Frank's writings derived from these visits, as Rogers explains, put forward a Pan-American cultural community, consisting of a "male" Anglo-North and a "female" Hispanic South, best embodied in Buenos Aires by Victoria Ocampo herself (2012a: 469). Despite the fact that such a conception actually betrayed Frank's gender prejudice (Ocampo also had disagreements with Ortega on the issue, as will be discussed), Ocampo was fascinated by his "transnational" conception of America which, in practical terms, translated in his project of promoting a flow of cultural exchange in the American continent: in opposition to the state of decay resulting from the Great War and its aftermath, America flourished against the stagnation of Europe. Ocampo recalls the meeting in the following terms: "I liked him [Frank] [...] This meeting marks an important event in my life. My interest in the United States, its writers, its cities, its way of life, was suddenly aroused" (Ocampo 1984: 50–51).

Frank's view of a Pan-American collective identity was summarised in his short-lived editorial project *Seven Arts* (1916–1917), as the Frenchman Romain Rolland explains in the first issue of the journal, in an article significantly entitled "America and the Arts" translated by Frank himself: "Rejoice in the founding of a magazine in which the American Spirit may seek and achieve consciousness of its nature and of its role. My faith is great in the high destinies of America [...] On our old Continent, civilization is menaced. It becomes America's solemn duty to uphold the wavering torch" (Rolland 1916: 47). Like Frank, Rolland lays out a picture of a decadent European culture that can be regenerated through American paths. In this view, Frank aligns himself with Ortega, whose work he had reviewed in the *Nation & Athenaeum* of London and who, in turn, published translations of Frank's work in his *Revista de Occidente*. As Gayle Rogers has suggested, Ortega's "wide-ranging and mutually influential dialogues with the American journalist and novelist, Waldo Frank, and the Argentine writer, publisher and feminist, Victoria Ocampo, evince a shared conviction that Europe might be resuscitated best in Madrid, New York, and Buenos Aires" (Rogers 2012a: 468).[8]

It was Waldo Frank who encouraged Ocampo to launch her own literary journal, and Ocampo credits him for doing so in "Carta a Waldo Frank" ["Letter to Waldo Frank"], published in the first issue of *Sur* in 1931. This letter signals Ocampo's preference for the public epistle as a genre, which she would also use in, among other occasions, in "Carta a Virginia Woolf" (1934), published in *Revista de Occidente*. The epistolary genre stands as an interesting choice, since it already reveals Ocampo's feminist agenda in her determination to irrupt in a male-dominated sphere from the very place of oppression where women had been relegated, the private realm. By showing a conscious preference for a genre traditionally regarded as the private expression of personal opinion and offering instead, powerful, insightful and well-informed criticism on public matters, Ocampo unfolds her feminist strategy, ultimately blurring boundaries between gendered private and public realms and insisting on the fact that the domain of the private can also have a public political dimension.

Ocampo's letter recalls her first meeting with Frank in 1929, celebrates their shared conception of America as a continent "yet to be discovered" (Ocampo 1931: 18), and relates Frank's insistence on Ocampo's capacity to lead the journal, along with the subsequent maturation of the idea—including Ortega's suggestion of a name for the journal over the phone. On 1 January 1931 the first issue of *Sur* was published; its editorial board included Jorge Luis Borges, María Rosa Oliver, Pierre Drieu La Rochelle, Alfonso Reyes, Pedro Henríquez Ureña, Waldo Frank and José Ortega y Gasset, among others (Ocampo 1967: 141), and Ocampo summarises her editorial agenda as follows: "Here is my project: to publish a journal principally concerned with American problems under various of its aspects, where those Americans who have something to say and those Europeans interested in America collaborate" (1967: 139)[9]. Benjamín Jarnés, one of Gasset's most prominent reviewers in *Revista de Occidente*, enthusiastically summarised, in 1931, the spirit of *Sur* as follows:

> This [*Sur*] is a magazine whose dynamic and vital line does not reject any foreign vigour, a magazine which belongs, according to its own editor, "to those who had gone to America, to those who think in America, and to those who are of America". That is why the magazine, thought in American and for the Americans, is so full of European thought, because it is also written for all good Europeans. (Jarnés 1931: 317)[10]

However, *Sur* was timidly received by most conservative factions of Argentine society: "The expected hostility surprises and hurts me, irritates and depresses me", Ocampo writes to Ortega (Ocampo 1980: 39).[11] *Sur* was often dismissed for its alleged intellectual elitism and for being too prone to focus on European culture: in a literary panorama dominated by little magazines such as *Proa*, *Prisma* and *Martín Fierro*, *Sur* encountered local resistance and was often condemned as "foreignizing", as King notes (1986: 4). Despite the fact that Ocampo's pioneering efforts were not always appreciated in her home country by her contemporaries, these would be acknowledged in years to come, as Borges had prophesised in 1961: "Ethically speaking, [*Sur*] has stood for democracy and against dictatorships; intellectually speaking, it has kept alive intellectual curiosity which is, perhaps, [...] the best traits of Argentineans" (Borges 1961 cited in King 1984: 30).[12]

As I have elsewhere argued (Lojo Rodríguez 2002: 239), the relevance of *Sur* and of its two related publishing houses—Editorial Sur and Editorial Sudamericana, founded alongside the journal at Ortega's and Sylvia Beach and Adrienne Monnier's suggestion to mitigate the enormous expenses that *Sur* represented[13]—was invaluable, not only in the Argentine cultural panorama, but in the Spanish-speaking world in general. On the occasion of the twentieth anniversary of *Sur*, the journal's secretary, Guillermo de Torre, recapitulates its literary achievements, such as anticipating the publication of D.H. Lawrence's *Lady Chatterley's Lover*, or the launching of translations published almost simultaneously with the originals, as was the case of Martin Heidegger's

¿Qué es la metafísica? [*What is Metaphysics*]. Argentine writer Óscar Hermes Villordo recalls this in the following terms:

> Thus it was *Sur* which published the first Aldous Huxley in Spanish, *Contrapunto* [*Point Counterpoint*]—which continues to be his masterpiece; the first D.H. Lawrence, *Canguro* [*Kangaroo*]; the first Malraux, *La condición humana* [*The Human Condition*]; the first Joyce, *Exiliados* [*Exiles*]; the first Virginia Woolf, *Un cuarto propio* [*A Room of One's Own*], *Orlando* y *Al faro* [*To the Lighthouse*]; the first Chekhov, *Las revelaciones de la muerte* [*Revelations of Death*]; the first Michaux, *Un bárbaro en Asia* [*A Barbarian in Asia*]. (Hermes Villordo 1993: 270)[14]

Victoria Ocampo and Virginia Woolf

Ocampo met Woolf in November 1934, at a Man Ray Exhibition in Bloomsbury which she attended at Aldous Huxley's suggestion, knowing that Virginia Woolf would be there. This first encounter, as well as the series of meetings to come afterwards, is recalled by Ocampo in a conference delivered at the "Association for the English Culture" in 1946, where she describes Woolf as "the most precious gift England has given me" (1956: 92). Ocampo's romanticised recollection of the writer conflates with Woolf's exuberant construction of the Argentinean's native country, which she may have drawn from common-place, imperial renderings of the peripheral. Ocampo invites her audience to imagine Virginia Woolf's beauty, a "mask which, though deprived of life and intelligence, were beautiful. Imagine that mask filled with life and intelligence to the point that it seems to have been modelled by them. Imagine all that and still you will not have imagined the charm of Virginia Woolf's face; a charm of the happiest union of the material and the spiritual in a woman's face" (1946: 92).[15] However, Woolf described Ocampo as one of "these opulent millionaires from Buenos Aires [...] very ripe & rich; with pearls at her ears, as if a large moth had laid a cluster of eggs; the colour of an apricot under glass" (Woolf 1982: 263), as an exotic gilded butterfly drawn from South American gardens (Woolf 1982: 348–349).

Such disparity in their mutual perception, in which class prejudice and imperial misconceptions intervene, will not prevent the inception of a fruitful collaboration between the two women. Despite Woolf's Eurocentric construction of Ocampo (Salomone 2006: 70) of which she was aware of, the Argentinean truly appreciated the way Woolf transformed the contemporary novel (1946: 96). In turn, Woolf was charmed by Ocampo's personality and background, her acquaintances (they discussed Ocampo's recent meeting with the *Duce* in Italy) and by her editorial project. When Ocampo returned to Argentina by the end of December, it was agreed that *Sur* would publish Woolf's work in the Spanish translation: "I think the Room is the best to begin on", Woolf advises Ocampo in a letter; "then, perhaps, if you want another, Orlando or The Lighthouse" (1982: 358).

Ocampo's first impressions after those early meetings with Woolf are immediately recorded in the Argentinean's essay "Carta a Virginia Woolf" ["Letter to Virginia Woolf"], published in *Revista de Occidente* in 1934, later to be reprinted as prologue to her first collection of critical essays, *Testimonios* [*Testimonies*] (1935). The prominent position of this essay in Ocampo's compilation already acknowledges Woolf's centrality in her own work, as she clarifies: "Your name, Virginia, is linked to these thoughts [...] All the articles compiled in this volume [...] entail a series of testimonies to my hunger" (1934: 171). Once more, Ocampo chooses as a genre a breed in between the epistle and the critical essay, which allows her to combine, as Woolf herself had done in her own essayist practice, personal commentary and critical impressions. In this letter, Ocampo's addressee comprises not only the real Woolf and her own imaginative reassessment of her person and of her work, but also a community of common readers bonded by a disinterested love for literature. In addition to this, Ocampo speaks from the confines of the private—thus mirroring Woolf's room of one's own—with a distinct and incisive message expected to be heard in a male-dominated public realm, thus articulating the private as political.

In "Letter to Virginia Woolf", Ocampo creates an atmosphere of warmth and confidence in Woolf's welcoming living-room, which sharply contrasts with the foggy dusk of the London night outside. Here the two women interrogate themselves aiming to build "a bridge of words" (1934: 171) to spare the cultural gap that initially separated them. Woolf features Ocampo as an exotic book to browse; in turn, the Argentinean's literary "hunger" finds an encouraging response in Woolf's exhortation to write "all kinds of books, hesitating at no subject however trivial or however vast" (172).

Ocampo's essay is also articulated as a political appropriation of Woolf's major premises in *A Room of One's Own* by applying the universality of Woolf's message to Ocampo's peripheral background and, in so doing, also dissenting from Woolf. For Ocampo, to write "as a woman" (173) inevitably entails the perception of writing as a cultural product which mirrors social and ideological tensions. In this sense, Ocampo—and unlike Woolf—sympathises with Charlotte Brontë's combatant "rage" which translates in her writing into a "moving imperfection" (174) which Ocampo identifies with her own, drawing a parallel between Brontë's nineteenth-century social background with her own conservative Argentine society, not dissimilar to that which had prevented Shakespeare's sister from flourishing in England. Ocampo's letter closes with the narrator's identification with Shakespeare's sister as a homage to the yet unwritten women's works which are in need to find "the propitious temperature for their need to flourish" (177) for, in vindicating their cause, Ocampo also vindicates her own (174).

Woolf praised Ocampo's essay—"I don't usually like appearing as a private person in print, but on this occasion I can find no fault" (1982: 365)—and encouraged her to pursue her aims further: "I'm so glad you write criticisms not fiction. And I'm sure it's good criticism—clear and sharp, cut with a knife, not pitchforked with a rusty old edge machine" (1982: 356). In so doing, Woolf also praised Ocampo's incisive and masterful combination of personal impression and critical judgement, which she herself was so fond of in her own critical practice as a means to defy the controlling, authoritative voice of contemporary male critics.

"Letter to Virginia Woolf" signals the inception of Ocampo's intense and fruitful relationship with Virginia Woolf, and opens up the path to the reception, appropriation and assimilation of British Modernism, in general, and of Woolf's *oeuvre*, in particular, in Spanish-speaking countries through Ocampo's inspiring readings, assessments, translations and dissemination of Woolf's works. The choice of the epistolary genre as a vehicle for the circulation of ideas, which amalgamates private and public cultural exchange, constitutes a major coincidental point in both writers, whose extensive letter-writing both challenged and reassessed epistolary conventions by questioning a gendered opposition between public and private domains.

On occasion of the death of Nobel-prize winner Gabriela Mistral in 1957—one of Ocampo's most influential and long-lasting literary figures—Victoria Ocampo published an interesting reflection on the nature and politics of letter-writing through recollections of her own correspondence with Mistral ("Gabriela Mistral in Her Letters"). In addition, the essay also publicly airs Ocampo and Ortega's disagreement regarding the role of men and women in public and private realms: "Ortega was of the opinion that the epistolary genre went together with femininity because the letter is addressed to only one person, not to everyone, and because, unlike men, women are made for intimacy. According to Ortega […] men and women can only reach their maximum expansion in two different atmospheres. For men, the public life; for women, the private life" (1957: 295).

Ortega clearly regarded the epistolary genre as the "natural" vehicle of expression for women, embodying the spirit of domesticity, dealing with private matters and addressing private relationships, which, in his view, explains both women's excellence in the genre as well as men's ineptitude to master epistles since "the maximum expansion of men and women is only achieved in different atmospheres" (295). Ocampo cleverly questions Ortega's rigidly-erected boundaries between private and public domains by carefully recalling her own correspondence with Mistral, Noailles and Woolf, which tackled a variety of subjects ranging from aesthetics and politics to private matters and personal impressions. In so doing, Ocampo puts forward a powerful argument in favour of blurring boundaries between private and public realms and against women's invisibility, articulating the private sphere as a space of resistance to patriarchal oppression.

In addition to this, Ocampo's "Letter to Virginia Woolf" offers inspiring views on Woolf's work issued from a peripheral, non-European perspective. In so doing, Ocampo assumes the perspective of the common reader, whose interest and reading for pleasure also implies the existence of a potential community of readers with whom she establishes, like Woolf herself, an affinity despite dissimilar cultural backgrounds and other possible impediments, which Woolf's universality and appeal has the power to dissolve.

Woolf in Translation

Back in Buenos Aires, Ocampo commissioned the translation of *A Room of One's Own* to one of her most promising collaborators, Jorge Luis Borges (Lojo Rodríguez 2016: 469), which would be published as *Un cuarto propio* in *Sur* between 1935 and 1936, and in book form in Editorial Sur in 1936, to be followed by *Orlando* in 1937.[16] On 30 October 1936 Borges had already published a fragment of his translation of *Orlando* in the journal *El Hogar* [*The Home*] (1936), as part of his "Synthetic Biographies" series. Borges was deeply impressed by Woolf's technical achievement in the novel, and was especially appealed by her masterful combination of historical and fantastic realms: "In *Orlando* there is also a concern with time [...] Magic, bitterness and happiness collaborate in this book [...] in which dream and reality alternate and find their balance" (Borges 1985: 123).[17] Borges's biographer, Emir Rodríguez Monegal, explains how his translation of *Orlando* was to become a seminal book in the South American literary tradition by its contemporary reassessment of "fantastic narratives", influencing writers such as Julio Cortázar, Gabriel García Márquez and Borges himself (1968: 128).[18]

On occasion of the publication of *Orlando*'s translation in July 1937 Ocampo gave a lecture at the "Sociedad de amigos del arte" entitled "Virginia Woolf, *Orlando* y Cía" ["Virginia Woolf, *Orlando* and Co."], which was published next year in *Sur*. Unlike Borges's analysis of Woolf's *Orlando*—which placed the emphasis on the novel's intersection between historical sites and magic realms—Ocampo focuses on Woolf's feminist message. In addition to this, "Virginia Woolf, *Orlando* y Cía" is also articulated as a literary statement of Ocampo's—and also Woolf's—a particular manner of understanding literary criticism, the essay as a genre and the relationship between women and fiction.

The essay's opening mirrors Woolf's cautionary words to her common readers in *A Room of One's Own* regarding the nature of truth and, in so doing, questioning a positivist conception of the essay as a piece of expository prose characterised by a succession of unquestionable and seemingly objective statements aiming at the reader's enlightenment: "I should never be able to fulfil what is, I understand, the first duty of a lecturer to hand you after an hour's discourse a nugget of pure truth to wrap up between the pages of your notebooks and keep on the mantelpiece for ever. All I could do was to offer you an opinion upon some minor point" (1992: 4).

Similarly, Ocampo opens up her talk by establishing a position of affinity with her audience: "I am going to speak to you as the 'common reader' of Virginia Woolf's work. I am going to speak to you of the image I keep of her. Do not expect to hear pure criticism; you'd be disappointed" (1938: 7)[19]. Ocampo defines such intimacy in terms which bring to mind Woolf's definition of the common reader in the homonymous essay inaugurating her first essay collection, significantly entitled *The Common Reader* (1925). Ocampo consciously recalls Woolf's famous definition in presenting the common reader as a non-authoritative figure that differs from the professional critic and the scholar "in reading only for pleasure, without having to worry about transmitting his/her knowledge. The common reader does not have a method, only a passion: reading" (1938: 46).[20]

Ocampo's essay unfolds to offer her personal reassessment of Woolf's *A Room of One's Own*, as well as a vindication of her own appropriation of Woolf's argument in terms of her own native country, where social, political and cultural impediments prevent women from having public recognition: "We must note [that things] have hardly begun to change for women. Jane Austen's gesture of hiding her manuscript under blotting paper when visitors or servants entered the room" (1938: 26).[21] Interestingly, Ocampo signals the construction of gender as a cultural process, questioning the naturalization of women's inferiority and social invisibility which respond to patriarchal oppression: "Women are not natural, obedient, nor chaste, nor perfumed or adorned, and they only come to be so by submitting to the most unpleasant discipline" (1938: 30).[22]

Farewells and Diaries

Only three years after the publication of *Orlando*'s translation in Buenos Aires, Virginia Woolf committed suicide. Ocampo wrote a moving obituary entitled "Virginia Woolf en mi memoria" ["Virginia Woolf in my Memory"] (1941), which intertwines personal recollection and literary echoes from her work, in tune with those "continuing presences" (1992: 148) Woolf had celebrated in *A Room of One's Own*. Yet Ocampo never stopped imagining Woolf and assessing her influence in her own work and in her contemporary cultural scenario: *a propos* of the publication in *Sur* of the translation of Woolf's posthumous *A Writer's Diary* in 1954, Ocampo collected a series of personal impressions on the writer entitled *Virginia Woolf en su diario* [*Virginia Woolf in her Diary*]. Yet Ocampo's essay is also articulated as a thorough, incisive examination of the various means which have served patriarchy to oppress and silence women. In this sense, Ocampo comments on Leonard Woolf's censorship of his wife's diary; Leslie Stephen's demands on his wife and daughters; and on numerous examples which have resulted in efforts to silence women's voices across the world. Ocampo's essay tackles the various "ways which reactions against the patriarchal dictatorship have taken" (1954: 41): Woolf's work, most notably *A Room of One's Own* and *Three Guineas*, embody one of the most effective and yet unsurpassed means of women's rebellion against oppression (1954: 52).

In the last pages of her essay, Ocampo reassesses Woolf's novels and technical achievements (her writing practice, reality and fiction, the nature of time, the experience of the ineffable and the limits of language), as well as her own private relationship with the writer: "My friendship with Virginia [was] unilateral, since I knew her and she didn't know me; she existed for me intensely and I was for her a distant shade in an exotic country produced by her imagination" (1954: 98).[23] Aware of the disparate relevance of the acquaintance for each one of them—for Ocampo, Woolf had been "London's most precious thing"; for Woolf, Ocampo had been a peripheral figure in every possible sense, "a smiling ghost, as my own country was" (1954: 94)—the Argentinean mocks Woolf's imperial preconceptions: "The ghostly idea which she [Woolf] had of Argentina amused me a great deal" (1954: 95). By doing so,

Ocampo consciously returns to the inception of their acquaintance, when Woolf had imagined both Ocampo and her own country in terms of beautiful butterflies, which revealed Woolf's Eurocentric prejudice in her combination of exoticism, beauty and estrangement: "Virginia imagined that I came from a city (Buenos Aires) where clouds of the most splendid butterflies follow us in the gardens and superbly tanned young men wear tropical garments and have cool drinks under brightly coloured umbrellas" (1946: 95).[24]

More than twenty years later, Ocampo was elected member of the Argentine Academy of Letters (1977), a recognition which Woolf herself could not have during her lifetime: "Virginia Woolf has written that until a short time ago women students could not enter the lawns of the great English universities, reserved for men. This will give you an idea of the distance that a woman a little younger than Virginia had to travel to arrive at Alberdi's chair in 1977" (1977: 82). In her speech, Ocampo acknowledged her literary debt to her American and European major influences, Gabriela Mistral and Virginia Woolf respectively, and in so doing, she revisits her first steps in literary criticism by returning to her essay "Carta a Virginia Woolf". As she had done in this early essay, Ocampo addresses Woolf again, using once more the public epistle which her contemporaries (most notably Ortega) had termed as an intrinsically woman's genre, subject to personal matters and ascribed to a private realm. Ocampo recalls this genre in her inaugural speech to serve in the most prestigious institution of Letters in Argentina, and she does so by celebrating her own writing practice, her life-enduring resistance to established conventions and her debt to, and admiration for, her friend: "[Woolf] wanted women to express themselves in any language, in any country, and about any subject however trivial or vast it may seem. In my dedication, I said to her: You say it is important for women to express themselves in *writing*. You encourage them to write *all kinds of books, hesitating at no subject* ... You find that men's books inform us rather imperfectly about them. In the back of our heads, you say, there is a spot the size of a shilling that we cannot see with your own eyes" (1977: 282). In this way, Ocampo acknowledges Woolf as a major inspiration that had triggered her own writing impulse, as many other women writers across time and cultures to speak for themselves in their own voice.

Victoria Ocampo was to die only two years after this speech. In her *oeuvre* and political convictions, she had shared with Woolf the ability to perceive "a poetic vision of things and beings" (Ocampo 1963: 76) and an "eagerness to remove barriers" (1977: 284), which crystallised in her insightful choices concerning her ambitious editorial project and her own writing practice.

Ocampo's journal run discontinuously from 1931 to the late 1960s: the journal's circulation in all Spanish-speaking countries functioned as a large engine which translated, published and promoted the work of a large number of Modernist writers and thinkers, such as Aldous Huxley, D.H. Lawrence, James Joyce and Virginia Woolf, among many others. Thought in American and for the Americans, Ocampo's *Sur* has to be regarded as a major agent in the circulation of Modernist works and ideas in Hispanic countries and, as such, as a crucial component in assessing the condition of Modernism.

Notes

1. "Yo era una lectora fácil, también voraz y omnívora. Lo malo era que no podía ir a una librería a comprar cualquier libro que me interesara [...] Ejemplo de esta censura sin motivos aparentes fue el secuestro de mi ejemplar de *De profundis* (Oscar Wilde) encontrado por mi madre debajo de un colchón, en el Hotel Majestic (París). Yo tenía diecinueve años" (Ocampo 1980: 61; my translation). All translations from the Spanish, unless otherwise indicated, are my own.
2. "En aquellos días, la actitud de la sociedad argentina hacia una mujer escritora no era indulgente. Lo que decía Jane Austen en el siglo XIX continuaba siendo cierto: 'Si una mujer es lo suficientemente desafortunada de saber algo, debe esconderlo lo mejor que pueda" [...] Por ello recibí una lluvia de insultos" (Ocampo 1981: 105).
3. Ocampo's "La laguna de los nenúfares" ["The Water-Lily Pond"] was soon to follow in Ortega's journal (1926), an inspiring composition in between drama, animal fables and fairy tales, which reveals Ocampo's daring attempt at blurring boundaries and established genres and modes.

4. "Es inútil que tú seas admirable si no vives lo *sustancial* de tu época
   [...] Victoria, *el cambio aún de aspecto que el mundo va a sufrir en cuatro
   o cinco años va a ser fantástico*" (Ortega 1974: 150–151).

5. "Señora, la manera de leer que usted ejercita no es injusta e indebida.
   Fuera necesario tranquilizarla a usted sobre ello. En primer lugar,
   *porque una mujer capaz de escribir y de pensar con tanta gentileza no se
   inquieta, de seguro, cuando comete una injusticia*" (Ocampo 1991: 207).

6. "Hace siete años tuvo usted la gentileza de escribir un epílogo a mi
   breve comentario de la Divina Comedia [...] Guardo de ese rasgo un
   recuerdo emocionado y agradecido" (Ocampo 1931: 17).

7. In her diary, Virginia Woolf herself recalls the two women's meeting
   as rendered by Ocampo: "And so to Mme de Noailles, dying of extin-
   guished vanity in a small flat. She lay in bed, bedizened, covered with
   dozens & dozens of veils & c: began plucking them off; was never still a
   moment; lighting lamps & putting them out; demanded worship; was
   not old, but had outlived her fame. Nothing wrong with her but the
   death of her great fame" (Woolf: 263–264).

8. As John King notices, Ocampo's *Sur* as an editorial project was also
   indebted to a whole tradition of literary magazines run by the male,
   Argentine oligarchy at the turn of the twentieth-century, as was the case
   of Paul Groussac's *La Biblioteca* [*The Library*] (1896–1897), Manuel
   Gálvez and Ricardo Olivera's *Ideas* (1903–1905) and most notably,
   Bianchi and Giusti's *Nosotros* [*Us*], whose values were progressively
   questioned by young intellectuals and *avant garde* writers gathering in
   Sur (King 1986: 14).

9. "He aquí mi proyecto: publicar una revista que se ocupe principal-
   mente de problemas americanos bajo varios aspectos, y donde colab-
   oren los americanos que tengan algo que decir y los europeos que se
   interesen en América" (1967: 139). All translations, unless otherwise
   indicated, are my own.

10. "Revista en cuya línea dinámica, vital, no se desdeña ningún vigor
    ajeno; revista que es—en palabras de la propia editora—"de los que
    han ido a América, de los que piensan en América y de los que son de
    América" [...] Por eso, la revista, pensada en americano y para los amer-
    icanos, está llena de pensamiento europeo, está también escrita para los
    buenos europeos" (Jarnés 1931: 317).

11. "La hostilidad prevista me sorprende y me hiere, me irrita y me dep-
    rime" (Ocampo 1980: 39).

12. "Alguien, en un provenir no lejano, tendrá el valor de reducir esta historia en sus grandes líneas y entonces resultará evidente la compleja y benéfica labor que *Sur* ha ejecutado en América. Éticamente, ha defendido la causa de la democracia frente a las dictaduras; intelectualmente ha mantenido viva esa curiosidad universal que, según declaré, es acaso el mejor rasgo de los argentinos" (*Cuadernos del Congreso por la Libertad de la Cultura*, 55 (dic., 1961, 20, cited in King 1984: 30).

13. In her article "Vida de la revista '*Sur*'", Ocampo explains how she followed Ortega's advice to found two publishing houses, Sur and Sudamericana, as a commercial strategy to mitigate the enormous expenses of the journal: "Como *Sur* daba un serio déficit, Ortega me aconsejó que publicara libros para amenguarlo. Su experiencia de la *Revista de Occidente* le había demostrado que los libros podían equilibrar las finanzas de una revista. La idea me pareció brillante y la puse inmediatamente en práctica. Pero, desde que la saqué, elegí (porque me gustaban) obras que otras editoriales no se atrevían a publicar por lo voluminoso y el riesgo de perder dinero que implicaban. Por ejemplo: *Contrapunto*, de Huxley, y *Tipos psicológicos* de Jung. *Kanguro*, de D.H. Lawrence" (1967: 144).

14. "De esta suerte le correspondió [a *Sur*] dar el primer Aldous Huxley en castellano, que sigue siendo su obra maestra, *Contrapunto*; el primer Malraux, *La condición humana*; el primer Joyce, *Exiliados*; los primeros Virginia Woolf, *Un cuarto propio*, *Orlando* y *Al faro*; el primer Chekhov, *Las revelaciones de la muerte*; el primer Michaux, *Un bárbaro en Asia*" (1993: 270).

15. "Imaginen ustedes una máscara que, aún sin vida, sin inteligencia, fuera hermosa. Imaginen esa máscara impregnada de vida y de inteligencia a tal punto que parece haber sido modelada por ellas. Imaginen todo eso y todavía se habrán imaginado mal el encanto del rostro de Virginia Woolf; encanto del más feliz encuentro de lo material y de lo espiritual en una cara de mujer" (Ocampo 1946: 92–93).

16. Borges teasingly alleged that his translation of Woolf's *A Room of One's Own* had been, in fact, his mother's: "Ahora voy a confiarle, ya que estamos solos los dos, un secreto, y es que ese libro lo tradujo realmente mi madre. Y yo revisé un poco la traducción, de igual modo que ella revisó mi traducción de *Orlando*. La verdad es que trabajábamos juntos; sí, *Un cuarto propio*, que me interesó menos [...] bueno, el tema, desde luego, es digamos un mero alegato a favor de las mujeres y el

feminismo. Pero, como yo soy feminista, no requiero alegatos para convencerme, ya que estoy convencido" (Ferrari and Borges 1982: 306). Borges's alleged "feminism" has been contested by some feminist critics (Ayuso 2004; Leone 2009; Willson 2005). For an assessment of Borges's practice as a translator see Ana Gargatagli's *Jorge Luis Borges y la traducción* (Barcelona: Servicio de publicaciones de la Universidad, 1993).

17. "En *Orlando* también hay la preocupación del tiempo [...] La magia, la amargura y la felicidad colaboran en ese libro [...] donde alternan el ensueño y la realidad y encuentran su equilibrio".

18. I have further explored the influence of Woolf's *Orlando* on South American magic realist writers in the article "Fiction: Magic Realism and Experimental Fiction. From Virginia Woolf to Jeanette Winterson" in *The Oxford Handbook of Virginia Woolf*, Anne Fernald ed. (Oxford: Oxford University Press, forthcoming 2018).

19. "Voy a hablarles a ustedes como 'common reader' [sic] de la obra de Virginia. Voy a hablarles de la imagen que conservo de ella. No esperen ustedes oír crítica literaria pura; se decepcionarían" (1938: 7).

20. "El 'common reader' difiere del crítico y del erudito en que lee exclusivamente por placer y sin preocupación de tener que transmitir sus conocimientos. No tiene un método sino una pasión: la lectura" (1938: 46).

21. "Conviene advertir que [las cosas] apenas empiezan a cambiar para las mujeres. Todas las que han escrito han hecho, de un modo u otro, el gesto de Jane Austen ocultando su manuscrito bajo un secante cuando los visitantes o los criados entraban en su cuarto" (1938: 26).

22. "Las mujeres no son naturales ni obedientes, ni castas, ni perfumadas, ni revestidas de adornos, y que solo llegan a serlo sometiéndose a la más molesta disciplina" (1938: 30).

23. "Y mi amistad con Virginia (tan unilateral, pues yo la conocía y ella no a mí; pues ella existía intensamente para mí y yo para ella fui una sombra lejana en un país exótico creado por la fantasía)" (1954: 98).

24. "Virginia se imaginaba que yo llegaba de una ciudad (Buenos Aires) en que nubes de las más espléndidas mariposas nos persiguen en los jardines, mientras jóvenes soberbiamente bronceados y de indumentaria tropical toman bebidas frescas bajo los quitasoles de colores" (1946: 95).

References

Ayuso, Mónica. 2004. The Unlike[ly] Other: Borges and Woolf. *Woolf Studies Annual* 10: 241–251.

Borges, Jorge Luis. 1985. Virginia Woolf: Una biografía sintética. In *Ficcionario: Una antología de textos*, ed. E. Rodríguez Monegal, 122–123. México: Fondo de cultura económica.

Ferrari, Óscar, and Jorge Luis Borges. 1982. *Diálogos*. Barcelona: Seix-Barral.

Gargatagli, Ana. 1993. *Jorge Luis Borges y la traducción*. Barcelona: Servicio de publicaciones e intercambio científico.

Hermes Villordo, Óscar. 1993. *El grupo Sur: Una biografía colectiva*. Buenos Aires: Planeta.

Jarnés, Benjamín. 1931. Sur. *Revista de Occidente* 96: 314–317.

King, John. 1984. Victoria Ocampo, *Sur* y el peronismo, 1946–1955. *Revista de Occidente* 37: 30–44.

———. 1986. *"Sur": A Study of the Argentine Literary Journal and Its Role in the Development of a Culture, 1931–1970*. Cambridge: Cambridge University Press.

Leone, Lea. 2009. A Translation of His Own: Borges and *A Room of One's Own*. *Woolf Studies Annual* 15: 47–66.

———. 2016. Woolf in Hispanic Countries: Buenos Aires and Madrid. In *A Companion to Virginia Woolf*, ed. Jessica Berman, 467–480. Oxford: Blackwell.

Lojo Rodríguez, Laura Maria. 2002. 'A Gaping Mouth, but No Words': Virginia Woolf Enters the Land of Butterflies. In *The Reception of Virginia Woolf in Europe*, ed. M.A. Caws and N. Luckhurst, 218–246. London: Continuum.

Meyer, Doris. 1979. *Victoria Ocampo: Against the Wind and the Tide*. Austin: University of Texas Press.

Ocampo, Victoria. 1931a. Carta a Waldo Frank. *Sur* 1 (1): 7–18.

———. 1931b. Contestación a un epílogo de Ortega y Gasset. *Sur* 1 (Fall): 17–52.

———. 1933 [1999]. "Anna de Noailles y su poesía". *Testimonios*. Buenos Aires: Sudamericana. 13–28.

———. 1934. Carta a Virginia Woolf. *Revista de Occidente* 46: 170–177.

———. 1935. *Testimonios I*. Madrid: Revista de Occidente.

———. 1936. Woman, Her Rights, and Her Responsibilities. *Testimonios II*, 251–267. Reprinted and trans. Doris Meyer in Victoria Ocampo: Against the Wind and the Tide. Austin: University of Texas Press, 228–234.

———. 1938. *Virginia Woolf, Orlando y Cía*. Buenos Aires: Sur.

―――. 1941. Virginia Woolf in My Memory. In *Against the Wind and Tide: Victoria Ocampo*, trans. D. Meyer, 235–240. Austin: University of Texas Press.

―――. 1946. A los alumnos argentinos. In *Testimonios: Tercera serie*, 90–100. Buenos Aires: Sudamericana.

―――. 1954. *Virginia Woolf en su diario*. Buenos Aires: Sur.

―――. 1956 [1990]. Adrienne Monnier. In *Testimonios V*, 99–105. Reprinted in Doris Meyer *Victoria Ocampo: Against the Wind and the Tide*, 223–227. Austin: University of Texas Press.

―――. 1957 [2003]. Gabriela Mistral in Her Letters. In *This America of Ours: The Letters of Gabriela Mistral and Victoria Ocampo*, trans. and ed. Elizabeth Horan and Doris Meyer, 293–313. Austin: University of Texas Press.

―――. 1963. Releer, reincidir, regraciar. *Revista de Occidente* 1: 72–79.

―――. 1967. Vida de la revista "*Sur*". *Revista de Occidente* 16: 129–150.

―――. 1971. Envío al Director de la *Revista de Occidente*. *Revista de Occidente* 34: 1–6.

―――. 1977. Women in the Academy. In *Against the Wind and Tide: Victoria Ocampo*, trans. D. Meyer, 278–284. Austin: University of Texas Press.

―――. 1980. *Autobiografía II. El imperio insular [Autobiography II: The Insular Empire]*. Buenos Aires: Sur.

―――. 1981. *Autobiografía III. La rama de Salzburgo [Autobiography III: The Salzburg Branch]*. Buenos Aires: Sur.

―――. 1984. *Autobiografía VI. Sur y Cía*. Buenos Aires: Sur.

―――. 1991. *Autobiografía*. Madrid: Alianza.

Ortega y Gasset, José. 1974. *Epistolario*. Madrid: Revista de Occidente.

Ortega y Gasset, Soledad. 1984. Victoria Ocampo al trasluz de una doble amistad. *Revista de Occidente* 37: 7–23.

Owen Steiner, Patricia. 1999. *Victoria Ocampo: Writer, Feminist, Woman of the World*. Albuquerque: University of New Mexico Press.

Rodríguez Monegal, Emir. 1968. Novedad y anacronismo de Cien años de soledad. *Revista Nacional de Cultura XXIX* 185: 3–21. Reprinted in *García Márquez: El escritor y la crítica*, ed. Peter Earle, 1981, 114–138. Madrid: Taurus.

Rogers, Gayle. 2012a. The Circulation of Interwar Anglophone and Hispanic Modernisms. In *The Oxford Handbook of Global Modernisms*, ed. M. Wollaeger, 461–476. Oxford: Oxford University Press.

Rogers, Gayle. 2012b. *Modernism and the New Spain: Britain, Cosmopolitan Europe, and Literary History*. Oxford: Oxford University Press.

Rolland, Romain. 1916. America and the Arts. *Seven Arts* 1 (1): 47–51.

Salomone, Alicia. 2006. Virginia Woolf en los *Testimonios* de Victoria Ocampo: Tensiones entre feminismo y colonialismo. *Revista chilena de literatura* 69: 69–87.

Willson, Patricia. 2005. *La constelación del Sur: Traductores y traducciones en la literatura argentina del siglo XX*. Buenos Aires: Siglo XXI.

Woolf, Virginia. 1982. *The Letters of Virginia Woolf IV*, ed. Joanne Trautmann and Nigel Nicholson. London: The Hogarth Press.

———. 1992. *A Room of One's Own*, ed. Morag Shiach. Oxford: World's Classics.

9

"But She Loved Her Roses (Didn't that Help the Armenians?)": Resisting Facts, Inventing Forms, Negotiating History in Virginia Woolf's *To the Lighthouse* and *Mrs. Dalloway*

Katerina Kitsi-Mitakou

Subject and Object

If art and literature aim at representing reality, modernism's contribution to mimesis was the philosophical awareness that an objective reality out there may not exist. This is clearly evident in the course that English fiction, for example, had followed from the eighteenth century to the first decades of the twentieth century. While eighteenth-century novelists were concerned about persuading their readers that their fictional tales were veritable testimonies of "real" people taken from "real" life (biographies, letters, autobiographies, etc.), and while the nineteenth-century novel still held its faith in objective reality despite that fact that it was beginning to admit that the accurate representation of reality was a complicated task, modernist writers doubted the very existence of reality itself.

Take for instance the first chapter of Book Fourteen from Henry Fielding's 1749 novel *Tom Jones*. His extradiegetic narrator explains

K. Kitsi-Mitakou (✉)
Faculty of Philosophy, School of English, Aristotle University of Thessaloniki, Thessaloniki, Greece
e-mail: katkit@enl.auth.gr

© The Author(s) 2018
A. Falcato and A. Cardiello (eds.), *Philosophy in the Condition of Modernism*,
https://doi.org/10.1007/978-3-319-77078-9_9

to the reader that the novel's task is to create a truthful image of reality: "The picture must be after nature itself" (TJ 656). The lengthy and explanatory title of the chapter: "An Essay to prove that an Author will write the better, for having some knowledge of the Subject on which he writes," leaves no doubts that knowledge can and must be achieved through observation of the narrated subject; as the narrator again remarks, "A true knowledge of the world is gained only by conversation, and the manners of every rank *must be seen* in order to be known" (656, emphasis added). But it's apparent that the novelist's perception of representation became more intricate, when in 1859, George Eliot, the most ardent supporter of English realism, acknowledged the limitations of her observant and insightful narrators. In what has been considered Eliot's realist manifesto, Chapter 17 of her first novel, *Adam Bede*, Eliot's narrator vows with passion that her task is not to "refashion life," or "straighten the noses," "brighten the wit" or "rectify [the] dispositions" of her characters. On the contrary, it is "to give a faithful account of men and things as they have mirrored themselves *in my mind*" (AB 328–29, emphasis added). This last phrase here introduces the epistemological question of whether and how knowledge of reality is possible, or whether we can rely on our sense perception to show us what reality is really like. Even if a writer's "strongest effort is to avoid any […] arbitrary picture[s]," the mirror of her or his mind, Eliot's narrator admits with honesty, will always be "defective," the outlines "disturbed," and the reflections "faint or confused" (AB 328), since one's mind/senses/perception can never function as perfectly transparent, neutral or impartial filters through which the world can be narrated.

When in the twentieth century, the mind was not only the metaphor for the writer's "defective mirror," but also her or his chief focal theme, the modernist novel introduced its readers to the metaphysical aspect of philosophy and questions related with the very nature of reality itself: What is the ultimate nature of reality? Is the everyday world real? In what space-time framework do we and the objects around us exist? Does reality exist a priori and independently of its observer? The new directions taken in scientific, philosophical and psychological discourses in the early twentieth century steered writers away from the factual world of everyday reality towards what Virginia Woolf called the "dark places of psychology" (MF 152) in ways that seriously questioned the importance of facts. In "Modern Fiction," one of the essays which comprise Woolf's modernist manifesto, the writers who insist on detailed descriptions of external reality, settings, the characters' appearance or a meticulously chronological account of everyday routine are dismissed as "materialists" who "write of unimportant things" (MF 147), or "slaves" to the conventions of fiction. Writers need urgently, Woolf advocates, to detach themselves from the triviality of external facts, which can by no means capture the essence of what can interchangeably be called "life or spirit, truth or reality" (MF 149).

It is interesting to observe that although modernism was an anti-philosophical movement in general (Lackey, "The Literary Modernist Assault on Philosophy" 51), in the sense that it shook the stability of intellectual thought, sought to highlight the non-rational aspects of the unconscious self and laid emphasis on the impossibility of attaining Truth, it participated in major metaphysical and epistemological concerns and even touched upon areas of moral and political philosophy. Drawing from the case of Woolf's novels: *To the Lighthouse* and *Mrs. Dalloway*, I would like to suggest that modernism can offer a significantly challenging contribution to basic philosophical questions related with what the world is, what one is able to know about it, and, finally, what one does about it.

Woolf's connection with philosophy is not one of love and devotion judging from her depiction of the male philosopher, Mr. Ramsay, in *To the Lighthouse*. Trapped in a sterile teleological *Weltanschauung*, Mr. Ramsay's understanding of the world is compared to that of repeating "every letter of the alphabet from A to Z accurately in order" (TTL 49). This proves to be a fatally sterile and callous method that leads him to a dead-end, obstructs his vision from seeing the beauty around him (TTL 97), and makes him an unsympathetic husband and father. Woolf's philosopher, absorbed by his bareness, never looks at things, but above things ("He did not look at the flowers, which his wife was considering, but at a spot about a foot or so above them." TTL 91), and when he does all he can do is pity this "Poor little world" (TTL 97). His philosophy is nothing but a linear process of arriving somewhere, and, immobilized as he is at Q ("he is stuck at Q" for the rest of his life TTL 49), all he can do is plunge his "beak of brass" into his wife's "delicious fecundity," begging for sympathy and crushing his son's dreams of sailing to the lighthouse (TTL 52). Pathetic Mr. Ramsay, however, has initiated his family into one of the most crucial philosophical debates of all times: "'Subject and object and the nature of reality'" (TTL 33), as his son Andrew perceives and explains it to the young artist in the novel, Lily Briscoe.

Rather than rejecting philosophy, as some critics have argued (Lackey, "Modernist Anti-Philosophicalism and Virginia Woolf's Critique of Philosophy"), as a discourse incompatible with the psychological narrative that modernists initiated, Woolf's novel accommodates, and even adopts, Mr. Ramsay's perspective in its own search for truth. For although philosophy and art may seem to be juxtaposed as two antithetical poles in Woolf's novel, represented respectively by the two opposing characters of Mr. Ramsay and Lily Brisco, the question of subject and object becomes recurrent in *To the Lighthouse* and throughout Woolf's work in general. Woolf's resistance to the factual "life of Monday or Tuesday," as she announces in "Modern Fiction" (150), or the trifling accuracy of material records, reflects Mr. Ramsay's insoluble puzzle which, in the mind of Andrew Ramsay, takes the form of a kitchen table when no one is there (TTL 33). The question of whether the kitchen table exists when it is totally unseen or unperceived by human agency haunts Lily's thoughts and ignites her imagination:

So now she always saw, when she thought of Mr. Ramsay's work, a scrubbed kitchen table. It lodged now in the fork of a pear tree, for they had reached the orchard. And with a painful effort of concentration, she focused her mind, not upon the silver-bossed bark of the tree, or upon its fish-shaped leaves, but upon a phantom kitchen table, one of those scrubbed board tables, grained and knotted, whose virtue seems to have been laid bare by years of muscular integrity, which stuck there, its four legs in air. Naturally, if one's days were passed in this seeing of angular essences, this reducing of lovely evenings, with all their flamingo clouds and blue and silver to a white deal four-legged table (and it was a mark of the finest minds to do so), naturally one could not be judged like an ordinary person. (33–34)

In the young artist's mind, the philosopher's kitchen table becomes a point of attraction only when perceived in relation to its origin, the tree, and its past: the scrubs, grains, and knots which are powerful inscriptions suggestive of its long eventful history. Lily's surreal image of the table suspended in the fork of a pear tree adds new dimensions to the "angular essences" that are the focus of the philosopher's observation. Moreover, her concluding rumination ("naturally one could not be judged like an ordinary person") is more complicated than just an indirect ironic remark about Mr. Ramsay's limited vision, as Lily makes an effort to identify with and remedy his shortcomings. Mr. Ramsay's colourless evenings of meditating on dull objects are retouched by Lily's pastels in her imagination and the object of his study, whether phantom or real, acquires new and fascinating qualities extending in time and space. Lily's creative adoption of a lifeless table and its transformation into an object of "muscular integrity" carrying its own knotty stories on its surface reflects her wish to invent ways to envelope Mr. Ramsay's philosophy and match it with her art rather than sever herself from it.

"Subject and object and the nature of reality" is, after all, the dominant theme in Part 2 of the novel, when the Ramsays have not returned to their summer house in the course of ten years and it is threatened with extinction. The narrator attempts to communicate the appalling void of absence and death through the materiality of the desolate house, its empty rooms, the fading roses on the wallpaper or the cracked china; can they endure when "there [is] scarcely anything left of body or mind by which one could say 'This is he' or 'This is she'" (TTL 172)? The question of whether the house will perish or persist iterates and reiterates (TTL 176), while a positive answer to it is an imperative pressing issue. Woolf's groundbreaking narrative mode of introducing all the momentous events during the ten-year absence of the Ramsays in detached epigrammatic reports, which appear in square brackets, questions the verity of the facts, their narratability, as well as their very bizarre relationship with the materiality of the summer house.

Never before in the history of the novel had human tragedy been so awkwardly squeezed in a few lines of dubious origin, as the thoughts/voices of characters and the voice of the narrator mingle to such a degree that it is impossible to tell them apart. Mrs. Ramsay's sudden death, Prue Ramsay's death in childbirth, and Andrew Ramsay's death by shell explosion in the trenches of France are wedged into the frame narrative which describes the falling apart of the house.

> [Mr. Ramsay, stumbling along a passage one dark morning, stretched his arms out, but Mrs. Ramsay having died rather suddenly the night before, his arms, though stretched out, remained empty.] (175)

> ....

> [Prue Ramsay died that summer in some illness connected with childbirth, which was indeed a tragedy, people said, everything, they said, had promised so well.] (180)

> ....

> [A shell exploded. Twenty or thirty young men were blown up in France, among them Andrew Ramsay, whose death, mercifully, was instantaneous.] (181)

This factual piece of information, introduced through the voice of the narrator, is associated with hearsay ("people said") and also loosely related with the unreliable point of view of the old woman who comes to clean the house after ten years, Mrs. McNab, and who is prone to drinking and gossiping (TTL 179). The tragic history of the Ramsay family is, for some reason, interconnected with the desolation of the house and its resistance to the "gigantic chaos" of nature and the "amorphous bulks of [universal] leviathans" (TTL 183). Objects, it seems, will remain, only if subjects are there to tell their human history and blend it with their materiality. It is the force of the two women, Mrs. McNab and her helper, Mrs. Bast, their aged stiff bodies working laboriously that exorcise the "clammy sea airs" and silence the giant shrieking voices that have been invading the house and threatening it to extinction.

But the whole process is a parody: it is a "rusty laborious birth" that the old women are involved in, as they "stooping, rising, groaning, singing, slapped and slammed, upstairs now now down the cellars" (TTL 190). And this mock birth is a hint of the narrator's futile efforts to represent reality—the mirror this time is not only defective; it is broken, as there are no more faces for it to hold on its glassy surface (TTL 176).

> That dream, of sharing, completing, of finding in solitude on the beach an answer, was then but a reflection in a mirror, and the mirror itself was but the surface glassiness which forms in quiescence when the nobler powers sleep beneath? Impatient, despairing yet loth to go (for beauty offers her lures, has her consolations), to pace the beach was impossible; contemplation was unendurable; the mirror was broken. (182–183)

Woolf's aversion to intact mirrors is pronounced more explicitly in a short story published two years after *To the Lighthouse*, entitled "The Lady in the Looking-Glass: A Reflection." The mirror in the story pries mercilessly into the central character's mind, prizes Isabella Tyson open as if she were an oyster, strips her life to its bare factuality—her senility, angularness, and friendlessness—and, consequently, eradicates any chance the character could have to reinterpret reality. Unlike the perfect mirror in Isabella's hall, the Ramsays' smashed mirror allows the narrator to unchain herself from the accuracy of fixed facts and approach loss through a communal and universal perspective, i.e., a blending of voices and a coming together of subjects and objects. Death in the Ramsay family is spoken through the decaying, rotting, and decomposing inanimate world in the Ramsay universe and filtered through an amalgamation of points of view. In *To the Lighthouse*, it is only this modernist broken mirror that can speak for the subjects' tragedy reflected on the broken world that surrounds them.

Building Tunnels of Solidarity

The idea of combining perspectives and worlds, which is masterly exhibited, as we have seen, in the second part of *To the Lighthouse*, is something Woolf had been experimenting on since the beginning of her writing career. In her effort to free herself from the "old tyrant" of fictional conventions and capture the evanescent spirit of character, her imaginary Mrs. Brown, as she calls her, Woolf realizes that character will never be caught unless the writer pays due respect to everyone and everything that surrounds her. But the modernists' approach should not be that of their immediate predecessors, she writes in her 1923 essay "Mr. Bennett and Mrs. Brown," meaning the Edwardian writers who slavishly strived to construct a superficial world based on insignificant material details. They have given us, she notes, a vast and vague sense of things in general and killed the idea of character in their accurately described mansions and perfectly sewn buttons. What a writer needs to do, according to Woolf, is observe how subjects and objects merge, shape and reform one another. In 1923, at the same time Woolf was articulating her theories on modernist fiction, she was also working on what became Woolf's first brilliant sample of modernist writing and a seminal modernist novel completed and published in 1925, *Mrs. Dalloway*.

The book indeed opens a new, "illustrious" and "epoch-making" chapter in the history of literature, for it gets as close to catching the core of character as ever before, and validates Woolf prophesies in "Mr. Bennett and Mrs. Brown" that eventually character will be captured (388). The key to this ground-breaking method is connecting voices, characters, times, subjects and objects, or, as Woolf records in her diary, building underground networks of solidarity that unite them all: "I dig out beautiful caves behind my characters; I think that gives exactly what I want, humanity, humour, depth. The idea is that the caves shall connect, & each comes to daylight in the present moment" (Diary 2 263).

The novel focuses on a single day in June 1923 in the life of Clarissa Dalloway, wife of a Conservative Member of Parliament, who makes preparations for a large social gathering that will take place at their house in the evening of that day. Although Woolf had dismissed reality and its "cheapness," this "disgusting" routine of getting from morning to afternoon to evening (Diary 2 248), she is exploiting it here to its fullest, as the clocks around London keep striking the hour and half-hour irrevocably, "councell[ing] submission," and "up[holding] authority" (MD 133). External time functions as a grid that brings characters together: it offers smooth transitions between their individual stories, as the same clock sound is heard by them all and reminds them of their schedules and obligations. At the same time, however, the narrative embraces the characters' inner paces and propensity to return to the past and mix it with the present moment. Although Big Ben spreads its leaden invincible circles in the air, there are clocks around London whose elasticity is reminiscent of Dali's melting watches (as depicted in his 1931 painting *The Persistence of Memory*) and offer a more humanized and feminine version of mechanical time. St Margaret's clock, for example, identifies with Clarissa's heart and expresses "languor and suffering" (MD 64): it "glides into the recesses of the heart and buries itself ring after ring of sound, like something alive which wants to confide itself, to disperse itself, to be, with a tremor of delight, at rest—like Clarissa herself ..." (MD 64). Clock time in the novel is reduced to an empty signifier unless it can beat to the pulse of the characters' internal rhythms and express their agonies and concerns.

Woolf's method of connecting caves is more explicitly pronounced in the narrator's effort to seize some of the different and incompatible sides of Mrs. Dalloway's self composed for the world into a diamond shape (MD 48). Clarissa's parts live in other people, places, times, or things, survive "on the ebb and flow of things ... she being part, she was positive, of the trees at home; of the house there ... part of people she had never met," while her life spreads like a mist between people she knew best (MD 11). She herself has adopted a transcendental theory, which leads her to believe that her being is not pinned on a fixed place and moment, but extends everywhere and has developed "odd affinities" even with people and places she has never met or visited in her life: "some woman in the street, some man behind a counter—even trees, or barns" (MD 200). Consequently, in order to know her or be able to portray her, a writer would have to throw light on practically everyone and everything, on her visible, but also invisible components, with the hope of discovering some of the hidden fractions of her personality.

Has Woolf set a spiteful trap for her narrator (and herself by extension) by assigning her an impossible task? Woolf's delight in ridiculing narrators is evident in her 1920 short story "An Unwritten Novel," a metafictional piece that questions the very process of writing stories. While narration here oscillates between present and past, glides through places and people the character could have met, and traces fragments that could compose her story, Minnie Marsh (or at least the character whom the narrator decides to call that) has the final say. Much like Freud's renowned "Dora," the patient who in 1900, while treated by him for aphonia, rejected his version of her family drama and walked out on him adding to his career a therapeutic failure, Minnie Marsh steps out of the train bringing the story to an abrupt and anticlimactic end. As the woman who was sitting opposite the narrator in a train compartment arrives at her destination, the narrator's world collapses when she realizes that she had never been the forlorn and isolated woman involved in the dramatic plots she had spun for her.

Her narrator in *Mrs. Dalloway*, however, knows better than to force her characters into restrictively predetermined scenarios. Aware that they have a life of their own and may refuse to live in the edifices writers build for them ("Modern Fiction" 147), the narrator here functions as a magnet that attracts the voices and thoughts of the characters and allows them to blend with each other and live together in the obscure tunnels she constructs for them. When still on page 100 of the book, Woolf was concerned that the character of Mrs. Dalloway was "too stiff, too glittering & tinsely" and realized that she could "bring innumerable other characters to her support" (Diary 2 272). Her loans from cubist art, the dominant avant-garde movement in art during the 1910s and 1920s, are apparent here. Familiar with the new artistic trends through her intimate affiliation with the artists and art critics of the Bloomsbury Group—her sister Vanessa Bell, Roger Fry, Clive Bell, and Duncan Grant—Woolf experiments with a kind of literary cubism and expands the narrative plane on various levels, and to its full, in the medley of voices, times, characters and spaces she creates, as already argued. At the levels of space and time, Clarissa's day in London on June 13, 1923, is combined through her memory with a day in June in 1889 at her summer house in Bourton; at the same time, at the level of plot, Mrs. Dalloway's day on June 13 is united with the last day in the life of Septimus Smith, a World War I shell shock victim whom she has never met. Although their lives are apparently disconnected, Clarissa and

Septimus converge at crucial issues and amplify both each other as well as the themes Woolf wishes to highlight.

It is at this point where Woolf's cubist aesthetics participate more distinctly in modern philosophical debates concerning questions related with how the personal and the political are indistinguishable, how interrelated one's life is with the lives of others, and, consequently, how precariousness is a condition that involves (potentially) all people. Woolf's decision, in the process of composing the novel, to spare her upperclass, middle-aged, sociable hostess from literal death by introducing the suicidal young war veteran who eventually kills himself, is an indirect comment on how unstable boundaries between apparently different categories of people are. Clarissa and Septimus are divided by class, status, age, gender, mental condition (sanity vs insanity), yet, they are joined in their overwhelming bonds with the Empire and with death. If Clarissa lives in the hub of London life, well-protected by authority, and giving parties attended by the Prime Minister, Septimus volunteered to save this glorious world and experienced the catastrophic effects of Empire politics in the trenches. And while Clarissa's perception of death is focused on the emptiness of her menopausal, frigid, and "shrivelled" (MD 39) body, Septimus has encountered the most horrendous aspect of death in the flames of the battlefield and the killing of his best friend.

In thinking of sexual politics together with war politics, Woolf unites the two characters in their otherness and raises awareness towards the common devastating effects of the dominant ideologies concerning war: femininity and masculinity. Despite their strong homosexual attractions—Clarissa to Sally Seton, her love from Bourton, or to women confessing her follies to her (MD 40–41), and Septimus to his friend Evans—they are both forced into the model of heteronormativity. They both fail, though, in their heterosexual marriages; Clarissa embodies the paradox of a virginal wife and mother (MD 40), defying thus stereotypical femininity ("breastless" and "unmaternal" as she is), while Septimus, who had developed manliness at war (MD 112), refuses to participate in what he considers the filthy act of copulation with his wife and "increase the breed of these lustful animals," i.e., human beings (MD 116). From their different points of view, Clarissa and Septimus are united in resisting imperial politics and their violent intrusion into their private lives.

And although it seems that Septimus is the one that crosses the borders erected by specific mechanisms of power (the Empire, war politics, his doctors, etc.) and is led to destruction through his insane and hallucinatory character, while Clarissa can escape from it all in her icy retreat up in the solitude of her attic room and increasingly narrow bed, she is as prone to annihilation as he is, as made clear in the final scene of the novel.

The two plots of Clarissa and Septimus, that run parallel throughout the novel, come together at her party in the end, when Septimus' death is announced by one of her distinguished guests. The safe boundaries between the two characters collapse, as Mrs. Dalloway withdraws to an empty room to deal with this sudden blow. In the narrator's comment (filtered through Clarissa's thoughts): "She had escaped. But that young man had killed himself" (MD 242); escape and annihilation become identical, as the second statement, introduced with the emphatic "but" coordinator, seems to invalidate the first one in this sentence sequence. His loss is felt in her flaming dress and burning body (MD 241), forced as she is to stand there in her mermaid-green evening dress, a hostess that has failed in her attempt to unite people: "Somehow it was her disaster—her disgrace. It was her punishment to see sink and disappear here a man, there a woman, in this profound darkness" (MD 243). Still, her flaming body announces a different kind of uniting, a joined state of instability, anticipating Judith Butler's twenty-first-century theories of precariousness as a common condition.

In her *Frames of War: What Is Grievable Life?*, a 2009 collection of essays exploring contemporary wars (especially those instigated by the Bush administration) and ways of curbing violence, Butler focuses on the concept of identity in difference while acknowledging an important Hegelian loan. "The subject," she writes, "is always outside itself, other than itself, since its relation to the other is essential to what it is" (49), and its survivability, she argues borrowing from Melanie Klein's psychoanalytic theory, is dependent on the body's capacity to connect with others through its separateness from them. "If I survive," Butler contends, "it is only because my life is nothing without the life that exceeds me, that refers to some indexical you, without whom I cannot be" (44). Clarissa's life as the wife of an MP is indeed reduced to nothingness unless illuminated by the death of an insane war veteran who, like her, can see the emptiness and vanity of the flag, the Empire, the Prime Minister, society, etc. If she survives, it is only through his (anti)heroic act of (passively) resisting duplicity and purposelessness; his death only can protect the "thing that mattered," the valuable, elusive core that brings people together:

> A thing there was that mattered; a thing wreathed about with chatter, defaced, obscured in her own life, let drop every day in corruption, lies, chatter. This he had preserved. Death was defiance. Death was an attempt to communicate, people feeling the impossibility of reaching the centre which, mystically, evaded them; closeness drew apart; rapture faded; one was alone. There was an embrace in death. (MD 241–242)

History: A Matter of Endless Negotiations

To what extent, however, can otherness be embraced? What are these forms of other life that can participate in this union? Woolf's sensitivity to forms of female otherness is evident throughout the book and her work in general. We are told, for example, that Clarissa's hold can reach out (like the branches of a tree) to the old lady in the house opposite hers; the woman stares at her as she is about to go to bed, Clarissa sees her, and recognizes her as a form of life distant from her circle but close to her aging and diminishing body. We also know that the narrative accommodates forms of life largely dehumanized, like "the veriest frumps, the most dejected miseries sitting on doorsteps" that "drink their downfall" and love London life as much as Mrs. Dalloway does (MD 4–5). Or, even more strikingly, the archetypal mother figure of the grey nurse made of sky and branches (MD 73), and the battered beggar woman reduced to a bodiless incomprehensible voice, "a mere hole in the earth, muddy too, matted with root fibres and tangled grasses" (MD 106). Endowed with femininity, these abject forms of life are a source of attraction given Woolf's feminist agenda. They relate to some of the lost voices in history, the anonymous women that Woolf attempts to recover more explicitly in subsequent works like *A Room of One's Own* or *Orlando*.

Yet, *Mrs. Dalloway* is not as sensitive to female voices coming from non-metropolitan areas, as Valerie Reed Hickman's recent article on Woolf's contribution to transnational feminism has argued. There is very little space for the female subaltern in the novel, which makes a swift appearance in Hugh Whitbread's letters to Peter Walsh when India is associated with chattering baboons and collies beating their wives (MD 226). "What we hear from the coolies' wives," Hickman contends, "is not their voices but, at most, the sound of their cries, or of their bodies being beaten. For Peter, and thus for us, it is only as mere objects—of his own gaze and ear, and of native violence—that they are worth noting; it is only as such objects that they signify" (62). It is important to clarify here, though, that it is not Peter's perspective that reduces the coolies' wives to mere objects/victims of violence, as Hickman notes, but Hugh's, whose superficiality and imperialist aura are clearly criticized throughout the novel. The suppression of the female subaltern in this passage is not adopted by Peter or the narrative voice; it is Peter who, while looking at Hugh in Clarissa's party, identifies him with "the snobbery of the English," the "privileged but secretive ... type of the English public-school man" (MD 226), and *remembers* that for Hugh, India was nothing but the sound of wild animals or coolies' wives.

While I agree with Hickman's conclusion that Woolf's understanding of transnational feminist issues is very restricted, a fact which consequently limits her ability to approach metropolitan others too—as the two are inseparable—I interpret her representation of otherness less as a failure and more as a "possibility" (Hickman's actual closing remark, 71) that invites new readings of history. Taking it from that point then, I would like to carry this argument further by drawing attention to a rather provoking extract from the book referring to a hot issue in the agenda of British foreign policy at the time the novel was written. Let us briefly be reminded here that Woolf's initial plan, as noted in a June 1923 diary entry, was to "criticize the social system" by bringing together two opposing perspectives: the sane and the insane (Diary 2 248). Clarissa and Septimus, as we have already seen, do indeed represent two different ways of coping, or failing to cope, with British government of the interwar period and are in their own ways victims of Empire politics; her precarity is underscored through Septimus's unstableness. It is interesting to observe, however, that Clarissa has difficulty in acknowledging, let alone sympathizing with, transnational victims of imperial politics, like the small Christian minority of Armenians that in 1923 had become a highly debatable issue in English parliamentary committees.

British involvement in the Armenian question had a long and complex history, dating as far back as the mid-nineteenth century when Britain began pressing the Ottoman Empire to grant equal rights to the Christian minorities that lived in its territories, in the hope of expanding its power in the Balkan region and the Middle East. Near the end of the nineteenth century, in the Treaty of San Stefano, Turkey and Russia concurred to let the Armenian nation settle in Russian territory, where it would have been safer from the attacks of the Ottomans (who claimed Armenians were a threat to their Muslim nation). The British, however, afraid that they might lose control in the area, interfered and cancelled the agreement. The Armenians, who were forced to remain on the grounds of the Ottoman Empire, became victims of a series of atrocities committed by the Turks that started in the 1890s and culminated in the genocide of 1915. Although Britain had originally promised to undertake the task of reforming Turkey, it was never seriously engaged in protecting the Armenians or in helping them establish a national home.

Leonard and Virginia Woolf were more than informed on the subject, which was a popular topic in *The Times,* the *Nation* and *Athenaeum* during the early 1920s, as Trudy Tate has already shown in her essay on "*Mrs. Dalloway* and the Armenian Question" (472). The Woolfs were also friends with an ardent exponent of the Armenian cause, the historian Arnold Toynbee, who had published Lord Bryce's speech, delivered in 1915 in the House of Lords, in his book *Armenian Atrocities: The Murder of a Nation.* Bryce was the first to bring the Armenian question to Parliament, arguing in his speech that those appalling massacres committed by the Turkish authorities wiped out three-fourths or four-fifths of the whole Armenian nation. "There is no case in history," Bryce maintained, "in which any crime so hideous and upon so large a scale has been recorded" (Toynbee 21).

Given the gravity of the Armenian question, as well as Woolf's awareness of it, it is surprising to observe that the topic is introduced in the novel as a passing remark interposed between Mr. and Mrs. Dalloway's daily routine: he has just offered his wife a bunch of red and white roses but has found it impossible to say he loves her; she remembers how she has repeatedly failed him as a wife; they engage in trivial talk about the people they met during the day, and as he is about to leave, the following conversation is quoted: "'Some committee?' she asked as he opened the door. 'Armenians,' he said; or perhaps it was 'Albanians'" (MD 156). Mrs. Dalloway's confusion between the Armenians and the Albanians testifies to her ignorance of the topics her husband is concerned with, and is followed by her thoughts that solitude and independence are important characteristics in a marriage:

> And there is a dignity in people; a solitude; even between husband and wife a gulf; and that one must respect, thought Clarissa, watching him open the door; for one would not part with it oneself, or take it, against his will, from one's husband, without losing one's independence, one's self-respect—something, after all, priceless. (MD 156)

The fact that Clarissa is not forced by Richard to be troubled with his affairs, but is allowed to remain at a safe distance from his world, justifies readings of the novel that trace a feminist vein in the way the Dalloway marriage is represented by Woolf. This "progressive rhetoric," however, according to Tate, is employed in a very cynical way by Woolf and "screens an absolute conservatism" (471) on Clarissa's part, who is totally indifferent to a major political problem, like the extermination of a whole population.

How cynical is the narrative towards Mrs. Dalloway though? Woolf's use of what Dorrit Cohn has termed "narrated monologue," i.e. the representation of a character's silent thought in narrated form (without the use of quotation marks) makes it hard to define the extent to which Clarissa's perspective is rejected or adopted. Blurring the line between narration and quotation, a narrated monologue usually tangles the narrator to attitudes of sympathy or irony towards a character, or even allows the narrator to oscillate between the two without settling anywhere. "Precisely because they [narrated monologues] cast the language of a subjective mind into the grammar of objective narration," Cohn writes, "they amplify emotional notes, but also throw into ironic relief all false notes struck by a figural mind. A narrator can in turn exploit both possibilities, even with the same character" (117). It is not easy to trace the exact spots of the narrator's sarcasm in the extract above, except perhaps in the extreme statement that "self-respect" in a marriage depends on the "gulf" between the two spouses. Although it would be hard to claim that Clarissa's inability to tell the difference between the Armenians and the Albanians is extolled by the narrator, it is not exactly clear that the narrator does not empathize with this attitude. As Ruth Livesey has argued, despite her affiliation with socialism through Leonard and the rest of the Bloomsbury Group, Woolf distanced herself from the ethical aesthetics of 1880s socialism, which preached "radical sympathy that sought to elide the individual in the name of solidarity" (135). Woolf was not willing to sacrifice her free individuality for others; sympathy was, after all, a quintessentially feminine characteristic in the nineteenth century, a sacred quality of "The Angel in the House" figure, whose ghost she had struggled hard to kill in her effort to write freely and discover the truth about her own experiences as a body ("Professions for Women" 2275).

Refusing to play the part of the unselfish, tender "Angel," flattering and serving others at a domestic, everyday level is hardly the same, however, with being dismissive of a major historical tragedy. But the question of whether Clarissa, or the text for that matter, *is* actually dismissive becomes more complicated in a passage following shortly after, where narrated monologue enables Woolf's narrator to weave in and out of several characters' minds and create textures whose threads are impossible to isolate:

He [Richard] was already halfway to the House of Commons, to his Armenians, his Albanians, having settled her [Clarissa] on the sofa, looking at his roses. And people would say, "Clarissa Dalloway is spoilt." She cared much more for her roses than for the Armenians. Hunted out of existence, maimed, frozen, the victims of cruelty and injustice (she had heard Richard say so over and over again)—no, she could feel nothing for the Albanians, or was it the Armenians? but she loved her roses (didn't that help the Armenians?)—the only flowers she could bear to see cut. (MD 157)

It is very tempting to classify the parenthetical question in this extract as sarcastically rhetorical given the fact that is beyond common sense: what could loving roses ever have to do with helping a nation of mass murdered refugees? Yet, there is more than cynical criticism of Mrs. Dalloway's indifference in the passage quoted above, as the Armenian genocide is not filtered simply through Mrs. Dalloway's confusion and lack of empathy, but through four (at least) dubiously conflicting and converging perspectives (Richard's, Clarissa's, the people's, and the narrator's).

Before taking a closer look at this intertwining of voices, let us consider that the association of the Armenian genocide with Clarissa's roses and its reduction to the dubiously expressed question of whether her love for roses helped their struggle can be read as a verification of Marxist characterizations of the novel as the art form of modern *bourgeois* culture *par excellence* which renders material circumstances invisible. For Marxist critics, like Walter Benjamin or György Lukács, the modernist novel, in specific, is so absorbed by individual consciousness, as evident in Mrs. Dalloway's case, that it has led literature to its destruction, and so "modernism means not the enrichment, but the negation of art" (Lukács 46). The late-twentieth-century critic Fredric Jameson, however, distances himself from Lukács' view that "modernism is some mere ideological distraction, a way of systematically displacing the reader's attention from history and society to pure form, metaphysics, and experiences of the individual monad" (255). Although for Jameson too, the novel is an instrument of capitalism obsessed with the self and endorsing a repressive political ideology, he believes that it can also function as an agent of unveiling ideological processes. Jameson's contribution to Marxist thought is the thesis that the tendency to privatize contemporary life is nothing but a symptom, as the division between the spheres of the social and the political, on the one hand, and the personal, on the other hand, is erroneous. As a poststructuralist Marxist, he believes that history is both real and always textual; his Marxist background infers that the reality of history cannot be disputed, as necessity never allows us to escape it, while his poststructuralist standpoint leads him to the conclusion that reality can be approached only through a series of (re)textualizations (67). So, even if reality is no longer visible in modernist texts, like in bourgeois life, it is always there; it has become, what Jameson terms, the "political unconscious."

In light of Jameson, let us return to Clarissa's roses and examine whether they can function as the novel's political unconscious, the repressed aspect of history lurking in the subtext, by laying emphasis on its form or narrative techniques, as that is what produces meaning after all in the case of the modernist novel. For Jameson, the novel is the end of genre in the sense that it is "a narrative ideologeme whose outer form, secreted like a shell or exoskeleton, continues to emit its ideological message long after the extinction of its host" (137). *Mrs. Dalloway* does not deny the materiality of the Armenian question—the maimed Armenians are there, even if only as a very awkward and reduced presence—but rather opens it to a variety of interpretations. And it is Woolf's modernist narrative techniques, her use of narrated monologue and the abandonment of a single controlling point of view, that become what Jameson calls the "textual determinants" of ideology (140).

The passage quoted above is less ambiguous at the points where people's judgment of Clarissa is presented in a direct quotation ("'Clarissa Dalloway is spoilt'"), or when Richard's opinion about the Armenians is filtered through Clarissa's ears and the narrator's voice in Free Indirect Speech ("Hunted out of existence, maimed, frozen, the victims of cruelty and injustice"). Does the text adopt any of these two perspectives, though? Is it settling towards the "spoilt" version of Clarissa, or does the use of inverted commas suggest a distancing from common opinion? And does the fact that Richard's words are given in Free Indirect Discourse indicate that his voice conflates with the narrator's at this point, or are his words adopted ironically by the narrator in order to expose the hypocrisy of Mr. Dalloway and the conservative party he represents? The committee he was about to attend was going to decide about the future of the Armenian people, who were to be deserted to their fate by the Great Powers in the Treaty of Lausanne signed in

July 1923. What can be read in the subtext here is that the British government *seemed* to show compassion for the genocide victims, but refused to take any effective measures for their support.

Clarissa's lack of compassion, on the other hand, is genuine, and it is almost impossible to tell with certainty whether this is not a position the narrator shares with her, given the degree of the literal endosmosis of the two voices. Even if the narrator is not muddled about Armenians or Albanians, but simply reflects Clarissa's befuddlement, it remains uncertain whether the parenthetical question is actually an attack on Clarissa's nonchalance or an earnest inquiry. It would not be extreme to argue for the latter, if we consider the fact that there is a similar passing reference to the Armenian question in a diary entry on December 26, 1929, where Woolf very provocatively compares her passion for trees with one's obsession with the barbarism of the Armenian massacres, and gives priority to trees over anything else. Sitting in her bedroom in Monk's House, Rodmell, Woolf enjoys the brilliant view of the downs and gets furious at the idea of the land being sold and exploited by a syndicate: "Cutting down trees & spoiling downs are my two great iniquities—what the Armenians were to Mrs. Cole [a headmistress in a school Leonard Woolf had attended]" (Diary 3 274, note 9).

This interweaving of voices and the absence of an orchestrating narrative viewpoint in Woolf's modernist novel expose the text to a variety of interpretations and render the very materiality of the historical event it refers to contextual. This is not to imply that the objectivity of the Armenian massacres is denied; for even if the text sides with the heroine's apathy, it doesn't settle there for good. Instead, it refuses to decide upon the question it poses, a question that recapitulates the crux of the argument against modernism's a-historicity: Can the selfish but candid indulging in aesthetic pleasure participate in major political concerns? *Mrs. Dalloway's* contribution to this debate is that history is evanescent and multisided. The cubist array of voices, which for some critics suggests the modernist novel's affiliation with a more democratic principle, highlights the open-endedness of historical events and their interconnectedness with private stories, and addresses the reader as an active agent of approaching plots. In connection with this, the underrepresentation of the Armenian genocide creates a substantial gap in the text and calls for the attention of the suspicious reader.

In a strangely prophetic way, for example, this undecidability of Woolf's text reflects the reluctance of foreign diplomacy to reach an agreement about the Armenian question. While Toynbee or Bryce early in the twentieth century, as well as historians and politicians who came after them, had infallible evidence that the Turkish authorities slaughtered the Armenian population in the hope of exterminating them, there have been incessant negotiations in the United Nations about whether these mass killings should be called "genocide." Turkey has never accepted this version of history and British diplomacy of the twentieth and even twenty-first-century has also been reluctant to do so. The representation of the Armenian question in *Mrs. Dalloway* anticipates exactly this neglect of and unresolvability around the issue. Moreover, the confusion between the Armenians and the Albanians, does not signify only Clarissa's lack of understanding of major political concerns; it also alludes to the atrocities committed in 1912–1913 by the Serbo-Montenegrins for the purpose of exterminating the Albanians. In that context, the conflation of the two nations is not a mistake, but an imaginative, constructive way of combining and cross-reading related facts in history. For the histories of what Butler calls "unrecognizable" or "ungrievable" populations, like Armenians, Albanians, Jews, Yugoslavians, Rwandans, etc., intersect at various points. In a remarkably ironic way, this passage is also predictive of a number of genocides that followed; it even foresees Hitler's reference to the Armenian Genocide before he embarked on the extension of the Holocaust in Poland in 1939: "Who, after all," he said, "speaks today of the annihilation of the Armenians?" The ambivalence of Woolf's text as far as its own position towards history is concerned suggests clearly that there is no other possible way of representing history except through a medley of contrasting perspectives, or, as Butler argues in the *Frames of War*, a series of endless negotiations. Clarissa's making love to her roses, in that sense, is a way of fertilizing facts and engaging the reader as an active agent in the production of meaning.

References

Bradbury, Malcolm, and James Walter McFarlane. 1978. *Modernism, 1890–1930*. Hassocks: Harvester Press. Print.

Butler, Christopher. 1994. *Early Modernism: Literature, Music, and Painting in Europe, 1900–1916*. Oxford: Clarendon Press. Print.

Butler, Judith. 2006. *Precarious Life: The Powers of Mourning and Violence*. London and New York: Verso. Print.

———. 2009. *Frames of War: When Is Life Grievable?* London and New York: Verso. Print.

Cohn, Dorrit. 1978. *Transparent Minds: Narrative Modes of Presenting Consciousness in Fiction*. Princeton: Princeton University Press.

Douglas, Roy. 1976. Britain and the Armenian Question, 1894–7. *The Historical Journal* 19 (1): 113–133. *Google Scholar*. July 27, 2016. Web.

Eliot, George. 1985. *Adam Bede. 1859*, ed. Stephen Gill. Harmondworth: Penguin [AB].

Fielding, Henry. 1982. *The History of Tom Jones, A Foundling: In Four Volumes*, ed. R.P.C. Mutter. Harmondsworth: Penguin [TJ].

Freud, Sigmund. 1997. Dora: An Analysis of a Case of Hysteria, ed. Philip Rieff. New York: Touchstone.

Goldman, Jane. 2004. *Modernism, 1910–1945: Image to Apocalypse*. Houndsmills and New York: Palgrave Macmillan. Print.

Hale, Dorothy J., ed. 2006. *The Novel: An Anthology of Criticism and Theory 1900–2000*. Malden, MA: Blackwell. Print.

Hickman, Valerie Reed. 2014. Clarissa and the Coolies' Wives: Mrs. Dalloway Figuring Transnational Feminism. *Modern Fiction Studies* 60 (1): 52–77, 222. *ProQuest*. June 11, 2016. Web.

Jameson, Fredric. 1983. *The Political Unconscious: Narrative as a Socially Symbolic Act*. London: Routledge.

Lackey, Michael. 2006. Modernist Anti-Philosophicalism and Virginia Woolf's Critique of Philosophy. *Journal of Modern Literature* 29 (4): 76–98. muse.jhu.edu. June 8, 2016. Web.

———. 2006. The Literary Modernist Assault on Philosophy. *Philosophy and Literature* 30 (1): 50–60. *Google Scholar*. June 21, 2016. Web.

Livesey, Ruth. 2007. Socialism in Bloomsbury: Virginia Woolf and the Political Aesthetics of the 1880s. *The Yearbook of English Studies* 37 (1): 126–144. From Decadent to Modernist: And Other Essays. Print.

McQuillan, Martin. 2000. *The Narrative Reader*. London and New York: Routledge. Print.

Nicholls, Peter. 1995. *Modernisms: A Literary Guide*. London: Macmillan. Print.

Nuttall, Jon. 2002. *An Introduction to Philosophy*. Cambridge: Polity. Print.

Tate, Trudi. 1998. *Modernism, History and the First World War*. Manchester: Manchester University Press. Print.

Toynbee, Arnold J. 1915. *The Armenian Atrocities: The Murder of a Nation, with a Speech Delivered by Lord Bryce in the House of Lords*. London: Hodder & Stoughton.

Walder, Dennis. 1990. *Literature in the Modern World: Critical Essays and Documents*. Oxford: Oxford University Press. Print.

Williams, Raymond. 1980. *Problems in Materialism and Culture: Selected Essays*. New York: Verso Books. Print.

Woolf, Virginia. 1981. *The Diary of Virginia Woolf. 1920–24*, ed. Anne Olivier Bell, vol. 2. Harmondsworth: Penguin [Diary 2].

———. 1982. *The Diary of Virginia Woolf. 1925–30*. ed. Anne Olivier Bell, vol. 3. Harmondsworth: Penguin [Diary 3].

———. 1984. Modern Fiction. *The Common Reader I*, ed. Andrew Mcneillie, 146–154. London: Hogarth Press.

———. 1988. Mr Bennett and Mrs Brown. *The Essays of Virginia Woolf, vol. 3: 1919–1924*, ed. Andrew Mcneillie, 384–389. London: Hogarth Press.

———. 1998a. *Mrs. Dalloway*. Oxford: Oxford University Press [MD].

———. 1998b. *To the Lighthouse*. Oxford: Oxford University Press [TTL].

———. 2003a. The Lady in the Looking-Glass: A Reflection. *A Haunted House: The Complete Shorter Fiction*, ed. Susan Dick, 215–220. London: Vintage.

———. 2003b. An Unwritten Novel. *A Haunted House: The Complete Shorter Fiction*, ed. Susan Dick, 106–116. London: Vintage.

———. 2012. Professions for Women. *The Norton Anthology of English Literautre*, vol. 2, 9th ed., ed. Stephen Greenblatt, 2272–2276. New York and London: Norton.

10

Virginia Woolf and *The Hours* (Stephen Daldry, 2002): Vulnerability, Performativity and Resistance

María José Gámez Fuentes and Rebeca Maseda García

As Ana Falcato states in the introduction to this volume, one of the core disputes among scholars of literary modernism to this day deals with questions related to the end of the modernist movement and the complete de-historicizing of the literary work, which, as indicated by her, have fundamental implications for postmodernist narrative frameworks. When speaking of the limits of modernism and postmodernism (either in philosophy, literature, or the arts) in relationship with

This chapter is part of the research project *La re-significación de la mujer-víctima en la cultura popular: implicaciones para la innovación representacional en la construcción de la vulnerabilidad y la resistencia* [The re-signification of women as victims in popular culture: implications towards representational innovation in the construction of vulnerabiity and resistance] (FEM2015-65834-C2-2-P, MINECO-FEDER), funded by the Spanish Ministry of Economy and Competitivity.

M. J. Gámez Fuentes (✉)
Universitat Jaume I, Castelló de la Plana, Spain
e-mail: gamezf@uji.es

R. Maseda García
Alaska University Anchorage, Anchorage, AK, USA
e-mail: rmasedagarcia@alaska.edu

© The Author(s) 2018
A. Falcato and A. Cardiello (eds.), *Philosophy in the Condition of Modernism*,
https://doi.org/10.1007/978-3-319-77078-9_10

215

feminism, however, we enter an exponentially more complex ground. A close analysis of the film *The Hours* (Stephen Daldry, 2002), a so-called postmodern text of popular culture that rewrites one of the main modernist figures, Virginia Woolf, and her seminal *oeuvre*, will be useful in elucidating how the feminine artistic and theoretical practices go beyond any bipolar categorization of modernism *versus* postmodernism. Revisiting Woolf's modernist conceptions of female subjectivity, under the postmodern filmic framework of a movie such as *The Hours*, opens up possibilities to bring the prevalence of feminist fundamentals under contemporary debates on the place of women in postmodern culture.

For this analytical and theoretical endeavour, Judith Butler's theory on the politics of performativity (Butler 1997) and the place of the gendered subject within discourse (Butler 1990) seems most illuminating. Butler's main contribution to feminist thought rests on her argument that categories of sex, gender and sexuality are culturally constructed rather than an innate quality of the subject; subject's identity is constructed through the iterative character of language. Thus, discourses establish the frames of intelligibility, which legitimate or sanction subjects according to their success in repeating the norm or failing to do so (Butler 1990, 1997). In this sense, subjects are vulnerable before the hegemonic grammar of recognition. However, it is also that performative character of subject(ificat)ion which opens the possibility to enact resistance by questioning and subverting the compulsion to repeat the ideal norm. This is precisely what the different female characters from *The Hours* attempt in different historical moments. By questioning (or undoing) frameworks of intelligibility of what being a woman means within the intra and extradiegetic contexts of the movie, *The Hours* manages to re-signify old feminist struggles within new paradigms of identity politics via popular culture.

(Post)Modern Trouble

The classification of cultural phenomena as belonging to Modernism, Postmodernism, Feminism and Postfeminism has been highly contested. Accomplishing clear and significant definitions has been a substantive part of contemporary theory and cultural practice (Abrams, Jameson, Giddens, Hutcheon, etc.). These discussions, as well as the validity or appropriateness of even using the categories and terminology used in the early postmodern criticism in a dialectical relationship with modernity, with the feminist critique, and their application to cultural practice, are still ongoing. Like any cultural movement that has enjoyed some longevity, there are many divergent definitions of modernism, postmodernism, feminism, etc. There are even opinions that define postmodernism as "that which cannot be defined". In order to define what is modern, postmodern or feminist, theoreticians have used them either as historical characterizations or theoretical approaches. Butler asks, "What does it mean for a term that has described a certain aesthetic practice to apply to social theory and to feminist social and political theory?" (1992: 5).

Terms like 'postmodernism', 'poststructuralism', and 'feminism' belong to a slippery descriptive field as they try to resolve differences between various positions at once by providing a term that would include them with all their modalities or permutations. Butler (1992), for instance, points out that we should be wary of grouping under the same rubric (of postmodernism and feminism) different frameworks and artistic practices. Is the effort to domesticate these theories under the sign of 'the same' a simple attempt to confer specificity to these positions? Butler wonders if this gesture of conceptual domination, which groups theories together under the headings of postmodern, responds to a "simple refusal to grant the specificity of these positions, an excuse not to read, and not to read closely" (1992: 5). That is, Butler continues, we keep trying to label the theories and practices of the past decades under the concept of 'postmodern' against its own dispersed nature. If one argues that the postmodern works as a unifying sign, then it is definitely a 'modern' sign, which is why one can debate for or against this idea of an overarching postmodernism. For instance, Lyotard argues that the modern and postmodern "are continually bound in a dialectical relationship, so that the postmodern supersedes the modern only in order itself to become the modern" (2003: 1131).

To add a further layer of complexity, there have also been ample discussions about differences between Modernism and Postmodernism in relation to gender (Hutcheon 1987; McHale 1987; Huyssen 1986; Jardine 1985; Moi 1985; Owens 1983; Derrida 1967). For instance, several critics situate modernity as the historical moment in which the 'law of the father' predominates; and Modernism as mainly masculine creative territory. Thereby, Owens (1983), Derrida (1967), or Jardine (1985) consider female creation as inherently postmodern: female discourse, in and of itself, possesses postmodern qualities inasmuch as they challenge the universality of the male point of view, and criticise the 'superior' narratives of the modern man (see Harris 2000; Suleiman 1991; Creed 1987). Owens (1983) regards postmodernity as a crisis in Western representation, its authority and its demands of universality. This crisis was advanced by the repressed and/or marginal discourses, feminism amongst them. The challenge to the universal-masculine discourse has been associated, in general, with the politics and creations of feminism, as well as with theories considered to be mainly postmodern (Butler 2015).

Notwithstanding, this marriage of feminism and postmodernism is troublesome. As Owens points out, although one of the highlights of postmodern culture is the presence of an insistent feminist voice—which "insistence on difference and incommensurability may not only be compatible with, but also [represent] an instance of postmodern thought" (1983: 61)—, "the absence of discussions of sexual difference in writings about postmodernism, as well as the fact that few women have engaged in the modernism/postmodernism debate, suggest that postmodernism may be another masculine invention engineered to exclude women" (1983: 61). This view is shared by different authors, such as Spivak (1988) or Irigaray (1977), for whom postmodernism makes women protagonists while rejecting their involvement in the critical debate (they speak specifically of Derrida's writings).[1]

Unable to escape the historicity of works executed by women, however, the question remains, what happens when various modernist female authors begin to alter that vision of the world where the values of the 'natural', 'the real', and the universal (all signalled as modernist attributes) are paramount? Do they stop being modernist? Can women artists be described as modernist or postmodernist?[2]

Since the 1970s, the feminist criticism has questioned the modernist tradition in an attempt to claim a parallel female tradition within. For instance, Minow-Pinkey (1987) argued that, in England, the characteristics associated with modernism were shared by both men and women artists. The modernist revolt strived to end the oppressive ideology of likeness of Victorian patriarchy, as well as the superficiality of the Edwardians, who failed to question it. This revolt represented the assertion of a radical alternative to (what contemporary feminists regard as) a phallocentric society and culture. For women, this conflict with the conventions of oppression was the main concern and, in fact, it was shared by both male and female artists. The formal features of the realist novel—narrative, plot, and character—were radically challenged, not only in postmodern theory, but also in the modernist literary practice itself. In Woolf, for instance, the feminist and modernist aesthetics converge, at least initially, in this attempt to challenge phallocentrism. In her essay of 1924, "Mr. Bennett and Mrs. Brown" Woolf complains that Edwardians such as H.G. Wells, Arnold Bennett and John Galsworthy:

> have developed a technique of novel writing which suits their purpose; they have made tools and established conventions which do their business. But those tools are not our tools, and that business is not our business. For us those conventions are ruin, those tools are death. (*Collected Essays* I, 330)

Other scholars, such as Toril Moi (1990) defended the correlation between modernism and feminism and postmodernism and postfeminism. If postmodernism (at least in the sense that Lyotard gives to the term) regards all meta-narratives, including feminism, as "repressive actions of metaphysical authority", then, what does postmodernist feminism mean? Moi preferred to use the term 'postfeminism' to cover different configurations of feminism and postmodernism today (1990: 368). For authors like Moi, if feminism is considered equally unifying—of all the experiences of women—then it can be considered as one of the meta-narratives or meta-discourses that characterize the 'modern'. The practice that ends the patriarchy-invented category 'woman' should be called 'post-feminist'. Lastly, following Irigaray,

Bellamy (1997) argues that categories such as 'modern' or 'postmodern' are made mostly to accommodate the male artistic tradition. Women artists have their own tradition and language hence such categorizations are inappropriate.

It is undeniable that feminism itself is a problematic notion as it designates a movement that takes many shapes in different contexts, and it contains multiple and contradicting forms. Feminism is not unitary; like postmodernism, it embraces multiple and contradictory forms. Even when sections of feminist thought fought the binary male-female distinction, many still preferred to remain under the banner of feminism inasmuch as it also allowed political grouping, which was indispensable in the defense and consecution of longed-for rights. The main generator of dissent among feminists still is that some of them work mainly in a theoretical ground, while others toil in the political arena. The latter criticize the deconstructive feminist gestures that seem to float free of a specific political context. In general, the difficulty some feminists have with postmodernity is clear: in order to achieve political goals the affiliation to the category of 'women' is necessary, even though this move forces them to subscribe to the binary equation created to sustain women's exclusion and abjection. Although feminism shares poststructuralists-postmodernists' tendencies—in their dismantlement of the universal (male) pretensions—it does not see its work as completed. Political activists' rejection of the notion of sexual indifference (or destruction of the categories man-woman) is noticeable in their insistence on the (real) cultural effects of sexual difference in social politics. Nowadays, many understand feminism as rigid and obsolete, identifiable with the suffragist movement or radical political agendas. Many theoreticians, however, continue to work within the feminist framework, understood as a broad and vibrant movement. Feminism does not end with the achievement of certain objectives; goals change with the passage of time.

The contradictions we find in different feminist factions were already identifiable in Woolf's work. She located herself within this contradiction between the defense of a feminist politics and the dissolution of the category 'woman'. On several occasions, she fervently defended the ideal of the transcendence of gender identities while, when discussing politics (opinions that potentially affected the public arena), she leaned towards a radical separatism between men and women: for her, they did not write similarly, nor have the same means nor were they expressed the same way. The importance of issues posited by Woolf about the constitution of gender and sexuality, and its relationship with identity, characterizes the moment when *The Hours* was produced; importance not only circumscribed to discussions in academic circles associated with women, gender, and LGTBQ studies, but also in the social sphere, the popular culture, the medical profession, politics, etc. It is in this continuity of Woolf's ideas in a product of contemporary popular culture, in this bridging between her thoughts (about women's vulnerability, performativity and resistance) and the same concepts that remain incumbent nowadays, that we access here to an understanding of the inappropriateness of speaking rigidly about modernism or postmodernism in relationship with gender.

The Hours

The film is based on Michael Cunningham's homonym novel (1998), which received the Pulitzer Prize. The choice of title is already indicating its connection to *Mrs. Dalloway*, as *The Hours* was Woolf's preliminary title. The British filmmaker Stephen Daldry—known for directing *Billy Elliot* (2000)—adapted it to the screen. The characters were interpreted by internationally well-known actresses and actors— Meryl Streep, Julianne Moore, Nicole Kidman, Ed Harris, Toni Collette, Claire Danes, Jeff Daniels, Miranda Richardson, Claire Danes, John C. Reilly, Linda Bassett and Eileen Atkins—, and the budget, production and distribution were characteristic of mainstream cinema. *The Hours* reached a commercial status; the novel broke record sales, and one of the film's interpreters, Nicole Kidman, won an Academy Award for best actress.

Although *The Hours* cannot be considered a biopic, per se (it does not follow entirely the genre conventions), its inspiration comes from the life of Woolf at the time when she was writing *Mrs. Dalloway*. In the film, there is a direct relationship between Woolf's life and her writing, and the impact of both on readers, particularly between a specific moment of her life (the creation of a particular work) and its influence on the lives of people from different historical junctures. Thus, the film focuses on three women whose lives are interconnected through the novel *Mrs. Dalloway*. The women are: Clarissa Vaughn (Meryl Streep), who lives in 2001 New York with her lesbian partner (Miranda Richardson) and daughter (Claire Danes), and is preparing a party for her AIDS-stricken friend and poet Richard (Ed Harris) who continually teases her by calling her Mrs. Dalloway; Laura Brown (Julianne Moore), who lives unhappily in 1950s California with her son (Jack Rovello) and her Second World War veteran husband (John C. Reilly), is expecting a second child and happens to be reading *Mrs. Dalloway*; Virginia Woolf (Nicole Kidman), who tries to come to terms with literature, illness and life in her 1920s England while she writes the novel. The connections between the stories of Laura and Clarissa with Woolf and *Mrs. Dalloway* are clear, but the relationship between Laura's and Clarissa's is revealed at the end of *The Hours*; Laura Brown is the mother of Richard. Each story takes place during a few hours of a day in June, but the film makes clear the relativity of time measurements; it avoids the traditional linearity, and expresses the possibility of the reproduction of a moment from the past in the present or the future. This strategy also highlights the identification between the characters from parallel universes.

This, and the intertextual relationship of *The Hours*—in the forms of citation, allusion, plagiarism, and diegetic transposition—, its collage/montage form, and the dialectic connection that it establishes with the spectator, can prompt us to define the film as postmodern. In addition, in terms of its content, *The Hours* responds to the postmodern practice of evading a unique point of view and offering a multiplicity of readings. The film depicts different lifestyles and understandings of our responsibilities to others and to ourselves. It offers multiple readings of the meaning and significance of being a woman, a mother, a lesbian, a partner, of having AIDS, of ending one's own life, of personal sacrifices, etc. The film creates a different construction of the reality in an attempt to grant meaning to it. All this manufactures a plurality of universes that configures—through montage—an eclectic landscape, a *collage* (Harvey 2002). Furthermore, the film has a coral protagonist

(Elsaesser 1999). Its characters move in parallel worlds or *heterotopias*, to use Foucault's concept (1972).[3] Its time organization is complex. Citations and the *mise en âbyme* ensure that viewers understand that what they are seeing is a story that has been previously told and, therefore, every description of reality is a construction and not the "truth". These aforementioned qualities of *The Hours* demand viewers to hold an active critical reception. The inherent ambiguity of characters and situations allows a reading/reception adapted to a precise particular moment/situation of each viewer (Eco 2002; Degli-Esposti 1998).

The film also uses, in a sense, the traditional narrative with its three-act structure of setup or exposition, confrontation, and resolution or denouement. This structure coincides with the hours of the day; the protagonists wake up to a world that requires they perform their assumed roles; during the day they provide plenty of proof of the constructed character of identity politics; and, at night, they make decisions that break with the expected subjectivity/identities. As Woolf's character argues while starting to write *Mrs. Dalloway*: "A woman's whole life in a single day. Just one day. And in that day her whole life".

The Vulnerability of the Gendered Subject Before the Grammar of Recognition

The Hours begins in Sussex, England, 1941. In a bucolic landscape with a river stream, we see a pair of bony nervous hands tying up the belt of a coat. The frames from her walk intercut with images of her hands writing while her voiceover is heard. She is writing her last words to her husband where she admits she can no longer bear the crises she suffers and the voices she hears so she has taken the decision of ending her life. The violin music increases its presence as we see her trembling hand holding the pen and in another scene getting closer to the river where she will finally drown herself. We see Virginia's body floating under the water and the overprinted title of the film. The film's depiction of Woolf's final act of defiance and self-determination, her suicide, opens, however, the door to the vulnerable lives of several characters, starting with hers. Their vulnerability seems to be linked to a failure to repeat properly the gendered grammar of intelligibility (Butler 1990). The film portrays this vulnerability through several instances. Mainly, the female characters appear to be overwhelmed, suffocated and/or crossed by the burden of roles traditionally associated to femininity. This is symbolised from the initial scenes where the protagonists are introduced through the eyes of others who watch over them while the women are lying in bed.

The film cuts to a residential area in Los Angeles, California, in the 1950s. A man (Dan Brown, played by John C. Reilly) arrives in a car with a bunch of flowers, and as he enters the house and snoops into a bedroom, he sees his wife sleeping. In parallel fashion, in Richmond, England, 1923, another one, Leonard Woolf (Stephen Dillane), goes into the house, where he encounters a doctor who briefs him on his wife's progress (he recommends tranquillity). The camera goes up to the first floor where Virginia lies awake in bed; she, as Laura Brown previously, pretends to be asleep. Clarissa, in New York City, 2001, is also seen as sleeping, but this time by her female partner. When the three of them wake up, Clarissa and Virginia seem uncomfortable with what they see in the mirror; Virginia even snorts. This feeling the mirror provokes acts as a synecdoche of the awkwardness (progressively unfolded in the film) originated by having to live up to the patriarchal expectations placed upon them. This mirror's reflections will be later impersonated through the characters of Kitty (Laura's friend and inadvertent object of desire who apparently embodies the feminine ideal of the time), Vanessa (Virginia's sister who seems to be the perfect hostess and mother) and Richard (Clarissa's friend and platonic love).

No wonder Laura delays getting out of bed, and while reaching for *Mrs. Dalloway*, looking tired, the gesture of her hand going to her chest transmits suffocation. She turns her face towards outside the left part of the frame as she, visibly removed from the mundanity of her surroundings, listens to her husband in the kitchen opening and closing cabinets. The insecurity before the ideal image of femininity is also translated through the women's bodies: they display insecure body movements, they frequently speak with soft and hesitant voices, and they are very prone to sighing.

As they begin to manifest their struggles the film's point of view shifts to them. The piano music that has been accompanying all along the intermingling of scenes begins to crescendo as the three women appear in a thoughtful stance in their respective settings, as if reflecting or gathering stamina to start facing the daily chores (symbolized through vases of flowers that are rearranged in their different intradiegetic times).

However, insecurity before quotidian patriarchal expectations is not the only source of vulnerability. The state, represented through the medical institution, also appears as an agent acting upon the women's apparently diminished subjectivity.[4] This control over women's lives based on their supposed frailty is also echoed through the relationships surrounding them. Virginia and Laura are treated as convalescents not only by doctors but also by their husbands; Virginia because of her mental breakdowns and Laura for her pregnancy. Moreover, these men seem to know what their respective wife's needs are. Leonard appears as the monitor of Virginia's single daily activities; she keeps him informed of her writing and emotional states and he advises her in what she should eat and do; Dan Brown treats Laura as a child not being able to do anything because of her pregnancy.[5]

In the same vein, Virginia's sister, Vanessa Bell or Nessa (as she is addressed in the film) seems to be maternally protective, but also slightly condescending. She reprimands her when she sees her dressed up in what she considers a non-conceited manner, and hears about her inability to manage the servants, as a lady-of-the-house (of her class) should do. Virginia's vulnerability is also heightened in a scene where a close-up shot shows her lying down on the ground staring and being stared at by a dead bird situated at eye level, emphasizing their identification. This horizontal position is paralleled by the next shot where we see Laura lying in bed. The similarities of positions between a dead bird, Virginia and Laura are symptomatic of Virginia's tragic finale and Laura's attempt at it. Laura's frailty is reiterated in the sequence when she goes to a hotel room in order to evade her reality, and to commit suicide. In this scene, a bird's-eye shot of her in the bedroom accentuates her insignificant figure in the middle of a huge and impersonal hotel room. She takes her sandals off and we see a close-up of her naked feet hanging from the bed because it is too high for her. Virginia and Laura are further connected in their vulnerability when a surreal scene shows the room where Laura lies starting to flood with water, echoing the manner in which Virginia Woolf ended her life. Laura will not end her life in a hotel room, though; and viewers witness further instances of her vulnerability. One scene towards the end of the film stands out, in this regard, for its despair. Dan is waiting in bed for his wife to come to him while she is sitting on the toilet silently crying, unable to face the very moment of intimacy her husband so eagerly expects. She gathers herself, wipes her tears away and resigned, as if going to a slaughterhouse, enters the bedroom.

Clarissa's vulnerability depends mainly upon her extreme reliance on other people's opinion of her, especially Richard's. For instance, the scene in the flower shop underscores the importance she gives to the shopkeeper's opinion; how she tries to justify her friend's work before a stranger's eyes talks about the weight of the others who interpellate us to fulfil certain expectations. Like *Mrs. Dalloway*'s homonym character, she apparently displays great superficiality; in fact, Richard quotes Woolf's novel by saying: "Oh, Mrs. Dalloway…always giving parties to cover the silence". It is problematic; the fact that she seems to be granting some legitimacy to Richard's appraisal of her life as trivial, only full of details, schedules, parties. The weight she gives to what Richard thinks of her life, along with how fulfilled she feels when she is with him, project a very reductionist image of her capabilities. Moreover, there is a further troubling aspect: the importance Clarissa concedes to her current platonic love relationship with him (platonic because he is gay) seems to be blocking her ability to see the importance of everything else she has in her life. The reminiscences of the heteronormative romantic relation they had in the past are a burden to her in the present.

Her daughter Julia seems to have understood this very well and, in a scene, gives an objectionable look to her mother who immediately has to apologize for dismissing the value of the rest of her life in front of Richard's judgement. In the conversation with her daughter, we realize that she confuses satisfaction with her life as a woman with satisfaction with life according to a concrete chronological time: for Clarissa, a middle-aged woman, the past was the best moment of her life. The pragmatism of young Julia is crushing when she says: "all you're saying is that you were once young". In any case, Clarissa insists in remarking on the intense 'sense of possibility' that she felt her youth. The past seems indeed the thing that stings Clarissa's heart as it is emphasized in another scene with her old friend, Louis (Jeff Daniels), where she ends up breaking into tears for all the feelings lost in the past that will never come back. In any case, the way she underestimates her current lesbian relationship, in comparison with the one she had with Richard in the past, underscores also the difficulties in valuing any love relationship beyond the heteronormative framework.

The Performative Character of Language

Beyond the constraints of the hegemonic framework and the vulnerabilities it creates, the film also underlines its constitutive character, the possibilities the iterative character of performing the established grammar of recognition may open, the problems associated with repeating the norm, and the fear of social sanction (if failing) (Butler 1990). For instance, when the maid interrupts Woolf's stream of consciousness, unmoved (and uninterested) by the maid's request, she asks Nelly to wait for her in the kitchen. Later, as she goes downstairs she hears the maids complaining about her mood swings. Virginia comes reluctantly in the kitchen. Her body movements speak of a discomfort which is accentuated by a scene in which the lady-of-the-house feels inadequate before the resolution of a maid that has been taking decisions regarding meals since her employer, so busy with her writing (says the maid), did not give instructions on how to proceed.

Laura also fails to display the 'naturality' of gendered identities. Her husband, instead, is the one preparing and serving breakfast to their son. Her fatigued tone of voice contrasts with her husband's cheerful voice. As soon as she waves goodbye to her husband from the living-room window (with a perfectly styled smile on her face), she turns silent and looking concerned to her son, who stands in front of her, silent as well. They sit at the table, uneasy and staring at each other in silence, until Laura, feigning resolution, breaks the uncomfortable moment by coming up with what she is going to do, what she is expected to do: make a cake for his father's birthday with her son's help. The cake, however, is quite deficient. She is angry about it, but has no time to dwell on it as her friend Kitty pops in. This scene is probably the most revealing regarding Laura's 'inadequacy' in performing the gendered feminine role. It is so because of the contrast between her and Kitty, the perfect 'Angel of the house'; she seems to represent femininity at its best. Well-groomed and attired, she jokingly comments on Laura's difficulties to make something that is so easy for everyone (obviously, she implies every woman): making a cake. In their superficial chatter, Kitty stresses the good time they will have at her husband's birthday celebrations at the country club. Laura comments on how good Kitty and her husband are in socializing and having friends. It seems as if Kitty's comments on the successful life she leads with her husband were only addressed to Laura for her to praise.

In this scene between Laura and Kitty, the masquerade of perfect femininity and blissful marriage is uncovered little by little, and, as Woolf proposed in her life and work, the film introduces a female communion. First, Laura states that this kind of life is what their men deserved after having been to a war. This opens the door to the audience to question if what we see is actually real or a façade constructed for the deserving ones. This unsettling aspect is reinforced by the fact that Kitty rapidly changes the subject by grabbing the book *Mrs. Dalloway* that is on the kitchen counter and wanting to know what it is about. As Laura explains that is about a woman who is throwing a party and seems confident but really she is not, we see more explicitly how the mask falls from Kitty: she is about to cry, obviously because she identifies with the statement made about the character. Kitty reveals to Laura she has a growth in her uterus, preventing her from getting pregnant, which, according to her, is what really makes a woman. She could perform every single mandate as a woman, she admits, but not getting pregnant makes her 'inadequate'. This could explain her overperforming of femininity. She continues expressing her fear of the medical institution and her fear of how her own husband will handle the whole thing (later we learn she will go alone to the hospital). Laura tries to comfort her putting her arms around her and kissing her forehead but she ends up in Kitty's mouth. Unaware of (or reluctant to admit) any sexual connotations, she says goodbye to an excitingly flushed Laura. Laura's son has witnessed the whole scene with his usual scrutinizing eyes. Confronted by his mother's question of what he wants when staring at her, he runs out while Laura, visibly in distress and filled with tears, throws the cake into the dustbin.

However, *The Hours* not only showcases women's failure to repeat the frames of intelligibility, but also men's, most notoriously Richard's. Daldry, by transferring *Mrs. Dalloway* to other epochs (mid twentieth and twenty-first century) and geographies (Los Angeles and New York), presents a new discourse about sexuality and gender; a discourse informed by the political, social and cultural advances in those terrains. The author opens, according to Hughes, the door to the expression of 'new voices'—women's, gays' and lesbians' (2004: 350). Hence, in the twenty-first century, it is Richard who talks about this situation in terms of a performance he has to display, which in turn, symptomatizes the performative character of one's persona before others and the performative character of subjectivity. Richard is fed up with having to look proud and brave for having AIDS. In the contemporary story, Richard is the one that shares a great deal with Virginia; they are both writers, are attended, loved and respected by someone—Clarissa and Leonard respectively, and both commit suicide in order to stop being a burden (as they explicitly express during the film) but, whereas the burden in Richard's case is due to a degenerative illness, the film displays that for Virginia it is related to her place as a woman.

Spaces of Resistance

If gender identity is a compendium "of repeated acts within a highly rigid regulatory frame that congeal over time to produce the appearance of substance", it follows that "it is open to intervention and resignification" (Butler 1990: 33). This brings us to the discursive possibilities inaugurated when contemplating non-normative signifying practices (Butler 1997: 72) that exclude the fetishist reduction of collective identities by the heteronormative discourse, and that open the doors to the discovery of new enunciate loci from which to speak. Daldry turns to the most talented feminist modernist writer, Woolf, to speak of the performative possibilities of language to construct agency and resistance.

In fact, it is in language that Virginia, Laura, and Clarissa find their meaning of life and the means to resist.

In the film, Virginia, Laura and Clarissa, once acknowledged as vulnerable before discourse, display different instances of playing within and despite the discourse/grammar of recognition. At the beginning of the film, Woolf sits in her bedroom and opens her writing notebook. At that moment, shots of Laura starting to read and Clarissa starting to write are juxtaposed. Virginia starts saying: "Mrs. Dalloway said she would buy the flowers herself". Laura appears reading the same sentence in the book and Clarissa utters the sentence in first person voice: "Sally, I think I'll buy the flowers myself". As we have seen, Laura and Virginia seem hopeless at performing their duties as mothers, wives, and/or ladies-of-the-house. Meanwhile, when they read and write respectively, they display certainty, happiness and resolution. We witness that contrast in Virginia's story in the film's first minute; our first impression of her is related to her frailty through the close-up of her bony shaky hands. However, this frame intercuts with a close-up of her hands again, although this time they are in a calmer state of slowly digging the pen in the ink: while writing she is in command. In an earlier scene, Virginia enters Leonard's studio and, interpellated by him, gives a brief report of how her night went ("uneventful, no headaches"). She lies about having had breakfast, and he insists tenderly but wearily that she should eat something. This mundane chitchat is of no interest to her, so she cuts it off, announcing that she might have a first sentence; writing is, thus, erected as her salvation.

The film also offers other spaces of resistance for these women. Virginia claims her agency in several instances, like when Nelly, the maid, seems bothered by Virginia's lack of interest in the choice of meals, Virginia requests to add ginger in the culinary plans and the snubbed maid has to go to London to comply with her desire. Despite her feelings of inadequacy, Virginia, masquerading as the lady-of-the-house, finally gets her desire. The following scene gives an acute sense of Virginia's situation, and conveys more clearly her resistance. We see her rushing out of the house in a concealed manner through the backyard, so that Leonard does not notice she is leaving toward the train station, seeking to escape from her contrived confinement. Through the ensuing dialogue between Leonard and Virginia, we witness not only the depth of his worry, but also the extent of her desperation. The subjective separation of how each of them views her sanity is represented through a long shot of both of them on the train platform; their figures standing opposite each other at the respective borders of the frame. Leonard adopts a very patronizing manner of talking to Virginia in order to reprimand her for not having informed him of her leaving, but also to remind her that they have the obligation to return to eat Nelly's dinner. Hearing the word 'obligation' triggers in Virginia an angry complaint about feeling under custody and imprisoned. Through her words we realize how powerless she feels under the care of the medical institution represented by all the doctors that continuously judge her supposedly best interests. Virginia pronounces that it is she the only one who understands her own condition. She vindicates her right to choose how to live her life, which includes their return to stimulating London. Defeated, Leonard consents to go back there.

Lastly, her last move of defiance will be her own suicide. Woolf herself often wrote about suicide in her letters and diaries, as well in her fiction, without neither romanticizing nor stigmatizing it. Woolf also freed several of her heroines from romance through spinsterhood or suicide. Within the film, Virginia's suicide emulates the escape from the patriarchal repressive order of fictional female protagonists in the nineteenth century literature—in the literary tradition of the Brontës, Jane Austen, or Emily Dickinson's poetry, even of Woolf herself in *The Voyage Out*. Feminist literary criticism analyzes the sacrificial plot as an alternative source of feminine power, the epitome of women's refusal to be integrated in a system that speaks of them/defines them, but ultimately keeps them speechless.

In Laura's case, nonetheless, the resistance takes a different shape. In the first instance, we only see her at peace in her reading encounters with Woolf's novel, *Mrs. Dalloway*. She seems to turn to Virginia Woolf's literature in order to be able to keep going; the reading of *Mrs. Dalloway* acting as a lifeboat and as a way to connect with a matrilineal memory of women's past resistances.

However, after Kitty's visit and the (socially disallowed) promise of female bonding through a kiss, she reaches bottom. Her determination makes her perform the household chores impeccably; we see a close-up of the finally well-made cake that she puts immaculately on the kitchen table. She appears adequately groomed and dressed, ready to go out. The kitchen is left clean and in complete order, she leaves her son with a neighbour, and drives away. The intensity of the piano music, in crescendo, while she drives carelessly, followed by the mysterious violins when she enters the hotel is a bad omen. She takes the bottles of pills out of her bag and grabs *Mrs. Dalloway* to lie down on the bed. Her end seems imminent but the audience's expectations will be frustrated via Virginia's writing agency. What Laura reads is articulated through the writer's voiceover which, in turn, corresponds to Woolf's thoughts while talking to her niece. Virginia admits to the latter that she was thinking about killing her heroine, but she changed her mind; instead she decides that if someone is to die, it is the male figure. Indeed, Virginia Woolf settled on Septimus as the sacrificial death in *Mrs. Dalloway*— and Cunningham/Daldry chooses Laura's son, Richard—freeing Clarissa (and Laura) from wishing to end her life. We see, in the next frame, Laura waking up in a scare and crying to herself that she cannot do what she pretended. Virginia announces to her niece she will have to kill someone else instead. Woolf thus rewrites an apparently 'unfit' woman's tragic destiny and gives her female character the option of finding a more empowering finale, as we will see.

The other alternative that the English writer posited was spinsterhood—highly vilified (mocked, insulted, and pitied) by Western culture—, and that is going to be Laura's pivotal decision: she chooses to desert her family. Her son, the Richard of the twenty-first century never forgave her for that and so, in his novel, she is portrayed as a 'monster' (as Julia, Clarissa's daughter, says). The subsequent narration, however, dismantles this idea that echoes the hegemonic scene of address. The unfolding dialogue between Laura and Clarissa, after Richard's funeral, breaks away from any configuration of Laura as a monster. Instead, the narrative makes us identify with her to understand the decisions she made. She admits having abandoned both of her children despite knowing that it was the worst thing a mother could do. In contrast, Clarissa shares that she wanted so much to be a mother, she did it on her own (in fact, the film has previously shown Clarissa and her daughter sharing an intimate moment, while lying in bed and caressing in a tender manner). Laura finds her very lucky and discloses to Clarissa how different she felt in relation to motherhood. For her, it was a question of not belonging, of wanting to kill herself. The extreme close-ups of Clarissa and Laura's faces as Laura tells her story act to engender the audience's sympathy. We hear that for Laura there was no choice: the family life she was leading was death for her and she chose to break free in order to find life. Again, the patriarchal discourse enters the scene of address: "No one is going to forgive me", Laura says unregretful, though.

Clarissa leaves the room as if needing some air after what she has heard. Her partner, Sally, follows her to their bedroom and Clarissa holds her face in her hands. She seems to be really looking for the first time, in the face what she has with Sally and kisses her passionately. Meanwhile, Laura's assumption of not being forgiven for relinquishing what she considered deadly motherhood is fissured by the narrative: Clarissa's daughter visits her in her own bedroom where Laura is getting accommodated for the night. Julia embraces Laura silently, apparently for no reason, but symbolizing an empathic bond. With a peaceful smile, Clarissa turns off the lights of the house to go to sleep and we hear Virginia's voiceover talking about looking life in the face and knowing it and loving it for what it is. This voiceover continues to the final image of the movie where Virginia gets into the river to drown herself.

Conclusions

A modernist literary figure *par excellence*, Virginia Woolf, has aroused interest and passions, particularly since the resurgence of public and critical attention to her life and work in the 1970s, propelled mainly by feminist scholars. Woolf's texts are essential material in the commentary and teaching of literary modernism, women's writing, feminist theory and gay and lesbian studies. Multiple disciplines have found, in Woolf, inspiration for their theoretical and practical corpora, and support for their particular postulations. What is it about Woolf that has allowed for such appropriation of her ideas, no matter how different (and at times opposed) the agendas are? It is Woolf herself, with her own contradicting beliefs, especially related to gender and art, who has allowed the use of her ideas in the support of different ideologies. She advocated for, and realized, the foundations for a specific feminine art and politics while, at times, she displayed a disbelief in the actual existence of two sexes. In intimate relationship with these contrasting points, she fluctuated between the certainty of the existence of female and male subjects, and the idea of the dissolution of identity.

Thus, Woolf's readers can find how certain aspects of her work respond to contemporary tendencies (so-called postmodern), specifically as she embraces complexity, and her ideas vary from an essentialist feminism to the deconstruction of gender, radical lesbianism, or androgyny as artistic ideals. These fluctuations are Woolf's hallmark and, according to several scholars, the hallmark of other modernist female writers as well (Minow-Pinkey 1987; Moi 1985). The inherent state of contradiction and paradox in Woolf's writing and the ideological content of her artistic expression, result in a close fit with the poststructuralist and postmodernist spirit. It is also similar to several lines of thought found within feminism from the early women's movement to the current time (Marcus 1997; Tuzyline 1997; Mcnaron 1992; Caughie 1991; Minow-Pinkey 1987). All factions claim Woolf as their authority, locating their aesthetics and politics—modern or postmodern, feminist or postfeminist—in hers.

Daldry's postmodernist film, *The Hours*, reclaims the Woolf that spoke of gender as social construct, and how this grammar of recognition posited women in the precarious task of having to live up to social/patriarchal expectations. In the film, old feminist struggles having to do with the vulnerability of the female subject before the violence of hegemonic frameworks are framed within a debate coming from identity politics. Woolf contended that centuries of social practice effectively divided humanity into two separate groups (male and female), grouping them in separate spheres, functions and roles and, consequently, modes of behaviour and thought followed suit. Such dichotomies inevitably limit individual perceptions. But she also believed identities to be masquerades after all: performances and culturally learned attributes.[6]

The nuances of such a subject(ificat)ion, impelled by the established norms of intelligibility, spark a conflict of identity; a crisis that Virginia, Laura and Clarissa suffer from in *The Hours*. These women, however, resist conforming to the social mores prescribed for them. The presentation of their stories is clearly marked by women's vulnerability; the narrative development entertains women's performativity of the roles assigned to them; and the denouement provides a kind of catharsis for the characters, or release of the tension and anxiety by focusing on the prevalence of their resistance. These ideas about women's vulnerability, performativity and resistance were paramount for Woolf and remain relevant in the postmodern world. The recovery of Virginia Woolf's life and work by *The Hours* undoubtedly illustrates how modernism and postmodernism are categories that must be questioned in relation to gender.

Like the protagonist of Virginia Woolf's *A Room of One's Own*, who remains outside the library but in the vicinity (without abandoning its perimeter), we see that the three women in the film are not within, but neither outside of, the structures of tradition, representation and the social world. The intermingling of the three women's lives in *The Hours*, as if echoing Woolf's own writing strategy, is the enhancement of inconclusiveness. Rather than denying contradiction, the protagonists embrace it, stopping to observe and analyse, rather than running towards a conclusion. This is an appropriate strategy paradigmatic of those who, having been denied a subjectivity (by virtue of being a woman), struggle to define themselves as subjects in a culture to which they do not belong. The film, following the writer's trail, opens up the possibility of resisting normative signifying practices, but not by insisting on the creation of a separate women's culture or by deconstructing the gender dichotomy itself but, in a very postmodern fashion, by undertaking both simultaneously: claiming differences while undoing them, assuming the shared vulnerability of women's experiences while resisting them in historicized performances.

Notes

1. Derrida (1967) juxtaposes Western discourse as "centrism" (logo-, phallo-, etc.) and deconstructive discourse as displacement or an offset of this centrism. According to Derrida, woman is the subject that has been displaced from the center; woman is "the other" and, thus, he privileges her figure. Derrida and Owens, however, are men. Therefore, a disconnection between this apparent privileging of women in the deconstructive discourse and the blatant subordination of women in the phallocentric speech occurs.

2. Umberto Eco echoes the new common practice to define cultural productions dating back to the early days as postmodern: "Unfortunately, 'postmodern' is a term *bon a tout faire*. I have the impression that it is applied today to anything the user happens to like. Furthermore, there seems to be an attempt to make it increasingly retroactive: first it was apparently applied to certain writers or artists active in the last twenty years, then gradually it reached the beginning of the century, then still further back. And this reverse procedure continues; soon the postmodern category will include Homer" (2002: 305).

3. Spaces that have more layers of meaning or connections to other places than immediately meet the eye. In general, it is a physical representation that approximates utopia or a parallel space that contains "undesirable" bodies to make a real utopian space possible (Foucault 1972).

4. Woolf herself suffered great oppression by the hands of numerous psychiatrists and doctors, whom she criticizes satirically in *Mrs. Dalloway* through the character of Septimus' psychiatrist, Sir William Bradshaw and general practitioner Dr. Holmes (Barrett and Cramer 1997: 164). She was treated with the 'rest cure', a therapy designed by Silas Weir Mitchell for 'hysterical' women. This therapy involved isolation, absolute rest in bed for up to six weeks, a rich diet that stimulated weight gain, and the absence of all intellectual activity. Showalter defined Mitchell as "an outspoken misogynist, whose methods punished 'deviant' and discontented women by forcing them into an allegedly therapeutic female role" (Showalter 1977: 274).

5. In the contemporary story, nonetheless, the character who is unwell is Richard, Clarissa's lifelong friend who is dying of AIDS and whom she tends to.

6. It is noteworthy to mention how the British psychoanalyst Joan Riviere developed her theory of the "Womanliness as masquerade" in 1929, and how this idea of femininity as performance has greatly influenced late twentieth-century feminist theory; for instance, Butler (1990) considers that the 'substantial person' is only the effect of socially instituted and maintained norms of intelligibility through which human subjects come to assume an identity; in her words, "an abiding substance is a fictive construction produced through the compulsory ordering of attributes into coherent gender sequences" (1990: 24).

References

Barret, Eileen, and Patricia Cramer (eds.). 1997. *Virginia Woolf. Lesbian Readings*. London and New York: New York University Press.

Bellamy, Suzanne. 1997. The Pattern Behind the Words. In *Virginia Woolf. Lesbian Readings*, ed. Eileen Barret and Patricia Cramer, 21–36. London and New York: New York University Press.

Butler, Judith. 1990. *Gender Trouble*. London: Routledge.

———. 1992. Contingent Foundations: Feminism and the Question of 'Postmodernism'. In *Feminist Theorize the Political*, ed. Judith Butler and Joan W. Scott, 3–21. London and New York: Routledge.

———. 1997. *Excitable Speech: A Politics of the Performative*. London and New York: Routledge.

———. 2015. *Senses of the Subject*. New York: Fordham University Press.

Caughie, Pamela L. 1991. *Virginia Woolf and Postmodernism: Literature in Quest and Question of Itself*. Urbana and Chicago: University of Illinois Press.

Creed, Barbara. 1987. From Here to Modernity: Feminism and Postmodernism. *Screen* 28 (2): 47–68.

Cunningham, Michael. 1998. *The Hours*. New York: Farrar, Straus and Giroux.

Degli-Esposti, Cristina. 1998. *Postmodernism in the Cinema*. New York and Oxford: Berghan Books.

Derrida, Jacques. 1967. *L'écriture et la différance*. Paris: Éditions du Seuil.

Eco, Umberto. 2002. Postmodernism, Irony, the Enjoyable. In *Postmodernism and the Contemporary Novel*, ed. Bran Nicol. Edinburg: Edinburg University Press.

Elsaesser, Thomas. 1999. Specularity and Engulfment. Francis Ford Coppola and Bram Stoker's Dracula. In *Contemporary Hollywood Cinema* (1st ed., 1998), ed. Steve Neale and Murray Smith, 191–208. London and New York: Routledge.

Foucault, Michel. 1972. *The Archaeology of Knowledge*, trans. A.M. Sheridan Smith. London: Tavistock Publications.

Harris, Andrea L. 2000. *Other-Sexes. Rewriting Difference from Woolf to Winterson*. New York: State University of New York Press.

Harrison, Charles, and Wood, Paul (eds.). 2003. *Art In Theory 1900–2000. An Anthology of Changing Ideas*. Oxford: Blackwell.

Harvey, David. 2002. Time-Space Compression and the Postmodern Condition. In *Postmodernism and the Contemporary Novel*, ed. Nicol Bran, 40–58. Edinburg: Edinburg University Press.

Hughes, Mary Joe. 2004. Michael Cunningham's *The Hours* and Postmodern Artistic Re-presentation. *Critique: Studies in Contemporary Fiction* 45 (4): 349–361.

Hutcheon, Linda. 1987. The Politics of Postmodernism: Parody and History. *Cultural Critique* 5: 179–207.

———. 1990. An Epilogue: Postmodern Parody: History, Subjectivity and Ideology. *Quarterly Review of Film and Video* 12 (1–2): 125–133.

———. 2001. *The Politics of Postmodernism* (1st ed., 1989). New York: Routledge.

Huyssen, Andreas. 1986. *After the Great Divide: Modernism, Mass Culture, Postmodernism*. Bloomington and Indianapolis: Indiana University Press.

Irigaray, Luce, 1985. *This Sex Which Is Not One* (1st ed., 1977), trans. Catherine Porter, 23–33. Ithaca, NY: Cornell University.

Jameson, Fredric. 1984. Postmodernism, or the Cultural Logic of Late Capitalism. *New Left Review* 146: 53–92.

———. 2003. The Deconstruction of Expression (1984). In *Art in Theory 1900–2000. An Anthology of Changing Ideas*, ed. Charles Harrison and Paul Wood, 1046–1051. Oxford: Blackwell.

Jardine, Alice. 1985. *Gynesis: Configurations of Women and Modernity*. Ithaca: Cornell University Press.

Lyotard, Jean-François. 2003. What Is Postmodernism? (published as "Résponse á la question: qu'est-ce que le posmoderne?" 1982 (trans. Régis Durand). In *Art in Theory 1900–2000. An Anthology of Changing Ideas*, ed. Charles Harrison and Paul Wood, 1131–1137. Oxford: Blackwell.

Marcus, Laura. 1997. *Virginia Woolf*. Plymouth: Northcote House & British Council.

McHale, Brian. 1987. *Postmodernist Fiction*. New York: Methuen.

Mcnaron, Toni. 1992. 'The Albanians, or Was It the Armenians?' Virginia Woolf's Lesbianism as Gloss on Her Modernism. In *Virginia Woolf*

Miscellanies: Proceedings of the First Annual Conference on Virginia Woolf, ed. Mark Hussey and Vara Neverow-Turk, 134–141. New York: Pace University Press.

Minow-Pinkey, Makiko. 1987. *Virginia Woolf and the Problem of the Subject: Feminine Writing in the Major Novels.* Brighton: Harvester Wheatsheaf.

Moi, Toril. 1985. *Sexual/Textual Politics: Feminist Literary Theory.* London: Methuen.

————. 1990. Feminism and Postmodernism: Recent Feminist Criticism in the United States. In *British Feminist Thought. A Reader,* ed. Terry Lovell, 367–376. Oxford: Basil Blackwell.

Owens, Craig. 1983. The Discourse of Others: Feminism and Postmodernism. In *The Anti-Aesthetic. Essays on Postmodern Culture,* ed. Hal Foster, 57–82. Seattle: Bay Press.

Showalter, Elaine. 1977. *A Literature of Their Own: British Women Novelists from Brontë to Lessing.* Princeton, NJ: Princeton University Press.

Spivak, Gayatri Chakravorty. 1988. Can the Subaltern Speak? In *Marxism and the Interpretation of Culture,* ed. Cary Nelson and Lawrence Grossberg, 271–313. Urbana: University of Illinois Press.

Suleiman, Susan Robin. 1991. Feminism and Postmodernism: A Question of Politics. In *Zeitgeist in Babel: The Postmodernist Controversy,* ed. Ingeborg Hoesterey, 111–130. Bloomington: Indiana University Press.

Tuzyline, Jita Allan. 1997. The Death of Sex and the Soul in Mrs. Dalloway and Nella Larsen's Passing. In *Virginia Woolf. Lesbian Readings,* ed. Eileen Barret and Patricia Cramer, 95–113. London and New York: New York University Press.

Woolf, Virginia. 1929. *A Room of One's Own.* London: Hogarth.

————. 1966–1967. *Collected Essays,* ed. Leonard Woolf. London: Chatto and Windus.

————. 1975–1980. *The Letters of Virginia Woolf,* ed. Nigel Nicolson and Joanne Trautmann. London: The Hogarth Press.

————. 1979a. *Women and Writing* (1st ed., 1931), ed. Michele Barrett. New York: Harcourt Brace Jovanovich.

————. 1979b. *The Diary of Virginia Woolf,* ed. Anne Olivier Bell. London: The Hogarth Press and Penguin Books.

————. 2000a. *Mrs. Dalloway* (1st ed., 1925). London: Penguin Classics.

————. 2000b. *Orlando, A Biography* (1st ed., 1928). London: Penguin Classics.

Part IV

Historical Perspectives

11

Finance Capital and the Time of the Novel or, Money Without Narrative Qualities

Mathias Nilges

"Money has lost its narrative quality the way painting did once upon a time," observes a character in Don DeLillo's 2003 novel *Cosmopolis* during a discussion of an "art form" for which there exists a word only in Greek, *Chrimatistikos*: "the art of money making."[1] In the age of finance capital, the famous Marxian formula M-C-M' that describes the relation between monetary accumulation and commodity exchange no longer appears to describe the dominant logic of the economic structure, nor is it able to provide us with a logical basis for mapping and narrating lived reality. In dominant finance capital, an era beyond the dominance of industrial production and even commodity production and exchange, the art of money making presents itself in its arguably purest form (pure in the sense that the logical structure of the value form and its universal equivalent, money, now stand at the forefront of the current mode of capitalism, having removed the centrality of the 'C,' the commodity that formerly mediated the process of monetary production

M. Nilges (✉)
St. Francis Xavier University, Antigonish, NS, Canada
e-mail: mnilges@stfx.ca

243

A. Falcato and A. Cardiello (eds.), *Philosophy in the Condition of Modernism*,
https://doi.org/10.1007/978-3-319-77078-9_11

and accumulation, from the equation). The equation is contracted to the relation M-M'—money is talking to itself. Yet, while this process of moving the fundamental value form and logic of the money form to the foreground of the capitalist process presents what can be described as an instance of purification—flows of capital in their purest form can be seen when examining the contemporary stock market or trade in futures—this purification results in an epistemological and narratological crisis: the logic of finance capital (along with its potential limits) has become more complicated to think about and to narrate. The purification of the art of money making generates a crisis for art in general and literature in particular. The form of thought in which the structural form of finance capital and the crisis of narrative form intersect is time. Time has served as the crucial plane upon which we could formerly narrate the logic of capital and money. Yet, the character in DeLillo's novel suggests, today, "money makes time. It used to be the other way around. Clock time accelerated the rise of capitalism. People stopped thinking about eternity. They began to concentrate on hours, measurable hours, man-hours, using labor more efficiently."[2] Thus, while the generation of clock-time, an abstraction that, via a fetishistic inversion that maps clock-time precisely onto the logic of the value form and the commodity fetish, allowed us to narrate money and capitalism, the temporal logic underlying the transition into dominant finance capital requires an accompanying process of acceleration in order to function that transcends the limits of the temporal episteme that determined previous stages of modern history. Since under finance capital the logic of time and money is inverted, transforming time into "a corporate asset" that "belongs to the free market system," we witness a narratological crisis that is connected to a crisis of temporal epistemology: the future is increasingly drawn into the present, or, as the character in DeLillo's novel suggest, "we used to know the present and not the future—this is changing,"[3] yet, the present, in turn, also becomes ever "harder to find."[4] What seems to be required in the face of the dominance of finance capital, which increasingly accelerates time and appears to absorb the future into the present, is precisely what DeLillo's character realizes as possibly the most significant epistemological project of the present: "a new theory of time" that can allow for a renewed possibility of narrating, understanding, and ultimately rigorously criti-quing finance capital. To understand finance capital is to develop new forms of narrating it, and to narrate finance capital is to engage with its temporal logic that underlies the current epistemological crisis that attaches a widespread millennialism and crisis of futurity (we live in an era, after all, in which popular culture and theoretical thought intersect on the terrain of the end times and, in the absence of a future imag-inary, turns either to apocalyptic or nostalgic narratives and lines of thought) to the seeming inability to think (the limits of) finance capital.

In what follows, I will illustrate the stakes of appreciating the rela-tionship between recent changes in our cultural and literary imagination that are determined by a crisis of futurity and narratology, and our abil-ity to think about finance capital. What, to put it more bluntly, happens to the cultural and literary imagination, as well as critical and theoret-ical thought, once our imagination has indeed become financialized? And further: what are the elements and consequences of what we may call a financialized imagination, and how can culture and, in particular, literature provide us with the means for probing the limits of such a form of thought? As indicated above, answering these questions requires a detailed engagement with the temporal logic of finance capitalism and its structures, and, as I will suggest, it is, in fact, precisely via litera-ture that we can find ways of exploring the limits and ways of thinking beyond the financial imagination that are largely lacking on contempo-rary theoretical production. Yet, before turning to the relation between finance capital and time that generates the above-mentioned crisis of our temporal episteme, let me briefly turn toward another novel pub-lished in 2003 that allows us to see the problem of narrating the time of finance capital in more detail. On the level of cultural production, this crisis presents itself as the impression of seemingly non-transcendable contemporaneity. In William Gibson's *Pattern Recognition,* global mar-keting guru Hubertus Bigend suggests in a memorable passage that,

> we have no idea, now, of who or what the inhabitants of our future might be. In that sense, we have no future. Not in the sense that our grandparents had a future, or thought they did. Fully imagined cultural futures were the luxury of another day, one in which 'now' was of greater

duration. For us, of course, things can change so abruptly, so violently, so profoundly, that futures like our grandparents' have insufficient 'now' to stand on. We have no future because our present is too volatile.[5]

Similarly, *Spook Country*, book two of Gibson's latest trilogy that consists of *Pattern Recognition* (2003), *Spook Country* (2007) and *Zero History* (2010), presents a world utterly devoid of true futurity, determined by a situation whose objects mark it as "terrible in its contemporaneity."[6] What we should note here is that these statements link the impossibility of change to both the present's volatility and the completion of a process of innovation that appears to exhaust the category of the new or what Ernst Bloch calls the "not yet." What, then, is the relationship between the terror of contemporaneity and the current crisis of futurity?

We find similar formulations in recent theoretical discourse. In 1994, in a passage that has since been adopted and popularized widely by Slavoj Zizek, Fredric Jameson writes that, "it seems to be easier for us today to imagine the thoroughgoing deterioration of the earth and of nature than the breakdown of late capitalism; perhaps due to some weakness in our imagination."[7] Already 30 years earlier, in a conversation in 1964, Ernst Bloch and Theodor W. Adorno noted a tendency that, as we shall see, has not simply increased in intensity but in fact has come to its structural conclusion, a tendency that helps us shed light on both the contemporary crisis of futurity and the connected relation between the financialized and cultural imagination. Both Adorno and Bloch note the pervasiveness of a "shrinking of utopian consciousness" that appears to be connected to the peculiar relation between "technological accomplishments" and "innovations to the totality." Both Bloch and Adorno agree that the present moment in history is defined by the fulfillment of longstanding utopian dreams (Adorno lists the examples of communication technologies and space travel). Adorno further notes:

insofar as these dreams have been realized, they operate as though the best thing about them had been forgotten—one is not happy about them. As they have been realized, the dreams themselves have assumed a peculiar character of sobriety, of the spirit of relativism, and beyond that, of boredom.[8]

What Bloch terms the "melancholy of fulfillment" Adorno describes in complimentary fashion as a central logical paradox in the structure of utopian thought that determines the relation to its object: "one sees oneself almost always deceived: the fulfillment of the wishes takes something away from the substance of the wishes."[9] The paradox of wish-fulfillment and banality registers primarily, as Bloch emphasizes, on the level of time and, once taken to its logical conclusion results in a situation that "consists largely only in a repetition of the continually same 'today.'"[10] And it is, as we shall see, the transition into full finance capitalism that fulfilled a series of wishes on the level of structure and totality and also in regards to the "technological accomplishments" that are central to finance capital's functioning—yet, not in the manner in which we may have hoped. In *A Singular Modernity*, Jameson describes the contemporary socioeconomic situation as characterized by what he calls the "standardization of everything," leading to "the persistence of sameness through absolute difference." The experience of "perpetual change" as one of the dominant conditions of postmodernity, Jameson argues, introduces at its climax the impression of ultimate homogenization and standardization. "What we begin to feel, therefore," he concludes, is that as a paradoxical result of the centrality of perpetual change in the context of postmodernity, "nothing can change any longer."[11] We are by now relatively familiar with the description of the material basis Jameson associates with the evacuation of the concept of the new. Jameson provides us here with a point of entry into the causes for the epistemological problem of the present with which we are concerned here. The exploration of this problem requires us to link forms of thought to their dialectical counterpart: the form of finance capital.

To further illustrate this point, let me turn for a moment to the recent work by Richard Sennett. The particular value of Sennett's recent critical production lies in the fact that it fuses cause and symptom. That is, Sennett's work provides us with an introduction to the socioeconomic structures of the present, as well with examples of the epistemological crisis arising from it, a crisis to which he, too, is not immune. Sennett's account of the "culture of the new capitalism" is structured around descriptions of loss that ultimately amount to descriptions of exhaustions of utopian projects. The most significant transition in contemporary society, according to Sennett, is that previous political and philosophical movements have exhausted themselves seemingly paradoxically precisely as a consequence of their fulfillment. The goals of the radicals of the 1960s have aligned themselves with those of the "rulers [of] today" and "history has granted the New Left its wish in a perverse form."[12] Previous struggles for liberation that grounded themselves in the rejection of paternalistic institutions (be they bureaucratic, social, or economic) have been emptied of their revolutionary content and become the logic of the present system of accumulation that is founded upon deregulation and productive instability that, as we shall see later in more detail, finance capital requires in order to function. Finance capital, that is, structurally fulfilled the wishes for the supersession of Fordist capitalism, though, of course, not in the manner in which the New Left had imagined this. Such a structural transformation, of course, cannot leave capitalism's social dimension untouched, and it is this social mediation of the structural logic of new capitalism that is Sennett's main concern. "The fragmenting of big institutions," Sennett writes, "has left many people's lives in a fragmented state," adding that, "if you are nostalgically minded—and what sensitive soul isn't?—you would find this state of affairs just one more reason for regret."[13] The transposition of a structural concern into an affective reaction, of course, strikes us immediately as logically not very rigorous, since the affective level immediately absorbs concrete historicity. Yet, this transposition is interesting, since it is representative of a common response to the problem of the standardization of difference that precisely recognizes a crisis of futurity in the present structures and responds to this crisis by substituting for true futurity the anti-dialectical and pseudo-historical category of nostalgia.

The category of time thus immediately enters into Sennett's analysis. Time becomes one of the main challenges of the present, according to Sennett. More concretely, the challenge is connected to what he perceives as the problem of constructing stable life-narratives, of "how to manage short-term relationships, and oneself, while migrating from task to task, job to job, place to place." "If institutions no longer provide a long-term frame," Sennett concludes, "the individual may have to improvise his or her life-narrative, or even do without any sustained sense of self."[14]

The result of the new capitalism, which Sennett associates with Schumpeter's notion of accumulation by "creative destruction," is the inability to formulate narratives of the future, since the present is determined by "unstable energy" that does not allow for stable teleologies.[15] Milgrim, one of the protagonists of Gibson's *Zero History* understands this point perfectly well. "Stasis is the enemy," he suggests, continuing: "stability's the beginning of the end." The logic of the nonexistent category of "order flow" perfectly encapsulates this point for Milgrim:

> It's the aggregate of all the orders in the market. Everything anyone is about to buy or sell, all of it. Stocks, bonds, gold, anything. … that information exists, at any given moment, but there's no aggregator. It exists, constantly, but it is unknowable. It someone were able to aggregate that, the market would cease to be real. … because the market *is* the inability to aggregate the order flow at any given moment.[16]

The notion of stability as the basis for futurity, confronts us as one of the dominant epistemological problems of our time, and it illustrates the direct link between the logic of finance capital, a temporal crisis, and the centrality of a degree of unknowability, at which point one aspect of the financialized imagination reveals itself as precisely such a constitutive inability to imagine. This also allows us to get a glimpse of one of the logical contradictions that lie at the heart of the current crisis that seemingly does not allow us to narrate finance capital and replaces a missing imagination of the future with nostalgia and the desire to return to a more map-able past.

There are, then, two key aspects of the temporal crisis that link time and the ability to know, or imagine, finance capital, and we may be able to supplement Jameson's diagnosis with a suggestion of what this weakness in imagination might be and how it is created. The first aspect, as we began to see above, is what we could with Jameson describe as the standardization of difference. As Gibson's novels suggest, the standardization of difference is at once key to the working of the finance market and a direct cause of the impression of an omnipresent contemporaneity, a present that absorbs the future into itself yet exists without duration or stability, thus making it impossible to think the future as difference. This problem is wonderfully explored in Benjamin Kunkel's 2005 debut novel, *Indecision*. The novel's protagonist, Dwight Wilmerding, suffers from abulia, the chronic inability to make decisions. This inability to make decisions, Dwight realizes, is to a large degree connected to his existence in the contemporary world, in which he is surrounded by difference yet unable to make meaningful decisions in the absence of differences that truly matter. After all, what really is the difference between the most recent smartphones, new TV sitcoms, or the most recent micro-manipulations of ubiquitous cultural genres? Dwight's inability to imagine the future and his inability to make decisions are linked, it turns out, since he seems to live in a time in which difference and change no longer exist in spite of, or, as we have seen, because of their ubiquity and full integration into the logic of capital (finance thus fully supersedes the structures of Fordist modernity that rested on standardization, regulation, and replication). To be sure, Kunkel's novel suggests, Dwight is surrounded by omnipresent difference, but none of these differences seem to matter, since they are all part of the same omnipresent contemporary moment of capitalism and thus not different at all. Hence, Dwight develops a romantic longing for life in communist Romania, for a past and for a situation in which capitalism had an other and, therefore, one could make decisions that mattered and that made a difference. At the same time, Dwight's inability to make decisions contains a second facet that is dialectically linked to the first. Dwight also suffers from what he believes to be a temporal disorder that does not allow him to make decisions: he is "unable to think the future until [he] arrive[s] there."[17] This inability to think the future, Dwight speculates, in turn appears to be related to what he considers to be an overly slow "temporal metabolism" that is "not equipped for the digestion of … postmodern life."[18] The second aspect of the crisis under examination, then, appears to be linked to a problem of speed.

The reason that life appears too contemporary (DeLillo) or terrible in its contemporaneity (Gibson) is logically related to Dwight's perception of omnipresent contemporaneity, of perpetual change and ultimate difference that robs us of true difference, and thus of the future and him of the ability to make decisions. And just as Cayce, the protagonist of *Pattern Recognition*, mobilizes a poignant quote by Dwight

D. Eisenhower whenever she is perturbed by the structural logic of our contemporary moment ("it's more the way it is now than it's ever been"),[19] the characters in *Cosmopolis* understand that the present of finance capitalism is characterized by a fundamental process of contraction and condensation. "Time is a thing that grows scarcer every day," a character in the novel observes.[20] It does so, the characters realize, since finance capital and the future are now one and the same thing, and that living in finance capitalism means living in the future. For the first time, it seems, the commercials we have been watching over the past decades are finally right: the future is now. Thus, when the characters in DeLillo's novel observe the activity on a street that is determined by delivery trucks, jewel and antique trade, and "hagglers and talebearers, the scrapmongers, the dealers in stray talk," they read the life and economic activity that takes place on the street as "an offense to the truth of the future."[21] The truth of the future, on the other hand, is legible to them via the bank towers they passed earlier, which, in contrast, were "designed to hasten the future. They were the end of the outside world. They weren't here, exactly. They were in the future, a time beyond geography and touchable money and the people who stack and count it."[22] Yet, suggesting that finance capital is the future and then concluding that one must live in the future in order to be a suitable subject for finance capitalism appears to be a tricky proposition. How, after all, is it possible to inhabit the future?

This problem, is turns out, is solved by the temporal and logical structure of finance capital itself. In order for the structure to function, it has to take place at an increasingly accelerated speed. Trades have to take place virtually instantaneously, and "real time" communication necessarily accompanies the rise to dominance of finance capitalism. Yet, there lies at the heart of real time communication an epistemological problem that necessarily maps onto the temporal problem connected to the money form as it presents itself in finance capitalism. As communication increases in speed and we reach the moment at which the temporal lag between sending and receiving, of transactions and trades has contracted to the point at which we perceive them as versions of immediacy, we in fact lose sense of the process of mediation that makes these processes structurally far from immediate. That is, at the moment at which we have access to real time communication and trade, time itself becomes not more but decidedly less real. Transactions, internet searches, and the exchange of messages occur in units of time we are no longer able to think, units that are so small that we no longer have analogies for them. We are still able to mobilize images such as "the blink of an eye" to assist us in the effort to think tiny differences between competitors' results in sports events, yet we are absolutely unable to truly think a unit such as the yoctosecond. As a consequence, at the moment at which time becomes as "real" as never before in the process of communicating and trading, time confronts us no longer as natural but in fact as the thing it truly is: an abstraction we externalize through a fetishistic inversion and then treat as though it confronts us as a natural, external given. The confrontation with its abstraction in the context of real time communication, however, undoes this inversion, and we are unable to see time as anything other than the arbitrary construction it truly is. It is in this limit of the temporal fiction that becomes visible at the climax of speed that time confronts us in its purest form as a form of thought, and herein lies the true moment of realism in real time communication: the moment of realism within the financialized imagination that undoes the fiction of capital. This, of course, as suggested above, maps precisely onto the confrontation with capital and the value and money form, which are revealed as pure abstractions and arbitrary constructions in the process M-M'. As a consequence, the fetishistic inversion and the fetishistic relation to money in the context of finance capitalism is undone. Indeed, as Paul Virilio suggests, such a situation may also force us to rethink the very definition of progress, thus ending modernity's (and modernism's) romance with this concept:

> In the nineteenth century, Progress meant the *Great Commotion* of the railways. In the twentieth century, it still meant more the *Great Speed* of the bullet train and the supersonic jet. In the twenty-first century, it means the *Instantaneity* of the interactive telecommunications of cybernetics.[23]

It is this process of acceleration that exhausts narratives of progress and speed in a context of rapidity that is perceived as instantaneity that also results in in what Virilio understands as a "sudden loss of memory" that carries with it a loss of imagination, which parallels the exhaustion of our "great progressive illusions."[24] As a result, "past, present and future contract in the omnipresent instant."[25]

The unthinkable speed with which the transactions of finance capital take place are the reason that finance capital is the future and simultaneously draws the future into the present—and, as DeLillo's novel suggests, at this moment "the present is harder to find" as well, which creates the perceived volatility of the present that determines Gibson's novels.[26] Similarly, Cayce's travels through the globalized space of finance capital no longer cause her to feel jet lag—time does not really matter here. Rather, Cayce experiences what she describes as "soul lag," the perception of a contradiction between the temporal requirements of finance capitalism and the speed of global transactions and the limits of human existence and imagination. Yet, DeLillo's novel stresses, "never mind the speed that makes it hard to follow what passes before the eye. The speed is the point."[27] And indeed the speed and the inability to think the actual transactions and flows of capital is the point, just as the inability to truly generate an aggregate of the flows of trade and instead accept the market's constitutive impossibility to be imagined is the point. Here, the seeming temporal and generic shift of Gibson's recent work (*Pattern Recognition* is the first of Gibson's novels not set in the future but in the present, and his turn to realism surprised many of Gibson's readers, who had come to associate him fundamentally with science-fiction and even more centrally with cyberpunk with whose invention Gibson is frequently credited) intersects with the formal contraction of DeLillo's recent novels (it is by no means an irrelevant point as regards the relation between the form of DeLillo's novels and the forms of thought and capital that are his subject matter that we see increasingly short, contracted novels—his 1997 novel *Underworld* is 827 pages long; *Cosmopolis* is 209 pages long; and his most recent novel, *Point Omega*, published in 2010 and an end point indeed, is a mere 117 pages long). Franco Berardi provides us with an account of the problem around which these novels revolve that suggests that we may be witnessing a moment in which finance capitalism reaches a threshold, a moment in which capital is not only unable to hide its most fundamental contradictions (the logic of the value and money form) but it is forced to operate in a manner that necessitates the hypervisibility of these contradictions. At this point, one of the central forces that regulates the relation between capital and its social dimension is that of imagination: the constitutively necessary inability to imagine the structure of finance capitalism stands in direct regulating opposition to the hypervisibility of its contradictions. Berardi regards Bill Gates' *Business @ the Speed of Thought* as a "contemporary formalization of this threshold," and suggests that what we are seeing in dominant finance capital is a process of radical contraction that weighs as heavily upon capitalism as it weighs on our imagination:

> Marx spoke of a tendency, a limit point in the process of the valorization of capital: the impossible possibility that capital might circulate "without circulation time," at an infinite velocity, such that the passage from one moment in the circulation of capital to the next would take place at the "speed of thought." Such capital would return to itself even before taking leave of itself, passing through all of its phases in a process encountering no obstacles, in an ideal time without time—in the blinding flash of an instant without duration, a cycle contracting into a point.[28]

It is this point, the point of time and the point of finance capital, which can be seen as DeLillo's point omega and seemingly as an endpoint for the imagination, narrative, and the novel.

And indeed, in such a situation, it is no surprise that we are witnessing not only novelistic contraction but also the turn away from narratives of the future and toward narratives of the present or the past, moments in which it was still possible to imagine the future and the concrete life narratives Sennett misses. The currently vibrant doomsday industry that ranges from a pervasive cultural attachment to (post-)apocalyptic narratives, the aftermath of which allows for the return to simpler times (usually also accompanied by the return to earlier gender politics and social arrangements) and the resurrection of clearly imaginable futures, to actual doomsday prepping and the simultaneous fetishization of the concept of "change" in a time in which difference and change determine every part of our lives and have become centrally operative principles of finance capitalism is but one of many symptoms of this situation. Replicating the logic of Bigend's account of the exhaustion of futurity as a result of the present's lack of stability, Sennett describes the "search for order" as a prominent social phenomenon in response to structural deregulation that attaches the desire to recover narratives of the future to a stable present.[29] Notably, the desire for a stable present is attached to a distinct form of nostalgia and, as a result, the anti-dialectical logical formulation is endowed with yet another dimension, that of regression. The solution to the problem of lacking access to the future that is barred by an oppressive sense of contemporaneity is sought in a return to the simulacrum of a past in which the formulation of narratives of the future was possible due to the existence of simple and stable structures upon which a project of transcendence and futurity could be mounted. The way into the future, blocked by the present, necessitates from this perspective a return to the past. It is clear to see at this point that the logic of apocalyptic narratives performs an important labor in the context of this form of thought. The function of the apocalypse is to free futurity from the grasp of difference, resolving the problems of a present by means of destruction and a "system-reboot" of sorts. This regressive and anti-dialectical reboot destroys the limitations of the present and simplifies the structural context to a degree that it once again allows for the formulation of narratives of the future. In this sense, the apocalypse is intended to resolve the epistemological problems that arise from a present characterized by the stasis of complexity and difference, and it is also at this point that we can see that the current wave of apocalyptic imagination is a necessary byproduct of, and an index of, profoundly new forms of alienation connected to the financialized imagination.

Yet, literature is and has been aware of this. In fact, as early as the 1980s, we can find not only literary representations of the rise of finance capitalism and of Wall Street-subjectivity, but also novels that deal with the emerging epistemological crisis that accompanies this transition in capitalism. In this respect, it is possible appreciate read Paul Auster's short (and rarely studied) 1987 novel *In the Country of Last Things* as a novel about the emerging contradictions of finance capital alongside other 1987 novels such as Tom Wolfe's *The Bonfire of the*

Vanities. The novel's plot and logic are driven by the departure from stability and the transition into a post-apocalyptic world "in constant flux," in which "nothing lasts."[30] Auster's novel describes one key aspect of the apocalyptic imagination as follows:

> so many of us have become like children again. It's not that we make an effort, you understand, or that anyone is really conscious of it. But when hope disappears, when you find that you have given up hoping even for the possibility of hope, you tend to fill the empty spaces with dreams, little childlike thoughts and stories to keep yourself going. (9)

Yet, as is the case for the multitude of contemporary cultural narratives that mobilize postapocalyptic narratives to carry out an operation of nostalgia that is born out of the inability to imaginatively engage with the present, there is little doubt in Auster's novel that this return to a childlike state is a decidedly negative development. Unless I am a child, acting like a child will not make me a child again. It will instead make me childish. In addition to this childish engagement with the present that determines the most regressive aspects of the financialized cultural imagination, Auster also foregrounds the pervasiveness of "death" as "the only way we can express ourselves" as fraught with the contradictions that reveal the anti-dialectical core of the nostalgic "language of ghosts" (10/11):

> the closer you come to the end, the more there is to say. The end is only imaginary, a destination you invent to keep yourself going, but a point comes when you realize you will never get there. (183)

Don DeLillo's *White Noise*, roughly published at the same time as Auster's *In the Country of Last Things*, provides another famous example of this epistemological crisis. "Is this the point of Armageddon?" a character in the novel asks, "no ambiguity, no more doubt."[31] Similarly, it is the famous "airborne toxic event" that "release[s] a spirit of imagination" (153) that seems to provide further evidence for the function of apocalyptic form (and DeLillo's brilliant engagement with the relation between death and the current stage of capitalism) in the context of the financialized imagination.

Literature, then, has for the last few decades already foregrounded one of the problems regarding the rise of finance capital that have only been registered recently by theoretical production. In his 2010 book *For a New Critique of Political Economy* Bernard Stiegler launches a direct attack on the lacking future imaginary that characterizes both the structure of finance capitalism and current efforts to deal with the global financial crisis. The present crisis, he suggests, "heralds the end of the consumerist model."[32] Yet, the rise of finance capitalism is plagued by a dark, inverted version of its own temporal logic that draws the future into the present. Current efforts to deal with the financial crisis remain attached to the past in a manner the novels listed above anticipate. Despite the fact that the consumerist model has reached its limits, Stiegler suggests, attempts at resolving the current crisis remain routed through the consumerist model and reduce investment to the effort to stimulate consumption and production. Yet, Stiegler argues, "the consumerist model has reached its limits because it has become systemically short-termist, because it has given rise to a systemic stupidity that structurally prevents the reconstitution of a long-term horizon."[33] Much like Sennett's nostalgia or the imaginative stupidity of current post-apocalyptic cultural narratives, finance capital suffers from the systemic stupidity of the dark twin of the financialized imagination it requires in order to function—a damaging version of a perpetual present, yet a perpetual present that is not brought about by accepting the unthinkability of market and speed, but by the reactionary desire for restoration and deceleration. This, Stiegler suggests, is "a pure and simple reestablishment of the state of things, trying to rebuild the industrial landscape without at all changing its structure, still less its axioms, all in the hope of protecting income levels that had hitherto been achievable."[34] Finance capitalism's main contradiction can, in this sense, be regarded as the financialized imagination. In order to function, financial capitalism requires the epistemological exhaustion of those forms of thought— first and foremost the temporal episteme—that structured much of modern life and that reached their climax in Fordist modernity. Yet, the financialized imagination also generates its own, dialectically connected, dark doubling, which we encounter everywhere in cultural production and economic crisis management alike.

To be sure, this epistemological and temporal crisis that is part and parcel of finance capitalism is no small matter. It is not merely another wave of perpetually entertaining instances of culturally and imaginatively toying with the demise of the planet (though, of course, such waves hardly ever occur in the absence of dialectically connected historical and sociopolitical tensions). As Christian Marazzi stresses,

> The theoretical analysis of financial market operations reveals the centrality of communication, of *language*, not as a vehicle for transmitting data and information, but also as a *creative force*. Communicative action is at the origin of the conventions, of the "interpretive models" that influence the choices and the decisions of the multitude of players operating in the markets.[35]

Put differently, the constitution, maintenance, and expansion of finance capitalism requires appropriate cognitive and interpretive models, and it is here that we see the true contradiction of the regression of the financialized imagination into its impoverished, regressive version. Expanding upon the work of Andre Orlean, Marazzi suggests the importance of understanding that "beliefs have a creative role." "What the actors think," he continues, "the way they represent the world, has an effect on prices and, therefore, on the relationships that economic actors weave among themselves."[36] This point may initially not seem very complicated. Yet, when combined with the line of argumentation this essay proposed, it is possible to suggest the following: the backlash against, and general (partially structurally necessary) impoverishment of, what we can call the financialized imagination, therefore, to put this point provocatively, can be understood to be centrally involved in the current crisis of capitalism, and it is in many ways the weight of the necessary, self-imposed imaginative horizon upon which finance capitalism relies that is crushing its very structure.

Everywhere, thus, we encounter calls for new models for political economy that not only describe the symptoms of the current crisis with which we are by now quite familiar—few cultural artifacts today are free from the contradictions of the financialized imagination—but that also provide us with an account of why we are seeing what we are seeing. Yet, theoretical production frequently appears as paralyzed by the temporal, epistemological crisis underlying the current perceived impasse as does the post-apocalyptic culture industry. But do we truly need another description of the ways in which we appear to live in the end times? It is here, I would suggest, that we can turn toward literature and, in particular, to the novel in order to think through the current seeming dead-end. In a sense, we may be finding ourselves in a moment that can be described as a time for the novel, as it is indeed the novel's time we may require once again. Narrativization, as Paul Ricoeur famously illustrates, is always also a process of "presentifying" an act of thinking external objectivity that is always also a temporal operation. The layers of the logic of this operation are captured especially poignantly for Ricoeur by the German word *Vergegenwaertlichen*, which means both to make something present and to call something into consciousness, to understand, to grasp. What is narrated, consequently, as Ricoeur shows, is "the temporality of life."[37] The problematic logic of the temporal and structural episteme of finance capitalism that presents itself also as a problem of narrative, I would like to suggest, can be explored on precisely this level, the level of narrative, that allows us to confront the current crisis not as an exhaustion but as yet another aspect of narrating temporality that always contains different forms of temporal and narratological (and thus ultimately epistemological) presentification. The search for a new political economy may thus be linked to an inquiry into the contemporary politics of literature, since, as Jacques Ranciere suggests in *The Politics of Literature*, "the expression 'politics of literature' ... implies that literature intervenes as literature in [the] carving up of space and time."[38] Literature does so as literature precisely in its engagement with time, an engagement that lies at the heart of the novel. In a recent essay, Cathy Caruth writes:

> The question of literary criticism in the twenty-first century carries with it an implicit meditation on the loss and survival of literature. As a thinking of its own survival, moreover, the literary and the criticism with which it is bound up pass beyond the traditional boundaries of literary discourse. For the future—and its possible absence—cannot be thought without literary forms of articulation that exceed the language in which

we refer to what we know. In turning back to literature, literary criticism turns forward the possibility, and possible disappearance of, a conceivable future.[39]

To turn to the novel in times of finance capitalism as a means of thinking through the purported impasses of the financialized imagination is to respond to Caruth's call for a mode of attention to literature that can provide a fundamental element of literary studies in the twenty-first century as well as, I hope to have shown, provide us with the linguistic tools for critique and thought Marazzi considers a fundamental element of our efforts to think and critique the logic of finance capitalism.

Notes

1. Don DeLillo, *Cosmopolis* (New York: Scribner, 2003), 77.
2. DeLillo, 79.
3. DeLillo, 86.
4. DeLillo, 79.
5. William Gibson, *Pattern Recognition* (New York: Berkley, 2003), 57.
6. William Gibson, *Spook Country* (New York: Putnam, 2007), 10.
7. Fredric Jameson, *The Seeds of Time* (New York: Columbia University Press, 1994), xii.
8. Ernst Bloch, *The Utopian Function of Art and Literature*, trans. Jack Zipes and Frank Mecklenburg (Cambridge: MIT University Press, 1988), 1.
9. Bloch, 1–3.
10. Bloch, 2.
11. Fredric Jameson, *A Singular Modernity* (New York and London: Verso, 2002), 15–18.
12. Richard Sennett, *The Culture of the New Capitalism* (New Haven: Yale University Press, 2006), 2.
13. Ibid.
14. Sennett, 6.
15. Sennett, 16.
16. Gibson, *Zero History*, 177. Emphasis original.
17. Benjamin Kunkel, *Indecision* (New York: Random House, 2005), 3.
18. Kunkel, 18.

19. Gibson, *Pattern Recognition*, 180.
20. DeLillo, 69.
21. DeLillo, 65.
22. DeLillo, 36.
23. Paul Virilio, *The Futurism of the Instant—Stop-Eject* (London: Polity, 2010), 70. Emphasis original.
24. Virilio, 70–71.
25. Virilio, 71.
26. DeLillo, 79.
27. DeLillo, 80.
28. Franco Berardi, *The Soul at Work—From Alienation to Autonomy*, (New York: Semiotext(e), 2009), 11.
29. Sennett, 22.
30. Paul Auster, *In the Country of Last Things* (New York: Faber and Faber, 1987), 1–2.
31. Don DeLillo, *White Noise* (New York: Viking, 1985), 137.
32. Bernard Stiegler, *For a New Critique of Political Economy* (London: Polity, 2010), 4.
33. Stiegler, 5.
34. Ibid.
35. Christian Marazzi, *Capital and Language—From the New Economy to the War Economy* (New York: Semiotext(e), 2008).
36. Marazzi, 28.
37. Paul Ricoeur, *Time and Narrative—Volume 2* (Chicago: University of Chicago Press, 1984), 78.
38. Jacques Ranciere, *The Politics of Literature* (London: Polity, 2011), 4.
39. Cathy Caruth, "Afterword: Turning Back to Literature," *PMLA* 125 no. 4 (2010), 1087–1088.

References

Auster, Paul. 1987. *In the Country of Last Things*. New York: Faber and Faber.
Bloch, Ernst. 1985. *The Principle of Hope*. Cambridge: MIT Press.
———.1988. *The Utopian Function of Art and Literature*, trans. Jack Zipes and Franck Mecklenburg. Cambridge: MIT Press.
Caruth, Cathy. 2010. Afterword: Turning Back to Literature. *PMLA* 125 (4): 1087–1088.

DeLillo, Don. 1985. *White Noise*. New York: Viking.

————. 2003. *Cosmopolis*. New York: Scribner.

————. 2010. *Point Omega*. New York: Scribner.

Dubey, Madhu. 2003. *Signs and Cities: Black Literary Postmodernism*. Chicago: University of Chicago Press.

Gibson, William. 2003. *Pattern Recognition*. New York: Berkley.

————. 2007. *Spooky Country*. New York: Putnam.

————. 2010. *Zero History*. New York: Putnam.

Jameson, Fredric. 1994. *The Seeds of Time*. New York: Columbia University Press.

————. 2002. *A Singular Modernity*. New York and London: Verso.

Kunkel, Ben. 2005. *Indecision*. New York: Random House.

Marazzi, Christian. 2008. *Capital and Language: From the New Economy to the War Economy*. New York: Semiotext(e).

Nilges, Mathias. 2009. We Need the Stars': Change, Community, and the Absent Father in Octavia Butler's Parable Novels. *Callaloo* 32 (4): 1332–1352.

————. 2010. The Anti-Anti-Oedipus: Representing Post-Fordist Subjectivity. *Meditations* 23 (3): 27–70.

Rancière, Jacques. 2011. *The Politics of Literature*. London: Polity.

Ricoeur, Paul. 1984. *Time and Narrative*, vol. 2. Chicago: University of Chicago Press.

Sennett, Richard. 2006. *The Culture of the New Capitalism*. New Haven: Yale University Press.

Stiegler, Bernard. 2010. *For a New Critique of Political Economy*. London: Polity.

Virilio, Paul. 2010. *The Futurism of the Instant: Stop-Eject*. London: Polity.

12

Marianne Moore and the Logic of "Inner Sensuousness"

Charles Altieri

Let me begin indirectly. The most capacious context for this essay on Marianne Moore is the fact that various aspects of contemporary Materialisms prove enormously useful in appreciating Impressionist painting. But my praise is primarily a means to get at how the Modernists' critiques of both Impressionism and Imagism take on considerable currency now, because these critiques provide imperatives for also exploring basic limitations in these New Materialist stances.[1] These explorations, in turn, call attention to significant feats of imagination defining values and producing experiences which cannot be aligned with any current version of materialism. Here I want to show how Moore's particular ways of engaging these values and experiences invoke distinctive powers of mind that are based directly on mental states at best only partially attributable to any dispositions of material properties. I also want to elaborate, through Moore, one way of taking seriously the entire Modernist project of stressing the powers involved in the act

C. Altieri (✉)
University of California, Berkeley, CA, USA
e-mail: altieri@berkeley.edu

© The Author(s) 2018
A. Falcato and A. Cardiello (eds.), *Philosophy in the Condition of Modernism*,
https://doi.org/10.1007/978-3-319-77078-9_12

of composition because of how they model modes of self-consciousness crucial for the displacing of representation as the primary ambition of poetry. Moore's work offers one highly intelligent elaboration of how consciousness can experience its own powers as it negotiates the intricacies of experience.

The best overall framework I can offer, in order to link Moore with more general Modernist tendencies, is one provided by Hegel's concept of the "inner sensuousness" basic to Romantic art (which cannot be identified entirely with Romanticism). This concept, elaborated in Hegel's *Lectures on Aesthetics*, affords two important complements to critical work attempting to define why Modernist art can still matter in contemporary culture. "Inner sensuousness" is still sensuousness, or that aspect of idealist concerns that can be translated into aspects of the life of the senses. As such, it allows us to develop ways of identifying with the artists and writers that challenge the emerging hegemony of rhetorics of materialism. And the concept of "inner sensuousness" directs us to a variety of acts of mind demanding high degrees of self-consciousness in the making and in our responding to the making, so the concept provides a significant defense for constructivist values. Moore is an ideal exemplar of this alternative mode of sensual life because of her efforts to evoke feelings that are not grounds for the conceptual labors of mind but continuous with them. Producing those feelings is, for her, a matter of bringing poetry as close to discursive prose as possible so that her constructions directly offer themselves as modes of thinking rather than as efforts to produce dramatic stagings of represented feelings. Poetry becomes continuous with powers of reflection grounded in both situations and arguments that occupy space in the real world.

I have to assume that my audience knows both the rhetoric behind Impressionist painting and the style sponsored by the rhetoric. Then they can judge the possible affinities with how the New Materialists stage the convocation of matter and mind—in documents ranging from the practical to the ecstatic. For examples of the practical, I correlate statements from the Introduction and the closing essay of *The Art of the Real: Visual Studies and the New Materialism.*

The common denominator of contemporary materialisms, realist or not, could perhaps be described as the belief that objects and things, in general, act outside of the regime of the signifier and have the potential to affect one another outside of any reference system (2).

In the most general terms, the new materialism asks us to rethink the "agency" of the world and the objects that populate it, while at the same time rethinking our own "agency" in terms of its human uniqueness. It asks us to think about a new kind of animacy, relatedness, and hierarchy in the world (172). In effect, the New Materialisms call attention to the plenitude that is the life of the senses. And they assign much of what had been considered a distinctive realm of consciousness to the agency responsive to a globalized animacy. The "Introduction" to Diana Coole and Samantha Frost's anthology giving the movement a name and a telos provides an elaborate development of what is involved in identifying with these new versions of agency:

> The prevailing ethos of new materialist ontology is consequently more positive and constructive than critical or negative; it sees its task as creating new concepts and images of nature that affirm matter's immanent vitality. Such thinking … avoids dualisms or dialectical reconciliation by espousing a monological account of emergent, generative, material being. … For materiality is always something more than 'mere' matter: an excess, force, vitality, relationality, or difference that renders matter active, self-creative, productive, unpredictable. (8–9)[2]

Finally the ecstatic mode cultivated by some New Materialist Work provides perhaps the best analogue to how the Impressionists seem to have idealized their own processes as events where the energies of composition merge with the intricate plenitude provided by the senses:

> Such theories thus introduce elements of creative contingency, meaning, difference, efficacy, and a limited freedom for improvisation or resistance into nature before cognition begins. … As a consequence, the human species, and the qualities of self-reflection, self-awareness, and rationality traditionally used to distinguish mind from the rest of nature, may now seem little more than contingent and provisional forms or processes within a broader evolutionary or cosmic productivity. (20)

One might say, in this context, that the great accomplishment of Impressionism was releasing the studio-bound painter's mind to its possibilities of identifying with the powers of light and the dynamic energies of nature's capacity to gather incredibly diverse particles into momentary wholes. But these very dynamics of mind made subsequent painters wonder if these intensities could ever be represented adequately by any kind of focus on natural appearance. This wondering, in turn, helps justify the range of Modernist critiques of Impressionism that could otherwise be dismissed as strategic self-interesting grumbling trying to make a place for whatever innovations the critic or painter deemed important. Let me first cite Hermann Bahr as he tries to create cultural roles for the various Expressionist movements coming to dominate the German art world:

> The newest school of painting consists of small sects and groups that vituperate each other, yet one thing they all have in common. They agree only on this point, that they all turn away from Impressionism, turn even against it ... Whenever Impressionism tries to simulate reality, striving for Illusion, they all agree in despising this procedure. (Bahr 1925) [117 art in theory]

Very few ambitious younger painters would disagree with Bahr. But we have to turn to defenders of Cubism like Albert Gleizes and Jean Metzinger to encounter more careful analysis:

> After [Manet] there was a cleavage. The yearning for realism was split into superficial realism and profound realism. The former belongs to the Impressionists ...; the latter to Cézanne. ... Here [in Impressionism] the retina predominates over the brain; they were aware of this and, to justify themselves, gave credit to the incompatibility of the intellectual faculties and artistic feeling. ... If [Cézanne] did not himself reach those regions where profound realism merges insensibly into luminous spirituality, at least he dedicated himself to the art of giving our instinct a plastic consciousness.

In many respects, this giving an instinct a mode of consciousness is my theme. Look at how the younger painters found inspiration in the shift from the retinal to the constructive. One could cite, for example, the whole of Braque's "Thoughts on Painting," from which I extract two concise statements: "the subject is not the object; it is the new unity, the lyricism which stems entirely from the means employed," and "The senses deform, the mind forms. ... There is no certainty except in what the mind conceives" (art 214–215). Then there is Guillaume Apollinaire teasing out another binary opposition between the retinal and the compositional: "Scientific cubism ... is the art of painting new structures out of elements not from the reality of sight, but from the reality of insight. All men have a sense of this interior reality. A man does not have to be cultivated in order to conceive, for example, of a round form" (189).

This catalogue in which I indulge becomes relevant for poetry because it helps understand why virtually all the major Modernist poets early in their career came to treat Imagism as also closer to a retinal art than any mode of work that is committed to presenting what can be thought of as the mental energy responsible for the dynamics of inner life. Williams remarked on the Whistleresque features of Imagism and Pound wrote in his great essay on Arnold Dolmetsch, "Impressionism has reduced us to such a dough-like state of receptivity that that we have ceased to like concentration. ... The whole flaw of impressionist or emotional music as opposed to pattern music" is that it is "like a drug" because it "works from the outside, in from the nerves and the sensorium upon the self" (LE 433–434). Finally, there is Stevens's "Metaphors of Magnifico" with its gradual collapse into mere images as "the meaning escapes" (CPP 16).

Critics have yet to ask with sufficient intensity what modes of experience, what values, and what plausible visions of our capacities as human beings we can see emerging because of this commitment to the mind's making—in poetry as well as in painting. Yet the question looms with increasing urgency because of the challenges the New Materialisms pose to any kind of discourse about mind that is not aligned with how material life shapes consciousness.[3] There are two probable reasons, beyond the turn of fashion, for this lack of intense questioning in relation to the reading of poetry. First, it is simply difficult to separate in art what Paul Klee called "the powers which do the forming" from the product that the form establishes (367). How can we separate the mental energies or inner life from where the emotions and thoughts are generated within material contexts not quite accessible to self-consciousness. I hope to address this issue as I interpret the three Moore poems in the conclusion to this essay— "An Egyptian Pulled Glass Bottle in the Shape of a Fish," "A Grave," and "An Octopus." But readings cannot be enough because the reliance of so many Modernist painters and writers on modes of spiritualism has become a substantial embarrassment, especially to those who love their work. So we need a second argument attempting to provide a defensible model for art devoted to critiques of the retinal principle and the reliance on representation which follows from that principle. This is where Hegel's account of "inner sensuousness" comes in because, as C.D Blanton pointed out to me, Hegel finesses his own idealism here. The binary is not between mind and matter but between two modes of sense—sense dependent on perception and empathy and sense dependent on those feelings and emotions that more directly involve the mind's creative activity. That binary in turn makes it possible to go beyond Hegel by treating all art that deals primarily with structural relations as involving a distinctive form of sensuousness because it asks us to concentrate on feelings directly emerging from those relations rather than deriving from the evocation of particulars. Why Moore so often relies on syllabics rather than speech rhythms will be a case in point.

Hegel's *Lectures on Aesthetics* define three major forms of art that capture the adventures of spirit as its place in history becomes increasingly articulate. First there are symbolic forms, represented primarily by Egyptian architecture, where artists can only manifest spirit in the work of deforming nature as spirit tries and fails to externalize its own felt imperatives to impose human shapes on external nature. Then there is the triumph of classical art. Here the spirit finds a home in the artist's capacities for sensuous representation—both of scenes and of images of the hero. There emerges complete harmony between spirit and its sense of having a site in which to dwell. But spirit cannot be content in the long run with defining itself in relation to external reality. So Romantic art finds a home for spirit in the inner life, in the inner sensuousness established by recognizing how spirit goes beyond representation to the conditions of desire and exalted feeling underlying the rendering of sense experience.

The following statements make clear how Hegel found in this alternative mode of sensuousness feelings that engage us in the compositional energies making works of art present considerably more than modes of picture thinking:

> Spirit does not stop at the mere apprehension of the external world by sight and hearing; it makes it into an object for its inner being which then is itself driven, once again in the form of sensuousness, to realize itself in things, and relates itself to them as desire. (36)

> These sensuous shapes and sounds appear in art not merely for the sakes of themselves and their immediate shape, but with the aim, in this shape, of affording satisfaction to the higher spiritual interests, since they have the power to call forth from all the depths of consciousness a sound and an echo in the spirit. In this way the sensuous aspect of art is spiritualized, since the spirit appears in art as made sensuous. (39)

I have to be careful here. I cannot claim that Hegel influenced Modernist poets, although ideas spawned by his work were part of European discussion of aesthetics in the first decades of the twentieth century. Instead I claim that Hegel on inner sensuousness provides one model for appreciating what the artists and writers were after in their rejections of retinal realism and "emotional music" deriving from outside the creative act. The concept of "inner sensuousness" has at least two important functions: First, this concept rationalizes both the self-consciousness and the impersonality basic to so much Modernist poetry because it transforms those features into distinctive modes of feeling that depersonalize how creativity emerges and so require us to separate the artifice from the dramatic situations in which the self might be implicated. From this perspective, creativity might be most fully experienced by distancing the empirical subject and stressing complex relational surfaces. Modes of making are the richest ways of aligning feelings to something like inner sensuousness responsive to something other than even the finest modes of picture thinking. And impersonality forces self-consciousness to engage with materials that demand shapes to experience more capacious and more penetrating than can be provided by how appearances make present to the senses. Second, the concept of "inner sensuousness" can be important as a model of valuing what the modernists achieve, because it locates entire domains of feeling and thinking that are compatible with naturalism but still do not fit any materialist account of how minds are constituted. And in that resistance to materialism, this approach to poetry clarifies also the work of contemporary poets like Geoffrey O'Brien and even Lisa Robertson who completely reject the epiphanic naturalist poetics that is the heir of Imagism.[4]

We might look initially at Moore's prose in order to see how attuned she is to what Hegel depicts. Here it helps to begin with her love affair with prose in figures like Hardy and Bacon. She imagines a prose that resists lyrical effusion, but at the same time has sufficient energy to make the reader's role considerably more than resting at the level of what the prose describes or summarizes. A prose base tilts writing toward emotions connected with judgment rather than sheer expressiveness. For Moore, there has to be accurate outer sensuousness before writing can be a matter of the inner life. So she writes to Yvor Winters, an ideal interlocutor on this topic, "For the litterateur, prose is a step beyond poetry I feel, and then there is another poetry beyond that."[5] Reaching this other poetry requires using a prose perspective so that one can resist the temptation to treat the world as mirror for the expressive self. Far better to cultivate a depressive "honesty" like Eliot's that at least makes him "a faithful friend of the objects he portrays; altogether unlike the sentimentalist, who stabs them in the back while pretending affection."[6] And H.D's poems rely on "an unequivocal faithfulness to fact" that frees the mind to develop a "reserve" that is "a concomitant of intense feeling, not the cause of it" (80). The cause is the active imagination making present through foregrounded technique "a fastidious prodigality—an apparent starkness which is opulence ... for the balanced speech of poetry" (113).

A sensibility founded on prose matters because it satisfies judgments about accuracy honoring the world's details and reducing the temptation to effusive ontology. More important, prose also matters because it prepares the way for that other poetry beyond the world of fact. That poetry approaches inner sensuousness because it is based not on observing details but on feeling relational structures within situations, which imagination proposes their own mode of reality. There is a special kind of imagination, found in Bacon and in W.C Williams, able "to see resemblances in things which are dissimilar" (56). For such writers, nature seems to invite a free play that extends its parameters without losing a sense of groundedness for the writer. To Moore, this involves the possibility of developing imaginative sites capable of presenting the actual within the real. Hence her eloquent responsiveness to the sculptor Alfeo Faggi:

> The preoccupation today is with the actual. The work therefore of Alfeo Faggi … is especially for the thinker, presenting as it does solidly and in a variety a complete contrast to the fifty-fathom deep materialism of the hour. Spiritual imagination … [seems] to derive feeling from the subject rather than having to bring feeling to it as in the theme which is palpable and easily comprehensible. (73)

"Such distilled impersonal spiritual force" affords "a reverence for mystery" which "is not a vague, invertebrate thing." This force produces the "only realm in which experience is able to corroborate the fact that the real can also be actual" (74). For Moore, there is an aspect of the psyche that longs for states where Platonic forms seem compatible with active analytic intelligence.

But she knows she cannot simply affirm Platonic metaphysics. If a work of art is to "acknowledge the spiritual forces which have made it" (CP 48), that acknowledgement must take place in a mode of sheer activity that has no foundation except a condition of experience. For her, such conditions of experience depend on the domain of compositional intricacy as establishing its own emotional field. H.D's sense of the mind as concomitant of intense feeling rather than its cause is one prime example of this distinctive site. We find that same sense of the space of writing in a letter about Joyce's *Dubliners* as "pretty nearly a manual … of the fundamentals of composition" (Letters, 164), in part because "the closing sentences of every one of the stories … haunts you and makes you investigate the mechanism of the writing" (Letters, 168). Williams is an even more powerful example because to read him is to enter a "self-imposed discipline" that "preserves the atmosphere of a moment, into which the impertinences of life cannot intrude" (59–60).

I want to flesh out these concerns of Moore's by testing how they produce variants of "inner sensuousness" in three distinctive poetic spaces that dramatize the continuing powers of modernist art to counter the rhetorics of materialism. The most radical counter to materialism might be the most elemental of Moore's concerns—the concern for how syllabics work differently from more expressive rhythms that appeal to the body's reception of what the mind composes. Moore's own creativity becomes one more ontological fact about her reaction to what of the scene her imagination can honor.

The syllabic scheme of "Egyptian Pulled Glass Bottle" is 4, 6, 12, 12 units in each of the two stanzas:

> Here we have thirst
> and patience, from the first,
> and art, as in a wave held up for us to see
> in its essential perpendicularity;

Then the second stanza:

> not brittle but
> intense—the spectrum, that
> spectacular and nimble animal the fish,
> whose scales turn aside the sun's sword by their polish[7]

On the discursive level, the poem is quite straightforward, almost too straightforward for those who like the kind of surface drama that sets an image in emotional context. "Here" in this sculpture, and perhaps in viewing this sculpture, we do not have an image in flux but an object proclaimed for its resistance to temporal drama. Analogously Moore suggests a huge gap between the inspiration for the poem as emerging from her own experience and the experience of the poem produced by the maker's intelligence and craft. Here the force of this craft depends on two levels of evocation. One is pictorial and associational: It seems that readers have to link thirst to the bottle and patience to the figure of fish out of its home in the water (and so thirsty in a different way)? The other is what the work in the artifact evokes, ultimately as a manifestation of the difference between life, where the fish might return to water, and art, where patience and thirst keep oxymoronic company as life and art long for completion in each other's condition. The second stanza then asserts the ways the art object produces its own version of life. "Brittle" is a condition of the artifact. "Intense" is a psychological condition, here appropriated for the art object's capacity to come alive as producing a spectrum of colors while evoking the scales by which sculpted fish resists the sun's violence.

But we have to see that on the discursive level the poem is as much promise as achievement. Where is the intensity? And what kind of actual power can the art work actually possess? What might enable it to establish resistance to the sun something more than a physical property of its polish? Perhaps the intensity begins with the intricate folds of reference for the deictic "here." "Here" refers not only to the indicated art object and its audience but to the properties of the poem and to how readers might negotiate those properties. The art object is, from the start, inseparable from acts of construction on the part of author and readers. That activity of construction, that location of intensity, consists mainly in how the manner of the poem puts the mind in matter and matter in mind—primarily by the work accomplished by two features of material presence—the enjambments and the dynamics of syllabic form.

The enjambments place the reader within the process of moving from line to line, as if they had to search for what might complete the line. Heavy enjambment abstracts language from ordinary utterance and makes it seem the responder is responsible for the product. In effect, enjambment compliments the ambiguity of the deictic and transforms "here" into a characterization of responsiveness: we have to see into the work rather than just see through it. This same process of addressing the reader's sense of constructing the meaningfulness she finds is sharply intensified by having to count syllables as one's means of fleshing out what gives the lines their physicality. Syllabics produce a relational force almost entirely dependent on the mind's agreeing to count elemental particles of meaning, almost as a reversal of quantum unpredictability.

Notice the weight syllabics establish for "patience." It is the only multisyllabic word among the first two lines. And that weight does not cancel the force of the rhyme but counters its powers of closure because there is now a competing system of aural organization. Perhaps this sense of responding to multiple constructed systems is one feature of art's perpendicularity. But that perpendicularity is only fully established by what the mind is asked to do with the pair of closing lines in each stanza. The sharp diversity between line 3, all monosyllabic, and line 4, with one word "perpendicularity" containing seven syllables, reminds us of just how intelligently poetry can play with its constitutive elements, and, in that process, sharply reinforce its central argument, as argument rather than image. Then, in the other stanza, the penultimate line brilliantly sets off the monosyllable "fish," by having intensely rhythmic multiple-syllable words as its contextualizing features. This insistence on artifice does not deny life but alters its status, so that the fish itself has to signify both its figural existence as a physical element and its powers as an art object to have its scales turn back the sun's sword. Then the way is prepared for another basically monosyllabic line, this time asserting[8] physicality on every level, just because it has the power to absorb all the mental play in the poem.[9] Even the two two-syllable words here produce an elegant balance for the two key operators in the poem—the power of polish to produce a transformation of the sun's sword.

"A Grave" is a much more intense and complicated poem that I think directly engages the phenomenon of negation as a means by which the mind registers its difficulties and adjustments as it tries to find a satisfying relation to the world of fact.[10] Some negation is governed simply by disappointed desire. But here the range and amount of negation suggests something else. The negations seem directly activities of mind's dialogue with itself as if feels its way into the recalcitrant materiality of this version of the sea:

> Man looking into the sea, ...
> but you cannot stand in the middle of this;
> the sea has nothing to give but a well excavated grave.
> ⋮
> moving together like the feet of water-spiders as if there were
> no such thing as death.
> The wrinkles progress among themselves in a phalanx
> beautiful under networks of foam,
> and fade breathlessly while the sea rustles in and out of the
> seaweed;

the birds swim through the air at top speed, emitting cat calls
as heretofore—
the tortoise-shell scourges about the feet of the cliffs, in motion
beneath them;

There are many features that I do not understand in this poem, although even my lack of understanding contributes to my fascination with it. Primary among these features is the form and the imagined setting. Why are syllabic counts continually being altered, and why are the lines in the last third of the poem all so expansive that they overrun the margin. Perhaps the lineation plays on the mind's needs here to find at least some awkward order for its tendencies to run over any boundaries that nature might set for it. And how does one understand the context for the first sentence? What is the relation between the first two general clauses and the use of the second-person. Who speaks and to whom?

What understanding I can muster depends on treating the poem's four sentences as the units providing structure for this overheated confrontation between the persons who look on the sea and the sea's refusal to give anything to that glance except a well-excavated grave. So I take the first sentence as sheer summary statement of the players—man, the desire to get to a lyric "you" as addressee, and the overall resistance of the sea to any of the distinctions about persons the poem seems eager to make. We may not know the dramatic situation from this sentence but we do have a pretty good idea of the dilemma "man" faces. And we realize that the negations in each of its two final lines will be an important feature of the confrontation with this sea-grave. (Perhaps only the power to wield these negatives can give consciousness any place at all in this situation.)

It should come as no surprise that the second sentence tries to change the focus from the sea as grave to the firs that line the shore. This speaking wants a lyric encounter and not this confrontation with the sea as grave. But the recalcitrance of the sea continues to fascinate, forcing series of analogies on the sentence that move from the trees saying nothing, to treating that saying nothing as a sign of repression, to the sea's refusal of any psychologizing for its identity as a collector, quick to return a rapacious look. That last line of the sentence returns to the fiercely impersonal indicative of the first sentence. So again, the third sentence begins by looking away, now in time rather than in space as odd negative versions of the imperfect tense dominate. And again, the sentence seems violently to yoke two separate domains—one concerned with others beside you and the other focusing on how the activity of the rowers reveals an unconsciousness that allows them to become so absorbed in the oars moving in the water than they can imagine that "there is no such thing as death." Here the negative is associated with the decision to pursue appearances rather than confront the reality of death.

It seems at first that the final sentence begins to revel in this unconsciousness by proposing all run-on expansive lines that treat the appearances of the surface as moments for imaginative reveling in the water and the versions of life which it sustains, so long as one does not regard anything more of the scene than conjoined appearances. Yet it seems that consciousness cannot stop also setting its own imperatives against what underlies those surfaces. Consciousness must try to dispel the comforts of being unconscious. This is why when Moore's gorgeous last sentence allows the ocean the subject position, everything changes. The responding mind cannot encounter these surfaces without finally drawing contrasts between the ocean that it enjoys seeing and the ocean that it knows can only be thought in negative terms because of its refusals to heed any lyrical demands, however long the lines become:

> The ocean
> advances as usual, looking as if it were not that ocean in which
> dropped things were bound to sink—
> in which if they turn and twist, it is neither with volition nor
> consciousness.

Notice how the negations do quite different kinds of work here. The first negation seems to sustain appearance by denying the truth of the nature of dropped things. Yet this negation can no longer support the illusion because it yields to the quest of mind all along to see what it also fears to see in the ocean's look. So the first negation generates the much more terrifying negations in the last line as the poem seems obligated to state what it has been resisting all along: the grave is absolute and mocks every hint that the sea can be a source of pleasure. The final negatives then seem the other side of a consciousness that cannot be content with appearances, even if it then has to confront its distance from the reality of death. There are simply no human predicates that we can apply in order to interpret this turning and this twisting. The only thing the sea offers is a sheer physical presence that makes one doubt that any full present tense can sustain what human beings need as sources of connection.

Yet "A Grave" may not want to have sheer bleakness dominate at the end. Those final negations also suggest that consciousness and even volition still have a place because they ultimately have imagined in this poem what completely resists their place in the natural order. Isolating the lack of volition and consciousness (with "consciousness" last) seems also to recognize their presence as forces that challenge all that a pure naturalism has to demand. There can be no doubt that matter wins. But matter does not explain the process of the poem, and hence the organization of inner sensuousness, especially the way consciousness struggles with the negatives that it also makes possible. So I think this utter emptying of any claim to pleasure by the end oddly confirms the significance of the passions that negation organizes, and even celebrates, as the difficult, focused attention by mind on mind's lack of congruence with sheer matter.

"An Octopus" takes us on a completely different mental journey from "A Grave"—to a model of plenitude based on identification rather than contrast. Here the mind's dynamics are most visible in its constant inventive elaboration of a space of resemblance linking quite disparate features of the scene, apparently by chance. But chance would not sustain this extended meditation. These lines celebrate the power to construct resemblances among sensations that are probably not given in the mode of sensation. Instead the play among resemblances allows the mind awareness of the feelings involved in being able to draw its own unique satisfactions from its capacities for synthesis. I cite two samples from the closing passage where the poem tries to test its own resources to articulate the multiplicity of effects and spatial relations establishing the mountain's uniqueness. The first celebrates the figure of the octopus as growing out of the poem's concern for proliferating the power of the various scenic details over the mind:

> Relentless accuracy is the nature of this octopus
> with its capacity for fact.
> "Creeping slowly as with meditated stealth,
> its arms seeming to approach from all directions," (CP 76)

And the second raises to figure the sheer power of those sensuous details:

> the white volcano with no weather side;
> the lightning flashing at its base,
> rain falling in the valleys and snow falling on the peak—
> the glassy octopus symmetrically pointed,
> its claw cut by the avalanche
> "with a sound like the crack of a rifle,
> In a curtain of powdered snow launched like a waterfall." (CP 76)

Let me try to summarize the relational features that this passage draws together. First there is the intensifying of quotations that have been spread throughout the poem. In T.S Eliot's poetry, quotations function as allusions that have pertinent and distinct meaning in their original contexts. Moore, on the other hand, incorporates statements by others so that they function primarily to bring the mountain into the space of discourse. There is no call to provide contexts evoked by the original statements in order to enrich the experience of the poem. What does enrich the poem considerably is the sense that what has been said becomes a part of the mountain: its physical force is as real in cultural space as it is in the observing. For the object as object can be modified by the thoughts and emotions that become a part of its record of its impact on the observers. The emotion becomes something that a collective body has fully experienced, so that it becomes a demand on the poet to make visible not only the mountain, but its power to move others to produce verbal correlates to what they see and think.

Taking up this challenge to render the experience of the mountain as cultural object requires not only description, but an effort to capture possible rhythms and orientations of focus that make this experience something that regularly moves other people. The reality of this mountain demands Cubist-like strategies that gather what it offers to various perspectives. Quotations afford some of these perspectives. But we cannot stop with the words of others. We have to see what they are seeing under an authority that helps us feel what generates the quotations in the first place. So, Moore weaves into the quotations a dialogue between how the mountain constitutes a magisterial space and how that space channels senses of temporal endurance. These quotations contrast intensely realized particulars like the trees with how these particulars are contained within the sense of the mountain as a whole "planed by ice and polished by the wind." Then this final passage has the language of the poet take over by testing what it can add to those quotations, before being once again subsumed in quotation. The movement here calls on resources that derive from dramatizing changes in perspective, from rendering the comprehensiveness of the experience as a whole because it solicits an intricate series of rhythmic devices, and from moving out beyond the space of perception to a self-conscious freedom of simile that may afford the ultimate value of paying close attention.

Think of the point of view in these last seven lines after the quotations as itself a mobile locus for intense self-reflexive feeling. First, the rendered point of view takes in the mountain completely as volcano; then it moves from base to valleys to peaks, only to return to the whole in the form of a sharply rendered and impressively accurate visual metaphor, the glassy octopus. We also have to recognize how the poem celebrates, through rhythmic intensity, the syntactic balance as it stresses its own capacities to honor how the details come together. There are few better integrated and balanced expressions of scope than "rain falling in the valleys and snow falling on the peak," the only line in the sequence that deploys a pronounced caesura. Here the rhythm brings the body to the mind's capacious grasp.

After this, Moore can prepare the stage for another kind of quotation. The poet's words culminate in the contrast between the vision of the whole as "glassy octopus" and a fascination with the metaphoric detail of the claw cut by the avalanche. Then the poet's words create almost a protective dome within which the quoted voice can exercise its pleasure in transposing quite particular impressions of the physical event of the avalanche:

> its claw cut by the avalanche
> "with a sound like the crack of a rifle,
> In a curtain of powdered snow launched like a waterfall."

Most of the quotations have taken up impressive general features of the experience the mountain affords. But this final quotation seems to do the poet's job better than the poet can in registering the impact of striking moments of attention. Here we have sensations of sound blending into a visual metaphor that in turn produces a dramatic simile. This mediation on capacious space permits also celebrating unique moments in time by which the mountain calls out to be appreciated. One hears the avalanche, or the condition of avalanche over time, before the mind develops metaphors for the sight, and for generating similes that give the feel for what this sight involves. Here the physical and hypothetical share the same kind of union as the quoted and the seen because the poem produces an affective field stressing the relationship between the facticity of the mountain and the imaginings that are fundamental to its sense of value.

Yet even this mode of satisfaction does not suffice. Moore seems to have thought that perhaps she had bound consciousness too closely to what was there to see. So, she changes the situation with one brilliant closing alliterative simile. The simile fits the scene and gives a momentary immediacy to an enduring condition. Yet it also accomplishes the more important task of celebrating at the end how the labor of accurate rendering earns, and has always earned, the freedom to produce figurative speech that simply continues the spirit of description by bringing the full resources of figurative language to bear as having been latent in this celebration from the start. Moore realizes modes of making that bring to bear the most visible, public, and concrete features of how activities generated by the making can complement the world of fact.

Perhaps what Impressionism needed all along was this attitude toward quotation. Such reminders of inner sensuousness shift the focus from the retinal to the social by reminding us of what is involved in fully satisfying the energies of consciousness to elaborate the significance of what is before it in ways that maintain a lively interchange between what construction allows the object and what the object invites as construction. And quotation, or the spirit of construction underlying quotation, allows a constant reminder that perpendicularity affords its own conditions of dialogue and participation.

Notes

1. I think some relations between Impressionism and the early Imagist collections are fairly obvious, primarily the commitment to how phenomena appear in a given moment and to the ideal of composition as fleshing out the moment where the composing mind feels at one with the actual energies of the natural scene. But I am also interested in criticizing indirectly the line of twentieth century poetry that develops Imagism's sense of developing single scenes or situations until one can resolve the feelings called up by a summary image. Moore thought of this kind of poetry as Romanticism by other means. I do not develop this argument much at all because I have done so in an account of Pound's resistance to the painterly logic of Imagism even in work within *Des Imagistes*. See my "Paul Stasi and Park".

2. Because this passage distinguishes excess of matter from mere matter, it provides a telling example of what Kenneth Burke in his *Rhetoric of Motives* calls "the paradox of substance." Burke argues that virtually any ontology will have to finesse the need to have its substance term, like matter, play two roles—the role of naming the nature of the stuff making up the world and the role of naming the vital principle that animates this stuff but also therefore cannot be reduced to what it animates.

3. I elaborate my objections to New Materialist arguments in my essay and review of Noble, see also Andrew Cole.

4. This is not to say that these contemporaries are not eager to write as allies of a general spirit of materialism, as is especially the case with Robertson. But their work issues difficult challenges that materialism address intricacies in how imagination constructs works of art.

5. Letters, 192. I have to add here that I have written about these three poems in previous essays, but not the same way or supported by the same arguments. I seem to be obsessed with getting these poems right. See my *The Art of Modernist Poetry* and my essay for Michael Soto.
6. The complete Prose of Marianne Moore, 35.
7. Collected Poems, 83.
8. I have to apologize for not copying Moore's poems more elaborately but copyright charges for them are exorbitant. So I will only cite the passages absolutely crucial for my argument. I have to hope that my readers will consult the two complete poems I talk about in an edition or online where they are readily available.
9. Mark Noble's *American Poetic Materialism*, shows all materialisms founder on the problem that the subject who is deconstructed by the play of matter has to have the traditional powers of a subject in order to make coherent descriptions of this incoherence. Here Moore plays on what mind can do to specify the significance of matter.
10. Given this difficulty, I am especially grateful to several critics who have engaged this poem, especially Jeanne Heuving, *Omissions Are Not Accidents* (Detroit: Wayne State 1992) and Jeredith Merrin, Re-Seeing the Sea: Marianne Moore's "A Grave" as a Woman Writer's Re-Vision. *Marianne Moore: Woman and Poet*, ed. Patricia Willis. Copyright © 1990 by the National Poetry Foundation, Inc.

References

Altieri, Charles. 2006. *The Art of Twentieth-Century American Poetry: Modernism and After*. Oxford: Wiley-Blackwell.
Bahr, Hermann. 1925. *Expressionism*, trans. R.T. Gribble. London: F. Henderson.
Burke, Kenneth. 1969. *Rhetoric of Motives*. Berkeley: University of California Press.
Coole, D., and S. Frost. 2010. *New Materialisms: Ontology, Agency and Politics*. New York: Duke University Press.
Gleizes, Albert, and Metzinger Jean. From Cubism. *Art Theory*. June 26, 2017. Web.
Hegel, J.F.W. 1975. *Lectures on Aesthetics*, 2 vols., trans. T.M. Knox. Oxford: Clarendon Press.
Heuving, Jeanne. 1992. *Omissions Are Not Accidents*. Detroit: Wayne State University Press.

Klee, Paul. 1969. *On Modern Art*. London: Faber and Faber.

Merrin, Jeredith. 1990. 'Re-Seeing the Sea: Marianne Moore's "A Grave" as a Woman Writer's Re-Vision'. In *Marianne Moore: Woman and Poet*, ed. Patricia Willis. Copyright © 1990 by the National Poetry Foundation, Inc.

Moore, Marianne. 1986. *The Complete Prose of Marianne Moore*, ed. Patricia Willis. London: Vicking.

———. 1951. *Collected Poems*. London: Macmillan.

Noble, Mark. 2015. *American Poetic Materialism: From Whitman to Stevens*. Cambridge: Cambridge University Press.

Pound, Ezra. 1968. *Literary Essays*, ed. and with an Introduction by T.S. Eliot. New York: New Directions.

Rothman, Roger, and Verstegen Ian. 2015. *The Art of the Real: Visual Studies and New Materialisms*. Newcastle upon Tyne: Cambridge Scholar Publishing.

Stevens, Wallace. 1990. *The Collected Poems*. New York: Vintage Books.

13

Intimidated Thought: The Novelistic Conditions of Modernism

Michael D'Arcy

In his recent book, C.D. Blanton suggests an underlying, if sometimes unstated, feature of recent work on nineteenth- and twentieth-century literature—a return to philosophical problems as informing the representational dilemmas of the literary culture of this period. More specifically, suggested here is the view of modernism as responding to philosophical problems inherited from Kantian and post-Kantian philosophy, namely the problem of empty forms, the inability of forms to engage with concrete life. On this account, modernist poetry suggests "the need to negotiate a crisis of knowledge formally," a project that leads to the series of "abstract instruments" of the modernist "negated epic." The conclusion Blanton draws is that "No literary form concerned with totality could ever remain merely literary," and this is because the larger issue here—of the limits of thought, of thought's separation from concrete life—is framed in terms of the "prior problem

M. D'Arcy (✉)
St. Francis Xavier University, Antigonish, NS, Canada
e-mail: mdarcy@stfx.ca

© The Author(s) 2018   **285**
A. Falcato and A. Cardiello (eds.), *Philosophy in the Condition of Modernism*,
https://doi.org/10.1007/978-3-319-77078-9_13

of the universal in bourgeois culture," as exemplified in the aporias of Kantian and post-Kantian philosophy.[1]

Of course, it is inaccurate to say that there is a priority assigned to philosophical problems in this strand of thought. In the critical tradition at issue here, following from Georg Lukács's seminal *History and Class Consciousness* (1923), it is recognized that the "crisis of knowledge" of Kantian and post-Kantian philosophy registers social and material conditions of modern culture—the reification of social life, the specialization and fragmentation intrinsic to regimes of social and economic organization. The aporetic scenario involved here is framed by Lukács as follows: "the specialization of skills leads to the destruction of every image of the whole" and yet "the need to grasp the whole—at least cognitively—cannot die out."[2] The problem of the absent or inexpressible totality is thus not just the philosophical problem of what to make of Kant's thing-in-itself, but also the problem of what Blanton calls "the epistemologically banished site of material determination,"[3] a social totality that modernist literature encodes even as it registers the impossibility of representing it. Following from this framework, recent scholarship on modernism provides various versions of the scenario of the absent totality: "the metabindungsroman encodes the impossibility of representing capitalism's never ending form via the offices of finite biographical form"; "a text strains to evince a field of reference that it cannot name."[4]

If this is familiar territory for those working in the field of modernist studies, it is useful for my purposes here to call attention to the specific philosophical background to the scenario of modernism's absent totality, as this allows us to frame the question of how this strand of critical thinking about modernism may be related to the notion of literary theory. By this latter term, I mean specifically accounts of literature informed by the twentieth-century turn to reflection on language and signifying systems—for example, the structuralism and poststructuralism that follows from the work Ferdinand de Saussure.[5] Responding, either implicitly or explicitly, to this question, recent materialist accounts of modernism suggest that this twentieth-century theoretical turn may be seen as a chapter in the history of literature's constitutive involvement with philosophical problems, or antinomies, formulated in the work of Kant and its aftermath. For example, referring to this post-Kantian "eidaesthetic itinerary" of literature, and to the apparent displacement of "traditional literature" by theory starting in the 1960s, Nicholas Brown writes, "the 'end' of literature would refer to the migration of its philosophical excess, the absolute to which each work refers without ever managing to contain, over into theory once and for all."[6] The suggestion here, then, is that theory, understood as the turn to reflection on language and signifying systems, is not necessarily incompatible either with the "eidaesthetic itinerary" of literature or the materialist project of thinking through the absent totality as a ground of literary production.[7]

There is, then, a relay suggested here between philosophy and theory in at least two senses. Theory takes over the eidaesthetic project located with literature in the wake of Kant; and, moreover, the emergence of theory is inscribed within an account of the antinomies of bourgeois thought and society instantiated in Kantian and post-Kantian philosophy. But this running together of philosophy and theory, this purported continuity between philosophical problems and the linguistic procedures of theory, does not sit well with prominent stands of twentieth-century theory. Paul De Man, for example, argues that literary theory "cannot be assimilated to" philosophy. The underlying interest of this insistence is familiar to readers of de Man—to resist the confusion between the operations of language and sensory intuition or perception. Literary theory, de Man writes, "emerges with the introduction of linguistic terminology in the metalanguage about literature. By linguistic terminology is meant a terminology that designates reference prior to designating the referent and...that considers reference as a function of language and not necessarily as an intuition. Intuition implies perception, consciousness, experience."[8] De Man's "The Rhetoric of Temporality" announces a similar linguistic reorientation of thought, away from "the dialectical relationship between subject and object": "this dialectical relationship is now located entirely in the temporal relationships that exist within a system of allegorical signs."[9] According to this line of thought, the advent of theory thus involves a shift from the philosophical problem of knowledge, conceived of in terms of a subject-object relationship—the problem, in other words, that subtends Lukács's account of the absent totality.

To refer to the notion of allegory here brings into view one crucial precursor of this strand of de Man's thought—Walter Benjamin's thinking about language. In his 1916 "On the Program of the Coming Philosophy" Benjamin calls for a linguistic reorientation of philosophy, one that departs from the overly limited conception of knowledge and experience descending from Kantian philosophy. The problem diagnosed here is the limitation of a "conception of knowledge as a relation between some sort of subject and objects," which involves an overly "shallow" vison of experience, a restriction of experience to the realm of appearances or phenomena, and thus to the forms and categories of the subject. As an antidote, Benjamin proposes that "A concept of knowledge gained from reflection on the linguistic nature of knowledge will create a corresponding concept of experience which will encompass realms that Kant failed to truly systematize," including, for example, "the realm of religion."[10] With this shift, the orienting terms and relationships are altered—instead of the scenario of knowledge or its limitations, organized around the subject-object problem, we get a linguistic scenario of reading, commentary, and citation. The activity of the subject is conceived of in these terms, rather than in terms of conceptual grasping, and this implies a form of receptivity or attentiveness—the subject must attend to the revelation of nature or spiritual being in language.[11] As in the case of de Man, this theoretical program, or linguistic turn, resists being amalgamated to the philosophical problem of knowledge subtending Lukács's account of the absent totality.

My point in drawing attention to this critical bifurcation is not to replace one theoretical tradition with another—arguing, for example, for a poststructuralist approach as opposed to a Marxist or materialist tack that takes important bearings from a reading of Kantian and post-Kantian philosophy. Rather, one of the interests of the following discussion is to show that within twentieth-century Marxist literary criticism, we see a shift from the subject-object problem of Kantian and post-Kantian philosophy to a linguistic reorientation of thought; and, in particular, I want to foreground problems of narrative form and accompanying dilemmas of reading in the work of Theodor Adorno. To be still more specific, my argument is that thinking through the problem of apparently excessive or purposeless description in the epic and the novel provides a path for Adorno to negotiate perceived impasses of philosophy. My discussion thus addresses an issue that has recently come to the forefront of thinking about nineteenth- and twentieth-century literature—that is, the status of apparently gratuitous detail or description.[12] Adorno's distinctive approach to this problem, I claim, is inseparable from a linguistic reorientation of philosophy, a shift that involves a mutation of the problem of knowledge underlying Lukács's accounts of the absent totality, as the work of philosophy is conceived as a practice of reading and reflection on language. The materialist motivation of Lukács's account of the antinomies of bourgeois thought is not relinquished here—the problem of the relationship between forms and material content still orients Adorno's linguistic turn of thought. It's just that this relationship between forms and material content is taken up as a problem of linguistic reference, rather than a problem of cognition understood on a model of sensible appearance or intuition.[13]

If this thinking through the dynamics of novelistic language serves as a response to impasses of philosophy, this suggests that this particular linguistic turn is not incompatible with the eidaesthetic project of literature that develops in the wake of Kant. My claim then is not that the linguistic turn of twentieth-century literary theory is necessarily inimical to a philosophical vocation for literature, the literary project of responding to antinomies formulated in philosophy. To say this much raises the question of how Adorno's novelistic linguistic turn, and my account of it, differs from the recent critical work referenced above in which the eidaesthetic vocation of literature converges with the linguistic turn of theory. As will become apparent in the discussion that follows, what Adorno's reflections on novelistic language provide is a framework to think beyond the scenario of representational failure that has oriented recent work on modernism hinging on the situation of the absent totality. Reading through Adorno's writings on the epic and the novel, it becomes apparent that he is not satisfied with this situation of representational failure and a turn to thinking through the dynamics of novelistic language is what allows him to gesture beyond this situation. Certain underlying motivations of this line of thought come into focus once we register its connections with Benjamin's linguistic turn. As with Benjamin's linguistic reorientation of philosophy,

Adorno's accounts of novelistic language, and the problem of reading that accompanies such language, are invested in developing a more expansive understanding of knowledge and experience—that is, beyond the overly circumscribed conception of knowledge and experience that undergirds accounts of the absent totality descending from Lukács.

In order to establish the specificity of Adorno's reading of novelistic language, I begin not with an account of modernism per se, but rather of nineteenth-century realism, Fredric Jameson's *The Antinomies of Realism*. To approach the relationship between modernism and philosophy in this way is not as incongruous as it may appear given that one of the implications of Jameson's book is that realism appears here as an inherently unstable form, subject to an undoing from within its own logic, and thus, as David Cunningham has noted, realism appears "increasingly as always already a kind of modernism in the making."[14] Jameson's book, as one would expect, turns on the scenario of the absent totality, even if this is largely implicit, recasting the absent totality, that which eludes narrative language, in terms of affective bodily states. Novelistic realism is seen here according to an opposition between a narrative impulse—which involves the linear temporality of succession with its characteristic verb tenses, such as the French simple past—and an antithetical "scenic impulse," instantiated in apparently superfluous description that disrupts the narrative and registers the claims of "affect" or "nameless bodily states." Jameson elaborates this opposition through reference to Roland Barthes's 1968 essay, "The Reality Effect": "This irreconcilable divorce between intelligibility and experience, between meaning and existence can be grasped as a fundamental feature of modernity...if it means something it can't be real, if it is real, it can't be absorbed by purely mental or conceptual categories."[15] Jameson's "scenic impulse," and the affect it registers, appears as a historically disruptive element, breaking apart the chronological temporality in which plot unfolds (the time of *récit*, the simple past in the French literary tradition), a disruption Jameson sees emerging around the mid-nineteenth century.[16]

Leaving aside the question of whether affect is the best term to describe this "contingency" that is inimical to narrative form, in order to bring into focus certain parameters of Jameson's argument we can notice a telling discrepancy between this account and Barthes's "The Reality Effect." In addressing apparently superfluous or meaningless details in nineteenth-century fiction, Barthes argues that such description functions as a signifier of "the category of the real," rather than an actual denotation of contingent contents. He thus sees concrete reality, as it is evoked, for example, in the literary and historical writing of the nineteenth century (Flaubert, Michelet), as an effect of signification, a "referential illusion," a disavowed "reality effect," rather than an index of an actual extra-textual immediacy or a reality external to signification. We have here then an example of a regressive "disintegration of the sign" in the name of a "referential plenitude," which runs contrary to Barthes's structuralist project invested in challenging the aesthetic of representation.[17] It is according to this analysis that Barthes speaks of the "mythic opposition of the true-to-life (the lifelike) and the intelligible," a formulation Jameson takes up in his description of the antinomy between "the narrative impulse" and the affect that de-structures nineteenth-century realistic fiction. In Jameson's hands, Barthes's "mythic" opposition between meaning and existence becomes "an irreconcilable divorce" between meaning and existence, intelligibility and the experience of "concrete reality."[18] What gets missed here is that for Barthes, this opposition is "mythic"—in other words, it is intrinsic to what Barthes calls "the ideology of our time." In his criticism of this ideology of representation, Barthes's structuralist procedure is to pull this discussion back into an analysis of the sign, of mechanisms of signification, against the countervailing cultural need to authenticate the real, in the name of a "referential plenitude."

At an initial level, we can see that we are dealing here with the difference between a structuralist moment in the thought of Barthes—in which the analysis of the mechanisms of signification, with a corresponding bracketing of the referent, is intrinsic to a critique of representation—and Jameson's Marxist appeal to a concrete material basis for cultural forms, a basis situated here in opposition to those narrative forms that both conceal and register that material basis. To come back to my point of departure, we can see this distinction as a fault line between the theoretical-linguistic turn informing Barthes's approach and the philosophically informed materialism of Lukács and

Jameson. What this difference comes down to, for our purposes, is two explanations of apparently meaningless details or description in fiction. Either these details are understood as part of an ideology of representation, mystifying reality effects, putting forth a phony unity of signifier and reference, pretending to directly access a self-evident concrete reality; or alternatively, gratuitous description is seen as an index of a material disruption of narrative form, conceived of, in Jameson's account, in terms of an intrusion of affect.

But there is an alternative approach suggested within twentieth-century Marxist literary criticism, a modernist thinking about narrative that, I want to argue, can be read as negotiating between the linguistic turn of theory and the philosophically inflected materialism descending from Lukács. I turn then to the work of Adorno, where apparently excessive narrative description is seen to function in a different way, that is beyond the choices of ideological mystification and formal disruption. In "On Epic Naiveté" (1943), which he composed with Max Horkheimer as part of the preparation of *Dialectic of Enlightenment* (1944), Adorno locates epic naiveté in digressions or descriptions that seem not to supplement narrative discourse, which Adorno insists is "characterized by general concepts," but to interrupt and suspend such discourse. The famous account of Achilles's shield in *The Iliad* serves as a paradigmatic example here, though Adorno's account indicates that he sees epic naiveté as manifest not only in works usually classified as epics but also in nineteenth-century poetry and fiction: "The impulse that drives Homer to describe a shield as though it were a landscape and to elaborate a metaphor until it becomes action, until it becomes autonomous and ultimately destroys the fabric of the narrative—that is the same impulse that repeatedly drove Goethe, Stifter, and Keller...to draw and paint instead of writing." Apparently purposeless details or descriptions, manifest in Homer and certain nineteenth-century literature, are read here as an index of an investment in the non-fungible, the non-exchangeable, the unique. Adorno thus sees epic naiveté as invested in the singularity of its referent and an aspiration to achieve an affinity between language and its referent: such naiveté involves "the element commonly referred to as objectivity or material concreteness...a stubborn clinging [*Halten*] to the particular when it has already been dissolved into the universal."[19]

At certain moments, this argument seems congruent with Jameson's account of the "scenic impulse" that de-structures nineteenth-century fiction, as when Adorno speaks of epic digression as destroying the fabric of the narrative. But the crucial distinction here is that for Adorno, epic naiveté, the proliferation of description or narrative digression, is located on the side of enlightenment; that is, epic naiveté actually supplements narrative discourse rather than dissolving it. He describes epic naiveté as an "anti-mythological enterprise," underlining that it acts as a corrective to narrative.[20] One way to understand this situation of epic naiveté as part of enlightenment is to register that for Adorno, epic naiveté is entangled with conceptual mediation and the problem of the separation between concepts and the non-conceptual, between forms and content. At the same time, epic naiveté expresses a fundamental aspiration of enlightenment: Adorno argues that epic naiveté's fixation on the singular, "what occurred once and only once," is "thought's innermost yearning, the logical form of something real that would not be enclosed by social domination and the classificatory thought modelled upon it: the concept reconciled with its object."[21]

We can frame the contradiction involved here in these terms: Adorno's epic naiveté clings to the particular in the interest of overcoming antinomies of bourgeois philosophy, such as the gap between forms and material concreteness. But this paradoxical enterprise occurs in a historical situation where the particular "has already been dissolved into the universal." Or in other words, there is a futility inscribed in the intention to access reality of epic naiveté: "The attempt to emancipate representation from reflective reason is language's attempt, futile from the outset, to recover from the negativity of its intentionality, the conceptual manipulation of objects, by carrying its defining intention to the extreme and allowing what is real to emerge in pure form, undistorted by the violence of classificatory ordering."[22] The naïve attempt to escape classificatory ordering or the mediation of the conceptual, is seen to be impossible—thought cannot escape from its structures. Framed in this way, epic naiveté appears as a somewhat pessimistic version of what Adorno elsewhere says about philosophy. We recognize the aspiration of epic naiveté—to allow "what is real to emerge in pure form"— in Adorno's description of philosophy and its constitutive naiveté in

Negative Dialectics: "A faith, as always subject to question, that philosophy would still be possible; that the concept could leapfrog the concept, the preparatory stages and the final touches, and thereby reach the non-conceptual, is indispensable to philosophy and therein lies something of the naiveté, which ails it. Otherwise it would have to capitulate and with it everything to do with the Spirit."[23]

Philosophy and narrative—the naiveté of philosophy and the naiveté of narrative language—thus seem to merge into each other, but at this point we can locate a bifurcation that enters Adorno's thought with the notion of epic naiveté. His description of the futility of epic naiveté, its impossible aspiration to access the real, suggests that this account is offering a version of the scenario of the absent totality or the antinomies of bourgeois thought diagnosed by Lukács. We are apparently dealing here, that is, with an account of the isolation of the forms of thought from their material conditions and the attendant limitation on representation and knowledge. But another path forward is also suggested briefly in "On Epic Naiveté." A narrative accounting of modernity is apparently offered here as a possibility, thanks, that is, to the functioning of epic naiveté: "only this kind of naiveté permits one to tell the story of the fateful origins of the late capitalist era."[24] The suggestion here is that storytelling or narrative may succeed in accounting for the reality of modernity where philosophical language does not.

This suggestion is fleshed out in Adorno's essay "Reading Balzac" (1961). The essay begins with the scenario of the absent totality, illustrated for Adorno in the situation of Balzac's *paysans de Paris*: "When the peasant comes to city, everything says 'closed' to him."[25] If thought is thus "locked out," unable "to grasp the totality of the real,"[26] what emerges in Balzac is not (or not just) a scenario of representational failure, but rather a "naïve" literary way forward in the face of this impasse: "sometimes however the compensatory fantasies of the naïve man are more accurate about the world than the realist Balzac is credited with being….it is as though every sentence of his pen were constructing a bridge into the unknown."[27] As in "On Epic Naiveté," in this reading of Balzac, the naiveté of narrative comes to the rescue in the face of the impasse of enlightenment, and we thus see here a reorientation of thought from a philosophical to a novelistic register.

This involves a linguistic shift. The task of philosophy, the task of thought to engage with totality, migrates to a non-philosophical, novelistic, use of language: "With the thunderbolt of citation Balzac brought society as totality, something classical philosophical economy and Hegelian philosophy had formulated in theoretical terms, down from the airy realm of ideas to the sphere of sensory evidence...art presumes to conjure up in perceptible form a society that has become abstract."[28] Adorno's work elsewhere suggests that this development is motivated by a historical situation in which the abstraction of philosophical language is not capable of engaging with experience. Or in other words, conceptual mediation has become too tainted with the danger of the "liquidation of the particular" in the name of the subsumptive tendency of the system, whether philosophical or socio-economic.[29] In view of this situation of philosophy, the way forward proposed by Adorno in "Reading Balzac" is perhaps surprising, given his well-known criticism of the false immediacy of realism and the pseudo-concreteness of existential phenomenology. This criticism follows from the recognition of the abstraction that is inherent in the predominance of exchange value within modernity, a historical situation in which society "has become abstract." In this situation, Balzac's conjuring up of society in perceptible form, or in other words, the concreteness of epic naiveté, is not supposed to be available. And of course aesthetic modernism, and Adorno's accounts of it in particular, are usually associated with a turn to abstraction, a turn which, on his account in *Aesthetic Theory*, "syncopates the overwhelming objectivity of the commodity character."[30]

The problem raised here then is how Adorno's naïve linguistic procedure avoids the danger of false immediacy that has been associated with realism. How exactly is the concretion of epic naiveté, which Adorno sees in Balzac, Goethe, Stifter, and Keller, distinguished from the deluded or mystifying version of immediacy Adorno warns about in the preface to *Minima Moralia*: "To speak immediately of the immediate is to behave much as those novelists who drape their marionettes in imitated bygone passions like cheap jewelry"?[31] We can also frame this question in terms of the problem of philosophical language. Adorno's shift away from philosophical or theoretical language to a more concrete or naïve language—in a discussion of Hegel's language Adorno writes,

"Philosophical language is patterned on naïve language"[32]—brings him uncomfortably close to Heidegger's attempts to escape traditional philosophical terminology. Given that this latter project is a principal target for Adorno, the question presents itself—what distinguishes Adorno's "naïve" use of language from the mystifying "pseudo concreteness" he located with existential phenomenology or other philosophical developments of his time (such as philosophical anthropology)?

It is here that we can circle back to the question of excessive detail or description. Adorno sees such excessive detail in Balzac as the mark of a literary mode he qualifies as "derived realism," a tendency Adorno sees not only in Balzac but also in "nineteenth century prose as a whole after Goethe." When description, or concrete detail becomes excessive, as it is in Balzac (according to Adorno), we move from a "primary" realism to "a more modern form of concreteness." This "derived realism" may be understood as a parody of realism, or a distorted imitation of it, which registers that actual realism capable of representing concrete experience in meaningful ways is not available: "Balzac uses the suggestion of concreteness. But is so excessive that one cannot yield to it naively, cannot credit it to the ominous richness of epic vision"; "The epic that is no longer in command of the material concreteness it attempts to protect has to exaggerate it in its demeanor, has to describe the world with exaggerated precision precisely because it has become alien." Adorno links this proliferation of description to Zola and, implicitly to modernism, given that Adorno claims this modern concreteness leads to "the dissolution of timer and action."[33]

If this procedure avoids a fetishizing of false immediacy or existentialism's pseudo concreteness, there is also here a response to Lukács's arguments in "Narrate or Describe?" (1936).[34] While he differs from Lukács in his situation of Balzac, to an extent Adorno's reading agrees with Lukács's conclusions about excessive description in nineteenth-century fiction. Lukács's argument that the excessive description of Flaubert and Zola is guilty of a capitulation to reification finds echoes in Adorno's reading of Balzac, where the novelist's "concretion" involves a fixation on the reified products of his society. On Adorno's account, Balzac's description replicates the proliferation of commodities and his novelistic language converges with the reification of the society he describes.

Adorno thus implicitly agrees with Lukács's point that excessive description in nineteenth-century fiction anticipates modernism. At the same time, this excessive description is reconfigured by Adorno in ways that are not envisaged by either Lukács or Jameson. Where each of these latter critics sees excessive description as a threat to the formal coherence of narrative, for Adorno, Balzac's excessive "suggestion of concreteness" contributes to the cognition of the artwork: "Art becomes knowledge."[35]

This formulation suggests a merging of narrative art and the cognitive task of philosophy, and we return here then to the scenario of the amalgamation of literary art and philosophy. It is important to recognize, however, that Adorno's reading of excessive description in the novel is intrinsically involved with a transformation of philosophy according to a linguistic reorientation of thought. I will return to "Reading Balzac" and "On Epic Naiveté" in due course, but in order to develop this claim, I want to initially consider the text where Adorno most explicitly announces his linguistic mutation of philosophy—his 1963 study, *Hegel*. Here Adorno suggests a project of bringing "the dialectic into language." "Philosophy," Adorno writes, "has to reflect on material concreteness, definition, and fulfillment, just as it has to reflect on language and its relationship to the matter at hand."[36] What this means, he goes on the state, is that philosophy tries to break out of its isolation from things in themselves, to express the "non-identical." While this recalls the naïve faith that is seen to be intrinsic to philosophy in *Negative Dialectics*, "to reach the non-conceptual," in the passage under consideration from *Hegel*, this philosophical impulse is explicitly linked to reflection on language and this involves the continuation of a reflection on language undertaken in *Dialectic of Enlightenment* (1944). Adorno's account in *Hegel* of the expressive pole of language, language's capacity to express the thing in itself, "the matter at hand," looks back to the analysis of language in *Dialectic of Enlightenment*, in which language is seen to involve a tension between an abstract, classificatory aspect, and a mimetic pole which involves an affinity between word and its referent.[37]

Developing this line of thought, Adorno's *Hegel* argues that Hegel's procedure tends to operate to the neglect of the expressive or mimetic pole of language, or in other words, "the abstract primacy of the whole" gets in the way of the "abandonment to the matter at hand."

And this problem, Adorno adds, can also be conceived in political terms: "Hegel's logic is not only his metaphysics; it is also his politics."[38] We can situate this problem in terms of Adorno's own confrontation with his historical moment: his work of the 1950s and 1960s suggests that the problem he faces at this particular historical juncture is not so much (or not only) how to avoid the lures of false immediacy, but rather how to remain faithful to the demands of the particular or the individuated, in the face of the subsumptive tendencies of system, whether this is seen as social or philosophical. For example, the Dedication to *Minima Moralia* admits that Hegel's method, with its abhorrence of anything isolated (that is, unmediated), "schooled *Minima Moralia*," but Adorno goes on to argue that philosophy, Hegel's in particular, has gone too far in the direction of the "liquidation of the particular" in the interest of "the primacy of the whole."[39] In *Hegel,* Adorno frames this situation in linguistic terms: the pole of rational transparency or classification, what Adorno calls "language as communication" or "communication dictated by the market," assumes an excessive weight on language, at the expense of the expressive pole.

The way forward suggested in *Hegel* is not to retreat to nominalism, but rather to reorient thought in terms of problems of reading, or what Adorno calls "literary presentation." We see the rational for this shift in Adorno's account of the difficulty of reading Hegel:

> Nothing can be understood in isolation, everything is to be understood only in the context of the whole, with the awkward qualification that the whole in turn lives only in the individual moments. In actuality, however, this kind of doubleness of the dialectic eludes literary presentation…This is why one has to make so many allowances for it in Hegel. That it cannot in principle achieve the unity of the whole and its parts becomes its weak spot.[40]

We see here the appearance of a fold between dialectic and literary presentation or the task of reading Hegel. The weaknesses diagnosed here of Hegel's literary presentation, and the reader's engagement with it, are precisely what recommends these textual operations to Adorno. If this literary presentation, this reading, involves a constitutive lack of unity between the whole and its parts, this avoids the coercive subordination of particularity to the abstract totality of the system. At the same time, this reconfiguration of thought in terms of literary presentation and reading does not involve an abandonment of the possibility of relationship between particular parts and the totality of the system; in fact, the ongoing negotiation of the tension between these two poles is just the process of reading. This negotiation is crucial for Adorno because to relinquish either pole of this process would be a capitulation of thought—either glorifying the abstract demands of the system, which would effectively be an apologetics for the tendency to domination of enlightenment; or a lapsing into nominalism, which, in hypostatizing the particular, would conform to bourgeois ideology.

The problem of knowledge, conceived of in terms of the concept-object relation, is reconceived as a problem of reading and narrative form. In each case, we are dealing with the question of how to relate forms to particular contents, but what changes with this shift to thinking through the operation of reading is that we move away from a scenario of knowledge conceived in terms of sensory intuition or appearance, to the dilemma of how to read narrative details, and this will bring us back in due course to the issue of gratuitous description in nineteenth-century fiction. At points, this project of reading does not even look like a project of attempting to reconcile particularity with the generality of a work or a meaning. Rather, the procedure of reading suggested here is to immerse oneself in textual details and still move beyond them, however slightly: "the art of reading him [Hegel] should take note of where something new begins, some content, and where a machine that was not intended to be a machine is simply running and ought not to keep on doing so. At every moment one needs to keep two seemingly incompatible maxims in mind: painstaking immersion in detail, and free detachment."[41]

This shift to operations of reading and literary presentation allows Adorno to conceive of forms of thinking that avoid, or at least soften, the domination inherent in the conceptual operations of enlightenment. The reading mode suggested here involves a subject that is not particularly productive or spontaneous, but rather attentive and receptive, "taking note of where something new begins," attending to the genuine novelty of content (*Inhalt*). At the same time, a "free detachment" is necessary for this process and thus the turn to reading involves a breaking down of the strict opposition between autonomy and heteronymy, between the productive subject of modernity and the receptive or passive subjectivity that has been taken as its antipode (for example, in accounts of the epic).[42] This reconceiving of subjectivity is also suggested if we register the emphasis on content (*Inhalt*) in Adorno's account of reading. Samuel Weber has called attention to the implications of Adorno's predilection for the notions of *Gehalt* (substance) and *Inhalt* (content), especially in his accounts of reading. Tracing the echo of the verb *halten* (to hold) in the words *Gehalt* and *Inhalt*, in contradistinction to the grasping (*greifen*) sedimented in the word *Begriff* (concept), Weber writes, "a holding action is not the same as seizing or grasping, *Halten* is not *Greifen*, *Gehalt* is not merely a synonym for *Begriff*. Against the tendency towards dialectical *Aufhebung*, Adorno insists on the necessity of immersing oneself 'in details' that precisely are not resolved or transcended through universal mediation."[43]

If we return to Adorno's accounts of epic or novelistic naiveté with these precisions in mind, the connections between literary naiveté and the linguistic turn developed in *Hegel* become evident. Epic naiveté, in its fixation on "objectivity or material concreteness," is characterized by fixation (*Fixierung*) on its object, the act of holding or clinging (*halten*), as opposed to grasping (*greifen*). Adorno deploys the terms *halten* and *Halten* recurrently to characterize the operations of epic naiveté—for example, recall that epic naiveté involves "a stubborn clinging (*Halten*) to the particular." But because this activity is situated as part of enlightenment, this holding operation of epic naiveté occurs in tension with a movement of abstraction—the clinging to the particular occurs "when it has already been dissolved into the universal." We can recognize here the dynamic of the reading procedure described in Adorno's *Hegel*—the tension between particularity and abstraction ("the universal") in epic naiveté anticipates the balancing between immersion in detail and detachment required in the reading of Hegel.

We come back then to the reading of Balzac, returning to the problem of excessive description in nineteenth-century fiction. For the most part, Adorno's "Reading Balzac" does not explicitly thematize reading in the way that he does in the last chapter of *Hegel*. The exception is the passage already discussed above, in which Adorno writes that Balzac's "suggestion of concreteness" is "so excessive that one cannot yield to it naively." This is, I would argue, a version of the reading operation described in *Hegel*, with its "seemingly incompatible" coupling of immersion in detail and detachment. Not yielding naively to Balzac's excessive detail is an act of readerly detachment. We can see this detachment, as it is worked out in *Hegel* and "Reading Balzac," as a minimal assertion of autonomy, but this particular assertion is also intrinsic to a reorientation of thought according to what Adorno in *Hegel* calls "literary presentation." What such presentation involves, in nineteenth-century fiction, is a realism when realism is no longer possible, an epic concreteness when such concreteness is no longer available, a turn to the sphere of "sensory evidence" when such evidence has become abstract and reified. If "literary presentation" and the reading of it, are thus intrinsically naïve, what this naiveté involves is not just doing something that is not strictly speaking possible—like reading Hegel, or concretely referring to objects—but also these literary operations betray a referential intention of language, an aspiration to connect language in a necessary (and not just conventional) way to materiality and experience. As we have seen, Adorno frames this referential intention in terms of a shift from the abstract language of philosophy, or what he calls "theoretically oriented writing," to a concrete language of description or "sensory evidence." This shift is naïve, given that language has become abstract under the conditions of modernity and thus the attempt to recover a non-reified concrete language is impossible, but this naïve referential impulse remains a defining characteristic of language, to allow "what is real to emerge in pure form."[44]

This naïve referential impulse, like Adorno's conception of reading, works to break down the opposition between the impositions of subjectivity and the passive, purely receptive, or visionary mode that has been seen as an antipode to the subject of modernity. To speak in terms of literary genres, Adorno is framing an epic impulse at the heart of the formal dynamics of the novel, and vice versa—a confusion, that is, between the productive subjectivity of the novel (modernity) and the absence of such productivity that has been taken to characterize the world of the epic.[45] At this point, we can also recognize that this ambiguity or confusion at the heart of Adorno's novelistic naiveté is intrinsic to a revised conception of experience, by which I mean that experience here is no longer confined to the forms and categories of the subject, as it is in Kant, but rather exceeds the intentions and forms of subjectivity. Or to be more precise, the opposition between subjective forms and objective content is placed in question in this revised conception of experience.[46] Adorno's naïve novelistic turn thus looks back on Benjamin's earlier linguistic reorientation of thought, which as we have seen, also framed a process of reading in terms of receptivity or attentiveness in the interest of moving beyond Kant's overly restrictive conceptions of knowledge and experience. But Adorno's reorientation of philosophy around the linguistic dynamics of the novel and the epic is also, we should note in conclusion, a scenario of the fragility of thought at the historical moment in which he is writing. It is this fragility that I aim to suggest with the title of this paper: intimidated thought is the ambiguous and fragile thought of the novel and its language, thought that throws itself away, that capitulates "to the superior power of reality,"[47] that destroys the fabric of the narrative. This may remain, however, the last best hope for philosophy: as Adorno writes at the conclusion of "Why Still Philosophy" (1962), "History promises no salvation and offers the possibility of hope only to the concept whose movement follows history's path to the very extreme."[48]

Notes

1. C.D. Blanton, *Epic Negation: The Dialectical Poetics of Late Modernism* (Oxford: Oxford University Press, 2015), 8–11.
2. Georg Lukács, *History and Class Consciousness: Studies in Marxist Dialectics*, trans. Rodney Livingstone (Cambridge, MA: The MIT Press, 1971), 103–104.
3. Blanton, *Epic Negation*, 8.
4. Jed Esty, *Unseasonable Youth: Modernism, Colonialism, and the Fiction of Development* (Oxford: Oxford University Press, 2012), 27; Blanton, *Epic Negation*, 10. See also Fredric Jameson, "Modernism

and Imperialism," in *The Modernist Papers* (London: Verso, 2007), 152–169.

5. Taking a broader historical perspective, one could suggest that the advent of literary theory may be traced to the emergence of a modern conception of literature whereby a text accounts for its own functioning and calls forth theoretical accounts of this functioning. On this point see Nicholas Brown, *Utopian Generations: The Political Horizon of Twentieth-Century Literature* (Princeton: Princeton University Press, 2005), 14–15.

6. Brown, *Utopian Generations*, 15. Blanton also sees theory as a chapter in the post-Kantian eidaesthetic vocation of literature. See C.D. Blanton, "Invisible Times: Modernism as Ruptural Unity," in *Modernism and Theory: A Critical Debate*, ed. Stephen Ross (New York: Routledge, 2008), 137–152.

7. If we look elsewhere, it's clear that others see a tension or bifurcation between the linguistic theoretical turn and scholarly work of a materialist bent. See, for example, J.M. Bernstein, *Against Voluptuous Bodies: Late Modernism and the Meaning of Painting* (Stanford, CA: Stanford University Press, 2006), 259–260; Raymond Williams, *Marxism and Literature* (Oxford: Oxford University Press, 1977), 42–44.

8. Paul de Man, *The Resistance to Theory* (Minneapolis: University of Minnesota Press, 2012), 8.

9. Paul de Man, Paul, *Blindness and Insight* (Minneapolis: University of Minnesota Press, 1983), 208.

10. Walter Benjamin, *Selected Writings*, 4 volumes, ed. Michael W. Jennings et al. (Cambridge, MA: The Belknap Press of Harvard University Press, 1996–2003), 1: 103, 108. This linguistic reorientation of thought is manifest in Benjamin's subsequent work, notably *The Origin of German Tragic Drama* and *The Arcades Project*.

11. From this orientation follows Benjamin's conception of the dialectical image—it is not an object of vision, intuition, or intentionality, but rather may be recognized in language. Walter Benjamin, *The Arcades Project*, trans. Howard Eiland and Kevin McLaughlin (Cambridge, MA: The Belknap Press of Harvard University Press, 2002), 462–463.

12. See, for example, Fredric Jameson, *The Antinomies of Realism* (London: Verso, 2013); Jacques Rancière, *The Emancipated Spectator*, trans. Gregory Elliot (New York: Verso, 2011), 107–132.

13. While a fuller elaboration of this point is beyond the scope of this essay, we can note that this line of thought converges in important respects with de Man's postulation that the linguistic terminology of theory is interested in "reference as a function of language and not necessarily as an intuition."

14. David Cunningham, "Time, Modernism, and the Contemporaneity of Realism," in *The Contemporaneity of Modernism: Literature, Media, Culture*, ed. Michael D'Arcy and Mathias Nilges (New York: Routledge, 2016), 50.

15. Jameson, *Antinomies of Realism*, 37.

16. Rancière makes a somewhat similar argument in his account of the "pensive image." Such images—Rancière cites as examples the "small visual scenes" in Flaubert's *Madame Bovary*—are at odds with the narrative sequence of the text: "The logic of visually no longer arrives to supplement action. It arrives to suspend or rather duplicate it" (123). Rancière, *Emancipated Spectator*, 123. For a discussion of this similarity between the accounts of Jameson and Rancière, see Cunningham, "Time, Modernism, and the Contemporaneity of Realism," 53–54.

17. Roland Barthes, *The Rustle of Language*, trans. Richard Howard (Oxford: Blackwell, 1986), 146–148.

18. Barthes, *Rustle of Language*, 146; Jameson, *Antinomies of Realism*, 36–37.

19. Theodor Adorno, *Notes to Literature*, trans. Shierry Weber Nicholsen (New York: Columbia University Press, 1991), 1: 24–26. Theodor Adorno, *Noten Zur Literatur* (Frankfurt am Main: Suhrkamp Verlag, 1958), 1: 50–55.

20. Adorno, *Notes*, 1: 25–26. This aspect of "On Epic Naiveté" is continuous with the project of *Dialectic of Enlightenment* to situate the epic on the side of enlightenment. This contrasts with Lukács's understanding of epic subjectivity and naiveté in *Theory of the Novel* and *History and Class Consciousness*, where epic and naïve thought are seen as non-reflective thought, oblivious to the conditions of capitalist modernity (the antinomies of bourgeois thought). The point that the epic is situated as part of the project of enlightenment is already suggested in Hegel's, *Aesthetics*. Max Horkheimer and Theodor Adorno, *Dialectic of Enlightenment: Philosophical Fragments*, ed. Gunzelin Schmid Noerr, trans. Edmund Jephcott (Stanford, CA: Stanford University Press, 2002). Hegel, *Aesthetics*, 2: 1045–1050.

21. Adorno, *Notes*, 1: 26.

22. Ibid., 27.

23. Theodor Adorno, *Negative Dialectics*, trans. Dennis Redmond (2001), http://members.efn.org/~dredmond/ndtrans.html, 7.

24. Adorno, *Notes*, 1: 26.
25. Ibid., 1: 121.
26. Adorno opens his 1931 lecture "The Actuality of Philosophy" with the assertion that under current conditions thought is unable "to grasp the totality of the real." Theodor Adorno, "The Actuality of Philosophy," *Telos* 31 (Spring 1977): 120.
27. Adorno, *Notes*, 1: 122.
28. Adorno, Ibid.
29. On this point, see Theodor Adorno, *Minima Moralia: Reflections on Damaged Life*, trans. E.F.N. Jephcott (New York: Verso, 2005), 15–18.
30. Theodor Adorno, *Aesthetic Theory*, ed. Gretel Adorno and Rolf Tiedemann, trans. Robert Hullot-Kentor (Minneapolis: University of Minnesota Press, 1997), 21.
31. Adorno, *Minima Moralia*, 15.
32. Theodor Adorno, *Hegel: Three Studies*, trans. Shierry Weber Nicholsen (Cambridge, MA: The MIT Press, 1993), 114.
33. Adorno, *Notes*, 1: 128–129.
34. Georg Lukács, *Writer and Critic and Other Essays*, trans. Arthur Kahn (London: Merlin Press, 1970), 110–148.
35. Adorno, *Notes*, 1: 129.
36. Adorno, *Hegel*, 101, 109.
37. Horkheimer and Adorno, *Dialectic of Enlightenment*, 12–13.
38. Adorno, *Hegel*, 93–94.
39. Adorno, *Minima Moralia*, 16–17.
40. Adorno, *Hegel*, 91.
41. Ibid., 94–95.
42. See, for example, Lukács, *Theory of the Novel*.
43. Samuel Weber, *Theatricality as Medium* (New York: Fordham University Press, 2004), 240.
44. As Peter Hohendhal notes, this conception of language departs from Saussure and the structuralism that followed from his work. The basic point here (though Hohendhal does not put it in these terms) is that, in contrast to Saussure, Adorno does not bracket the referent. Peter Uwe Hohendhal, "Adorno: The Discourse of Philosophy and the Problem of Language," in *The Actuality of Adorno: Critical Essays on Adorno and the Postmodern*, ed. Max Pensky (Albany, NY: State University of New York Press, 1997), 67.
45. Apparently alluding to Lukács's account of the epic in *Theory of the Novel*, *Dialectic of Enlightenment* frames this confusion as follows:

"Odysseus, like the heroes of all true novels after him, throws himself away in order to win himself." Horkheimer and Adorno, *Dialectic of Enlightenment*, 38–39.
46. On this point, see Adorno, *Hegel*, 138.
47. Theodor Adorno, *Notes*, 1: 36.
48. Theodor Adorno, *Critical Models: Interventions and Catchwords*, trans. Henry W. Pickford (New York: Columbia University Press, 2005), 17.

References

Adorno, Theodor. 1958–1965. *Noten Zur Literatur*, 3 Volumes. Frankfurt am Main: Suhrkamp Verlag.
———. 1977. The Actuality of Philosophy. *Telos* 31 (Spring): 120–133.
———. 1991–1992. *Notes to Literature*, 2 Volumes, trans. Shierry Weber Nicholsen. New York: Columbia University Press.
———. 1993. *Hegel: Three Studies*, trans. Shierry Weber Nicholsen. Cambridge, MA: The MIT Press.
———. 1997. *Aesthetic Theory*, trans. Robert Hullot-Kentor and ed. Gretel Adorno and Rolf Tiedemann. Minneapolis: University of Minnesota Press.
———. 2001. *Negative Dialectics*, trans. Dennis Redmond. http://members.efn.org/~dredmond/ndtrans.html.
———. 2005. *Critical Models: Interventions and Catchwords*, trans. Henry W. Pickford. New York: Columbia University Press.
———. 2005. *Minima Moralia: Reflections on Damaged Life*, trans. E.F.N. Jephcott. New York: Verso.
Barthes, Roland. 1986. *The Rustle of Language*, trans. Richard Howard. Oxford: Blackwell.
Benjamin, Walter. 1985. *The Origin of German Tragic Drama*, trans. John Osborne. New York: Verso.
———. 1996–2003. *Selected Writings*, 4 Volumes, ed. Michael W. Jennings et al. Cambridge, MA: The Belknap Press of Harvard University Press.
———. 2002. *The Arcades Project*, trans. Howard Eiland and Kevin McLaughlin. Cambridge, MA: The Belknap Press of Harvard University Press.
Bernstein, J.M. 2006. *Against Voluptuous Bodies: Late Modernism and the Meaning of Painting*. Stanford, CA: Stanford University Press.
Blanton, C.D. 2008. Invisible Times: Modernism as Ruptural Unity. In *Modernism and Theory: A Critical Debate*, ed. Stephen Ross, 137–152. New York: Routledge.

————. 2015. *Epic Negation: The Dialectical Poetics of Late Modernism.* Oxford: Oxford University Press.

Brown, Nicholas Brown. 2005. *Utopian Generations: The Political Horizon of Twentieth-Century Literature.* Princeton: Princeton University Press.

Cunningham, David. 2016. Time, Modernism, and the Contemporaneity of Realism. In *The Contemporaneity of Modernism: Literature, Media, Culture*, ed. Michael D'Arcy and Mathias Nilges. New York: Routledge.

De Man, Paul. 1983. *Blindness and Insight.* Minneapolis: University of Minnesota Press.

————. 2012. *The Resistance to Theory.* Minneapolis: University of Minnesota Press.

Esty, Jed. 2012. *Unseasonable Youth: Modernism, Colonialism, and the Fiction of Development.* Oxford: Oxford University Press.

Hegel, G.W.F. 2010. *Aesthetics*, 2 Volumes, trans. T.M. Knox. Oxford: Oxford University Press.

Hohendahl, Peter Uwe. 1997. Adorno: The Discourse of Philosophy and the Problem of Language. In *The Actuality of Adorno: Critical Essays on Adorno and the Postmodern*, ed. Max Pensky, 62–82. Albany, NY: State University of New York Press.

Horkheimer, Max, and Theodor Adorno. 2002. *Dialectic of Enlightenment: Philosophical Fragments*, trans. Edmund Jephcott and ed. Gunzelin Schmid Noerr. Stanford, CA: Stanford University Press.

Jameson, Fredric. 2007. Modernism and Imperialism. In *The Modernist Papers*, 152–169. New York: Verso.

————. 2013. *The Antinomies of Realism.* New York: Verso.

Lukács, Georg. 1970. *Writer and Critic and Other Essays*, trans. Arthur Kahn. London: Merlin Press.

————. 1971. *History and Class Consciousness: Studies in Marxist Dialectics*, trans. Rodney Livingstone. Cambridge, MA: The MIT Press.

————. 1996. *The Theory of the Novel: A Historico-Philosophical Essay on the Forms of Great Epic Literature*, trans. Anna Bostock. Cambridge, MA: The MIT Press.

Rancière, Jacques. 2011. *The Emancipated Spectator*, trans. Gregory Elliot. New York: Verso.

Weber, Samuel. 2004. *Theatricality as Medium.* New York: Fordham University Press.

Williams, Raymond. 1977. *Marxism and Literature.* Oxford: Oxford University Press.

14

A Quotation from Seneca Is Missing: About a So-Called Poem for Children

Jerónimo Pizarro

I recently included in an anthology of 18 poems (*Todos los sueños del mundo*, 2012), and before that, in an exposition ("Fernando Pessoa: el mito y las máscaras", 2011), a poem I always considered as one of the greatest Pessoa signed with his own name, even though back then I did not have the data to understand it completely. What I did know was that it was not a musical poem as were many of the symbolist compositions of the *Songbook*, a book Pessoa worked on for a long time and never published. I am speaking of the poem "Liberty", written during the last year of the poet's life, 1935, which begins with a mnemonic leading to an inexistent quotation: "a quotation from Seneca is missing". Most editions, including the critical edition, leave out this note arguing its lack of interest because it is not part of the poem but only "a note the poet would replace with the effective epigraph" (Prista, in Pessoa 2000: 441). I myself once imagined a game, and suggested, in a note, that the exclusion of the quotation could be understood as an expression of liberty itself: "it could be a deliberate emptiness, one

J. Pizarro (✉)
Universidad de Los Andes, Bogotá, Colombia

© The Author(s) 2018
A. Falcato and A. Cardiello (eds.), *Philosophy in the Condition of Modernism*,
https://doi.org/10.1007/978-3-319-77078-9_14

309

of the liberties of the author or 'Liberty'" (in Pessoa 2012: 129). And for a time, paying attention to my own perplexity, I used the poem of March 16, 1935 to discuss with my students the famous triad of literary criticism that Umberto Eco revisited: the author's intention, the text's intention and the reader's intention (Eco et al. 1992). I would ask for the meaning of the poem from the author's perspective, from the perspective of the text itself, or from the reader's perspective, and we would always fail to achieve a proper explanation for that introductory note that we all supposed, as Luís Prista, to be a "note which would eventually be replaced with the proper epigraph, some phrase from Seneca the poet would still come up with" (Prista 2003: 220). I will write out the poem here, including the note so many editions remove:

LIBERTY

(a quotation from Seneca is missing)

What a delight
Not to fulfil a task,
Have a book
and not read it!
To read is annoying,
To study is nothing.
The sun gilds
Without literature.
The river flows, night or morn,
Without an original edition.
And the breeze, she
Is so naturally early
She takes her time and has no hurry.

Books are paper painted with ink.
To study is something in which the distinction
between nothing and nothing at all is indistinct

It is so much better, in the mist,
for King Sebastian to wait,
may he come or not!

Great are poetry, kindness and dance...
But the best in the world are children,
Flowers, music, moonlight, and the sun, who sins
when instead of creating, he dries.

More than this
Is only Jesus Christ
Who knew nothing of finances
Nor was reported to have books...

(118-55^r)[1]

This poem seems to lead to idleness, underestimating studies, at the same time as it suggests, in a tone that brings Alberto Caeiro's poetry to mind, that "the sun gilds | without literature".[2] I always enjoyed discussing these verses with my literature students. We would have problems when it came to the hermetic references to King Sebastian and Jesus Christ. Many interpretations of the poem were based on redemption and messianism. Some students focused on childhood and "surrendered", just like Manuela Nogueira, Pessoa's niece, to a verse of the poem, "But the best in the world are children", which seemed to be a perfect epigraph for a book for children. Actually, Manuela Nogueira named an anthology of poems and texts of Fernando Pessoa, supposedly for children, with the phrase: *The Best in the World are the Children* (1998),[3] adding the definite article to "children" which was not there in the original line, as Luís Prista noticed (2003: 222). But was the poem really intended to be a celebration of childhood and were the learned references to Sebastianism and Christianism simple allusions that any Portuguese child would understand? How far can the liberty of the critic reach, may he be a conservative critic as Eco, or irreverent as Derrida?

Curiously enough, and following Manuela Nogueira, many other compilers included the poem "Liberdade" among their selection of poems for children. The poem appears in at least four books that may be found in the library of the Casa Fernando Pessoa as José Correia informed me in 2014:

Nogueira, Manuela (2015). *O Melhor do Mundo são as Crianças*. Antologia de poemas e textos de Fernando Pessoa para a infância. Lisboa: Assírio & Alvim, p. 7.

Pais, Amélia Pinto (2011). *Fernando Pessoa, O Menino da sua Mãe*. Porto: Ambar, 2007; Porto: Areal Editores (com novas ilustrações), pp. 78–79.

Gomes, José António (2008). *Poesia de Fernando Pessoa Para Todos*. Ilustrações de António Modesto. Porto: Porto Editora, p. 21.

Judice, Manuela (2007). *O Meu Primeiro Fernando Pessoa*. Ilustrações de Pedro Proença. Lisboa: Dom Quixote, s/n. de pp.

I confess my students were always somewhat perplexed when, at a certain point, I explained that the poem appeared in books for children published in Portuguese speaking countries. The perplexity arouse because not all of them considered the poem to be for children in the first place and some even found some irony in it. What would be the best reading of "Liberdade"? We never arrived at a consensus, and we did not need to.

Some months ago, I watched, for the second time, a documentary (*Second-Rate Poetry* 2012) about the consolation prize the government of António de Oliveira Salazar gave to *Message* (1934), the only book published by Fernando Pessoa during his lifetime—the *English Poems* are much to short to be technically considered a book. At a certain moment of his speech, when Salazar announces the censorship of some liberties, I noticed the actor representing Salazar's character pronounced a quotation from Seneca. Still in the movie hall, I sent José Barreto an IPhone message: "What is the phrase of Seneca that Salazar quotes in his speech during the prize-giving ceremony in 1934?" The answer hit me as a *eureka*: "Excerpt of the text read by Salazar during the prize-giving ceremony on February 21, 1935, in which he justified censorship and the imposition of guidelines for writers and artists: '… But would any evil fall upon the world if writing better and especially reading better brings to writing less? Today, as in Seneca's criticism, 'dissertations and chronicles decorate the room of the idle, in shelves that reach the ceiling'".[4] This phrase is surely the quotation Pessoa meant to include as an epigraph of "Liberdade". The dating is also correct: the speech was from the 21st of February and the poem from March 16, 1935. There is another piece of important information that has probably been forgotten for too long: Jorge de Sena, who published a famous series of three anti-Salazarist poems in *O Estado de São Paulo* on August 20, 1960: "Antonio de Oliveira Salazar", "This Mister Salazar"/and "Poor Thing" explained in 1974, that: "Among the papers of Fernando Pessoa (not those in the legendary suitcase, but in another one which nobody knew about and which the family of the poet generously loaned us for examination) we found some years ago this sequence of three, with the poem 'Liberdade' (published in *Seara Nova* in 1937), with the satire 'Yes, it is the New State, and the People'" (Sena 2000: 255; cf. Saraiva 1981; Sousa 1988).

(I open here a necessary parenthesis: the *eureka* moment I experienced at the movie hall just lasted some weeks because I had only found again what Luís Prista had already discovered between 2000 and 2003, and published in the article I quoted here and that he gave me in 2005 at the Portuguese National Library. I had read the article, but I partially forgot it: I could remember the text because of its criticism of Manuela Nogueira's book—which I knew about in 2005—and not because of the discovery of Seneca's phrase. I was fascinated by this meticulous text in which he managed to criticise in so many pages the absence of the article "*the*" placed before "children", and my memory did not hold that other very precious issue: the discovery of the missing epigraph. Anyway. Let us continue…)

"Liberdade", which was well understood by the directors of the *Seara Nova* journal, circulated secretly in 1935 until they managed the censorship to accept it in 1937. After it was published by Manuela Nogueira in the book *The Best in the World are the Children* (1998) it was read as being less ironical, lighter and even pedagogic, which led to further mistakes. Out of its context, dispossessed of its material body and of its epigraph, and placed in books of commercial print run, "Liberdade" ceased to be a hymn to Liberty, a flag that preceded the Revolution of the Carnations, and it turned into a poem which showed how much Pessoa loved children. I do not wish to say he did not, but I think this case properly exemplifies how the sense of a text, and especially a political text, can hardly be understood without attending to the history and context of its publication and circulation, not to mention the philological importance of the place where the document is found, the localization of a document in an archive or the material characteristics of the text.

To illuminate these aspects, I believe Luís Prista's article, which I have quoted already several times, "The Best in the World are not the Children", is decisive. I read it once again while I was writing this text. First, Prista rescues a statement of Pedro da Silveira that is important because it proves that the poem "Liberdade" was written to be published and that it was rejected by the censorship in 1935, before it was published in 1937. This is the statement, published in July 1974, after the revolution of the 25th of April:

> Today, it is finally possible to reveal what before the 25th of April was absolutely impossible.
> At least since 1932, one of the young cafe friends of F. Pessoa was Manuel Mendes. It was to him the poet gave the recently finished typescript of the poem "Liberdade", so he could publish it, if he so wished, and the *Seara* journal consented. It consented; but the pencil of the censor, facing the last stanza (*More than this | Is only Jesus Christ | Who knew nothing of finances | Nor was reported to have books...*), could not stand the third verse: "Who knew nothing of finances". The serviceman with the pencil thought it was an allusion to... Salazar. Only two years later another censor left it through. This is the edifying story of Fernando Pessoa as a...posthumous collaborator of the *Seara Nova*. ("Additional note" to Jorge de Sena, "Four Anti-Salazarist Poems of Fernando Pessoa", *Seara Nova*, nº 1545, July 1974, p. 20).
>
> (*apud* Prista 2003: 224)

Thus, Pessoa could have been a collaborator of the *Seara Nova*, the only thing that stopped him was the power of censorship. Second, Prista establishes a very illuminating chronology of 1935.

January 19	The Law Project for the Secret Associations is presented
February 4	Fernando Pessoa publishes the article "Secret Associations"
February 21	Salazar's speech during the prize-giving ceremony of the SNP [Ministry of National Propaganda]

March 14	Article of Rolão Preto closes press controversy
March 16	"Liberty"
second decade of March	"Salazar is a Piggy Bank"
March 29	"António de Oliveira Salazar"
March 29	"This Mister Salazar"; "Poor thing"
April 4	"Kill the Bigger Lice"
April 5	Discussion and approval of the law project
after the 5th	"Solemnly"
[1935]	"To the National Broadcasting Station"
July 29	"Yes, it is the New State, and the People"
August 18	"They Say the Zoo"
[second semester]	"I Spoke about the 'Salty Sea'"
November 8	"My Poor Portugal"
November 8–9	"Love Poem in New State"
November 30	Death of Fernando Pessoa

(Prista 2003: 231)

As it may be noticed, the anti-Salazarist poems of Pessoa—the most popular—are from the 29th of March 1935; and "Liberdade" is dated March 16 of the same year. This would be enough to agree with the appreciation of José Barreto: "In my opinion, "Liberdade" is not the same kind of anti-Salazarist poem as the poems that follow it, even though it includes attacks directed towards the dictator and was provoked by his speech. This is: it is less explicit, it is somewhat hermetic when compared to the satirical poems of 1935 aimed at Salazar. The difference lies in the fact that this poem was actually written to be published, as the orthographic factor of the typescript also proves (118-55ʳ) to be different than usual. The other anti-Salzarist poems of 1935 could, obviously, never have been published".[5] Actually, "Liberdade" seems to clear the way for an incredible anthology of more or less political poems that Pessoa, to protect himself, kept in his trunk and only shared with some of his friends.

Finally, let us refer to the historical importance that Pessoa gave to the speech Salazar pronounced on the 21st of February 1935 during the prize-giving ceremony of the Ministry of National Propaganda, which Pessoa did not attend. In a rough draft of a letter from the

30th of October 1935 for Adolfo Casais Monteiro, Pessoa wrote (as George Orwell in his *Animal Farm*) that, since that speech of Salazar, "we came to know, all of us who write, that the restrictive rule of the Censorship 'you cannot say this or that' had been replaced by the rule of the soviet Power 'you must say that or this'. And he adds: "In other words, everything we write not only has not to contradict the principles of the New State (that I ignore), but also has to be subordinated to the guidelines set by the advisors of the already mentioned New State" (Pessoa 1998: 282; file number 114¹-36). Or as he states in another uncompleted and never sent letter addressed to the general Óscar Carmona, re-elected president without an opponent on the 17th of February 1935, "Up to now the Dictatorship had not had the shamelessness of, turning its back to all true politics of the spirit—i.e., put the spirit above politics—intimidating those who think, obliging them to think with the State's head, which has no head, or intimidating those who work, obliging them to work ~~with the learned animality of the Corporate Chamber~~ freely as they are ordered" (in Cunha 1987: 126; file number 92 M-33ʳ). For Fernando Pessoa, Salazar's speech of the 21st of February 1935 marked an historical cleavage. It was the moment in which the "learned animality" of the pigs began to impose guidelines and to change the seven commandments, recalling Orwell's novel again…

In this context, and not forgetting that Salazar was appointed as minister of finance, is there not another echo to the reading of the final lines of the poem?

> More than this
> Is only Jesus Christ
> Who knew nothing of finances
> Nor was reported to have books…

Jesus Christ, in opposition to Salazar, "knew nothing of finances"—supposing Salazar would have been a good regent of the Chair of Economic Politics and Finances and a good minister—and, not regarding the learned ignorance of the politicians, in misty times, Pessoa says, the best would be to wait for a super-Camoens (to bring back King Sebastian):

It is so much better, in the mist,
for King Sebastian to wait,
may he come or not!

In "Liberdade", Pessoa ironically assumes the character of the "idle man" "*preguiçoso*" from the quotation of Seneca addressed by Salazar ("it is in the houses of the laziest men that you will see a full collection of orations and history with the boxes piled right up to the ceiling"/ "*em casa dos sujeitos mais preguiçosos poderás encontrar tudo quanto há de discursos e de obras históricas em prateleiras que se erguem até ao tecto*"),[6] just as he will assume, in the series of three anti-Salazarist poems, the character of the "nostalgic dreamer of depression and decadence" (based on an accusatory fragment of the same speech by Salazar). Later on, he would sign the "Love Poem in New State"—I owe this indication to José Barreto—with another accusation made by the Salazarist power to the opposition: "the communist-Masonic demo-liberalism". In the already referred poems of 1935, Pessoa does not deny these accusations, on the contrary, he assumes them as a way of provocation, as who says: "That is what I am, so what?". Following José Barreto's interpretation, which I agree with, "Liberdade" turns into a provocative praise of the idleness the dictator finds in the intellectuals of the opposition. It is not an open combat poem, as the others, but a poem of veiled provocation.

So, could it be that the poem which supposedly was for children has turned out to be an adult's poem inspired by a speech Salazar gave on the 21st of February of 1935? The answer is yes. With this stated, it is still convenient to clarify some issues about our posthumous liberties. Without the intention of denying or censuring in any kind of way any other reading of the poem, I think it is evident that any critical work that does not exclude Seneca's quotation—and a critic may always argue that Pessoa himself did not include it—must start from two unavoidable facts: the quotation from Seneca (that Salazar took from *De tranquillitate animi*) and the allusion to the "finances" in the last stanza of the poem lead us, without doubt, to Salazar and his speech of the 21st of February, 1935. In this context, the question asked by Prista ("Why did the poet never get to type in the quotation"), is, actually, not only pertinent but even fascinating, even though it might never find an answer. Prista ventures two hypothesis: "Maybe because he was looking for the exact Latin text. Or because Pessoa was trying to play with Salazar's erudition, "A quotation from Seneca is missing" assumed the incapacity to quote a classic and thus was a taunt that should be published?" (2003: 237). I admit, simply, that the poet probably never came to find the original phrase, because the book of Seneca is not in his private library.[7] However, today it seems to me clear that the epigraph would have to be found—as it actually did—more so in the speeches of Salazar than in the works of the Roman moralist, as, by the way, Richard Zenith did, when he suggested as a possible epigraph a passage of the letter 51 from the *Letters to Lucilius*: "Do you know what liberty consists in? In not being a slave of anything, of any need, of any eventuality; in fighting face to face with fortune" (in Pessoa 2006: 485).[8] And what shall we do now with this disturbing poem? Shall we remove it from the school manuals and from the wide spread editions?[9] I hope not. That would be an anti-aesthetic and dictatorial gesture. However, I think it is clear the readers of those books would gain a lot if the quotation from Seneca was included in the corpus of the poem, if the verses were properly set and if a basic contextualization of the poem was given. Then it would be possible to begin to write, as an exercise, provoking poems against different kinds of authoritarian regimes disguised as poems for children. Was not Pessoa himself a pretender, and could we not, profitably, teach children to pretend? Let us leave the challenge in the air.

Notes

1. On the back of the page there are two notes: «Quando essa typa William Shakespeare | Ia a cambalear p'ra casa» e «There is no reason to suppose that I am worse...» (118-55ᵛ).
2. «Doura» or «doira». The autograph reads «doura», even though the typescript referred above contains modernized forms: «biblioteca», «Cristo», «indistinta», «literatura» and «crianças» *versus* «bibliotheca», «Christo», «indistincta», «litteratura» and «creanças»; and, more, «coisa», instead of «cousa» (*apud* Prista 2003: 220–221).

3. In the first part of the book the author uses, "without quoting", as Luís Prista explains with detail (2003: 221–222), «a collection of ten poems 'that Fernando Pessoa wrote for children'». I am talking about the anthology organized by João Alves das Neves, *Comboio, Saudades, Caracóis*, illustrated by Cláudia Scatamacchia and published in São Paulo by FTD in 1988. The title of the second edition of *The Best in the World are the Children/O Melhor do Mundo são as Crianças* (1998) is *My Uncle Fernando Pessoa/O Meu Tio Fernando Pessoa* (2015) and one also may find, on page 66, the poem "Liberty".

4. Personal communication which preceded *On Fascism, Military Dictatorship and Salazar/Sobre o Fascismo, a Ditadura Militar e Salazar* (2015). For a direct translation from Latin to English: "Consequently it is in the houses of the laziest men that you will see a full collection of orations and history with the boxes piled right up to the ceiling" (248–249). Retrieved from: http://www.loebclassics.com/view/seneca_younger-de_tranquillitate_animi/1932/pb_LCL254.249.xml.

5. Personal communication.

6. I use the translation of professor José António Segurado e Campos, omitting only some repetitions which intend to clarify the text (*apud* Prista 2003: 238).

7. See this passage of Luís Prista's article: "Did Pessoa ever look for the Latin passage among the books of his personal library? In the bookshelf that belonged to the poet, nowadays in the Casa Fernando Pessoa, there are three volumes with Lucius Annaeus Seneca's works—the two volumes of *Seneca's tragedies* (*with an English translation by Frank Justus Miller*, London and New York; William Heinemann-G.P. Putnam's Sons, 1917) and a book that includes the opuscule *Apocolocyntosis* (*with an English translation by W.H.D. Rouse*; London and New York; William Heinemann-G.P. Putnam's Sons, 1916; in the first part of the volume we find *Petronius*, with a translation by Michael Heseltine)—, none of them contain annotations or underlinings made by Pessoa. It would not be there where he could find the phrase he was interested in, which appears in the dialog *De tranquillitate animi* (cap. 9, §7): '*Apud desidiosissimos ergo uidebis quidquid orationum historiarumque est, tecto tenus exstructa loculamenta*'" (2003: 238).

8. Zenith corrected that information in 2013; please notice the summary of the meeting that took place at the Faculty of of Social and Human Sciences of the University of Lisbon: "Fernando Pessoa and the New State". http://bookcasefilms.blogspot.pt/2013/02/debate-na-fcsh-fernando-pessoa-e-o.html.

9. I will quote here a note from Luís Prista's article: "In her Master's dissertation, *The School Anthology for Portuguese Education* (Braga, Universidade do Minho, 1987), Maria Sousa Tavares gives a list of the texts that were most frequently included in anthologies for children in 7th grade primary school and 3rd grade secondary, from 1905 to 1997. In one of her collections, related to periods following the 25th of April, 'Liberdade' is the poem of Fernando Pessoa that the Manuals prefer, and the 21st amongst all other authors [...] Bear in mind that the programs of 7th grade, unlike those of other grades, do not require the reading of texts of Pessoa" (2003: 221).

References

Cunha, Teresa Sobral. 1987. Fernando Pessoa em 1935. Da ditadura e do ditador em dois documentos inéditos. In *Colóquio-Letras*, no. 100, November–December, 123–131. http://coloquio.gulbenkian.pt/bib/sirius.exe/issueContentDisplay?n=100&p=123&o=r.

Eco, Umberto, Richard Rorty, Jonathan Culler, and Christine Brooke-Rose. 1992. *Interpretation and Overinterpretation*, ed. Stefan Collini. Cambridge and New York: Cambridge University Press.

Nogueira, Manuela. 2015. *O Meu Tio Fernando Pessoa*. Preface by Richard Zenith. Famalicão: Centro Atlântico.

Pessoa, Fernando. 1998. *Cartas entre Fernando Pessoa e os Directores da "Presença"*. Edition and Study by Enrico Martines. Edição Crítica de Fernando Pessoa, Série Branca ["Estudos"], vol. 2. Lisboa: Imprensa Nacional-Casa da Moeda.

———. 2000. *Poemas 1934–1935*, ed. Luís Prista. Edição Crítica de Fernando Pessoa, Série Maior, vol. 1, Tomo V. Lisboa: Imprensa Nacional-Casa da Moeda.

———. 2006. *Poesia do Eu*, ed. Richard Zenith, vol. 2. Lisboa: Assírio & Alvim. Obra Essencial de Fernando Pessoa.

Pessoa, Fernando, Porfirio Barba-Jacob. 2012. *Todos los sueños del mundo | Todos os sonhos do mundo. Poemas*. Bilingual Edition with Preface and Notes by Jerónimo Pizarro, trans. Jerónimo Pizarro and Gastão Cruz, Collaboration, Paloma Fernández. Medellín: Tragaluz.

Prista, Luís. 2003. O melhor do mundo não são as crianças. In Ivo Castro and Inês Duarte (orgs.), *Razões e emoção. Miscelânea de estudos em homenagem a Maria Helena Mira Mateus*, 217–238. Lisboa: Imprensa Nacional-Casa da Moeda.

Sena, Jorge de. 2000. Os poemas de Fernando Pessoa contra Salazar e contra o Estado Novo [1974]. em *Fernando Pessoa & Cª Heterónima* (*estudos coligidos 1940–1978*). Third Edition, Revised and Amended [1.ª ed. 1982], 255–261. Lisboa: Edições 70.

Also See

Pessoa, Fernando. 2011. *Associações Secretas e Outros Escritos*, ed. José Barreto. Lisboa: Ática. Obras de Fernando Pessoa, Nova Série.

———. 2015. *Sobre o Fascismo, a Ditadura Militar e Salazar*. Edited by José Barreto. Lisboa: Tinta-da-china. Colecção Pessoa.

Saraiva, Arnaldo. 1981. Fernando Pessoa e Jorge de Sena. *Persona*, no. 5, Porto, Centro de Estudos Pessoanos, Abril de 1981, 23–37.

Sousa, João Rui de Sousa. 1988. Fernando Pessoa e o Estado Novo. *JL, Jornal de Letras, Artes e Ideias*, no. 310, 14 de Junho, 10–13.

Part V

Dystopias of the Self

15

The Well Is Not the World: William Golding's Sense of Reality in *Darkness Visible*

Stephen Mulhall

At the beginning of her very useful paper on William Golding's novels, Barbara Everett notes that his writing can be hard to talk about critically—a point certainly confirmed by my recent reading in the vast secondary literature surrounding Golding's work, which tends either to point at particularly powerful passages rather than explaining how they exercise such power, or to invoke possible sources and structures of significance whose relation to the relevant primary text is so speculative as to render them entirely external to that text's effects. Everett takes this resistance to serious criticism to be internal to the nature of Golding's enterprise: 'The novels dissolve, on the one hand, into their own critique, which the interested can only re-echo; and on the other, they take the form of theory's opposite, an undiscussable whole world peculiarly substantial in itself, thingy and definite'.[1] If Golding's work resists even the theory-resistant literary critic in this way, how much more resistant is it likely to be to the philosopher, so often viewed

S. Mulhall (✉)
University of Oxford, Oxford, UK
e-mail: stephen.mulhall@new.ox.ac.uk

© The Author(s) 2018
A. Falcato and A. Cardiello (eds.), *Philosophy in the Condition of Modernism*,
https://doi.org/10.1007/978-3-319-77078-9_15

(and sometimes rightly) as not only the source for but also a paradigm of the more theory-laden forms of such critique?

On reflection, however, both the literary critic and the philosopher might resist both branches of Everett's intuitively plausible accounting. On the one hand, why *must* 'the interested' (whether interested in the novels or their criticism) re-echo lines of critical evaluation to be found in the novels themselves, as opposed to critically evaluating them or identifying other possible lines of criticism? And on the other hand, the mere substantiality of a novel's world need not, on the face of things, render it the opposite of theory, let alone undiscussable (given that not all critical discussions of fictive worlds need be theoretical).

But of course, Everett's claim is that Golding's worlds are '*peculiarly*' substantial: and this peculiarity has something to do with their wholeness (call it their self-sufficiency), as if they were not so much composed of things as themselves thinglike ('giving a pleasure close to that of a beautifully crafted handmade toy' [GP, 111]). This is why their author can 'achieve a degree of mimetic reality, of fidelity to sense-experience, not surpassed in recent fiction' (GP, 112)—a 'sense of reality' that is 'not in itself identical with reality' but in a way exceeds it. For these thing-like worlds possess 'an intensity and coherence' of a kind that the real world does not and could not possess, since 'only a certain permeability in the real makes existence possible for us at all' (GP, 112). Everett thus implies that a fictive world is discussable in her literary-critical sense of that term only insofar as we experience it as permeable to us, as permitting us to reach into it, even to find it habitable—an environment within which we might live, move and have our (literary-critical) being.

In this paper, I will build upon Everett's intuitions about the excessive sense of reality Golding achieves and about the relation between permeability and criticism, whilst rejecting her general characterization of Golding's worlds as uniformly impermeable. In so doing, I'm driven by the need to properly acknowledge the particular Golding novel which has obsessed me ever since I read it when it first appeared in 1979: *Darkness Visible*.[2] For the fictive world with which it confronts us patently does not conjoin intensity and coherence in the manner of Golding's first five novels (culminating in *The Spire*). It certainly manifests intensity, but in a peculiarly substantial way, thingy and definite, in itself rather than as a qualification of some other feature of that world (such as its coherence); indeed, its intensity appears to be a function of its refusal to cohere, even of a certain kind of willed or ragged permeability. My critical account of *Darkness Visible* (which primarily engages with its first Part) grows out of this permeability or seaminess of its fictive world, and in so doing, it takes up an invitation that I claim is extended by the world-maker himself. In one way, therefore, my account may be said to re-echo something that that text already knows about itself; but what it thereby identifies is not a self-interpretation into which the novel tidily dissolves, but rather an aspiration that it can neither meet nor relinquish.

Walls Are Windows

Darkness Visible appeared fifteen years after *The Spire* (and twelve years after the three inter-linked novellas published under the title *The Pyramid*)—by far the longest period of silence in Golding's career. Whatever the personal reasons for this (and John Carey's recent biography[3] identifies a long struggle with writer's block, the damaging effect of a negative review of *The Spire*, an accident at sea in which Golding and his family were very nearly killed, a developing drink problem), it also suggests a phase of artistic reflection—taking stock, considering what had been achieved and what new achievements might be possible or at least worth attempting. *The Pyramid* had already declared Golding's willingness to contest the restrictive allocation of his work to the genres of myth and fable; its narrative unfolds in roughly contemporary social circumstances (that of a small English town named Stilbourne). In *Darkness Visible*, he takes on the larger task of assessing the condition (not of Britain but) of England—of finding his own terms for expressing and evaluating the sense of social, cultural and political decline, or decay, by which so many people in England seemed gripped in that decade (as the radical energies of the sixties dissipated and the spirit of Thatcherism crystallized).

The English town at the heart of *Darkness Visible* is called Greenfield, and it contains an ironmonger's of character named Frankley's. Early in the nineteenth century, it moved into rickety buildings next to the towpath of the newly-cut canal; it thrives until the convulsions of the First World War, after which decline sets in and accelerates inexorably, despite various attempts to avert it by diversifying the goods it sells and its ways of selling them, until in the late seventies the business closes and the building is demolished. Frankley's is thus 'an image in little of society at large', by virtue of its 'complex disorder of ancient and modern' (DV, 42): the shop gradually buried itself under the accumulating sediment or remainder of each new generation of over-stocking; and each internal re-arrangement of departments remodelled a building that was already an architectural palimpsest when Frankley's first came to occupy it:

> The buildings were indeterminate in date, some walls of brick, some tile-hung, some lath and plaster, and some of a curious wooden construction. It is not impossible that parts of these wooden areas were in fact medieval windows filled as was the custom with wooden slats and now thought to be no more than chinky walls. Certainly there was not a beam in the place that did not have here and there notches cut, grooves and an occasional hole that indicated building and rebuilding, division, reclamation and substitution, carried on throughout a quite preposterous length of time. (DV, 38)

One innovation marks the point at which Frankley's tips from vigour to decline. After the First World War 'the place grew a spider's web of wires along which money trundled in small, wooden jars' (DV, 39): each shop assistant would propel the money and receipt for a transaction to a central cashier, who would return the change by the same means, with bells marking each stop on the jar's travels. Hence the decreasing levels of trade are marked by increasing periods of silence, which—combined with the muffling effect of the building's construction—ensure that every so often 'a jar would hiss over [a] customer's head like a bird of prey, turn a corner and vanish in some quite unexpected direction' (DV, 39). When a new Mr. Frankley abolishes the overhead railway, seeing it as a slur on the elderly, august shop assistants, and reintroduces separate tills, it becomes clear that the spider's web had done two things.

First, it had accustomed the staff to moderate stillness and tranquillity; and second, it had so habituated them to the overhead method of money sending and getting that when one of these ancient gentlemen was offered a banknote he immediately gestured upwards with it as if to examine the watermark. But this, in the evolution or perhaps devolution of the place, would be followed by continuing silence and a lost look while the assistant tried to remember what came next. (DV, 39–40)

Consider the overhead railway as an image, in little, of the spiritual life of the larger society within which Frankley's conducts its business. Then we might conclude that spiritual life blossoms in response to the moral convulsion of a world war; that affairs of the spirit take on a more predatory aspect the less often we traffic in them; and that their elimination on the grounds of respect for individual dignity in fact engenders disorientation, hollowing out a previously meaningful (even joyful) gesture language.

Now consider Frankley's as an image, in little, of the text that contains it. Then we should expect that text to be fundamentally concerned with spirituality as called forth by the extremities of war, liable to misinterpretation in malignant terms, and requiring expression in a language of gestures but crippled or deformed in the drive towards that expression by the disorientation of those to whom that language now belongs. Indeed, since the inheritors of this language— both characters and author—are also inhabitants of the society for which Frankley's goes proxy, the means of expression for which they are groping will have the same palimpsestic quality as that of their preposterously ancient society—the same layers of overlapping sedimentation, the same overstocking, the same subjection to unceasing 'rebuilding, division, reclamation and substitution' (DV, 38). In that sense, the key obstacle confronting anyone seeking a viable contemporary spiritual language may be the sheer multiplicity of available terms or modes of discourse rather than their absence: the problem is not the absence of spiritual concepts but how to recover a meaningful personal and collective means of spiritual expression from a bewildering, historically diverse and ineliminably hybrid profusion of such concepts.

It is this condition in which one of the novel's central characters—Matty—finds himself; and its first Part is devoted to recounting his attempts to make sense of his spiritual vocation, to himself and to post-war English (and, briefly, Australian) society. But the author of this recounting is himself in a condition analogous to Matty's: for to recount Matty's struggle to articulate both his understanding of himself as a prophet, and the prophetic visions to which he is subjected, is itself to attempt to articulate a prophetic vision of the condition of England; and the nature of this task, as well as the responsibilities taken on by anyone claiming the authority to engage in it, is conditioned by exactly the circumstances Matty confronts.

There is, of course, an apparent difference between the two tasks: for where Matty directly claims spiritual authority for his visions, and so for the actions they authorise, Golding claims (need only, and perhaps can only, claim) artistic authority for his vision of Matty's spiritual life. *Darkness Visible* is not a sacred text, but rather a literary text about the sacred (both textual and extra-textual). Hence the novel's epigraph: '*Sit mihi fas audita loqui*'. With these words, Virgil seeks permission from the gods to relate his vision of the Underworld into which Aeneas travels, in the company of the Sibyl and under the protection of a golden bough of mistletoe. If Matty is Golding's Aeneas, then Golding is Virgil: his authority is poetic.

But in registering that distinction, Golding also problematizes it. For these words of Virgil call on the gods to allow him to articulate a vision of Hell: in other words, this Roman poet presents his literary enterprise not only as having a spiritual subject-matter but also as subject to spiritual authorization—quite as if the poetic and the sacred are inextricably woven into one another, internally related. It thereby appears to be an essential part of Golding's vision that our disorientation in relation to religious concepts includes, or entails, a disorientation with respect to the inherent otherness of the religious and the poetic—one which leaves us no longer open to the claim of each to be the other's particular or intimate other. After all, Roman texts were (perhaps until yesterday) as much a part of the cultivated English mind as the texts of Ancient Greece and Christianity—as indeed was much of what eventuated in Western culture from their interaction. So if Virgil's *Aeneid* is part of the palimpsest that constitutes contemporary English culture, so too is the idea of the spiritual and the poetic as inter-penetrative. But the only way to validate that assumption is to attempt to activate that cultural resource. So the success of Golding's enterprise will turn on whether or not that attempt finds acknowledgement in his readers—on whether or not we can see what he means by invoking such reference points, and so see what he claims to see by their means.

A Structure Builds Itself Up

The opening sequence of *Darkness Visible* is rightly regarded as one of its most powerful. It describes a group of firemen who watch incredulously as a small boy walks out of an inferno of blazing buildings during the London Blitz. Since the fire is of such intensity that it melts lead and distorts iron, it seems impossible that any human being could have sur-vived it, but—although Matty is badly burned on the left side (so that even extensive plastic surgery leaves one side of his head bald and his left ear a purple stump)—he survives, and is eventually despatched from the hospital to Foundlings School in Greenfield.

This sequence insistently raises a question about what kind of being this boy is: he appears to 'condense out of the shuddering backdrop of the glare, and at the moment of his appearance he seemed to one of the watching firemen 'to be perhaps not entirely there—to be in a state of, as it were, indecision as to whether he was a human shape or merely a bit of flickering brightness. Was it the Apocalypse? Nothing could be more apocalyptic than a world so ferociously consumed' (DV, 15). This fireman is a bookseller, and one described as suffering 'from a romantic view of the classical world' (DV, 11); so this conceptual lens from the New Testament is no more and no less natural to him than that of Pompeii, or of seeking a piece of wood to placate Pan when he first glimpses Matty (DV, 12). And the hybridity of his interpretative framework is emphatically continuous with that of his narrator (as well as with the nature of the preposterously old country's capital):

There was an area east of the Isle of Dogs in London which was an unusual mixture even for those surroundings. Among the walled-off rectangles of water, the warehouses, railway lines and travelling cranes, were two streets of mean houses with two pubs and two shops among them. The bulks of tramp steamers hung over the houses where there had been as many languages spoken as families that lived there. But just now not much was being said, for the whole area had been evacuated officially and even a ship that was hit and set on fire had few spectators near it. There was a kind of tent in the sky over London, which was composed of the faint white beams of searchlights, with barrage balloons dotted here and there. The barrage balloons were all that the searchlights discovered in the sky, and the bombs came down, it seemed, mysteriously out of emptiness. They fell in or round the great fire…

Under the tent of searchlights a structure had built itself up in the air. It was less sharply defined than the beams of light but it was far brighter. It was a glare, a burning bush through or beyond which the thin beams were sketched more faintly…

The drone of bombers was dying away. The five-mile high tent of chalky lights had disappeared, been struck all at once, but the light of the great fire was bright as ever, brighter perhaps. Now the pink aura of it had spread. Saffron and ochre turned to blood-colour. The shivering of the white heart of the fire had quickened beyond the capacity of the eye to analyse it into an outrageous glare. High above the glare and visible now for the first time between two pillars of lighted smoke was the steely and untouched round of the full moon—the lover's, hunter's, poet's moon; and now—an ancient and severe goddess credited with a new function and a new title—the bomber's moon. She was Artemis of the bombers, more pitiless than ever before. (DV, 9, 13)

Most obviously, these passages elicit conviction by their precision at the purely descriptive level: they allow us to see in a literal sense, to see what the firemen standing on the edge of what was no longer part of the habitable world would have seen. But the fourth sentence of the passage (and of the book) subverts this literality, or perhaps it subverts our sense of what it is for words and sentences to be literally employed. It asserts that there was a tent in the sky over London—not that the searchlight beams and barrage balloons looked like a kind of tent, but simply that there was one (the kind composed of beams and balloons). But Golding does not just prefer metaphor to simile, a literal falsehood to a truthful comparison;

he goes on to write as if the falsehood were simply, literally true, as if its metaphorical validity immediately authorized its availability for purely descriptive purposes—proceeding, for example, to describe the extinguishing of the searchlights as the striking of a tent. And no sooner has talk of a tent become the new benchmark for literal truth than it engenders a new dimension of metaphorical significance. The fire is presented as having built itself up under the tent, as if expanding into the accommodation provided for it; and no sooner does it fill that structure than it is re-described (not as like but) *as* a burning bush—quite as if the idea of the tent as living quarters for a desert people immediately engenders a vision of it as providing shelter for the Ark of the Covenant, which in turn discloses the fire as the self-sustaining manifestation of God's appearance to Moses. From now on, the fire simply *is* a burning bush; and the literal truth of that characterization, in turn, licenses the later metaphorical characterization of its attendant smoke as 'two pillars', those marks of divine protection afforded the Israelites in their desert journey out of Egypt.

In this way, the most outrageously imaginative characterizations of the real become bare denotations of its actuality: the literal truth about things answers to the most extravagant of metaphors. Poetry is truth-telling, a means of entering more deeply into reality rather than of wandering away from it; and more specifically, ancient poetic forms of truth-telling are not only not made redundant by modernity: by disclosing their utterly contemporary usefulness, they disclose hitherto unsuspected ranges of their meaning. The moon of the bombers still merits the name 'Artemis', but reveals a degree of pitilessness in that divinity (and in reality) that earlier moon-worshippers could not have imagined.

From the outset, then, this novel deploys concepts from different layers in the spiritual palimpsest of English culture; but in the case of the tent and the burning bush, those elements also serve a reflexive purpose. For one can think of the strict geometry of the tent as the narrative structure of the novel in which it is presented, and the burning bush as the vision of spiritual reality (of reality as spiritual) it is designed to invoke and accommodate, even if it is fated to be first melted and ultimately dismantled or struck by that vision—the poetic equivalent of the string that is frayed and broken by divine music, as Matty's spiritual elders put it in one of his own visions (cf. DV, 238). Just as God's fiery self-manifestation to Moses requires a bush in or on which to burn, so any vision of divine fire needs a linguistic and literary medium; but unlike the Creator, the artistic creator cannot prevent his creation from consuming that which conjures and contains it.

Going for Ever, Sideways

During his time in hospital, Matty's relationship to language is presented as being as unusual as language's relation to him. First there is his name, or rather the curious business of his acquisition of a name, its assignment being the responsibility of an office that, working through the alphabet in rotation, had just made use of the letter 'v'.

> The young wit who was given the job of using 'w' suggested 'Windup', her chief having displayed less than perfect courage in an air raid. She had found she could get married and still keep her job and she was feeling secure and superior. Her chief winced at the name and drew his pen through it, foreseeing a coven of children all shouting 'Windup!', 'Windup!' He made his own substitution, though when he looked at what he had written it seemed not quite right and he altered it. There was no obvious reason for doing so. The name had first jumped into his mind with the curious effect of having come out of empty air and of being temporary, a thing to be noticed because you were lucky to be in the place where it had landed. It was as if you had sat silently in the bushes and—My!—there settled in front of you the rarest of butterflies or birds which had stayed long enough to be seen and had then gone off with an air of going for ever, sideways, it might be. (DV, 17)

As its final, syntactically strained sentence makes clear, this passage operates within the assumption that the relation between name and bearer is non-arbitrary. Philosophers and other theorists of language may tell us that names are not sentences, *a fortiori* neither apt or inept characterizations of the object or person they denote; but the depth of our resistance to such assertions is already evident in the ease with which we see the malicious joke in the young wit's coining of the name 'Windup' in honour of her chief: if we didn't intuitively regard names as fitting their bearers, why would we so unquestioningly accept the idea that a person's name might woundingly declare an unflattering aspect of his character? But it is not just that the chief experiences his eventual choice of name for Matty as somehow right for him: it is that the way in which the final sentence articulates that experience (thereby hovering undecidably between his way of experiencing it and the narrator's way of imagining that experience) involves treating Matty's rightful name as if it were a thing, and indeed the very thing it names.

According to this baptismal narrative, there is a moment of (non-original, alphabetically guided) invention, then a substitution, then an alteration, before Matty's name is settled on; and it is no sooner settled on than it is subjected to slippage in other's mouths throughout the novel (into 'Wandgrave', 'Wheelwright', 'Windgraff', 'Windrave' and so on), until his full name is finally bestowed upon him only as the final moments of his life are described (DV, 247). That name is Matthew Septimus Windrove—so even the chief's initial substitution is not *ex nihilo*, since the 'Wind' element is retained throughout, and we might well suspect that the intermediate version was 'Windgrove'. One could say, then, that Matty's name—taken as a linguistic element in the baptismal passage, and in the novel as a whole—literally is unceasingly mutating, on the move, possessed of an air of moving on for ever sideways. But the final sentence portrays his name as in truth unchanging and everlasting; what is temporary is rather its availability, which is a function of its willingness to grace us with its presence and our willingness to be receptive to that presence. The right name arrives, and then departs, but it never mutates; the office's preliminary revisions are rather increasingly successful attempts to reshape our language to accommodate it, to receive an apt impression of its own beautiful, independent life. In fact, Matty's rightful name is portrayed as if it *were* that which it names, as if it were its bearer; after all it is Matty himself whom we have already been invited to think of as the rarest kind of human creature (if he is even human at all), someone whose inhabitation of this world is momentary, his presence a fortunate but temporary phase in an endless journey that passes orthogonally through our locale. According to the final sentence, then, Matty's name is Matty, and Matty is his name: this act of naming penetrates to the essence of the being named, just as Adam in the Book of Genesis is authorized by God to give each creature its rightful name.

But whilst the passage operates within this Adamic assumption of fusion between name and bearer, its author simultaneously exploits the difference between the two. He tells us that Matty's rightful name is rare, beautiful, even partaking of eternal life, but he doesn't tell us what that name is until the novel's climax; he earns initial credit for his claim by virtue of the rare beauty of the passage in which the claim is made, but he builds upon that beginning by exploiting the long period of non-disclosure in two ways. First, he depicts Matty's nature and life in such a way that it can claim to manifest the rare beauty that results from participation in eternity; but the continuing mystery of his real name simultaneously leads the reader to feel that a crucial piece of the puzzle about Matty's nature and life is always missing. As a result, when his rightful name is revealed, its claim to the rare beauty of eternal life can now draw on the sustained achievement of that long and complex portrayal of its bearer, and at the same time it appears as the culminating element in that portrait—the nominative detail that goes proxy for the whole (appearing just as Matty's life reaches its apotheosis). Name and bearer thereby become mutually implicating, inextricably interwoven: what Matty's name means to us is indistinguishable from what Matty has come to mean to us, both part of that meaning and the whole of it. Matty is Matthew Septimus Windrove (the seventh chapter of Matthew's Gospel, and, in particular, its seventh verse, that exemplary articulation of the mighty wind of the Holy Spirit, which drives him to rove restlessly between places and countries, and perhaps also leaves him riven, both body and soul); Matty is his name.

Toads and Their Jewels

So much for language's relation to Matty; what of Matty's relation to language?

> As the various aids to recovery were removed from him and he began to speak more, it was observed that his relationship to language was unusual. He mouthed. Not only did he clench his fists with the effort of speaking, he squinted. It seemed that a word was an object, a material object, round

and smooth sometimes, a golf ball of a thing that he could just about manage to get through his mouth, though it deformed his face in the passage. Some words were jagged and these became awful passages of pain and struggle that made the other children laugh. After his turban came off in the period between the primary work and what cosmetic work was possible, the ruin of his half-raw skull and blasted ear was most unappealing. Patience and silence seemed the greater part of his nature. Bit by bit he learnt to control the anguish of speaking until the golfballs and jagged stones, the toads and jewels passed through his mouth with not much more than the normal effort. (DV, 17–18)

Coming immediately after the baptismal narrative, this passage continues to envision words as material objects, whilst leaving it unclear how far that vision is the narrator's and how far it is merely the narrator's way of capturing Matty's experience of language (which means leaving the distance between Golding and his protagonist as ours to determine). But no sooner has the narrator translated his own metaphorical equivalence between words and golf balls or jagged stones into a tool for literal description than he offers a new metaphorical equivalence on that basis: golf balls and jagged stones are aligned with toads and jewels. Did these toads and jewels just leap into Golding's mind out of thin air, no more than a glancing and temporary alternative means of expression; or are we here privileged to observe an exotic form of words establishing a further staging post in its unending journey through English language and culture? In defence of the latter possibility, I adduce three sources for these toads and jewels—three layers of the English cultural palimpsest as embodied in one cultivated poetic mind.

First, there is the ancient folk-myth about toads—that their ugly exterior hides something of great value. Golding's passage (by interrupting Matty's increasing mastery of words with a reminder of his physical condition) certainly invites us to apply the myth to Matty himself—that visibly ugly creature who contains a jewel of great worth, the divine fire out of which he originally condensed. But the passage directly applies this image not to Matty but to the words coming out of his mouth, all of which are presented as if emerging through a communicating passage from his interior, and so as all expressive of his interior jewel.

This relates his divine fire to language, the Word to words; but it simultaneously discriminates within the field of language by identifying as jewels only those words which cause him pain and anguish to pronounce or exteriorize—the jagged stones (for the paratactic juxtaposition of the two metaphorical pairs offers the toads as equivalents of the golf balls). So speaking the Word, communicating it to others by externalizing its jewel-like nature will necessarily demand awful passages of pain and struggle from the speaker—indeed, deforming physical contortions.

The second source is *As You Like It*, and an early speech by Duke Senior:

> Now, my co-mates and brothers in exile,
> Hath not old custom made this life more sweet
> Than that of painted pomp? Are not these woods
> More free from peril than the envious court?
> Here feel we not the penalty of Adam,
> The seasons' difference, as the icy fang
> And churlish chiding of the winter's wind,
> Which when it bites and blows upon my body
> Even till I shrink with cold, I smile and say,
> 'This is no flattery: these are counsellors
> That feelingly persuade me what I am.'
> Sweet are the uses of adversity,
> Which like the toad, ugly and venomous,
> Wears yet a precious jewel in his head;
> And this our life, exempt from public haunt,
> Find tongues in trees, books in the running brooks,
> Sermons in stones, and good in every thing. (II.i.1–17)

Shakespeare's character here invokes the ancient myth for new purposes. Most immediately, he presents adversity as something whose venomous ugliness brings about a sweet consequence—just as Matty's subjection to adversity will ultimately bring forth goodness. But the nature of that adversity is highly specific: the reverse the Duke suffers is banishment from court to the Forest of Arden, hence from urban civilization to the rural heartland of England—an early example of the Shakespearean green world that provides perspective on ordinary life and the means to transform it. Matty's obdurate resistance to contemporary social conventions is thereby presented as a potentially transfigurative attachment to the truly fundamental dimension of life—the basic bodily rhythms of the human animal's life form.

The particular sweetness the Duke prophesies also resonates with Golding's portrayal of Matty: for he associates inhabitation of the green world with access to the true language of nature, and so to true language—for the native tongue of the natural world is presumably the most truly apt expression of the nature of things, thus the one language in which words make manifest the essence of every thing of which they speak, and indeed make it manifest as good. The Duke's way of claiming that there is such a language even takes on the lineaments of that of which it longingly speaks: for each synonym it deploys for that language alliteratively bonds itself to each exemplary instance of the nature which speaks it—trees have tongues, but brooks have books, and stones sermons. Each of his words for language mirrors and so points us towards the respect in which each of our existing words for each natural thing already incarnates its nature. What the green world gives us is thus not a new language, but a proper appreciation of our old language as always already penetrating to the essence of things. This finding of the language of nature is, in fact, a refinding of our natural language (specifically of English, since these alliterative alignments involve the material properties of English words). In Matty's terms, the jewels of his spiritual language make manifest the divine fire out of which all creation is forged (although it will not be until the séance in Part Three that his words, and so words as such, will reveal their divinity (DV, 232–233).

But the Shakespearean context problematizes any attempt to derive from the Duke's speech a straightforward endorsement of the Adamic myth of language by which *Darkness Visible* appears to be orienting itself. This is because that speech is an exercise in the familiar literary genre of pastoral, bequeathed to the Renaissance by classical antiquity, according to which Nature stands opposed to art, and is to be praised for its very artlessness (its refusal of painted pomp, its embrace of the reality of the seasons and the body). But this genre suffers from what A.D. Nuttall has called a 'central psychosis': the fact that it is in art that the artless is celebrated.[4] The pastoral is a product of urban life, as the Duke is the product of the court; its generic identity is a poetic articulation of the very mode of existence it condemns. The paradox is evident in the Duke's attempt to dispraise language by praising the language of nature; as one of his courtiers immediately points out, he has translated 'the stubbornness of fortune into so quiet and sweet a style' that it constitutes an exemplary instance of that against which he claims to be taking a stand. It does not follow that the Duke, or any other pastoral poet, does not genuinely love the simple green world; but the very success of his loving depiction of it only confirms his exile from it.

Is the same true of the play in which the Duke makes this speech? Shakespeare plainly attempts to avoid the trap, since *As You Like It* not only contains a critique of the Duke's pastoralizing, but offers a counter-version of it, by making its green world real in a way that the Duke's speech does not: for it contains genuine rustics, of the earth earthy—such as Audrey, Corin and William, the rawness of whose imagery and existence mounts a counter-attack by nature against pastoral's defeat of nature by style. When Corin tells us 'that the property of rain is to wet and fire to burn; that good pasture makes fat sheep; and that a great cause of the night is the lack of the sun' (III.ii.23–28), his wisdom approaches tautology, but precisely because of that it conveys a strange strength and fullness of meaning; it is no less a deployment of words than the Duke's speech, but perhaps it approaches more nearly the linguistic condition to which the Duke's polished alliterative allusions to the tongue of the trees or the stone's sermons self-subvertingly advert.

So by alluding to this play, does Golding's talk of toads and jewels align him more with the Duke, or with the Duke's creator? How far does *Darkness Visible*'s Greenfield collude with the classical models and modes it draws upon (including that of pastoral), and how far does it disrupt or displace them, in order to find or re-activate the reality to which they aspired? Is Matty an artful representation of spiritual artlessness, or the real thing, in all its raw harshness? Like Shakespeare's generation of a genuinely English pastoral out of a critique of its prior forms, Golding's regeneration of raw spirituality (call it an English spiritual) out of a collage of inherited spiritual forms cannot avoid a version of Nuttall's pastoral psychosis: for both inevitably create a new artistic form, one which engenders a realistic effect rather than reality itself. It does not follow that either artist does not love what each aspires to depict; but it does mean that both confront the apparent paradox that their success in depicting it only confirms their exile from it. The real question is: can any artist, and indeed any human being, hope for anything other than exile—whether from pastoral or from spiritual reality—in our present cultural condition, or indeed in any cultural conditions we can recognize as pertinent to art?[5]

The third source invoked by Golding's toads and jewels is one of Hans Christian Andersen's fairytales or fables, 'The Toad' (1866). The youngest, smallest and ugliest member of a family of toads who have tumbled into a well is frustrated by the restrictions of their admittedly safe environment; having imbibed her mother's tale of the precious jewel that one family member carries in her head, she declares that she certainly doesn't possess it, before climbing out of the well to explore the larger green world surrounding it. She meets a variety of more or less threatening inhabitants of that world—a disgusted farmer, some welcoming frogs, a hubristic caterpillar, a poet and a naturalist (the former saving her from the latter's specimen jar)—until the head of a family of storks take her to their rooftop nest, a final voyage that she thinks indicates their willingness to have her join their coming migration to Egypt but which is, in fact, a result of their need for food.

> 'I must go to Egypt' said she.. 'All the longing and all the pleasure that I feel is much better than having a jewel in one's head'.
> And it was just she who had the jewel. That jewel was the continual striving and desire to go upward—ever upward. It gleamed in her head, gleamed in joy, beamed brightly in her longing...
> The Stork's beak pinched her, and the wind whistled; it was not exactly agreeable, but she was going upward—upward towards Egypt—and she knew it; and that was why her eyes gleamed, and a spark seemed to fly out of them.
> 'Quunk!—ah!' The body was dead—the Toad was killed! But the spark that had shot forth from her eyes; what became of that? The sunbeam took it up; the sunbeam carried the jewel from the head of the toad. Whither?

Ask not the naturalist; rather ask the poet. He will tell it thee under the
guise of a fairy tale…
But the jewel in the head of the toad?
Seek it in the sun; see it there if you can.
The brightness is too dazzling there. We have not yet such eyes as can
see into the glories which God has created, but we shall receive them
by-and-by; and that will be the most beautiful story of all, and we shall all
have our share in it.[6]

Andersen's adaptation of the ancient myth transfigures the jewel from
an object to a drive—the continual striving and desire to go upward; it
is what one might think of as a perfectionist intimation that the well
is not the world, that another, better state of the world always lies just
beyond the limits of the world one currently inhabits. There is no final,
complete or attained state of that world and so of the self or soul that
inhabits it; rather, there is either a lethal willingness to accept one's
currently attained world, or a refusal ever to regard any attained world
as final or complete. The little toad's vitality lies in her striving, not in
anything she already possesses or might come to possess; otherwise put,
it is the impossible desire to become one with the incomprehensibly
transcendent sun, which is at once beyond the gaze or reach of mortal beings and yet always already one with those beings insofar as they
yearn for it.

But Andersen also tells us that the incomprehensible nature of jewel
and sun can nevertheless be comprehended—if not by the naturalist
then by the poet, and in the form of a fairy tale (*this* fairy tale). What
grants this genre its power is, however, its willingness to acknowledge
that its own grasp of this dazzling brightness takes the form of acknowledging its own utter inadequacy in comparison with another mode of
story-telling, that of God's narrative for creation and for human beings
within it. And just as we shall all have our share in that most beautiful of stories, so the fairytale's portrayal of the jewel's participation
in the sun is successful only by declaring its own willing dependence
upon, and so its ultimate participation in, the Christian story of the Son
(the Father and the Holy Spirit). By declaring its own nothingness in
relation to that divine narrative of (and doing so in terms provided by

the sacred texts which convey it, such as 'Now we see through a glass darkly; presently we shall behold Him face to face'), it identifies the mode of its participation in that narrative—namely, that of withdrawing any claims to authority of its own by crediting such authority as it may presently have to another Author. Since its nothingness is manifest only in relation to that unattained but attainable narrative perspective, any proper declaration of that nothingness relates it and its readers to that other perspective, and so makes of itself a way into that divine story—a spark thrown off its dazzling sun.

It becomes increasingly clear as Part One of *Darkness Visible* develops that Matty can only become himself precisely by such an act of directed or dialectical self-abnegation—by declaring himself as nothing in relation to the God of the Old (and New) Testaments, and thereby aspiring wholly to identify his life with the Christian form of life, to become an individual in whom that impossibly perfected story condenses or crystallizes. But the author of *Darkness Visible* makes no such vow: Christian concepts and traditions remain prominent throughout the text, but they are frequently interwoven with (and sometimes put into conflict with) resources deriving from other layers of the cultural sedimentation that helps constitute the English society out of which it was written.

This is evident in the very phrase whose palimpsestic significance we are currently delineating: Golding's toads and jewels inherit and revivify ancient folk-myth, the pastorals of classical antiquity and Shakespearean revaluation, and European fairy tale. He thereby acknowledges his indebtedness to the genres of myth and fable, whilst presenting them not as limits upon his present project but as elements in a broader field of its poetic resources—more specifically as conventions that his project aspires to reconstruct in order better to realize their orienting aspiration to represent the reality of things. But this heterogeneity of genres also shows that, unlike Andersen, Golding resists the subordination of poetry to any particular religious authority, the absolute subsumption of his literary authority within that of Christianity; he is not Aeneas but Virgil, not a religious visionary but rather the artistic envisioner of Matty's religious visions. And yet: when Golding reaches the point of envisioning the Hell that Matty seeks to avert but which is as integral to his religious sensibility as Heaven—when in Parts Two and Three he follows Sophy, the metaphysical twin of twentieth century terrorism, from her initial nihilistic intuitions to her whole-hearted creative imagining of their realization in the world—the question of his authority to relate what he has seen unavoidably recurs. Virgil asks divine permission to say what he has seen of the Underworld; when that request re-appears as the epigraph to Golding's novel, to whom does he imagine that it is directed, and in what spirit?

Vulnerable Skin

By the end of his stay in Australia, Matty's agonizing struggle to find a way of meaning Christian words and deeds—to find himself in those religious resources—comes to a climax.[7] After the apparently castrating crucifarce or crucifixion he undergoes at the hands (or feet) of an Aborigine named Harry Bummer, he performs his own version of the Old Testament prophetic practices of Elijah and Ezekiel in downtown Darwin, to disruptive effect; and before returning to England, he searches for somewhere low down, a place at once hot, fetid and supplied with water, in which he can undertake a ritual (at once final and initial or initiatory). Watched only by uncomprehending frogs and lizards, he strides into and through a deep, isolated pool at night-time, dressed only in a chain fastened around his waist from which heavy steel wheels are slung, and holding a lit, antique lamp over his head; at the mid-point, his head is wholly submerged, with only the hand and arm grasping the lamp remaining above the surface of the water. Once he reaches the other side, he heaves the lamp four times at each point of the compass; then he goes on his way (DV, 72–76).

Matty remains silent throughout, but his actions speak for themselves: more precisely, they *say* themselves, as Wittgenstein puts it when characterizing what he calls a gesture language, or the gestural dimension of language.[8] The medium and the message are one; what it signifies and its mode of signification are inextricable. One might say that Matty's actions are perfectly adapted to their purpose: their meaning would be altered or diminished if any element of the ritual were other than it is (intuitively, the shape and raw material of the steel wheels matters as much as their weight, as does the old-fashioned design of the lamp). On the other hand, the significance of those actions in that place is importantly dependent on the wider context within which the ritual is performed; in particular, our sense of its meaning is inseparable from our knowledge that Matty is performing it, and so from everything we know about Matty's life up to this moment (which means pretty much everything in *Darkness Visible* up to this point). These are not contra-dictory responses, any more than saying of the expression in someone's eyes that it is unique and that it expresses what it expresses only in the context of her face.

When Wittgenstein discusses Sir James Frazer's account (in *The Golden Bough*) of the annual ritual in which the priest-king of Nemi is slain by his successor, he offers the following response:

> Put that account of the King of the Wood at Nemi together with the phrase 'the majesty of death', and you see that they are one.
> The life of the priest-king shows what is meant by that phrase.
> If someone is gripped by the majesty of death, then through such a life he can give expression to it.—Of course this is not an explanation: it puts one symbol in place of another. Or one ceremony in place of another. (RFGB, 3e[9])

One way of giving expression to our understanding of Matty's ritual would be to put it together with the following passage: 'and the light shineth in darkness and the darkness comprehendeth it not'; another would be to put it together with the phrase 'you have been baptized with water; you shall be baptized with the Holy Spirit'. Either phrase might crystallize what is compelling about Matty's ritual, and so about his life; or they might leave us cold, dissatisfied. But even if they satisfy us, it is not by finding a non-ritualized or unceremonial equivalent for the meaning of the ritual; they rather amount to the substitution of one ritual symbol or ceremonial gesture for another. Such phrases, insofar as they capture the impression the ritual makes, do not so much repre-sent its meaning as re-enact it: one might equally well say that the ritual gives expression to what grips us about the words. Each is the other's explanation; the meaning of both is equally ceremonial or gestural.

If we acknowledge this ritual and these phrases (both from the beginning of John's Gospel) as one, then we acknowledge an internal relation between the meaning of the ritual and the meaning of Christianity; but this ritual is not a Christian rite, not a rite of passage into or within the Christian church—it is Matty's remaking of Christian elements into a language that articulates what he (prophetically) feels, something that he has just distinguished from what he (prophetically) sees (DV, 71). The same holds of his culminating spiritual insight, during his employment as a caretaker at Wandicott House, an exclusive private school outside Greenfield. Having just had his sexual potency restored by a dream in which Sophy appears as the woman in the Apocalypse (to which he responds by dancing to the sound of Beethoven's Seventh, the symphony Wagner ceremonially characterized as 'the apotheosis of dance'), he has a vision in which his fellowship with his two spiritual elders is revealed, and all three throw down their crowns at the feet of a great spirit in white, who will stand behind the schoolchild Matty has been asked to guard, and whom he will save from a terrorist kidnap attempt. Surely here, one might think, the intense colours of his spiritual passion have finally come neatly and evenly to fill in the outlines provided by the Christian story (cf. DV, 22); but even here, those outlines are broken—the specificities and exclusivities of doctrine bypassed, the orthodoxies of liturgy and rite dispensed with. Christianity remains Matty's sole spiritual language until the end; but he works only with those elements that work for him, and is more than willing to fuse or stitch them together with any extra-Christian elements that also seem to work.

How does Golding make his depiction of Matty's immersion ritual so powerfully impressive—conveying its ceremonial meaning without lapsing into attempts to explain or summarize that meaning non-ceremonially? His description of Matty's actions is both like and unlike the book's opening description of his entry into the world. They are alike, in that this scene comes vividly to life primarily by an absolutely receptive transcription of its external physical details, so that the reader seems to be standing at the edge of the pool observing everything that happens; every element of deed and context exhibits itself before our eyes in such a way that we are simultaneously convinced that the man's purpose is utterly inscrutable (because hidden away inside his head, a point of view from which Golding scrupulously excludes us) and utterly transparent (wholly manifest in what the man does). But unlike the opening account of the Blitz, this radically external description reduces its metaphorical content to the barest minimum—no tents or bushes, no goddess of the outback, nothing figurative that is no sooner invoked than deployed as if literally true. Any reasonable natural scientist or anthropologist could accept the descriptive resources employed here; but the result is that the basic constituents of the natural world disclose themselves as capable of being (even perhaps as always already) irradiated with spiritual meaning.

Crucially, however, before this vivid transcription of the ritual, Golding writes a kind of prologue to it—two long paragraphs cast in predominantly subjunctive or counterfactual form, in which the narrator imagines someone walking into this hidden environment, and reports on what every available sense would have supplied such a person:

> Human feet would have felt the soft and glutinous texture, half water half mud, that would rise swiftly to the ankles and farther... The nose would have taken all the evidence of vegetable and animal decay, while the mouth and skin... would have tasted an air so warm and heavy with water it would have seemed as if there was doubt as to whether the whole body stood or swam or floated. The ears would be filled with the thunder of the frogs and anguish of nightbirds...
>
> Then, accustomed to the darkness by a long enough stay and willing—it would have to be by sacrifice of life and limb—to trade everything for the sight, eyes would find what evidence there was for them too. It might be a faint phosphorescence round the fungi on the trunks of trees... or a swift flight of sparks flashing between tree trunks...
>
> By then, feet that had stayed that long would have sunk deep, the mud moving to this side and that, the warm mud; and the leeches would have attached themselves down there in an even darker darkness, a more secret secrecy and with unconscious ingenuity, without allowing their presence to be felt would have begun to feed through the vulnerable skin.
>
> But there was no man in that place; and it seemed impossible to one who had inspected it from far off and in daylight that there ever had been a man in the place since men began. (DV, 73)

Suppose we were to put this passage together with the following sentence from the Book of Genesis: 'And the earth was without form, and void; and darkness was upon the face of the deep': we would, I think, see that they are one. But it is not just that the distinct natural elements of the scene blur and blend into one another (liquid earth, watery air, animal decay), to the point that natural form as such dissolves; a similar effect simultaneously occurs at the level of narrative form. For what begins as an act of imagining what someone else—no-one in particular—might experience quickly dissolves into an act of imagining what such experience would have been like for the narrator, and one so intensely detailed and penetrating that it quickly takes on the aspect of a report from someone who really did walk into the pool in the encroaching dark, even someone who is currently standing—all senses alert—in that softly glutinous water. In this way, distinct imaginative acts blur into one another, and acts of imagination blur into transcriptions of experience.

The uncanniness of all this compels the narrator to think of his imaginary person in the pool—that is, himself—as risking life and limb for the experience, and to associate his imaginative residence in the water with suffering leeches to feed silently on him. Here, the blurring or blending goes into reverse: the realities conjured up by the narrator's imaginative capacity to penetrate the experiences of others now begin to penetrate him, disclosing the porousness of his own identity and beginning to leech his lifeblood. Why this sudden sense of lethal vulnerability? Because the narrator's act of imagination places him in the very position that Matty will occupy later that night: it is a kind of trial effort, a preliminary attempt at taking on Matty's perspective or view on the world, becoming that incarnation of 'the Spirit of God moving upon the face of these waters' for which the previously cited verses of Genesis directly prepare the way. This (un)holy essay is something from which the narrator withdraws as a seeming impossibility, but an impossibility encountered specifically from the point of view of someone who had inspected it in daylight—from Matty's perspective.

In short, Golding tries to imagine the context and core experience of the ritual from Matty's point of view, and the experience so disturbs him that he denies its very possibility and retreats to the perspective of an observer for the ritual itself. He experiences his own character, when driven by deep spiritual feeling to inscrutable but exquisitely apt ritual gestures, as threatening to drain away his creator's vitality; he fears the uncanny porousness of his imagination to its own creations, and in particular the secret ingenuity with which this imaginative creation threatens to destabilize every boundary or limit within and between authorial self and authored world—to dissolve the structure of reality altogether. What lesson should Golding's readers draw from this ceremonial double gesture of immersion-and-withdrawal about the porousness of the barrier between themselves and the world of *Darkness Visible*—about the risks of allowing its creator to draw us into that world? And remember: the protagonist of this ritual scene is Matty—the good man, the prophet, the saint. What might happen when we are invited to imagine Matty's opposite, his dark twin?

The Rabbit, or: sit mihi fas audita loqui

At the end of Part Three, Sophy's plot to kidnap a child from Wandicott House School is falling apart: her terrorist sister has hijacked the plan (together with Sophy's boyfriend) for her own purposes; the arrival of unlooked-for visitors means that the stable room in which she grew up cannot be used to incarcerate the kidnapped child; and Matty has anyway forced her key accomplice to abort the kidnap itself. Having been ejected from the stables, but before discovering that the kidnap attempt has failed, in the depths of the countryside outside Greenfield, her attention is caught:

> There was a loud thumping noise in the hedge and it stopped her dead. Something was bouncing and flailing about and then it squeaked and she could make out that it was a rabbit in a snare, down there by the ditch that lay between the towpath and the woods. It was flailing about, not knowing what had caught it and not caring to know but killing itself in an effort just to be free, or it may be, just to be dead. Its passion defiled the night with grotesque and obscene caricature of process, of logical advance through time from one moment to the next where the trap was waiting. (DV, 249)

Still before receiving the bad news from her accomplice, but ecstatic at the sight of the conflagration at Wandicott House painting the sky red, 'she saw what the last outrage was and knew herself capable of it. She shut her eyes as the image swept round her' (DV, 251). Within that image is the kidnapped boy, now incarcerated in the stinking toilet of an abandoned, rotting barge she had previously explored on the towpath outside Greenfield. The child's arms are bound behind his back, as are his feet and knees; more ropes hold him on either side to the boat's walls, and a huge pad of sticky stuff covers his mouth and cheeks. His violent struggles against those bonds 'sound like a rabbit thumping' (DV, 251), and are redoubled when he hears her voice; but somehow, as she enters the confined space, inhales its disgusting smell of ancient and fresh urine, and removes the child's jersey and shirt, her boyfriend's commando knife is in her hand.

> She swept her hand over his naked tum and belly button, the navel my dear if you must refer to it at all and she felt paper-thin ribs and a beat, beat, thump, thump at left centre. So she got his trousers undone and held his tiny wet cock in her hand as he struggled and hummed through his nose. She laid the point of the knife on his skin and finding it to be the right place, pushed it a bit so that it pricked. The boy convulsed and flailed in the confinement and she was or someone was, frightened a bit, far off and anxious. So she thrust more still and felt it touch the leaping thing or be touched by it again and again while the body exploded with convulsions and a high humming came out of the nose. She thrust with all the power there was, deliriously; and the leaping thing inside seized the knife so that the haft beat in her hand, and there was a black sun. There was liquid everywhere and strong convulsions and she pulled the knife away to give them free play but they stopped. The boy just sat there in his bonds, the white patch of elastoplast divided down the middle by the dark liquid from his nose. (DV, 252)

Few commentators fail to note this passage, although only in passing, and those who do go into more detail typically misdescribe what actually goes on: they report Sophy as castrating the boy, or as stabbing him through his genitals.[10] These critical lapses are striking, and deeply significant. Specifically, they occlude the fact that Sophy stabs the child through the heart, which the passage repeatedly describes as leaping and thumping, thereby presenting it as going proxy for the boy's whole body (as it thumps and leaps in its confinement), and so characterizing both heart and body in terms first applied to the trapped rabbit in the ditch—a creature already identified with Sophy herself, the human animal whose obscene passion defiles the night as she flails hysterically in her desire to be free, or to be dead. These commentators thereby fail to note that Golding equates her murder of the child with self-murder, understanding it as an attempt to annihilate not just that frightened anxious, far-off part of her self that retains some connection with goodness, but her existence as such, which she conceives of as nothing more than an grotesque and obscene caricature of process or narrative.

This specific failure of vision is also, however, a way of averting one's critical gaze from the scene as a whole; it is a way of covering it up and so of ushering it off-stage even whilst appearing to do the reverse. Just like those who can hardly bring themselves to mention the scene at all, such critics deny its true reality, and so participate in the general critical reluctance to admit that we have indeed read every word of it, and so that Golding has compelled us to read every word of it. He has here exercised his unequalled imaginative powers in such a way that Sophie's imagining of the final outrage appears to us as the narrative of an actual event, and our reading of it is as a kind of participation in that event. The boundary between imaginative representation and reality dissolves within the world of the novel, together with the boundary between that imagined world and its readers; and we experience both dissolutions as the result of that world's creator's willingness to dissolve the boundary between himself and his creation—to immerse himself in the reality of Sophy's evil, which means devoting his imagination to making that evil real in a way which seriously problematizes Everett's bracingly clear-headed distinction between reality and a literarily-engendered sense of reality.

Put this account of child-murder together with the phrase 'darkness visible', and you see that they are one. But if this scene really epitomizes the meaning of the novel's title, and so of the novel itself, why has no critic of the novel ventured to quote extensively from it, let alone to cite it in its entirety? If to do so is to experience once again what it depicts, and so to inflict it on those who read that criticism, one can hardly blame them. Such a refusal is, after all, the most direct way of registering the perception (at once critical and moral) that this scene is ob-scene, something whose outrageous content ought really to remain off-stage (as the etymology of the term requires) because, staged in this way, it literally makes a deep impression on us: as one of Coetzee's characters puts it when confronted with an analogous case of the literary representation of evil, 'it made an impress on me the way a branding iron does. Certain pages burn with the fires of hell'.[11]

If we will not quote this passage—this exemplary element of the palimpsest that is *Darkness Visible*—we seem to imply that Golding should not have created it, and so should not have created the whole fictional world for which it goes proxy (however much praise we lavish on every other aspect of that world); but if we do quote it, we seem to risk violating basic tenets of literary criticism and morality alike (by failing to keep what is, precisely insofar as it is poetically successful, beyond the pale of rightful representation). But we might rather think of such citation as the critical equivalent of the creative strategy at work in Golding's depiction of the pool ritual—that is, as one of immersion-and-withdrawal. For if a critical immersion in Sophy's vision reveals the artistic means by which Golding creates in us the sense that this evil is no literary artefact but the thing itself, it necessarily reveals that impression to be a literary creation or effect, and thereby allows us to withdraw from any identity-threatening participation in it.

On that basis, would some of my readers extend retrospective permission for me to relay what William Golding saw on his visit to the Underworld? Others might rather stay true to their initial sense that these pages really do burn with the fires of hell, and conclude that this text genuinely disables criticism. Golding himself vowed never to talk about *Darkness Visible*, and he was true to his word. Many readers will take this as a ceremonial gesture intended to encourage a similar act of self-abnegation by those whose passionate interest in the text is precisely what tempts them to talk about it critically; but I think there are ways of acknowledging that gesture without so taking it—for example, by finding ways of talking critically about the novel which bring out the fact that, and the ways in which, it says itself. Do I need to add that I may be wrong?

Notes

1. 'Golding's Pity', in J. Carey (ed), *William Golding: The Man and His Books* (London: Faber and Faber, 1986), p. 110—hereafter 'GP'.
2. London: Faber.
3. *William Golding: The Man Who Wrote Lord of the Flies* (London: Faber, 2009).
4. A.D. Nuttall, *Shakespeare the Thinker* (New Haven: Yale University Press, 2007), p. 231.
5. For more on this issue, in relation to modernist realism as a project in the arts and in philosophy, see my *The Wounded Animal: J.M. Coetzee and the Difficulty of Reality in Literature and Philosophy* (Princeton, NJ: Princeton University Press, 2009), especially chapters 9 and 10.
6. Quoted from the translation at http://hca.gilead.org.il/the_toad.html.
7. If the present essay could contain another essay, this would be the point to explore the connections between Golding's Matty and Stanley Cavell's interpretation of Kierkegaard's diagnosis of Magister Adler, the defining question of which is 'How far a man in our age may be justified in asserting that he had a revelation?'—that is, whether anything any longer could conceivably count for us as a revelation of the Christian God. Matters of spiritual disorientation, empty forms of life, and the internal relations between religion, politics and art prove central to answering that question. Cf. 'Kierkegaard's *On Authority and Revelation*', in *Must We Mean What We Say?* (Cambridge: Cambridge University Press, 1976).
8. For more on this, cf. my *Inheritance and Originality* (Oxford: Oxford University Press, 2001), Part One, Sects. 45–46.
9. 'Remarks on Frazer's *Golden Bough*' (ed) R. Rhees (trans.) A.C. Miles (Doncaster: Brynmill Press, 1979).
10. Cf. V. Tiger, *William Golding: The Unmoved Target* (London: Marion Boyars, 2003), p. 195; M. Kinkead-Weekes and I. Gregor, *William Golding: A Critical Study of the Novels* (London: Faber, 2002), p. 252, respectively.
11. J.M. Coetzee, *Elizabeth Costello* (London: Secker and Warburg, 2003), p. 171. I discuss this episode in more detail in Chapter 12 of *The Wounded Animal* (op. cit.).

References

Andersen, H.C. *The Toad* (1866—Quoted from the Translation at http://hca.gilead.org.il/the_toad.html).

Carey, J. 2009. *William Golding: The Man Who Wrote Lord of the Flies*. London: Faber.

Cavell, S. 1976. 'Kierkegaard's On Authority and Revelation'. In *Must We Mean What We Say?* Cambridge: Cambridge University Press.

Coetzee, J.M. 2003. *Elizabeth Costello*. London: Secker and Warburg.

Everett, B. 1986. 'Golding's Pity'. In *William Golding: The Man and His Books*, ed. J. Carey. London: Faber and Faber.

Golding, W. 1979. *Darkness Visible*. London: Faber.

Kinkead-Weekes, M., and I. Gregor. 2002. *William Golding: A Critical Study of the Novels*. London: Faber.

Mulhall, S. 2001. *Inheritance and Originality*. Oxford: Oxford University Press.

———. 2009. *The Wounded Animal: J.M. Coetzee and the Difficulty of Reality in Literature and Philosophy*. Princeton, NJ: Princeton University Press.

Nuttall, A.D. 2007. *Shakespeare the Thinker*. New Haven: Yale University Press.

Tiger, V. 2003. *William Golding: The Unmoved Target*. London: Marion Boyars.

Wittgenstein, L. 1979. *Remarks on Frazer's Golden Bough*, trans. and ed. A.C. Miles and R. Rhees. Doncaster: Brynmill Press.

16

Pictorial Decorum

Jonathan Gilmore

Introduction: Continuity, Discontinuity and Artistic Autonomy

In this chapter I wish to explore, through a particular problem in the philosophy of art, a constant tension that shapes aesthetic theory. The philosophical problem is the nature of artistic decorum (the notion will be explained below). The tension is between (i) the pull of conceptions of art that stress its *continuity* with life: e.g., those frameworks that seek to show how the visual, auditory, affective, cognitive, rational, and evaluative dimensions of works of art instantiate and can be explained by appeal to modes, concepts, and categories of experience generally; and (ii) the pull of approaches that stress *discontinuity*, e.g., those that seek to identify distinctive or peculiar conditions of artistic experience, such as proprietary "artistic emotions," artistic cognition, and so on, that are not of the same kind as their everyday counterparts.

J. Gilmore (✉)
CUNY Graduate Center and Baruch College, New York, USA
e-mail: jonathan.gilmore@me.com

© The Author(s) 2018
A. Falcato and A. Cardiello (eds.), *Philosophy in the Condition of Modernism*,
https://doi.org/10.1007/978-3-319-77078-9_16

The emphasis on continuity in the philosophy of art realizes itself in various forms of reduction; dissolution of paradoxes through showing some putatively paradoxical behavior to be no more remarkable than ordinary behavior; and aspirations to greater explanatory power, theoretical simplicity, and often greater opportunity for empirical investigation, especially via the tools of cognitive science that were developed to study general affective, cognitive, and behavioral dispositions, not just those that come into play in our encounters with art. Finally, a hallmark of such continuity is the reference to art, in general, as a more primary explanandum than, say, particular styles, forms, movements, media, or techniques of art (let alone a particular work of art).

The emphasis on discontinuity, by contrast, is expressed in the identification of potentially *sui-generis* experiences of art, such as a kind of knowledge art alone can furnish or Schopenhauer's claim that music represents joy in general, not the everyday emotion that a person may have in response to some object or state of affairs; the stress on what may be ineffable in our engagement with art, not tractable in ordinary modes of measurement and scientific analysis; the autonomy of art in several registers; the essential embeddedness of certain kinds of expression in their artistic forms or media (as in the putative heresy of translation vis-à-vis poetry, or in Hegel's insistence that the thoughts which art expresses as a vehicle of Spirit's development do not exist prior to their expression via art.[1]); and, the emphasis on how aesthetic judgments can be objective while necessarily taking a first-person subjective form in which no reliance on authority or testimony is licit. Finally, such discontinuity tends to see individual works of art as potential counterexamples to general moral, metaphysical and epistemic theories, rather than as objects that call for redescription so as to eliminate whatever putative features made them seem to be exceptions calling for a distinctive analysis. For some thinkers, such as Flaubert writing in 1857, art's alternative to ordinary experience is a kind of refuge: "Life is a thing so hideous," he writes, "the only way to endure it is to escape it…by living in art." For others, art's disconnection from the real world is evinced in a *sui generis* kind of experience. Thus, in his lectures on literature, Nabokov cautions us to see each work of art as the "creation of a new world," and to approach it as "something brand new, having no obvious connections with the world we already know." In some approaches, that sui generis experience putatively furnished by works of art is said to entail that they possess a meaning that cannot be expressed or conveyed invariantly across different forms.[2]

In this essay I don't, of course, try to resolve that tension between continuity and discontinuity, a tension that may indeed be constitutive of our relation to art, at least since the advent of Modernism. My more modest goal is to offer an account of a particular kind of evaluation of art that expresses that tension. This is a judgment of art that sees it as failing, in some sense, in virtue of standards that it sets for itself. This kind of judgment, which I associate with considerations of artistic decorum, embodies both the idea of continuity that art is subject to general norms that apply to all sorts of (non artistic) objects and experiences, and the idea of discontinuity that works of art should be evaluated with reference to their "own laws"—to criteria that emerge from the art itself.

Pictorial Decorum

A familiar way of criticizing an artistic representation is to say that it misrepresents its subject. Sometimes this is meant to suggest that the representation shows the subject (a person, an object, a scene, etc.) in a way that elicits false beliefs about the subject. But such misrepresentation may also occur when a subject is represented in a way that "doesn't do justice" to it, or in a way said to be "inapt," "unfitting," "unseemly," "unsuitable," or otherwise wrong. In such cases, the charge is not so much that the depiction shows the subject in ways that are inaccurate, as that it shows the subject in ways that the subject doesn't warrant.

In what follows I ask what it means to judge a work of art as failing to depict its subject in an appropriate way. I refer to such a judgment, when applied to visual art, as one of *pictorial decorum*. Such decorum concerns how the subjects of a picture ought to be represented. However, it is unclear what kind or kinds of normativity are at issue when we consider whether a picture represents its subject in the right way. That a subject warrants being shown possessing certain properties because it has those properties, may be only one of many considerations in determining whether a pictorial representation is apt. As we will see, aesthetic, moral, cognitive and other considerations may also constrain whether the attribution of certain features to a subject is justified.

In "Pictorial Subjects and Modes of Depiction" and "Three Defects in Depiction" of this chapter, I describe a variety of cases that exemplify ways in which a work fails to render its subject in an adequate way. I look at three significant (but not exhaustive) kinds of reasons often introduced to justify the judgment that a work's form is inappropriate for its subject: (i) expressive reasons, (ii) cognitive reasons, and (iii) moral or political reasons. To say that a work exhibits a violation of decorum for expressive reasons is to hold that the subject is not rendered in an apt way given what meaning or expression the work is intended to convey. To say that a work's form doesn't fit its subject for cognitive reasons is to judge that the subject is rendered in a way that elicits a false understanding of the subject. Finally, to assert that a subject is misrepresented in moral terms is to suggest that it is shown from an immoral or politically objectionable point of view. In "Concepts, Saliencies, and Point of View", I ask how such violations of pictorial decorum are registered or embodied in the work of art. In other words, what property of the form in which a subject is represented grounds the violations of decorum? I propose that violations of pictorial decorum are instantiated in works of art as conflicts between *what is made salient* by the style, manner, or form of depiction and our *conception* (or broadly construed concept) of the object depicted.

Pictorial Subjects and Modes of Depiction

I begin with two examples of a failure of fit between style and subject. The first comes from a famous conversation that took place around 1961 in which Andy Warhol asked his friend Emile de Antonio what he thought of two paintings of Coca-Cola bottles that Warhol had recently completed. One displayed the soda bottle in the unembellished "cold" and formal manner that would later emerge as central to Warhol's style of Pop Art; the other, however, featured a frenetic cross-hatched surface with the kind of gestural brushstroke that a cutting-edge artist in

New York might have unreflectively adopted while under the sway of the still dominant style of Abstract Expressionism. De Antonio, who is the source of the story, wrote, "I said to Andy, 'Why did you do two of these? One of them is so clearly your own. And the second is just kind of ridiculous because it's not anything. It's part Abstract Expressionism and part whatever you're doing.'...that was almost the birth of Pop. Andy did it."[3]

Although Warhol did not immediately heed that appraisal, its justification soon became clear. For the "abstract expressionist Coca-Cola bottle," (Arthur Danto's appellation) was a stylistic mistake: the manner in which Warhol painted the work was inappropriate for its subject, even if it took the later emergence of Pop Art for the disjunction in that work between form and subject to be clear. In the Pop version of the Coca-Cola bottle painting, the style shows the depicted subject in a way commensurate with that subject's nature: the soft drink that is ubiquitous, the same for everyone, desired as much for brand-name as for taste, was aptly rendered in the hard-edged, anonymous, instantly recognizable and legible style of commercial advertising. By contrast, the representation of the bottle in a style associated with gestural brushstrokes, spontaneous composition, built-up surfaces and nonfigurative aims offers a point of view on the advertised image of the mass-produced soft drink that it does not seem to warrant. My second example of a failure of decorum is seen in Francisco Goya's major royal portrait of 1800, *The Family of Carlos IV*. It is a likely presumption in accord with such commissions that Goya intended to represent the monarch in a suitably flattering light.

However, the picture's awkward rendering of its subjects makes it difficult to see what it expresses as consistent with that aim. A viewer expects that picture would cast the royal family in a manner that conveys a putatively natural nobility, however what the picture actually shows is a rather ugly and undignified assembly with a puffed-up comportment and self-conscious ostentation in their dress. The elevated status of the royal family is no doubt indicated or symbolized by the appropriate trappings of dress and décor, but that status is not embodied in, or *shown* by, the picture. That is, we can infer to the status of the individuals from what we see, but we don't see an expression of that status in the picture. The nineteenth-century critic Théophile Gautier reportedly described the painting as looking like "the corner baker and his wife after they won the lottery."[4] Goya's manner of representation foregrounds certain features of the King and his family but those features seem inconsistent with how the subjects should be seen.

To explain such failures of fit, we might look to how style and subject were conceived in ancient accounts of rhetoric and decorum. From Aristotle, we learn that in describing something metaphorically, we must use the terms that are appropriate to the object, just as "we must consider, as a red cloak suits a young man, what suits an old one; for the same garment is not suitable for both."[5] And from Horace we learn of the three levels of style: plain, middle and lofty, the subjects that they are respectively fit to render, and the end (education, delight, moving an audience) each is directed toward.[6] These ancient treatments of decorum may be construed as offering only aesthetic imperatives, driven as they are by considerations of what construction of speech from the audience's point of view would appear (that is, merely *seem*) to be correct and thereby deliver the sought after response. But as the classical accounts' explanations of why a given style must not be used for a given subject make clear, the considerations that grounded the choice of an appropriate style were bound up with assumptions about the nature of, and hierarchy among, things themselves. The problem with appealing to these accounts in a general explanation of pictorial decorum, however, is that they only *describe* or catalog the aptness of style to subject, without explaining what that aptness consists in. We want to know what justifies the claim that some manner or style of representation is wrong for some subject or subject-type. What accounts for a failure of decorum?

In what follows, I will use the term *subject* to identify what a depiction refers to, or purports to refer to (as in cases in which the subject does not exist). And I will use the terms *manner, mode, style,* and *form* to identify the way in which a given subject is represented.[7] Some writers identify that distinction as between the subject of a work and its *content*. An advantage of that way of employing "content" (instead of "form" or "manner," "mode," and so on) is that it makes plain the analogies among the way a picture has a content and the ways other sorts of representations, such as linguistic and mental representations, have content. So just as we might ask, Is the content of this picture adequate to what in the world it depicts? we might ask, Is the content of my belief adequate to what in the world it represents? However, this notion of content is too narrow from the standpoint of making sense of pictorial decorum. The terms "form" "manner" or "mode" of representation are more appropriate, because they apply more broadly, capturing elements of a representation that, while not part of the content of the representation, nonetheless attribute features to the subject that is represented. A gigantic portrait may impute grandeur to the subject that the portrait represents, without the content of the depiction playing a role in that attribution. Furthermore, many features of a work of art do not attribute properties to its subject but may, nonetheless, provoke the charge that the subject should not be shown in that way. Consider, for example, the outcry in response to the 1997 *Sensation* exhibition in London for its display of Marcus Harvey's portrait of the child killer Myra Hindly composed from stamped or stenciled child's hand prints used (pointillist fashion) like basic units of color. The subject herself may have been sufficiently offensive to instigate the protests that ensued, but it was the emergence of the murderer's image from the impressions of children's hands that made the representation of her so unsettling. Here the concerns over the manner in which the subject was represented went beyond considerations of the content of the representation. The problem was the *medium* of representation. We may consider only a belief's content in judging the adequacy of the belief to its subject; but in the case of pictures, other considerations may play a role in whether the representation is apt. This point reflects a general feature of our interest in artistic representations qua artistic representations: we care not just for what is "said" or expressed about a subject by a representation, but, how that meaning is disclosed via the medium of the representation, that is, how it results from the manipulation of the medium.

One final caveat: How to describe the conditions under which a picture may be recognized as, may refer to, or purport to refer to, what it represents is addressed by several competing theories of depiction.[8] However, in the cases that follow, I take it for granted that even if a work's form may be inadequate to its subject, the depiction of the subject is secured. That is, my concern is not under what conditions depiction is achieved, but under what conditions the *right manner* of depiction is or is not achieved. A radically inapt depiction of a subject might never be recognized as of that subject, and, indeed, may fail to refer to the subject at all. However, the violation of pictorial decorum I discuss in what follows is not a general failure to produce a representation of a subject (such as when the wrong subject is mistakenly depicted), but a more particular failure to produce a representation of the subject that is appropriate or fitting.

Three Defects in Depiction

With those distinctions in hand, we can now look at just three of the many kinds of reasons that may be introduced in a judgment that a representation fails to suit its subject. These are expressive reasons, cognitive reasons, and moral reasons.

In the cases of the Warhol and Goya paintings discussed above, the reasons purporting to justify the failure of fit are *expressive*. That is, the flaws of those paintings are of a communicative sort. Each work instantiates an inadequate solution to the problem its creator encountered in how to represent his subject in a way that would express what was intended. This is just the familiar problem of an artist not finding a satisfactory way of saying what she wants to say. Aptness of depiction is a kind of achievement from which a work of art may fall short. In some cases, the problem is explained by how the artist planned her work, that is by how she thought of her aims. In other cases, the problem is due to the execution or realization of those plans. A work designed to be moving or profound may fail due to an inadequate technique. And a highly developed craft or perfect execution may not be able to save an inchoate or simplistic idea. Finally, some means that once allowed the successful achievement of a given end, may no longer suffice. An artist in the West, for example, who adopts a style whose period is over may not be able to express through that style what was expressed by those who originally formed it. Even if, for example, the nineteenth century Pre-Raphaelites had succeeded in adopting what they construed as the style of art before the Renaissance—in the course of which they thought art lost its sincerity, simplicity, and integration with human feeling—they couldn't form the medieval style as artists of the middle ages had. For such medieval artists did not express via their style an anti-modern nostalgia for preindustrial times. Artists who resurrect a style don't just use it but, unlike the earlier artists, invariably refer to it as well.[9] In any case, even if an artist knows what she wants to express, there is no guarantee that the discovery of adequate means of expression will ever occur.[10]

A work of art may also exhibit a disjunction between represented subject and manner of representation for cognitive reasons. One sees this in, for example, cases in which the style of a work conveys false propositions about its subject or solicits toward its subject a distorted point of view. Most of Vigée Le Brun's paintings of Marie-Antoinette show the Queen with the conventional formality, regal air, and reserve characteristic of public images of the monarchy in the *ancien régime*. However, one important work from 1787 displays her sitting among her children as an exemplar of maternal tenderness and *sensibilité*. That composition, unlike the more conventional portraits, was roundly denounced when it was exhibited in the Salon. For the point of view on the Queen that the picture offered was rejected as artificial, being inconsistent with the haughty and extravagant identity she was endowed with in the public mind.[11] Contrast this with the case of Goya's portrait of King Carlos, which was *expressively* flawed in failing to show what Goya intended it to show. Lebrun's portrait, by contrast, realizes the expression it was designed to have. The objection of audiences was that what was expressed didn't seem true to life.

Lebrun's painting was perceived by viewers as a misrepresentation of part of the actual world. But we should not assume that the cognitive adequacy of a representation is always, or even often, a matter of isomorphism in properties between subject and representation. For a work may stand to its object not only as a visual representation, but as an expression or exemplification, and it may be in terms of those latter relations that its cognitive adequacy is judged. So there may be no isomorphism in properties between a beautiful work and the ugly subject that it represents as such; between a profound representation and the superficial reality that it captures; or between a striking image and the bland or non-descript person it depicts. For the beautiful work may accurately express but not happen to show the ugliness of its subject, and the profound work may express the correct view that its subject is superficial, without the work being superficial itself.[12] When Warhol described the imagery of his paintings and silkscreens in saying that he "see[s] everything that way…[with] a kind of mental Braille, I just pass my hands over the surface of things" he was describing not so much his work, which was deep, as the superficial aspects of reality that it disclosed.[13]

A work of art may also be interpreted as cognitively misrepresenting a subject that exists in only a fictional sense. A film, for example, may present its hero as offering a deeply romantic and moving demonstration of his love (via the musical score, the effects he has on other characters, the extended close-up shots of his yearning eyes, and so on) even though that behavior would be identified by any objective standard as overwrought or clichéd. A painting may depict Helen of Troy in a manner that alludes to her supreme beauty, as shown, say, in a come-hither expression, a shimmering aura, and the stunned gaze of others, while inadequacies or peculiarities of the painter's technique nonetheless prevent us from seeing in the depiction a face that could launch a thousand ships.[14] A narrative may describe some sequence of events as if they were full of deep foreboding when any suitably sophisticated reader would find the unfolding of events predictable. Finally, an artist may inadvertently depict Hercules as wimpy, unicorns without horns, Little Red Riding Hood as wayward and culpable, or Satan as well-meaning but just misunderstood. If such representations were not intended to be counter-to-type or expectation, their failures would be of a cognitive sort.[15]

In some cases, moral reasons explain how a work of art may not represent a subject in an appropriate form. Even great admirers of the often astonishingly beautiful photographs by Sebastião Salgado of refugees, laborers, and others suffering from famine and human depredation have worried that they might solicit the wrong (contemplative or pleasure-seeking) point of view on the abject subjects they represent. Thus, for example, the critic Ingrid Sischy indicts Salgado for being too concerned "with the compositional aspects of his pictures—and with finding the 'grace' and 'beauty' in the twisted forms of his anguished subjects. And this beautification of tragedy results in pictures that ultimately reinforce our passivity toward the experience they reveal."[16]

Likewise, when the photographer Nicholas Nixon began in the late 1980s to exhibit a series of highly precise portraits of people dying from AIDS-related illnesses, viewers did not dispute the empathetic aims of the work, nor the visual accuracy of the series' depictions of its subjects' deteriorating bodies, but many held that the works failed to do justice to their subjects for showing them in a reductive manner, as if their disease was the most significant aspect under which they should be seen.

Finally, when the Colombian artist Fernando Botero, who is known for his popular paintings and sculptures of happy, chubby men and women, sought to respond to the news reports of US soldiers' abuse of inmates at Abu Ghraib, he created a series of gory paintings of anguished and tortured prisoners loosely based on the notorious photographs from the Iraqi prison. The problem in those paintings is that his sunny and sanitary style—so appropriate for his usual subjects—cannot fully accommodate the awfulness of the events the work refers to, and thus his stilted compositions fail visually to rise to the indignation he wants them to express. In that respect they veer close to being exploitative.

In each of these cases, the realization in a work of a morally or politically acceptable end is compromised by a morally defective execution or means. Of course, there are a wide variety of ways in which a picture may represent a subject in an immoral manner. Surreptitious photography, objectifying and obscene depictions, cruel caricatures, and showing a person in modes that her own self-representation would not sanction, are some of the many ways of creating a humiliating depiction. However, the interesting cases from the standpoint of understanding the nature of pictorial decorum are those that have at least morally neutral aims but, nonetheless, fail to depict their subjects in a morally acceptable manner.[17]

It should be noted that those different types of decorum—expressive, cognitive, moral or political—may be interdependent. When fifteenth-century artists sought to absorb the lessons of classical art, but worried that adopting its pagan style—using the form of Apollo to represent Jesus, for example—might compromise their work's contemporary Christian subject matter, their concerns for decorum were simultaneously expressive, cognitive, and (in their sense) moral as well.

Likewise, a moral realist might say that a failure to match form to subject from the moral or political perspective is just a cognitive failure of a certain kind (a failure in knowledge of what is morally required).

I hasten to emphasize that in all these cases, the charge that the subject is rendered in an unfitting or inapt manner admits of two interpretations. One is that the lack of fit is explained with reference solely to the nature of the subject; the other is that the lack of fit is due to the nature of the subject and the point, purpose, expression or meaning of the work. My concern here is with the second interpretation of pictorial decorum, that is, with constraints on how a subject should be represented that are supplied by virtue of what the work is designed and created to show or express.

In line with the first interpretation, one might hold the view that works of art ought to represent their subjects in a manner that promotes some particular value or realizes a certain end. One might argue, for example, that art ought to afford aesthetic pleasure; reflect progressive political aims; educate; flatter a sitter's vanity; promote love of country; expose tyranny; demonstrate the power of art; and so on. Under some conditions, evaluating a work of art as art with reference to its realization of one or more such goods or ends might be appropriate—as, for example, in those historical contexts in which art was commissioned and created to contribute to such ends. But it is very difficult to plausibly defend any evaluative norm as applying to a work of art by virtue of it belonging to its kind.

The narrower construal that I adopt allows us to appeal to constraints on appropriate representation that apply in virtue, not of any putative essence of art qua art, but of what a particular work of art is meant to achieve. Thus (on the construal of pictorial decorum I adopt) to claim that a work represents a subject in an inapt way presumes that the work has a certain meaning, expression, point or purpose with reference to which that way of representing the subject is wrong. The objectifying and demeaning portrayal of women that contemporary feminist art historians find in many Old Master paintings may be grounds for the ethical criticism of those works. But as those works were likely intended to reflect their assumptions about gender, they may not exhibit any failure of fit between their subjects and their forms. They may be morally defective, but not, as such, artistically so. By contrast, we presume that such depictions of abject individuals as those by Salgado, Nixon, and Botero (as well as by other artists such as Diane Arbus) are not meant to be exploitative, even if their way of rendering their subjects leaves them open to that charge.

In any case, not just any lack of fit between a subject and the manner or form in which it is represented instantiates a violation of pictorial decorum. For in some instances such a lack of fit may be conducive to realizing certain artistic ends. The greatness of *Don Quixote* as a picaresque novel for example, rests in part from the lack of fit between the style or form of the chivalric romance and the subject that is represented. Had Cervantes' work not meant, in part, to satirize a certain epic genre—that is, if it had a different meaning—we would find the subject a rather inadequate protagonist for the work's vehicle. So, the interesting cases from the standpoint of pictorial decorum are those in which the form of a work does not do justice to its subject *in light of the artwork's meaning* (expression, point or purpose).

I've described above how a work's form may be judged (in light of its meaning) not to fit its subject for expressive, cognitive, moral, and political reasons. No doubt, other reasons for a failure of fit could be introduced as well.[18] The question in what follows is what grounds such judgments of violations of decorum. Under what conditions does a work represent its subject properly and under what conditions does it not? Given that we are speaking of a conflict between form and subject, the phenomenon cannot be traced exclusively to one side or the other. Decorum is a relational concept and thus any adequate explanation of pictorial decorum would need to attend to both form and subject in relation to one another.

Concepts, Saliencies, and Point of View

One proposal for how to characterize the conflict between the subject of a work of art and its manner of being shown is to see it as arising from a failure of the appearance of the subject to fit within the constraints imposed by our *concept* of the subject. Kant posits a particular relation of this sort in section 16 of the *Critique of Judgment* where he suggests that the concept of an object is internally related to what sorts of appearances with (or under) which it can be judged as beautiful. There Kant's distinguishes between what he calls "free beauty" and "dependent beauty" (also translated as "adherent beauty"): a judgment attributing free beauty to an object "does not presuppose a concept of what the object is [meant] to be" whereas a judgment of dependent beauty "does presuppose the concept of the purpose that determines what the thing is [meant] to be, and hence a concept of its perfection…" In surveying examples of what may be judged to possess free beauty, Kant refers to flowers, birds, crustaceans, music not set to words, "designs *à la greque*, the foliage on borders or on wallpaper, etc.," each of which he says can be judged as beautiful without any reference to the concept of what it is supposed to be. Dependent beauty, by contrast, is exemplified for Kant in the beauty of a human being, a horse, or a building, as he sees these kinds of thing being such that the concepts of their respective purposes, or ends, putatively determine under what conditions (i.e., with what sort of appearance) they can be judged as beautiful.

There are a variety of competing interpretations of this notion of dependent beauty, each with some textual support; however, one central way of understanding the idea is that it is associated with decorum in the appearance of an object. The idea, as explained by Geoffrey Scarre, is that when we judge whether an object is beautiful, we "should ask ourselves whether it is fitting that an object of its type should possess whatever features make it beautiful."[19] So, Kant writes, "much would be liked directly in intuition to be added to a building, if only the building were not [meant] to be a church. A figure could be embellished with all sorts of curlicues and light but regular lines, as the New Zealanders do with their tattoos, if only it were not the figure of a human being." (section 16.5).[20] Here, the concept of an object constrains what sorts of appearances are appropriate to it. If a particular cathedral is beautiful, there is a sense in which it is beautiful *as* a cathedral, as what an object of that kind is supposed to be.

If Kant were right in identifying such a species of beauty, that would point to another kind of constraint on pictorial decorum—an aesthetic constraint, that is, a specification of how a work's form may not fit its content for reasons drawn from what makes something beautiful. The problem is that this would require subscribing to a theory of beauty as being more than a perceptual or sensory quality and there are good reasons to resist that view. One reason is that it seems we can see or judge something as beautiful without committing to any beliefs about what kind of thing it is, its causal sources, or its purpose or use. Another reason is that non-perceptual uses of the term "beautiful" can be best interpreted as indirect ways of praising something for being meritorious in some other sense, or as an exemplary instance of its kind. If, to the contrary, beauty is taken to be purely a perceptual property (even as it supervenes on non-perceptual properties), we can still say that some works ought to, or ought not to, represent their subjects in a beautiful form. However, the relevant reasons will then not be aesthetic but of another sort, e.g., expressive or moral.

Arthur Danto's account of "internal beauty," for example, suggests that sometimes the beauty of a work of art is a constituent of the artwork's meaning, as in, for example, the way the beauty of an elegy solicits a certain kind of attitude toward its content. The beauty of another work of art may be merely externally related to the work of art, i.e., such that it plays no essential role in the constitution or expression of the work's meaning. And, sometimes, given the meaning of a work, one or more particular kinds of beautiful form would be inappropriate.[21] When the original, largely neoclassical, design for the United States Holocaust Memorial Museum was radically changed to counter any perceived association of the building with triumphal or imperial architecture, even the critics of the original plan did not dispute that a neoclassical style could be independently beautiful or visually pleasing. However, they felt that it would be inappropriate, given the Museum's identity, to render it in that style, which might have "looked more like a monument to the perpetrators than to the victims."[22] Here the nature of that institution is defined in part by its purpose. And that nature constrains how it *should* appear. That judgment against the rejected Neoclassical style rested on moral reasons. However, it is worth remarking that, given that a moral failure in the museum's design would have also counted as an architectural failure, the normative aspect of that judgment is aesthetic as well.[23]

The above considerations suggest that any constraints that exist on when a subject is rendered beautifully are not drawn from considerations of what constitutes beauty per se, but from moral, political, expressive, and other concerns over when beauty, or a particular kind of beautiful form, is appropriate. However, we can make use of the relationship that Kant introduces in a more general fashion, as capturing how, when we judge the adequacy of a thing's appearance (that adequacy *not* here being limited to whether the appearance is beautiful) we do so via reference to a quasi-conceptual mental representation of the thing.[24] I will refer to such a mental representation as a *conception*. Used here simply as a general catch-all term, our conception of a thing may be composed of various beliefs, expectations, concepts (on a classical model), prototypical or stereotypical associations, assumptions of essential or central attributes, identifying roles or functions, and so on.[25]

I want to suggest that we can explain our judgment that there is a lack of fit between a work's subject and its manner of representation as consisting in a lack of fit between our conception of the subject and the point of view on the subject that the representation makes visible. By "point of view" I mean a way of seeing the subject with certain of features made salient and others downplayed or eliminated. The famous 1831 caricature of France's King Louis-Philippe as a pear, for example, made salient the coincidence of the King's head with the shape of a pear, large at the bottom and narrow at the top. Emphasizing his fat jowls and tiny head, the image implied he was both gluttonous and stupid. Here, the point of view the image adopted toward its subject did not visually falsify that subject, so much as make salient certain features of the subject at the expense of others in order to evoke our derisive response. When such foregrounded features of the subject are radically unusual (such as in Jonathan Swift's description of the skin of the gigantic women that Gulliver sees with loathing) such a point of view may interfere with the identification of the subject. But, typically, what a point of view does is present a recognizable subject as looking (and in consequence being) a certain way. Viewers of Lebrun's portrait of Marie-Antoinette approached it with a conception of queens as majestic, aloof occupiers of a dynastic role, not as individuals with their own domestic identities. And they thought of Marie Antoinette, in particular, in such a way that her notorious personal vices were central among her features (i.e., as explaining her other features; as being essential to her, and so on). None of those qualities of queens, in general, or Marie-Antoinette, in particular, precluded her possessing the qualities of material tenderness and at-home modesty (she's adorned only with a pearl necklace) that the portrait tried to make salient. But the painting failed to make those latter features *sufficiently* salient such that the point of view on the Queen they comprised was persuasive or vivid enough to replace the point of view on the Queen viewers already had. The point of view offered by the portrait is associated with a structured set of saliencies in which the qualities of Marie Antoinette's domestic life were central, and the qualities associated with her notorious public life were made peripheral. However, that ordering of significance among the qualities attributed to her was rejected in favor of the conception of the Queen that viewers already had. In that way, the failure of the painting to get audiences to see the Queen as it was designed is like the failure of a metaphor or simile to succeed in getting its listeners to see one thing in light of another.

The phenomenon of an object seen from a particular point of view that is correlated with certain saliencies is not restricted, of course, to pictorial contexts. For features may be brought to saliency through any number of processes that get one to look at something in a given way, with certain emphases, or as having a certain aspect. Prompted by a simple analogy, ostensive reference, or by occupation of a literally different point of view in space or time, we may come to see something in a particular manner, as like another thing, or in light of certain prominent features. Accounts of metaphor, in particular, often stress how they do not so much attribute qualities directly to an object as prompt a listener to take a distinctive perspective on the object. Max Black, for example, calls the perspective that a metaphor offers a "filter," and Richard Moran speaks of metaphor as offering a "frame."[26]

The important difference (for present purposes) between our ordinary experience of finding certain features of our environment salient and finding features in art salient, is that works of art are typically *designed* to direct viewers toward finding certain features as salient in what the works represent. The works of art *present* their subjects from a certain point of view, that is, with some features already made salient and ordered in relations of significance or relevance.[27] And a condition of our properly understanding a work of art is that we see the saliencies in its subject it is designed to show, rather than just any features that may emerge as significant because of our own interests (the way Swann in Proust's novel idiosyncratically judges paintings by Vermeer in terms of their represented figures' resemblance to his friends). To the extent that works of art are intended to convey any particular expression, experience, or meaning, they not only limit the features of their subjects that they present to viewers, but foreground certain of those features, or sets of features, and diminish others.[28]

Noël Carroll describes works of art, principally texts, in this way as "prefocused." His point, drawing on cognitive theories of emotions, is that works of art generate emotional responses from audiences through describing or depicting events, situations and characters in ways that make salient the features of those objects that are appropriate grounds (or criteria) for the emotion solicited.[29] For example, we can assume that an appropriate criterion of fear is what is harmful, i.e., fear is appropriately directed toward something that, from one's point of view, can be categorized as posing harm. Unlike objects in the real world, which typically are not created so as to be identifiable as harmful, an object in a work of art that is designed to provoke fear is depicted in such a way that those of its features that would tend to cause audiences to categorize the object as harmful are made salient.[30] Once audiences recognize the object with those saliencies, and thus under that categorization (with certain other conditions satisfied), they typically respond with the appropriate emotion. Carroll goes on to explain how such "emotionally governed perception casts its object in a special phenomenological light" which holds our attention to those emotion-appropriate features of the subject and directs our attention toward other features of the object that sustain that emotional response.[31]

That works of art may be prefocused (i.e., designed so as to present their subject with certain emotion-criterial features already spotlighted), explains not only how our emotional responses to such works are actually generated by the work, but how they can be objectively in accord with it. But that account need not be limited to just emotional responses, for it applies as well to other attitudes figuring in an objective or work-governed response to the content of a work of art. A work of art may represent its subject with features made salient so as to both cause and provide the justifying grounds for a wide range of attitudes, points of view, or cognitive forms of appraisal such as credence, approval, offense, respect, distain, mockery, worship, disregard, interest, and so on.

Carroll and others tend to describe the responses that a work of art solicits as external to the work, that is, they describe the attitudes relevant to the interpretation of a work as what the work is designed to solicit, elicit, provoke, generate, and so on, in audiences. But this does not seem to properly locate those attitudes. For when a work solicits a given attitude in audiences toward what it represents, this is because the work already embodies that attitude toward what it represents. A work of art does not just represent its subject, it unavoidably represents it from a certain point or points of view, both in literal terms of what spatial perspective or perspectives is offered on the subject, and in terms of what is shown as significant in the subject, what is diminished, and what evaluative properties are attributed or withheld from the subject. If a work is designed so as to solicit a particular attitude toward its subject, then that attitude is registered within the work explanatorily prior to the role it has in being solicited from audiences. Indeed, it is because such attitudes or points of view are registered within the work that there is some objective constraint on what counts as adopting the right interpretative stance or stances with respect to the significance or meaningfulness of the events, objects, or states of affairs the work represents.[32]

Of course, a work may be designed such that it expresses one type of attitude toward what it represents but, in being so designed, provokes in audiences an attitude of a very different kind. Swift's *A Modest Proposal* is written so as to project an attitude of calm, rational endorsement of its content, but it is designed to provoke in readers an entirely different attitude of revulsion for what the satire exposes about their inhumane views. And a visual work of art, such as Robert Colescott's *George Washington Carver Crossing the Delaware* (a parody stocked with racist-caricatures of Emmanuel Leutze's history painting) may show a subject from a racist point of view, but that is clearly not the work-as-a-whole's point of view, for such caricatures are critically directed at a bigotry in the culture at large. These kinds of cases don't count against locating the relevant attitudes associated with a work inside the work. For in such instances we have to distinguish between the *work of art's* attitude, and the attitude that is only part of the work's content.[33] That is, the approving tone of Swift's satire and the racist point of view of the painting do not characterize the attitudes of the works as a whole, only the attitudes that we would attribute to an implied narrator or its pictorial analog. The attitude the work expresses toward what it represents may be constituted by features of the work that include the attitude of an implied narrator or spectator, but need not be identical to it. We discover the *work's* point of view in part through assessing the points of view of the represented and implied attitudes it contains.

It is by virtue of the saliencies that are correlated with a given point of view that there can be a clash between the subject of a representation (the object or person referred to by the depiction) and the manner in which the subject is represented. That is, there are, on the one side, the features that we take to be essential to or typical of the subject. And, on the other side, there are the saliencies that are produced by the manner of representing that subject. These two sets of features, or their respective orders of emphasis, may be inconsistent. One possible result of such a clash is that we as audiences reject the saliencies supplied by the picture, in which case we say it is the wrong or inapt form. However, an alternative outcome is that the saliencies supplied by the form or manner of representation become dominant, forcing us to modify or replace our concept of the subject. In that case, the work of art may not be judged to be a violation of decorum (a failure to represent the subject in the way that is warranted) because it changes how we understand what is warranted.

Indeed, one of the ways in which a work of art may be said to change how we see the world, or what we see existing in it, is by succeeding in substituting the saliencies that emerge from its portrayal of a subject for the saliencies with which the subject is usually understood. Oscar Wilde's quip that London wasn't foggy until Whistler painted it suggests how works of art may direct our attention to a subject's features that we had seen but weren't salient for us until they were represented that way. Tolstoy writes of how Vronsky commends Mikhailov's portrait for capturing Anna Karenina's "sweetest inner expression" even though Vronsky, Tolstoy wryly notes, "had learned of that sweetest inner expression of hers only from this portrait. But the expression was so true that he and others thought they had always known it."[34] When Picasso famously depicted Gertrude Stein using the style of an African mask, he offered a frame or perspective on her that both elicited a new way of seeing her visual features, and reorganized one's perspective on her non-visible features as well. When challenged that his portrait didn't look like Stein, Picasso is said to have replied, "it will."[35] Here art gives the rule to nature, rather than nature giving the rule to art.[36] When the subject of a representation, such as Stein, comes to be standardly associated with the features that a given style makes salient, it is akin to the production of a dead metaphor: one so apropos that it takes the place of other formerly "normal" ways of conceiving something.

This account of when we judge there to be a violation of pictorial decorum may seem to describe only the phenomenology or experience of looking at a depiction. But sometimes our conception of a subject is indeed reflective of what we would count as an essential property of the subject or of what is most significant in the subject from a given point of view—the way, e.g., the autonomy of a person is significant from a moral point of view. A particularly effective manner of representation may make other features of the subject salient, such that we come to see the subject in terms of those saliencies that override the saliencies that are grounded in the nature of the subject itself. In such a case, there is a temptation to say that the work instantiates a violation of decorum, even if our experience of it doesn't indicate any distance between how the subject is shown and how it should be shown. A work of art may render human beings in ways that seductively emphasize the identity of their flesh as delicious meat, but there are perhaps moral reasons and innate dispositions for why we typically do not and should not see human bodies in that way, with such saliencies, that is, from such a point of view.

Notes

1. "And it was not as if these were already there, in advance of poetry…and then later were only clothed in imagery by artists and given an external adornment in poetry; on the contrary the mode of artistic production was such that what fermented in these poets they could work out only in the form of art and poetry" (LFA 102; VA 141).

2. The proposal that works of art allow us an exclusive access to, and exposure of, specifically, emotions is significantly advanced in Collingwood, *Principles of Art*. See also Wittgenstein's suggestive remarks in *Philosophical Investigations* (§531): "We speak of understanding a sentence in the sense in which it can be replaced by another which says the same; but also in the sense in which it cannot be replaced by any other (Any more than one musical theme can be replaced by another.) In the one case the thought in the sentence is something common to different sentences; in the other, something that is expressed only by these words in these positions (Understanding a poem.)" (2001: 122).

3. Another version of the remarks is reported in Jesse Kornbluth, "Andy," *New York*, March 9, 1987, p. 42. See also Benjamin Buchloh, "Andy Warhol's One-Dimensional Art" in his *Neo-Avantgarde and Culture Industry* (Cambridge: MIT Press, 2000), pp. 461–529.

4. This remark is discussed by Edward J. Olszewski, *Artibus et Historiae*, vol. 20, no. 40, p. 184, pp. 169–185.

5. Aristotle, *Rhetoric*, Book III, chap. 2.

6. For example, "A comic subject is not susceptible of treatment in a tragic style, and similarly the banquet of Thyestes cannot be fitly described in the strains of everyday life," *Ars Poetica*, pp. 89–98.

7. In what follows, I focus on primarily figurative works of art that represent concrete (i.e., not abstract) objects. But there are other relations between depiction and depicted subject that partake of abstraction. An abstraction can depict an abstract subject; an abstraction can depict a concrete subject; a figurative work can depict an abstract subject; and a figurative work can depict a concrete subject.

8. Some distinct approaches are found in Nelson Goodman's semiotic account that sees images as purely conventional and denotative in the way they represent (*Languages of Art*. Hackett Publishing, 1976); Malcolm Budd's account of resemblance as a necessary but not sufficient

feature of representations ("How Pictures Look," in D. Knowles and J. Skorupski, (eds.), *Virtue and Taste* [Oxford: Blackwell, 1993]); Richard Wollheim's theory of "seeing-in" as a special perceptual skill that is conceptually and historically prior to, and explanatory of, pictorial representation (*Art and Its Objects*, 2nd ed., [Cambridge University Press, Cambridge, 1980); supp. Essay V., and *Painting as an Art* [Thamas and Hudson, London, 1987]; Christopher Peacocke's account of depiction as wholly a function of perceptual experience ("Depiction," *The Philosophical Review*, 96 ([1987], pp. 383–410); Kendall Walton's theory that in appreciating a picture we use it as a prompt to imagine that we see in reality the object that the picture depicts (*Mimesis as Make-Believe* [Harvard University Press: Cambridge, 1990). The theory that pictorial recognition draws on just the ordinary perceptual abilities that allow the recognition of things outside pictures is advanced by Flint Schier, *Deeper into Pictures* (Cambridge University Press, 1986); Dominic Lopes, *Understanding Pictures* (Oxford University Press, 1996). Lopes offers a "hybrid" theory of pictorial reference that accommodates intuitions from both perceptual/recognitional and causal accounts.

9. See my *Life of a Style: Beginnings and Endings in the Narrative History of Art* (Cornell University Press, 2000).

10. A repeated failure to discover such means might raise the question of whether there really is any particular content in what the artist is trying to say. The title of Merleau-Ponty's essay "Cezanne's doubt" alludes to this possibility of an artist working in an unconventional style potentially failing to create work that has any communicable meaning. Cezanne, according to Merleau-Ponty, "speaks as the first man spoke and paints as if no one had ever painted before," "Cézanne's Doubt," in Hubert L. Dreyfus and Patricia Allen Dreyfus, trans., *Sense and Non-Sense* (Evanston, IL: Northwestern University Press, 1964), p. 19. For an interpretation of that remark, see my "Between Philosophy and Art," in Carman and Hansen, (eds.), *The Cambridge Companion to Merleau-Ponty* (Cambridge: Cambridge University Press, 2005), pp. 291–318.

11. See Simon Schama, "The Domestication of Majesty: Royal Family Portraiture, 1500–1850," *Journal of Interdisciplinary History*, vol. 17, no. 1 (summer, 1986), pp. 155–183. Critics scorned the picture as a forced and unpersuasive image of tenderness, and compared it unfavorably to other portraits of mothers and their children, including one of the painter herself with her daughter.

12. It was for cognitive reasons that Hegel claimed art had to harmonize its subject and its form: "the content which is to come into artistic representation should be in itself qualified for such representation." Without such harmony, Hegel suggests, the content of art (which he identifies across the board with Spirit) may be misrepresented in a "form antagonistic to its nature. Hegel adds that in art, unlike nature, the external shape or appearance of art exists for our apprehension: "[f]or this reason alone are content and artistic form fashioned in conformity with one another," Hegel, *Aesthetics: Lectures on Fine Art*, trans. T.M. Knox, vol. 1 (Oxford University Press, 1975), pp. 70–71.

13. Gretchen Berg, "Andy: My True Story," *Los Angeles Free Press*, March 17, 1963, p. 3.

14. See the sulky Helen in a painting by the Pre-Raphaelite Frederick Sandys (Walker Art Gallery, Liverpool). A.S. Byatt's fictional novel *Possession* suffers from the fact that while the story revolves around a poet of immense gifts, the poor quality of his poem that the novel presents (written, of course, by Byatt herself) seems inconsistent with the poet's renown. Contrast that with the *perfectly*-achieved middling quality of the poem Vladimir Nabokov attributes to his fictional poet of a minor reputation in the novel *Pale Fire*.

15. It would be a defense against such complaints on cognitive grounds for an artist to say she meant to depict those fictional entities in such a-typical ways. For an attempt to show an internal connection between the artistic or aesthetic assessments of a metaphor for aptness with a semantic assessment of its truth, see Hills, "Aptness and Truth in Verbal Metaphor."

16. The remark continues, "to aestheticize tragedy is the fastest way to anaesthetize the feelings of those who are witnessing it. Beauty is a call to admiration, not to action," Ingrid Sischy, "Good Intentions," September 9, 1991 *The New Yorker*. This echoes Walter Benjamin's charge in his "Author as Producer" that the artists associated with the *Neue Sachlichkeit* (an emotionally cool style of apparently objective literary and photography depictions) "make human misery an object of consumption." Benjamin accused specifically the picture book by Albert Renger-Patzsch entitled *The World Is Beautiful* with "turning abject poverty itself…into an object of enjoyment."

17. See my "Ethics, Aesthetics, and Artistic Ends" (*Journal of Value Inquiry*, vol. 38, no. 3, 2011) on the difference between images of humiliation and humiliating images, and the depiction-related reasons why a picture may be morally defective.

18. Adorno criticizes Brecht's anti-totalitarian play *Arturo Ui* on political grounds, saying that while the play is motivated by appropriate politically sympathies, it nonetheless represents Fascists in the wrong form: as buffoons. For that portrayal, Adorno suggests, construes Fascism as an accident or aberration, not a phenomenon explained by contemporary social institutions. He attacks Chaplin's *The Great Dictator* (1940) for similar reasons: the film, he says, "loses all satirical force, and becomes obscene, when a Jewish girl can bash a line of storm troopers on the head with a pan without being torn to pieces. For the sake of political commitment, [an accurate picture of] political reality is trivialized," Adorno, "On Commitment."

19. Geoffrey Scarre, pp. 357–358. Paul Guyer's account of this relation, which I adopt here, is that Kant's examples suggest that "the relation between the purpose and dependent beauty is a negative one: the purpose functions to constrain the forms which may produce the harmony of the faculties but *not* to fully determine them (Paul Guyer, *Kant and the Claims of Taste*, p. 247).

20. By section 48, Kant concludes that all artistic beauty is dependent beauty: when we declare a work of art beautiful, "then we must first base it on a concept of what the thing is [meant] to be, since art always presupposes purpose in the cause (and its causality)."

21. Danto, *The Abuse of Beauty: Aesthetics and the Concept of Art* (Open Court), 2003. See also, my "Internal Beauty," *Inquiry*, vol. 48, no. 2 (2005), pp. 145–154.

22. Edward Linenthal, in his study of the debates around the creation of the USHMM. Quoted in Brett Ashley Kaplan, *Unwanted Beauty: Aesthetic Pleasure in Holocaust Representation*, p. 162.

23. At the inauguration of Rachel Whiteread's memorial to the Austrian victims of the Holocaust, Simon Wiesenthal warned those assembled that the site "should not be beautiful but should hurt." It might be odd to see as beautiful the cast concrete mausoleum-like structure, composed of four walls bearing impressions of 65,000 identical books with their spines turned inward, but Wiesenthal's injunction stemmed from the recognition that seeing the memorial as beautiful would wrongly imply that its relationship to the public is supposed to be harmonious, when its actual function is to be a standing indictment and reminder of what the nation had allowed.

24. There is, of course, a difference between asking what appearance is appropriate for a given object and what appearance is appropriate for the object as represented in a picture, and it may be that there are

normative constraints that apply to the appearance of an actual object that do not apply to the appearance given to the thing when represented in a picture.

25. So we can define the concept of a bachelor in terms of unmarried and male. But we would explain our *conception* of a bachelor in a way that would preclude or qualify its application to such people as the Pope, men in long-term relationships, teenagers, recent widowers, and so on. I should note that even if a conception of x is different from the concept of x, that concept may still have an ineliminable stability function in allowing different conceptions of x (over time, in different contexts) to serve as conceptions of the same thing. The concept of a bird, for example, may be what fixes the reference of our various conceptions of a bird. For defenses of competing theories of concepts, see Margolis and Laurence, (eds.), *Concepts* (MIT Press, 1999), pp. 189–206.

26. Black 1962; Moran 1989. See the concept of salience used in the explanation of metaphor in Andrew Ortony, "Beyond Literal Similarity," *Psychological Review* 86 (1979), pp. 161–180.

27. For elaborations of the notion of a point of view in terms of an operator that identifies only certain features of a given context as relevant in one's judgment or deliberation, see Robert Brandom, "Points of View and Practical Reasoning," *Canadian Journal of Philosophy*, vol. XII, no. 2, June 1982, pp. 321–333; A.W. Moore, *Points of View* (Oxford: Oxford University Press, 1997); Antti Hautamäki, *Points of View and Their Logical Analysis* (Helsinki: Philosophical Society of Finland, 1986). On the objectivity of perceptual saliences see, Clotilde Calabi, "Perceptual Saliences," in David Woodruff, ed., *Phenomenology and the Philosophy of Mind* (Oxford: Clarendon Press, 2005), pp. 253–269.

28. Visual presentations may be "reductive" in this sense: for they depict their subjects from one or more points of view from which the qualities that the subject possesses are presented as being essential to the subject. Although the construal of concepts as prototypes is highly controversial, pictures are often interestingly like prototypes in not just depicting a thing, but depicting it *as if* its visible qualities are necessarily or typically possessed by it (or as if the object is a central example of its kind).

29. Such emotions are taken to be cognitive to the extent that they are comprised both of beliefs and feelings. And such emotions are taken to be rational to the extent that they are directed at those things that serve as criterial for them (e.g., the emotion of fear is directed at those things that are harmful, the emotion of pity is directed at people who

suffer undeservedly). This view that emotions present the world to us as having criteria value-laden features is defended in different forms in P.S. Greenspan, *Emotions and Reasons: An Inquiry into Emotional Justification.* (New York: Routledge, 1988); R. de Sousa, *The Rationality of Emotion* (Bradford Book, 1990); R.C. Roberts, "What an Emotion Is: A Sketch," in *The Philosophical Review* (1988), pp. 183–209.

30. Exceptions from the natural world would be those animals evolutionarily endowed with an appearance that has the function of warding off competitors or predators.

31. Carroll, "Art, Narrative, and Emotion," in Mette Hjort and Sue Laver, (eds.), *Emotion and the Arts*, p. 203. See also my "Aptness of Emotions for Fictions and Imaginings," *Pacific Philosophical Quarterly*, 2011.

32. Gregory Currie analyses the appropriateness of a reader's emotional response to a work of fiction as a matter of what he calls *congruence*: a fit between the reader's emotional response and the emotion expressed in the work. Currie distinguishes between being knowing what response is congruent with the work, and knowing whether that response is warranted on artistic grounds by the work. Currie, *The Nature of Fiction* (Cambridge University Press: 1990), p. 215 and passim.

33. See Robert Stecker, "Apparent, Implied, and Postulated Authors," *Philosophy and Literature* 11 (1987), pp. 258–271.

34. p. 477, Penguin Classics.

35. Roland Penrose reports the perhaps apocryphal story.

36. For an account that stresses art's way of developing novel forms for expressing new meanings, see Richard Eldridge, "Form and Content: An Aesthetic Theory of Art," *British Journal of Aesthetics*, vol. 25, no. 4, 1985: 303–316. Despite their overarching critique of claims for the cognitive status of literature, Peter Lamarque and Stein Olsen remark that that literature "constitutes its own form of insight" implying it can be cognitive in a way peculiar to literature (*Truth, Fiction, and Literature* [Oxford: Oxford University Press, 1994], 408–409).

References

Aristotle. 1995. *Rhetoric*, ed. Jonathan Barnes. Princeton, NJ: Princeton University Press.

Berg, Gretchen. 1963. Andy: My True Story. *Los Angeles Free Press*, March 17, p. 3.

Black, Max. 1962. *Models and Metaphors: Studies in Language and Philosophy.* New York: Cornell University Press.

Brandom, Robert. 1982. Points of View and Practical Reasoning. *Canadian Journal of Philosophy* 12 (2): 321–333.

Buchloh, Benjamin. 2000. Andy Warhol's One-Dimensional Art. In *Neo-Avantgarde and Culture Industry*, 461–529. Cambridge: MIT Press.

Budd, Malcolm. 1993. How Pictures Look. In *Virtue and Taste*, ed. D. Knowles and J. Skorupski. Oxford: Blackwell.

Calabi, Clotilde. 2005. Perceptual Saliences. In *Phenomenology and the Philosophy of Mind*, ed. David Woodruff, 253–269. Oxford: Clarendon Press.

Carroll, Noël. 1997. Art, Narrative, and Emotion. In *Emotion and the Arts*, ed. Mette Hjort and Sue Laver, 190–211.

Currie, Gregory. 1990. *The Nature of Fiction.* Cambridge: Cambridge University Press.

Danto, Arthur. 2003. *The Abuse of Beauty: Aesthetics and the Concept of Art.* Chicago and LaSalle: Open Court.

de Sousa, Ronald. 1990. *The Rationality of Emotion.* Cambridge: Bradford Book.

Eldridge, Richard. 1985. Form and Content: An Aesthetic Theory of Art. *British Journal of Aesthetics* 25 (4): 303–316.

Gilmore, Jonathan. 2000. *Life of a Style: Beginnings and Endings in the Narrative History of Art.* New York: Cornell University Press.

———. 2005a. Internal Beauty. *Inquiry* 48 (2): 145–154.

———. 2005b. Between Philosophy and Art. In *The Cambridge Companion to Merleau-Ponty*, ed. Taylor Carman and Mark B.N. Hansen, 291–318. Cambridge: Cambridge University Press.

———. 2011. Aptness of Emotions for Fictions and Imaginings. *Pacific Philosophical Quarterly* 92: 468–489.

———. 2011. Ethics, Aesthetics, and Artistic Ends. *The Journal of Value Inquiry* 45 (2): 203–214.

Goodman, Nelson. 1976. *Languages of Art.* Indianapolis: Hackett Publishing.

Greenspan, Patricia S. 1988. *Emotions and Reasons: An Inquiry into Emotional Justification.* New York: Routledge.

Guyer, Paul. 1979. *Kant and the Claims of Taste.* Cambridge: Harvard University Press.

Hautamäki, Antti. 1986. *Points of View and Their Logical Analysis.* Helsinki: Philosophical Society of Finland.

Hegel, George Wilhelm Friedrich. 1975. *Aesthetics: Lectures on Fine Art*, trans. T.M. Knox, vol. 1. New York: Oxford University Press.

Kaplan, Brett Ashley. 2007. *Unwanted Beauty: Aesthetic Pleasure in Holocaust Representation*. Chicago: University of Illinois Press.

Kornbluth, Jesse. 1987. Andy: The World of Warhol. *New York Magazine*, March 9, 38–49.

Lamarque, Peter, and Stein Haugom Olsen. 1994. *Truth, Fiction, and Literature*. New York: Oxford University Press.

Lopes, Dominic. 1996. *Understanding Pictures*. New York: Oxford University Press.

Margolis, Eric, and Stephen Laurence. 1999. *Concepts*. Cambridge: MIT Press.

Merleau-Ponty, Maurice. 1964. Cézanne's Doubt. In *Sense and Non-Sense*, trans. Hubert L. Dreyfus and Patricia Allen Dreyfus. Evanston: Northwestern University Press.

Moore, Adrian William. 1997. *Points of View*. New York: Oxford University Press.

Moran, Richard. 1989. Seeing and Believing: Metaphor, Image, and Force. In *Critical Inquiry*, vol. 16, no. 1 (Autumn), 87–112. Chicago: The University of Chicago Press.

Olszewski, Edward J. 1999. Exorcising Goya's «The Family of Charles IV». In *Artibus et Historiae*, vol. 20, no. 40, 169–185. Krakow: IRSA.

Ortony, Andrew. 1979. Beyond Literal Similarity. *Psychological Review* 86: 161–180.

Peacocke, Christopher. 1987. Depiction. *The Philosophical Review* 96: 383–410.

Roberts, Robert Campbell. 1988. What an Emotion Is: A Sketch. *The Philosophical Review* 97 (2): 183–209.

Scarre, Geoffrey. 1981. Kant on Free and Dependent Beauty. *British Journal of Aesthetics* 21 (2): 351–362.

Schama, Simon. 1986. The Domestication of Majesty: Royal Family Portraiture, 1500–1850. *Journal of Interdisciplinary History* 17 (1, Summer): 155–183.

Schier, Flint. 1986. *Deeper into Pictures*. Cambridge: Cambridge University Press.

Sischy, Ingrid. 1991. Good Intentions. *The New Yorker*, September 9, pp. 89–95.

Stecker, Robert. 1987. Apparent, Implied, and Postulated Authors. *Philosophy and Literature* 11: 258–271.

Tolstoy, Leo. 2003. *Anna Karenina*. London: Penguin Classics.

Walton, Kendall. 1990. *Mimesis as Make-Believe*. Cambridge: Harvard University Press.

Wollheim, Richard. 1980. *Art and Its Objects*, 2nd ed. Cambridge: Cambridge University Press.

———. 1987. *Painting as an Art*. London: Thames and Hudson.

Wittgenstein, Ludwig. 2001. *Philosophical Investigations*. The German Text, with a revised English translation, trans. G.E.M. Anscombe. Oxford: Blackwell.

17

'Navegar é preciso; viver não é preciso': The Impossible Journeys of Kierkegaard and Pessoa

Bartholomew Ryan

In the *Critique of Pure Reason*, Immanuel Kant looked and leaned out over the edge of philosophical reason and epistemology, but held his balance. He seemed to be warning future philosophical and poetic explorers of the dangers in going further out into the mind's imagination when he wrote:

> This land, however, is an island, enclosed in unalterable boundaries by nature itself. It is the land of truth (a charming name), surrounded by a broad and stormy ocean, the true seat of illusion, where many a fog bank and rapidly melting iceberg pretend to be new lands and, ceaselessly deceive with empty hopes the voyager looking around for new discoveries, entwine him in adventures from which he can never escape and yet also never bring to an end. (Kant 1999: 339/B295)

The dramatic philosopher Søren Kierkegaard—animated by poetics, and the dramatic poet Fernando Pessoa—"animated by philosophy"

B. Ryan (✉)
New University of Lisbon, Lisbon, Portugal
e-mail: bartholomewryan@fcsh.unl.pt

© The Author(s) 2018
A. Falcato and A. Cardiello (eds.), *Philosophy in the Condition of Modernism*,
https://doi.org/10.1007/978-3-319-77078-9_17

(Pessoa 1966: 13),[1] did not heed Kant's warning and sailed out to the "broad and stormy ocean" in order to discover further the depths of the modern human self which, with each journey and excavation, became ever more elusive, multiple, plural and unstable. They pioneered a new form of exploration—the voyage in the interiority of the human self. This hazardous journey is central to their philosophical and poetic vocation and legacy, and distinguishes them as modernists from the age of the Renaissance and Antiquity.

The task of this essay is to analyse and compare the impossible journeys of Kierkegaard and Pessoa, who appropriate many of the motifs of the traditional explorer who engages in espionage, disguise, daring, shipwrecks and bordering on madness, and, in doing so, forge an authorship exploding into multiplicity. The title—"Navegar é preciso; viver não é preciso" ('to sail is necessary; to live is not')—is a term borrowed by Pessoa from the fourteenth century poet Plutarch who rendered it from the Latin "*Navigare necesse est; vivere non este necesse*". Although Pessoa attributes this phrase to Jason and the Argonauts; according to Plutarch, this was supposedly shouted out by Pompey the Great in the first century to his men on his ships to set sail despite a very violent storm at sea. This expression is to be taken up as a mantra for the second coming of the Argonauts—this time as the Portuguese explorers of the fifteen and sixteenth centuries, as an inspiration to sail despite the danger, seek adventure and grapple with the unknown, the *terra incognita*, in and beyond the great oceans. The epic poet of the Portuguese maritime age, Luís Vaz de Camões, wrote in the national poem: "Count nothing impossible!" [*Impossibilidades não façais*] (Camões 2001: 196/1980: 316 [Canto IX: 95]). The age of literary modernism heralds in the third coming of the Argonauts— Pessoa and his heteronyms. Pessoa transforms "navegar é preciso; viver não é preciso" so that the exploration is directed to the depths of the so-called soul and to discover instead the self as subject—if there is one ever to be found. Some of this voyage had already been navigated and performed by the Christian philosopher Kierkegaard a century earlier.

There are many ways and avenues to link these two complex writers,[2] but here I bring them together to show how they pioneer a new way of being explorers by rediscovering and analysing the concepts of interiority and subjectivity. And although there are other modernist writers who have been masters of interior travel, Pessoa and Kierkegaard present their project very consciously by playing themselves alongside the actual explorers of exteriority. Joyce did write *the* interior odyssey of the twentieth century, but the protagonists' and author's journey in and outside that novel is also one of exterior travel. Literary modernism began to emerge at the end of the nineteenth century which witnessed the European frenzy for the last vestiges of undiscovered landscapes. This was the last phase of colonization, exploration and exploitation of uncharted regions in the frantic "scramble for Africa" in the era of Stanley and Livingston; and where the great botanists of the Victorian age such as Bates, Wallace and Spruce explored the impenetrable jungles of the Amazon. We will see how the ages of exploration are transformed in Kierkegaard and Pessoa.

Mirroring each other in literary and philosophical modernism, Kierkegaard and Pessoa are both encountering the abysses of modernity and are sometimes almost switching disciplines with Kierkegaard becoming overtly poetic and Pessoa overtly philosophical. However, we often find Pessoa at his most philosophical in his poetic heteronymic writings; and Kierkegaard at his most poetic in his most philosophical pseudonymous publications. Caeiro speaks of and to the poets and the philosophers, writing against philosophy while at the same time being perhaps Pessoa's most philosophical poet; and Kierkegaard remains a thinker contra philosophy, a poet contra aesthetics, and a Christian contra Christendom, while, at the same time, applauding the poet for wrenching us out into the middle of life (Kierkegaard 1993: 73/SKS8, 180), while one of his pseudonyms admits that he is only practicing dialectics (Kierkegaard 1983: 90/SKS4, 180). They are joined together as paradoxical writers for paradoxical times in coming to despise the onslaught and disintegration of modernity as well as being its most profound and enduring exponents. In the structure of modern conscious experience, Kierkegaard and Pessoa manage to achieve to write in such a way that they become at the same time and, crucially, on the same level, three aspects and voices of narrative: the subject, the author (as pseudonym, heteronym and orthonym), and the philosophical and poetic creator. In their journey in interiority, the instability of identity with both the literary and philosophical subject becomes endless and infinite.

The Adventure of Imagination, Impossibility and Interiority

In Georg Lukács' essay *The Theory of the Novel*, written at the same time as the birth of Pessoa's greatest heteronyms and the writing of Joyce's *Ulysses*, its author separates interiority and adventure from each other on the eve of his leap into Bolshevism (Lukács 1971: 66). Defending the likes of Kierkegaard and Pessoa from Lukács' later Marxist scrutiny, their journey in interiority is synonymous with adventure and which they view as great feats of exploration alongside the exterior voyages of the Colombuses and Magellans of human history. In a desperate search to find a home, Lukács leaves Kierkegaard and the experimental modernists behind, evocatively and astutely describing the Dane's quest: "Yet life's gift was mere deception; it could never after all, give him reality, but only lure him deeper and deeper, with every appearance of victory and success—like Napoleon in Russia—into the all-devouring desert" (Lukács 1974: 40). Perhaps, today, after Lukács' own perilous journey into the desert of Stalinist Russia, and after modernism and now living through the many spheres of post-modernism, we can return again to Kierkegaard and Pessoa and need not be so afraid of the homelessness of the self and unstable identities of the subject that so greatly unsettled Lukács.

Kierkegaard's pseudonym Johannes de silentio declares that "he who expected the impossible became the greatest of all" (Kierkegaard 1983: 16/SKS4, 113); and Pessoa's "semi-heteronym" (Pessoa 2001: 258) from *The Book of Disquiet*—Bernardo Soares—states: "I love impossible landscapes" (Pessoa 2015: 129). These two authors—Kierkegaard and Pessoa—never really go anywhere as adults in the exterior world, but journey far and wide in interiority. However, what distinguishes them is that Kierkegaard's idea of the impossible is the pursuit of Christian faith which his pseudonym Vigilius Haufniensis defines as "the inner certainty that anticipates infinity" (Kierkegaard 1980a: 157/SKS4, 456); while Pessoa's "impossible universe" (Pessoa 2006: 169) is his burning imagination embracing all kinds of faiths. If, from a Kierkegaardian point of view, Pessoa is judged to be stuck in the aesthetic stage, it is important to note that for Pessoa, not unlike Nietzsche or Joyce, the aesthetic and the spiritual are often synonymous. And for both Kierkegaard and Pessoa, life remains mediocre at best when it is outside the realm of poetry, religiousness or philosophy. Thus, Kierkegaard's pseudonym Johannes Climacus declares: "Between poetry and religiousness, worldly wisdom about life performs its vaudeville. Every individual who does not live either poetically or religiously is obtuse" (Kierkegaard 1992: 457/SKS7, 415); and Soares writes that "Only poets and philosophers see the world as it really is, for only to them is it given to live without illusions" (Pessoa 2015: 241).

Both Kierkegaard and Pessoa were suspicious of traveling and would have been horrified at the way most of us travel today. Outside of Denmark, Kierkegaard only visited Berlin on two occasions, and wrote *Fear and Trembling, Repetition* and most of *Either/Or* there. One wonders what might have happened if he found himself living in Andalucia, India or Mozambique for a year! Perhaps Kierkegaard would have loved to have travelled more and he was no doubt extremely productive when in the rare occasion he did, and he confesses in his journal to being a poet and the necessity of travel: "I am a poet. I must travel" (Kierkegaard 1996: 383/Pap. X I A 273). And although Pessoa lived for almost a decade as a child in South Africa, when he returned to Lisbon, he never visited any other country and there is no evidence that he was even in Porto, and yet he is probably the most radically cosmopolitan poet from Portugal. Of course, his fictional heteronym, Álvaro de Campos did all the travelling for him—as the Sensationist naval engineer who sailed all over the world. The point is, however, that for Kierkegaard and Pessoa they were always travelling—through their great imaginative power and as great urban walkers. Thus, to be a poet, one needn't and shouldn't go anywhere. For Kierkegaard, the poets were travelling now because they had lost their grasp of the interior journey: "[...] while the poets, merely in order to entertain their readers, ramble around Africa, America [...] so that soon a new continent must be discovered if poetry will not have to declare 'I pass'. Why? Because inwardness [*Inderligheden*] is being lost more and more" (Kierkegaard 1992: 287/SKS7, 262).

For Pessoa, the age of exploration was over; in the age of literary modernism, it was time to travel inward. The relationship between the hero and the poet was now transformed. So, while both still hung onto the redeeming quality and interdependent relationship of the poet and the hero, there is no longer the traditional swashbuckling hero and epic poet of Antiquity and Renaissance; rather there is the elusive, incognito hero and the masked poet or philosopher. Subverting the narrative even further, the poet and hero are one—the poet becomes the hero and the hero is the poet—in their most important creations/authors, such as Campos, Caeiro, Johannes Climacus and Anti-Climacus. In "The Tobacco Shop" [*Tabacaria*] (written in 1928 and published in 1933), originally called "March in Defeat", Álvaro de Campos—as hero and poet makes a triumph of a life in defeat and failure, revealing the audacious interior adventures he has undertaken:

> I've done more in dreams than Napoleon
> I've held more humanities against my hypothetical breast than Christ.
> I've secretly invented philosophies such as Kant never wrote
> But I am, and perhaps will always be, the man in the garret,
> Even though I don't live as one.
> [*Tenho sonhado mais que o que Napoleão fez.*
> *Tenho apertado ao peito hipotético mais humanidades do que Cristo,*
> *Tenho feito filosofias em segredo que nenhum Kant escreveu.*
> *Mas sou, e talvez serei sempre, o da mansarda,*
> *Ainda que não more nela*] (Pessoa 1998: 175)

In one fell swoop, he claims to have surpassed the genius of the political, religious and philosophical realms. Campos "conquered the whole world before getting out of bed" (Pessoa 2006: 175). Yet, he begins the poem by saying (probably Pessoa's most famous opening lines): "I'm nothing/I'll always be nothing./I can't want to be something./ But I have in me all the dreams of the world" [*Não sou nada./Nunca serei nada./Não posso querer ser nada./À parte isso, tenho em mim todos os sonhos do mundo.*] (Pessoa 1998: 173).

To go on their impossible, interior journeys, all Kierkegaard and Pessoa need are two things: a window and the imagination. Soares writes: "If I imagine, I see [...] If I imagine it, I create it" (Pessoa 2015: 376); and Johannes Climacus writes in his unfinished autobiography: "He did not require forests and travels for his adventures but merely what he had: a little room with one window" (Kierkegaard 1985: 124/SKS15, 22). One of the most touching and revealing passages in Kierkegaard's authorship is in the unfinished work called *Johannes Climacus* when the author, most likely Climacus writing in the third person shows his father also to be a person of great imagination and facilitator of the interior journey. When not able to go out, the father would take the little boy by the hand and then walk around the room where the father would transport them to a walking tour through Copenhagen (Kierkegaard 1985: 120/SKS15, 19). The author in question refers to the father as one who "was capable of everything", of having "the magic art" and an "omnipotent imagination" who "was able to fashion everything" (Kierkegaard 1985: 120/SKS15, 19). The child learns from the father, and the window become the portal, gateway and threshold for the impossible, interior journey to begin. Both Benjamin and Adorno were struck by this passage and included it in their analysis of the *flâneur* and interiority.[3] In the following paragraph, the child by his window is soon taking off on his imaginary journeys alone:

Outside the one window in the living room grew approximately ten blades of grass. Here he sometimes discovered a little creature running among the stems. These stems became an enormous forest that still had the compactness and darkness the grass had. Instead of filled space, he now had empty space; he stared again but saw nothing except the enormous expanse. (Kierkegaard 1985: 121/SKS15, 20)

For Pessoa, the motif of the window is often present in his greatest poet-explorers—Caeiro, Campos and Soares. It is by the window that the poem "The Tobacco Shop" takes place and where most of Caeiro's collection of poems "The Keeper of Sheep" are supposedly written. And like Climacus, Soares never ventures out of his home town but travels far and wide in his imagination:

Whoever has crossed all the seas has only crossed the monotony of him-self. I've crossed more seas than anyone. I've seen more mountains than are on Earth. I've passed through more cities than exist, and the great riv-ers of non-worlds have flown sovereignly under my watching eyes. If I travelled, I'd find a poor copy of what I've already seen without taking one step. (Pessoa 2015: 124)

Pessoa's "experimental journey" (Pessoa 2015: 313) and Kierkegaard's "venture in experimental psychology" (Kierkegaard 1983: 125/SKS4, 7) is a philosophical, poetic and spiritual excavation of the human self. And in their objective to be pioneers in their thought and art, the interior journey is to live "more intensely, more widely and more turbulently than those who live externally" (Pessoa 2015: 373).

Kierkegaard and Dr. Peter Wilhelm Lund

Kierkegaard is haunted by an exterior explorer—the brother of his two sisters' husbands: Dr. Peter Wilhelm Lund. The now famous explorer and paleontologist left Denmark in 1825 to explore the jungles of Brazil to study the flora and fauna. He returned three years later, but then set off for Brazil again in 1832 and discovered fossils of previously unknown animals such as the saber-toothed cat in limestone caves in the region of Minas Gerais. He also studied and greatly appreciated the ancient rock paintings within the caves. But it was in 1843 where he made his greatest discovery: he found the bones of human beings lying beside extinct remains of animals that were thought to live long before humans. A year after this ground-breaking discovery, Lund ceased working and yet remained in the small town of Lagoa Santa in Minas Gerais for the next thirty-five years until his death in 1880, never to return to Europe again. Today, there is a town in Minas Gerais named after him, and he is considered the father of both paleontology and archaeology. What happened at that moment of discovery in 1843? This finding was greatly celebrated by Darwin, but did it shatter Lund's Christian faith?[4] The adventures and story of Dr. Lund fascinated the young Kierkegaard and, although little has been written about this relationship and influence in Kierkegaard's authorship, it would haunt him throughout his own life of discovery.

Kierkegaard really begins his life as a writer in the summer of 1835 at the age of twenty-two when he makes his famous journal entry in Gilleleje on the 1st August, declaring his goal to "find a truth which is truth *for me*, to find *the idea for which I am willing to live and die*" (Kierkegaard 1996: 32/Pap. I A 75); and when he writes his letter, never to be sent, to P.W. Lund on the 1st June,[5] inspired by the exterior journey to begin his own interior journey. Thus, he begins the letter with these words: "You know how inspiring I once found it to listen to you and how enthusiastic I was about your description of your stay in Brazil" (Kierkegaard 1987: 453); and after reflecting on Faust, the natural sciences and theology, he concludes with these words:

> How fortunate you are to have found in Brazil a vast field of investigation where every step offers strange new objects and where the cries of the rest of the learned republic cannot disturb your piece. To me the learned theological world seems like the Strandvej on a Sunday afternoon in the season when everybody goes to Bakken in Dyrehven: they tear past each other, yell and scream, laugh and make fun of each other, drive their horses to death, overturn, and are run over. Finally, when they reach Bakken covered with dust and out of breath—well, they look at each other—and go home. (Kierkegaard 1987: 458)

Lund obviously had a great effect on the young Kierkegaard when he met him, and he continued to be a source of fascination and comparison throughout his adult life as the increasingly lost and mysterious inner life of the bachelor Dr. Lund living in the interior of Brazil came to parallel Kierkegaard's. Thus, fifteen years later, a lonely Kierkegaard will return to reflecting on Lund when he writes in his journal: "Today it occurred to me that my life resembles his. Just as he [Dr. Lund] lives out there in Brazil, lost to the world, condemned to excavating antediluvian fossils, so I live as though I were outside world, condemned to excavating Christian concepts" (Kierkegaard 1996: 501/Pap. X 3 A 239). And less than a year before his death, Kierkegaard returns to Lund one final time, on 3 December 1854:

To travel to South America, to descend into subterranean caves to excavate the remains of extinct animal types and antediluvian fossils—in this there is nothing ironic, for the animals extant there now do not pretend to be the same animals.

But to excavate in the middle of 'Christendom' the types of being a Christian, which in relation to present Christians are somewhat like the bones of extinct animals to animals living now—this is the most intense irony—the irony of assuming Christianity exists at the same time that there are one thousand preachers robed in velvet and silk and millions of Christians who beget Christians, and so on. (1970: 277–278)

Jonathan Lear quotes this passage in an essay as one of the best straightforward examples of irony in his entire writings (Lear 2010: 146). Lear contends that for Kierkegaard, using the archaeological metaphor, existence is "not mere biological life", and that it shows Kierkegaard placing irony and the art of pretending as central to being human, of which he had become the master by the time of writing this passage. Similarly, but going one step further, Pessoa's Soares contends that "The superior man differs from the inferior man and his animal brothers by the simple trait of irony" (Pessoa 2015: 135). We find in Kierkegaard's passage once again the interior journey contrasted with the exterior one, and also Kierkegaard's bitterness at the state of Christianity in nineteenth century Denmark and the irony of his existence and work. Kierkegaard never loses his passion for irony—from the publication of his thesis *The Concept of Irony* in 1841, to the pseudonymous enterprise of deception, masks and multiple perspectives, and then to the late journal entry under his own name. Another irony might be that it is only when Dr. Lund makes his greatest scientific discovery and triumph that his Christian faith is rattled and that is when his career of exterior exploration ends. Alone in those caves of Minas Gerais and gazing at the mysterious rock paintings led him onto an interior, inward journey which would last another thirty-five years living in retirement in the small town of Lagoa Santa.

The presence of Lund's explorations enters Kierkegaard's published works too, memorably in perhaps his most opaque and painful work— "Guilty/Not Guilty" in *Stages on Life's Way*.

When I was a child, a little pond in a peat excavation was everything to me. The dark tree roots that poke out here and there in the murky darkness were vanished kingdoms and countries, each one a discovery as important to me as antediluvian discoveries to the natural scientist. (Kierkegaard 1988: 363/SKS6, 337)

Here we have an example of Kierkegaard's approach anticipating Walter Benjamin's philosophy of ruination. With the ear of the poet, the gaze of the religious writer and the mind of the philosopher, Kierkegaard—whether as Quidam here or Climacus elsewhere—can be in a vast forest by simply looking at a blade of grass or tree root. This is why Climacus sighs that inwardness is being lost more and more in the philosophers and the poets, but not with the scientist. The modern age now worships the scientist but the real poet and philosopher are still essential though much rarer. This is exactly what Pessoa also believes and has no doubt that he is up to that task of being a poet. Inspired by and mirroring Dr. Lund, Kierkegaard has to take the journey inward as a poetic philosopher. In an omitted line from *The Concept of Anxiety*, Kierkegaard, thinly disguised as Vigilius Haufniensis, perhaps thinking again of Dr. Lund, notes that he "has taken and is taking only an inland journey" [*Indenlandsreise*] (Kierkegaard 1980a: 179). There is another implicit reference to Lund in the Brazilian jungles when in *Fear and Trembling*, published the same year that Dr. Lund makes his greatest discovery, Johannes de silentio makes his own investigative journey in trying to understand Abraham's three-day voyage to Mount Moriah who could be viewed as a murderer, a madman, or the knight and father of faith for the three major monotheistic religions of the West. Johannes de silentio distinguishes the Victorian age of exploration in botany and exotic lands with his own task: "Generally, people travel around the world to see rivers and mountains, new stars, colourful birds, freakish fish, preposterous races of mankind; they indulge in the brutish stupor that gawks at life and thinks it has seen something. That does not occupy me" (Kierkegaard 1983: 38/SKS4, 133). What absorbs Kierkegaard and all his pseudonyms then is that which is overlooked and of which perhaps Dr. Lund lost or gained out there in the limestone caves of Lagoa Santa. Thus, the last pseudonym to publish—Anti-Climacus—expresses what is at stake and what the whole task of Kierkegaard's authorship is about: "The greatest hazard of all, losing the self, can occur very quietly in the world, as if it were nothing at all. No other loss can occur so quietly; any other loss—an arm, a leg, five dollars, a wife, etc.—is sure to be noticed" (Kierkegaard 1980b: 32/SKS11, 148).

Pessoa and the Portuguese Argonauts

Kierkegaard has Dr. Lund to help him set off on his inward journey from the letter of 1835 to the last lonely reflections in his journals; Pessoa has the formidable and world-famous Portuguese navigators from the fifteenth and sixteenth centuries as his model. Camões celebrates the audacity of the Portuguese Argonauts in *The Lusíads*, writing: "Open the gates to that vast ocean / Which you navigate with such courage" [*Abrindo a porta ao vasto mar patente, / Que com tão forte peito navegais*] (Camões 2001: 224/1980: 351 [Canto X: 138]) Where can the Portuguese go after opening up the world? In the twentieth century, during the demise of Empire and in a world where the ocean has been conquered, Soares declares along the forgotten streets of Lisbon: "now we will master the psychological ocean" (Pessoa 2015: 366). This modern Argonaut is most clearly expressed in a section included in Richard Zenith's edition of *The Book of Disquiet* when the author audaciously claims:

> Your ships, Lord, didn't make a greater voyage than the one made by my thought, in the disaster of this book. They rounded no cape and sighted no far-flung beach—beyond what daring men had dared and what minds had dreamed—to equal the capes I rounded with my imagination […] Your argonauts grappled with monsters and rears. In the voyage of my thought, I also had monsters and fears to contend with. (Pessoa 2015: 115)

Like both Kierkegaard and Nietzsche in philosophy before him, Pessoa now embarks on a voyage of the human subject and shattering the concept of selfhood in literature. Not dissimilar to Quidam's discovery of "vanished kingdoms and countries" in the dark tree roots in a little pond in *Stages on Life's Way*, Soares voyages deep into his imagination simply by observing the most insignificant things along the streets of Lisbon, writing that "there's infinity in a cell or a desert" (Pessoa 2015: 86), and that the "geography of our consciousness or reality is an endless complexity of irregular coasts, low and high mountains, and myriad lakes" (Pessoa 2015: 288).

A drug-addled Campos had humorously summed up the paralysis of the Portuguese after their heroic age in his first major poem "Opiary": "I belong to that class of Portuguese / Who, once India was discovered, were out / Of work" [*Pertenço a um genero de portugûeses / Que depois de estar a India descoberta / Ficaram sem trabalho*] (Pessoa 2006: 150). Immediately after encountering Pessoa's most cherished heteronym— the 'master'[6] Alberto Caeiro, Campos is reborn and steps up to the task to equal the Portuguese Argonauts with his own great poem, the "Maritime Ode". It is a masterpiece of the imagination and the idea of *"navegar é preciso; viver não é preciso"* in literary modernism, appropriating motifs from the epic seafaring voyages for the modern fragmented and plural self. Standing on the riverbank in Lisbon, Campos expresses his "cyclonic, Atlantic being" (Pessoa 2006: 177) by penning this great work that rivals Camões as a supreme poem in the Portuguese language. His master—Caeiro—had planted the seed for the task ahead for Campos in one of the central poems of "The Keeper of Sheep" which also has a dramatic and transformative effect on Pessoa and Ricardo Reis:

I'm the Discoverer of Nature.
I'm the Argonaut of true sensations
I bring to the Universe a new Universe,
Because I bring to the Universe its own self.
[*Sou o Descobridor da Natureza.*
Sou o Argonauta das sensações verdadeiras.
Trago ao Universo um novo Universo
Porque trago ao Universo ele-próprio] (Pessoa 2006: 43)

No longer needing nor able to circumnavigate the world, Pessoa and his heteronyms, like Kierkegaard and his pseudonyms, make the world circumnavigate around him and his creative imagination.

After Caeiro, Campos tries to feel everything, thus becoming the self-proclaimed Sensationist. Soares dreams of crossing over to the other side of the Tagus River but never does because "When one feels too intensely, the Tagus is an endless Atlantic, and Cacilhas another continent, or even another universe" (Pessoa 2015: 112). Kant has opened the floodgates by making a Copernican revolution in philosophy "by assuming the objects must conform to our cognition" (Kant 1999: 110/Bxvi); Kierkegaard and Pessoa continue this Copernican revolution by making the object and subjects—both real and unreal—conform to their cognition and to their incognito selves. There is a controlled finitude to Kant's philosophical exploration who knows and respects the boundaries of the mind; but there is a void of infinitude in Pessoa's and Kierkegaard's endless dissection and exploration of the human self as multiple. Pessoa takes the myth-making of the Portuguese 'discoveries' in the sea without end and uses it for his particular subject which is itself an ocean without end. This is implicit for the poet throughout his national collection of poems called "Message" [*Mensagem*]: "That the sea with limits is for Greece or Rome: / The limitless sea is Portuguese" [*Que o mar com fim será grego ou romano: / O mar sem fim é português*] (Pessoa 1998: 274). Little did the cartoonist (P.C. Klæstrup) know or foresee (or perhaps he did!) how Kierkegaard's thought would be received and reread in the centuries following his own when he drew a caricature for the scandal sheet *The Corsair* in Copenhagen in 1846 to ridicule Kierkegaard. It is an image of Kierkegaard standing at the centre of a circle surrounded by various objects, landmarks, items and symbols—the whole world revolving around the philosopher, capturing Kierkegaard's peculiar, radical Copernican revolution. Perhaps Ricardo Reis remained immobile and incognito in Brazil, whose life is left to our imagination, and a physically frail Caeiro lived as a simple recluse in a small house on a hill outside Lisbon; nonetheless Campos speaks for them all in a nameless poem when he travels on a train, watching strangers get off and concludes: "And my heart is a little larger than the entire universe" [*E o meu coração é um pouco maior que o universo inteiro*] (Pessoa 2006: 253).

Madness, Shipwreck and the Quixotic Quest

For Kierkegaard and Pessoa, Dr. Lund and the Portuguese Argonauts travel on the verge of insanity, on a quixotic quest without end ("You observed the Argonaut's mad ambition/to tame the sea with sail and oar" [*Vistes aquela insana fantasia/De tentarem o mar com vela e remo*] Camões 2001: 124/1980: 226 [Canto, VI: 29]),–often becoming shipwrecked—literally in the case of the Portuguese explorers, or becoming a shipwreck of the mind—in the case of Dr. Lund. All of these elements are inserted into their philosophical and literary endeavour. Although viewed as a philosopher and Christian author, what largely inspired Kierkegaard were three key literary figures of European modernity on the brink of madness: Don Quixote, Faust and Hamlet. They are all on impossible journeys, and are also encapsulated in Pessoa's approaches and visions. Hamlet is haunted by the ghost of his father and is plagued by the shadow of madness, procrastination and death. He becomes Shakespeare's most famous creation, open to endless interpretation, and which Joyce wickedly has one of the characters in *Ulysses* say that "Shakespeare is the happy hunting ground of all minds that have lost their balance" (Joyce 2008: 239). Faust is the insatiable seeker of knowledge and truth whose selfhood in divided, and who looks "into man and into the secret hiding places of the earth" (Kierkegaard 1987: 454), and whom both Kierkegaard and Pessoa wanted to write a book on. Neither succeeded; instead, Kierkegaard's fragments on Faust end up scattered mostly in *Either/Or*, *Fear and Trembling* and *Johannes Climacus*; and Pessoa's unfinished poem *Faust: A Subjective Tragedy* is an unfinished blank verse drama divided into acts and interacts [*Entreactos*] and remains a mess even by Pessoa's standards.[7] And then there is Don Quixote, who goes on the ultimate impossible adventure, living in a dreamscape and battling windmills who he imagines to be giants, and in the process, his creator, Cervantes, forges the first modern novel. All three iconic literary figures are often assumed mad, mentally divided, and highly imaginative explorers, becoming representatives and symbols for the troubled modern human being. In their 'impossible journey' in literature and philosophy, Pessoa and Kierkegaard appropriate the three into startling, singular works to ignite philosophical and literary modernism.

Much of the voyages of the Portuguese navigators were often deemed quixotic and crazy. In his romantic biography of Fernão de Magalhães (better known to the world as Magellan), Stefan Zweig writes: "[…] thus from a reasonable point of view the boundless expansion of Portugal was an absurdity, a dangerous form of quixotry" (Zweig 1938: 20). Soares' passages are often quixotic in his interior dreamscape, where objects are transformed, and the impossible is always prioritized and celebrated. Under the title "A Voyage I never made", an early fragment that can be attributed to the first heteronym of *The Book of Disquiet*—Vicente Guedes—before Soares takes over, the elusive author writes:

> I visited New Europes and was greeted by different Constantinoples as I sailed into the ports of pseudo-Bosporuses. It baffles you that I sailed in? You read me right. The steamer in which I set out came into port as a sailboat […] that's impossible, you say. That's why it happened to me. (Pessoa 2015: 462)

The author pursues his quixotic voyage of the interior of the modern human mind on the frontier of madness: "We were, in that moment, no more than wayfarers between what we had forgotten and what we didn't know, knights on foot defending an abandoned ideal" (Pessoa 2015: 324). Madness seems to be an anonymous shadow throughout Pessoa and Kierkegaard's life as both were worried that they may indeed go mad, and Kierkegaard's successful brother and his brother's only son went insane (Lyby 2009: 206), and there were also examples of madness in Pessoa's family. Pessoa wrote (in English): "One of my mental complications—horrible beyond words—is a fear of insanity, which itself is insanity" (Pessoa 1966: 6). Many years later, in the year of his death, Pessoa confesses that his "heteronyms have their origin in a deep-seated form of hysteria" (Pessoa 2001: 254). Following the Romantics, genius and madness travel side by side in Campos' poem "The Tobacco Shop"; while truth and madness are sometimes synonymous with Kierkegaard, for they are linked by inwardness or as Climacus writes: "[…] lunacy and truth are ultimately indistinguishable, because they may both have inwardness" (Kierkegaard 1992: 194/SKS7, 178). However, Kierkegaard and his fictions may be saved because Climacus in a footnote to the citation above writes that "madness never has the inwardness of infinity". Kierkegaard and Pessoa, keeping lunacy at bay and aware of the presence of madness in their family, open their minds and writing to the inwardness of infinity. For Climacus, Don Quixote remains mad because he "is the prototype of the subjective lunacy in which the passion of inwardness grasps a particular fixed finite idea" (Kierkegaard 1992: 195/SKS7, 179). For Climacus and Kierkegaard, the absence of inwardness is also lunacy, revealing the disintegrating dialectical journey of his thought.

When we think of Kierkegaard's "inwardness of infinity" and Pessoa's poetic authorship of fragments piled up upon fragments, the writing is without end. Climacus' *Concluding Unscientific Postscript to the Philosophical Fragments* is a finished, published book but it rambles on as the pseudonymous author as idler states that his sole objective is "to make difficulties everywhere", who makes Christian faith even more elusive than it was before, and who classifies his great book as "superfluous" (Kierkegaard 1992: 618/SKS7, 561). The book remains ironic to the very last page, giving the last word to his mischievous editor— Kierkegaard—who claims no responsibility for the book or all the pseudonymous authors except for being both "the secretary and, quite ironically, the dialectically reduplicated author of the author or the authors" (Kierkegaard 1992: 627/SKS7, 571). Kierkegaard continues to be the self-declared reader rather than the author of his books (Kierkegaard 1998: 11/SKS13, 19); and for Climacus, "the absence of a conclusion is expressly a qualification of inwardness" (Kierkegaard 1992: 289/SKS7, 264). After publishing *Concluding Unscientific Postscript*, Kierkegaard writes in his journals on how Cervantes' *Don Quixote* could have been an even greater masterpiece if he had left it inconclusive:

> It is a sad mistake for Cervantes to Don Quixote by making him sensible and then letting him die. Cervantes, who himself had the superb idea of having him become a shepherd! It ought to have ended there. That is, Don Quixote should not come to an end; he ought to be presented as

going full speed, so that he opens vistas upon an infinite series of new fixed ideas. Don Quixote is endlessly perfectible in madness, but the one thing he cannot become (for otherwise he could become everything and anything) is sensible. Cervantes seems not to have been dialectical enough to bring it to this romantic conclusion (that there is no conclusion). (SKS20, 107/VIII I A 59)

For Kierkegaard and Pessoa, they are navigating through a shipwrecked age. Kierkegaard calls his era the "age of disintegration" in an extraordinary passage in the journals from 1848 (Kierkegaard 1996: 350/Pap. IX B 63: 7); and *The Book of Disquiet* has a passage that the editors put as the first paragraph of the "non-book, or impossible book" (Lourenço 2010: 197) where Soares describes his era as the age without faith (Pessoa 2015: 11). Joyce memorably summed up the feeling amongst some modernists of the twentieth century: "It is an age of exhausted whoredom groping for its god" (Joyce 2008: 198). Again, the Portuguese Argonauts for Pessoa and the explorations and fate of Dr. Lund and the state of Christendom in the nineteenth century provide the motif for shipwreck to be taken into their styles, strategies and approaches for their philosophical and literary endeavours. The Portuguese empire was undone when the sea was won (Pessoa 1998: 273/1979: 59), and Pessoa writes in what was probably to be included in *The Book of Disquiet*: "Shipwrecks? No, I never had any. But I have the impression that I shipwrecked all my voyages, and that my salvation lay in interspaces of unconsciousness" (Pessoa 2015: 473). Thus, in his impossible, interior journey, Pessoa with all his heteronyms, remains the 'man in the garret' or the 'Man from Porlock' who interrupted Coleridge's writing of what could have been his masterpiece. Instead, Coleridge's poem "Kubla Khan" exists as a fragment, a ruin of which Pessoa obsessed over.[8] This is Pessoa's shipwrecked universe, such that his master's (Caeiro) cosmology is revealed in the forty-seventh poem from "The Keeper of Sheep" where it is declared that "Nature is parts without a whole" (Pessoa 1998: 65); and Pessoa concludes his cycle of poems on the Portuguese Age of Discovery—the only collection of poems to be published by him—with the statement: "All is scattered, nothing is whole" [*Tudo é disperso, nada é inteiro*] (Pessoa 2006: 382/1979: 106).

If Pessoa is the "man in the garret", Kierkegaard is the *Extraskriver*—the supplementary clerk or extra-writer (Kierkegaard 1983: 7/SKS4, 103). He constructs a philosophy of fragments or crumbs (*Smuler*), which we witness explicitly in the motto to *Concluding Unscientific Postscript*, the title of *Philosophical Fragments*, and in the subtitle of *Either/Or* ("A Fragment of Life"). Climacus explains that "the 'fragment' [*smule*] of uncertainty helped Socrates, because he himself helped with the passion of infinity" (Kierkegaard 1992: 202/SKS7, 185). Whether masking as the assistant bookkeeper (Soares) or the hilarious bookbinder (the editor of *Stage on Life's Way*), they are both traveling—to quote Campos—"a broken gateway to the Impossible" (Pessoa 1998: 176).

Espionage, Disguise and Multiplicity

A whole book could be written on this last point linking Kierkegaard and Pessoa as explorers of the impossible and interiority. The multiplicity of the self through Kierkegaard's pseudonyms and Pessoa's heteronyms is the most obvious connection between the two of which some work has been done already.[9] However, in relation to the two explorers of interiority's "*navegar é preciso; viver não é preciso*" in philosophical and literary modernism, I conclude this essay by focusing on espionage and disguise that leads to a plurality and multiplicity of the self rather than a death of the subject. I am aware of some of the difficulties in bringing these two authors together in terms of their different use of language, their ultimate goals, the areas they are working in, and the reader they are trying to reach. Pessoa can be less rigorous than Kierkegaard in the free use of the words soul, self and subject—which can often have different etymologies or meanings (*alma* and *Sjel*, *selv* and *Eu/si*, *nada* and *Intet*). Kierkegaard is a moral and religious writer whose goal is to act as a corrective to Christendom; while Pessoa is first and foremost a poet whose duty and objective is to write daring new literary forms. What brings them together here again is that they both play out their authorship as a form of espionage and disguise and often allow their fictional writers to attain more depth and life than their real selves. Their strategies, often getting the better of them, is an unfolding of the elusive human self which is transformed into a plurality. Their interior journey is extremely modern because it opens up a multiplicity of pathways which remain open to interpretation, and the journey is contradictory, paradoxical and incomplete. Soares famously writes: "By delving within, I made myself into many" (Pessoa 2015: 92); and before any of Kierkegaard's pseudonymous writings are conceived, he confesses in the letter to Dr. Lund:

> Here I stand like Hercules—not at a crossroads—no, but at a multitude of roads, and therefore it is all the harder to choose the right one. Perhaps it is my misfortune in life that I am interested in far too many things rather than definitively in any one thing. (Kierkegaard: 1987: 455)

Almost twenty years later, after all the pseudonymous writings have been published and trying to be more direct in his writing, Kierkegaard still confesses to his journals that "it is disguise that is my passion" (Kierkegaard 1996: 636/Pap. XI 2 A 251).

When Campos writes that "we must operate on the soul" (Pessoa 2001: 83), and Climacus states that his task is "make difficulties everywhere (Kierkegaard 1992: 187/SKS7, 172), they go on to create a multiplicity of voices or polyphonic universe at a rapid rate that leaves the reader reeling as they venture further out into Kant's "broad and stormy ocean". Pessoa's heteronyms often express it better than Pessoa when Campos writes in "The Tobacco Shop": "I invoke my own self and find nothing" (Pessoa 1998: 176). Even when Kierkegaard unmasks and departs from the pseudonymous authorship, it seems that the mask indeed has stuck to his face,[10] where once he was "hiding for the time being in the cautious incognito of a *flâneur*" (Kierkegaard 1996: 351/Pap. IX B 63:7); a year before his death he admits that "unrecognizability is my life" (Kierkegaard 1996: 636/Pap. XI 2 A 251). Of course, the groundless, incognito self has been present to us long before Kierkegaard,[11] and Schopenhauer had already evocatively depicted the search for the inner self leading us to a "bottomless void" and "a wavering and unstable phantom" (Schopenhauer 1966: 187). But it is the conscious attempt by Kierkegaard and Pessoa to journey and analyse this "bottomless void" knowing that they are diving into a bottomless ocean, that sets them apart and which has left the exploration of the self richer for it, and which links them to philosophical and literary modernism. They both disperse and unleash the different aspects of the self, which is both a philosophical and literacy stroke of brilliance but also, crucially, to encourage the reader to begin to interpret him or herself and envision all the impossible journeys that he or she can undertake. Thus, Soares, writes: "I'm a navigator engaged in unknowing myself" (Pessoa 2015: 104).

I concur with Eduardo Lourenço's conclusion to his essay on Kierkegaard and Pessoa when he writes that "If Kierkegaard was the 'spy of God', Pessoa was the 'spy of nothing'" (Lourenço 2008: 201). They are supreme metaphoric and myth-making writers; at the same time, they are trying to capture the existential reality of being mortal human beings. They are sailing rather than living, acting out their lives and writing in disguise and as deceivers—as spies. "Spies of God" derives from Shakespeare's *King Lear* which is in the last speech that Lear says to Cordelia before she is brought away to be executed, and which the passage is also used by Kierkegaard in his ominous journal entry known as "the great earthquake" (Kierkegaard 1996: 117/Pap. II A 805). The motif of the spy will stay with Kierkegaard—via Climacus' spy in *Concluding Unscientific Postscript*; as one of 'God's spies' playing out his "godly satire" in his 'report to history'—*The Point of View* (Kierkegaard 1998: 17/SKS13, 24); and in his journals when he says, "I am like a secret agent" (Kierkegaard 1996: 322/Pap. IX A 190). Kierkegaard's pseudonyms are more than just pseudonyms as they share different ways of life and points of view than Kierkegaard, and quote and refer and socialize with each other—much like Pessoa's heteronyms. The *flâneur* whom Kierkegaard admits pretending to be is a traveler into the interior, an observer and a spy. Of course, all great writers are in a way spies, but Kierkegaard's pseudonyms are especially proud of this vocation and enjoy it—to the point of voyeurism. The pseudonyms of watchmen, seducers, explorers, poets, hermits and preachers—Victor Eremita, Johannes the Seducer, Johannes de silentio, Constantin Constantius, Johannes Climacus, Vigilius Haufniensis, Frater Taciturnus, Anti-Climacus, Inter et Inter, etc.—are all to varying degrees spies navigating the multiplicity of the self.

As spy or secret agent, indirect communication is everywhere, epitomized in the title page of *Fear and Trembling*, which contains double and triple secrets for the message to safely get to its receiver. The name Johannes de silentio is printed on the title page as the pseudonym who attempts to speak of the impossibility and silence of faith; the author proclaims that he is neither a poet nor a philosopher but calls the book a "dialectical lyric"; and the book's motto from Hamann is another example of indirect communication where the indirect message delivered by the messenger from the father to the son to kill the enemy is understood by the son but not the messenger. And of course, the content is explicitly probing the double secrecy between God and Abraham and between Abraham and his family, as well as implicitly probing the double secrecy between the author and his posthumous reader and between the author and his life (his father and his ex-fiancé). We are left foundering again like the shipwrecked Argonauts and are reminded of the opening two words of *Hamlet*—"Who's there?"—where Kierkegaard remains, by turns, incognito, the masked multiplicity of the self, the philosophical loafer with cigar, the troubled religious poet searching for the purity of heart to will one thing, and one of 'God's spies'.

Kierkegaard and Pessoa are in the state of flux, in movement, subjective, sailing—temporarily being (*estar*); rather than in the state of being (*ser*) static, permanent, objective. Thus, Campos sums up Pessoa's literary enterprise: "*Estar é ser. Fingir é conhecer-se*" (Pessoa 2014: 448). The first sentence is difficult to translate as we only have one word for the verb 'to be' in the English language for both the temporary and permanent state. But Zenith does well to translate these two sentences as: "Where we are is who we are. To pretend it to know ourselves" (Pessoa 2001: 200). The first sentence locates and defines the human being as constantly in motion; while the second sentence reveals that the conscious decision to feign and deceive is the key to knowing oneself. Perhaps, finally, Kierkegaard is held back and anchored or governed by Christianity. Climacus's dictum that "truth is subjectivity" (Kierkegaard 1992: 189) can be interpreted in the Christian sense that "only the truth the *builds up* [*opbygger*] is the truth *for you*" (Kierkegaard 1992: 252/SKS7, 229). This 'truth' signifies interiority and inwardness, or as: "*an objectivity uncertainty, held fast through appropriation with the most passionate inwardness*" (Kierkegaard 1992: 202/SKS7, 186). But "Truth is subjectivity" can also take on a life in a non-Christian and non-moral sense: to be an existential motto that opens up a multiplicity of possibility, relativism and possible chaos. Thus, Climacus writes later in the same book (and which Sartre later took note of): "The subjective thinker is not a scientist-scholar; he is an artist" (Kierkegaard 1992: 351/SKS7, 321). Pessoa follows the latter interpretation, entering the post-modern where every possibility is welcomed, and the self is dissected and dissolved in Kant's "stormy ocean". Thus, Campos' mandates to the philosopher and poet of the future are quite similar in the demand for infinite multiplicity and contradiction. Thus, the philosopher

> will become the interpreter of crisscrossing subjectivities, with the greatest philosopher being the one who can contain the greatest number of other people's personal philosophies. Since everything is subjective, every man's opinion is true for him, and so the greatest truth will be the inner-synthesis-summation of the greatest number of these true opinions that contradict one another. (Pessoa 2001: 83)

Pessoa, Caeiro and Soares are aware of the potential lunacy in being a philosopher but in their "experimental journey" are drawn to the dangers, isolation and absurdity of the contemplative life.[12] Pessoa remains at play with both philosophy and literature, where the pursuit of perfect art is the goal; Kierkegaard, though at play with literary and philosophical forms, is always pursuing and attempting to salvage the Christian faith. Like Campos' philosopher, the task of the artist is to engage in the multiplicity and dispersal of the self in a non-moral sense (that is why Kierkegaard, Nietzsche and Joyce knew that laughter was essential for survival):

> The greatest artist will be the one who least defines himself, and who writes in the most genres with the most contradictions and discrepancies. No artist should have just one personality. He should have many, each one

being formed by joining together similar states of mind, thereby shattering the crude fiction that the artist is one and indivisible. (Pessoa 2001: 84)

***

Kierkegaard and Pessoa have offered various pictures and narratives of the self, as well as showing the reader and themselves the plurality and multiplicity that is inherent and unleashed when we explore the depths of human consciousness and embracing and playing with various masks and possible selves on the journey. It is not a safe or recommended path, as we have witnessed the difficulty also in other explorers of the impossible in philosophy and literature—such as Nietzsche's endless questioning and transformative philosophy that may have led ultimately to the shipwreck of his mind; or Joyce's seventeen year, isolated *tour de force* culminating in *Finnegans Wake*, that hardly anyone is capable or bothered to read. However, today, we are fortunate to have their works still ahead of us because they expand rather than reduce, or reify, the human imaginative self. Kierkegaard's and Pessoa's interior journey is impossible but goes on, in that the self, subject and soul cannot be fully fathomed; and the heroic gesture in modernism is that they still try to navigate through the "broad and stormy ocean", and what we find, with patience, are complex, paradoxical works that open up the concept of the human self that questions both philosophy and literature, and enriches them both.

Notes

1. I have already made the case that Kierkegaard is first and foremost a "dramatic philosopher" in an article called: "Kierkegaard's Experimental Theatre of the Self", published in *From Hamann to Kierkegaard: First Workshop of the Project Experimentation and Dissidence* (e-book), eds. José Miranda Justo, Elisabete Sousa, Fernando Silva, Universidade de Lisboa, 2017, 79–98. http://experimentation-dissidence.umadesign. com/wp-content/uploads/2016/11/From-Hamann-to-Kierkegaard_e-book.pdf.

In a letter written to João Gaspar Simões in 1931, Pessoa explicitly calls himself a "dramatic poet"—like Shakespeare: "The central point of my personality as an artist is that I'm a dramatic poet; in everything I write, I always have the poet's inner exaltation and the playwright's deperson-alization. I soar as someone else – that's all" (Pessoa 2001: 247).

2. I have written elsewhere in an article on Kierkegaard and Pessoa by briefly going through various links and possible connections: "There are so many striking parallels to the interests and strategies of Pessoa and Kierkegaard – such as their lifelong fascination with the elusive Faust, the obsession with the interval and borders/margins, the conversation with, and reverence for, Shakespeare, the strategic othering of oneself for plurality and multiplicity, the creation of different voices and masks for different modes of life, their obsessive exploration of tedium and boredom, their abiding love and appropriation of fairy tales, their brief experience with romance and flirtation with love letters, their assimila-tion of theatre, and their vast unpublished workshop of fragments and notes. Here are two writers who don't write "proper" books per se, who are paradoxically pretending and deceiving in an attempt to be honest, and who leave to posterity some of the most penetrating excavations of the self ever undertaken by a writer. Of course, there are differ-ences – Pessoa is expressively pagan; Kierkegaard a neurotic Christian. Kierkegaard appropriates forms of literature towards his religious faith; Pessoa uses philosophy for his aesthetic endeavour" (Ryan 2013: 116).

3. Benjamin quotes this paragraph from *Johannes Climacus* in the work in progress chapter—"The Flâneur"—in the incomplete *Arcades Project*. Leading into the passage, Benjamin writes, "So the flâneur goes for a walk in his room" (see Benjamin 2002: 421); and after the passage, concludes, "Here is the key to the schema of *Voyage autour de ma cham-ber*." This work is by Xavier de Maistre, published in 1794, which the editors of *The Arcades Project* describe as "experiences undergone dur-ing a period of imprisonment when, as a soldier in the Piedmontese army, the author was being held in Turin and had to find compensation in mental traveling (Benjamin 2002: 986). Adorno cites Kierkegaard's passage in his section on inwardness and the *intérior* in his book on Kierkegaard, and comments: "Thus the flâneur promenades in his room; the world only appears to him reflected by pure inwardness. Images of interiors are at the centre of the early Kierkegaard's philo-sophical constructions" (Adorno 1989: 41). (For more on the *flâneur*,

interiority and inwardness in relation to Kierkegaard and Benjamin and Adorno, see Ryan 2014: 135–148, 179–193.)

4. The Danish author Henrik Stangerup takes this approach in his evocative novel on Dr. Peter Wilhelm Lund's story (Stangerup 1988).

5. Scholar and translator Emanuel Hirsch sees this letter as part of what he calls the "Faustian letters"—one of Kierkegaard's early projects which would have been a series of letters by a pseudonymous Faustian doubter (see Kierkegaard 1987: 662). Curiously and revealing another link between the two, Pessoa's first major heteronym, Alexander Search, is also a Faustian figure, who shares the same birthday as Pessoa, wrote only in English, and made a written pact with 'Jacob Satan' (see Pessoa 2001: 15).

6. Both Pessoa and Campos explicitly refer to Caeiro as their master: Campos begins his unfinished "Notes for the Memory of my Master Caeiro" with—"I met my master Caeiro" (Pessoa 2001: 38); and Pessoa, in his famous letter to Adolfo Casais Monteiro on 13 January 1935, writes that, regarding Caeiro, "my master had appeared in me" (Pessoa 2001: 257). As an aside, Adolfo Casais Monteiro translated *The Concept of Anxiety* in 1936, a year after the death of Pessoa, but there is still no proof that Pessoa read Kierkegaard.

7. For an excellent philosophical analysis of Pessoa's *Faust*, see Gusmão, Manuel; *O Poema Impossível: O "Fausto" de Pessoa*, Lisboa: editorial Caminho, 1986.

8. Pessoa published a small piece in 1935 called "A Man from Porlock", which discusses the enigmatic figure who supposedly interrupted the writing of Coleridge's 'Kubla Khan'. Pessoa calls this man from Porlock the "unknown interrupter" who showed up and "obstructed a communication between the abyss and life" [*esse interruptor incógnito, a estorvar uma comunicação entre o abismo e a vida*] (Pessoa 2000: 491/2005: 54).

9. I have already presented papers on the role of communication and the plurality of the subject in Kierkegaard and Pessoa, such as "Criando um Mito: Ficções Verdadeiras em Kierkegaard e Pessoa", Colóquio Internacional O Dia Triunfal, Gulbenkian, Lisbon, March 2014; and "Theatres of the Self with Kierkegaard and Fernando Pessoa", at the Jubilee International Congress 200 Year Anniversary, Reconsidering Kierkegaard in a Global World, Copenhagen, May 2013. See Antonio M. Feijó and Elisabete M. de Sousa's article "Fernando Pessoa: Poets and Philosophers" for more on Pessoa's possible connections to Kierkegaard, in Stewart, Jon (ed.) *Kierkegaard's Influence on Literature,*

Criticism and Art, Tome 5, v. 12: The Romance Languages and Central and Eastern Europe (*Kierkegaard Research: Sources Reception and Resources*), Surrey: Ashgate, 2013. See also, Bellaiche-Zacharie, Alain; *Pensée et exitence selon Pessoa et Kierkegaard*, Louvain: Presses universitaires de Louvain, 2012. Other articles that have been published in Portugal linking Kierkegaard and Pessoa in the past include: de Freitas, Filipa; "Nietzsche, Kierkegaard e Pessoa: a existência do poeta", in *Nietzsche e Pessoa: Ensaios* (eds.), Bartholomew Ryan, Marta Faustino, and Antonio Cardiello, Lisboa: tinta da China, 2016, pp. 223–254; Ryan, Bartholomew; "Into the Nothing with Kierkegaard and Pessoa", in *Kierkegaard and the Challenges of Infinitude: Philosophy and Literature in Dialogue*, edited by José Miranda Justo, Elisabete M. de Sousa and René Rosfort, Lisboa: Centro de Filosofia da Universidade de Lisboa, 2013, pp. 115–128; Ferro, Nuno, "Kierkegaard e Tédio", in *Revista Portuguesa de Filosofia*, no. 64, 2008, pp. 943–970; Oliveira Silva, Luís; "Estética e Ética em Kierkegaard e Pessoa," in *Revista da Faculdade de Ciências Sociais e Humanas da UNL*, Lisbon: Universidade Nova de Lisboa, 1988, pp. 261–272; Lourenço, Eduardo; "Kierkegaard e Pessoa ou a Comunicação Indirecta," in *Fernando Rei da Nossa Baviera*, Lisbon: Imprensa Nacional Casa da Moeda, 1986, pp. 121–144, and "Kierkegaard e Pessoa ou as Máscaras do Absoluto," in *Fernando Rei da Nossa Baviera*, Lisbon: Imprensa Nacional Casa da Moeda, 1986, pp. 97–109; and Hatherly, Ana; "Fernando Pessoa—retrato encontrado em Søren Kierkegaard," in *Actas do II Congresso Internacional de Estudos Pessoanos*, Porto: Centro de Estudos Pessoanos, 1985, pp. 263–277.

10. See Campos' lines in "The Tobacco Shop": "When I went to take off the mask, / It was stuck to my face" [*Quando quis tirar a máscara, / estava pegada à cara*] (Pessoa 1998: 177/2002: 324).

11. See, for example, Fernando Gil's brilliant essay on the Portuguese Renaissance poet Sá de Miranda (Gil 2009). Five hundred years before the disquieting poets of the twentieth century such as Pessoa or Trakl, Sá da Miranda captured the uneasiness and instability of the human self, where, as Gil writes, "the self is a shadow without a body, and as we shall soon read, *shadows cannot be grasped*" (Gil 2009: 206).

12. See, for example, when Soares writes: "Metaphysics has always struck me as a prolonged form of latent insanity" (Pessoa 2015: 84); or when Caeiro says that "philosophers are lunatics" [*os filósofos são homens doidos*] (Pessoa 2006: 31).

References

Adorno, Theodor W. 1989. *Kierkegaard: Construction of the Aesthetic*, trans. Robert Hullot-Kentor. Minneapolis, MN: University of Minnesota Press.

Benjamin, Walter. 2002. *The Arcades Project*, trans. Howard Eiland and Kevin McLaughlin. Cambridge, MA: Harvard University Press.

Camões, Luis Vaz de. 1980. *Os Lusíadas*, edição organizada por Emanuel Paulo Ramos. Porto: Porto Editora.

———. 2001. *The Lusíads*, trans. Landeg White. Oxford: Oxford University Press.

Gil, Fernando. 2009. *The Groundless Self*, trans. Kenneth Krabbenhoft, in Gil Fernando and Helder Macedo. *The Traveling Eye: Retrospection, Vision, and Prophecy in the Portuguese Renaissance*, 205–249. Dartmouth, MA: Center for Portuguese Studies and Culture, University of Massachusetts Dartmouth.

Joyce, James. 2008. *Ulysses*. Oxford: Oxford World's Classics.

Kant, Immanuel. 1999. *Critique of Pure Reason*, trans. and ed. Paul Guyer and Allen W. Wood. Cambridge: Cambridge University Press.

Kierkegaard, Søren. 1970. *Søren Kierkegaard's Journals and Papers*, vol. 2, F-K, trans. and ed. Howard V. Hong and Edna H. Hong. Bloomington: Indiana University Press.

———. 1980a. *The Concept of Anxiety*, trans. and ed. Reidar Thomte. Princeton: Princeton University Press.

———. 1980b. *The Sickness unto Death*, trans. and ed. Howard V. Hong and Edna H. Hong. Princeton: Princeton University Press.

———. 1983. *Fear and Trembling/Repetition*, trans. and ed. Howard V. Hong and Edna H. Hong. Princeton: Princeton University Press.

———. 1985. *Philosophical Fragments/Johannes Climacus*, trans. and ed. Howard V. Hong and Edna H. Hong. Princeton: Princeton University Press.

———. 1987. *Either/Or. Part I*, trans. and ed. Howard V. Hong and Edna H. Hong. Princeton: Princeton University Press.

———. 1988. *Stages on Life's Way*, trans. and ed. Howard V. Hong and Edna H. Hong. Princeton: Princeton University Press.

———. 1992. *Concluding Unscientific Postscript to Philosophical Fragments*, vol. 1, trans. and ed. Howard V. Hong and Edna H. Hong. Princeton: Princeton University Press.

———. 1993. *Upbuilding Discourses in Various Spirits*, trans. and ed. Howard V. Hong and Edna H. Hong. Princeton: Princeton University Press.

———. 1996. *Papers and Journals: A Selection*, trans. and ed. Alastair Hannay. London: Penguin Books.

———. 1997–2013. *Søren Kierkegaards Skrifter* (cited throughout the essay as SKS which is followed by the volume). 28 Text Volumes and 28 Commentary Volumes, ed. Niels Jørgen Cappelørn, Joakim Garff, Jette Knuden, Johnny Kondrup, and Alastair McKinnon. Copenhagen: Gad Publishers.

———. 1998. *The Point of View of My Work as an Author*, trans. and ed. Howard V. Hong and Edna H. Hong. Princeton: Princeton University Press.

Lear, Jonathan. 2010. The Force of Irony. In *The Force of Argument: Essays in Honour of Timothy Smiley*, ed. Jonathan Lear and Alex Oliver, 144–164. New York: Routledge.

Lourenço, Eduardo. 2008. Kierkegaard e Pessoa ou a comunicação indirecta. In *Fernando Pessoa: Rei da Nossa Baviera*, 167–201. Lisboa: Gradiva.

———. 2010. The Book of Disquietude, Suicidal Text. In *Here on Douradores Street: Essays on Fernando Pessoa*, 197–215, selected and trans. Ronald W. Sousa. Providence, RI: Gávea-Brown.

Lukács, Georg. 1971. *The Theory of the Novel*, trans. Anna Bostock. Cambridge, MA: MIT Press.

———. 1974. *Soul and Form*, trans. Anna Bostock. Cambridge, MA: MIT Press.

Lyby, Thorkild C. 2009. Peter Christian Kierkegaard: A Man with a Difficult Family Heritage. In *Kierkegaard and His Danish Contemporaries. Tome II: Theology, Kierkegaard Research: Sources, Reception, and Resources, Volume 7*, 190–210, ed. Jon Stewart. Surrey: Ashgate.

Pessoa, Fernando. 1966. *Páginas Íntimas e de Auto-Interpretação*, ed. Georg Rudolf Lind and Jacinto do Prado Coelho. Lisboa: Ática.

———. 1979. *Mensagem*. 13.a edição. Lisboa: Ática.

———. 1998. *Fernando Pessoa & Co: Selected Poems*, trans. and ed. Richard Zenith. New York: Grove Press.

———. 2000. *Crítica: Ensaios, Artigos e Entrevistas*, edição Fernando Cabral Martins. Lisboa: Assírio & Alvim.

———. 2001. *The Selected Prose of Fernando Pessoa*, trans. and ed. Richard Zenith. New York: Grove Press.

———. 2005. *The Education of the Stoic*, trans. and ed. Richard Zenith. Cambridge: Exact Change.

————. 2006. *A Little Larger Than the Entire Universe: Selected Poems*, trans. and ed. Richard Zenith. London: Penguin Books.

————. 2014. *Obra Completa. Álvaro de Campos*, edição de Jerónimo Pizarro e Antonio Cardiello, Lisboa: tinta da china.

————. 2015. *The Book of Disquiet*, trans. and ed. Richard Zenith. London: Penguin Books.

Ryan, Bartholomew. 2013. Into the Nothing with Kierkegaard and Pessoa. In *Kierkegaard and the Challenges of Infinitude: Philosophy and Literature in Dialogue*, ed. José Miranda Justo, Elisabete M. de Sousa, and René Rosfort, 115–128. Lisboa: Centro de Filosofia da Universidade de Lisboa.

————. 2014. *Kierkegaard's Indirect Politics: Interludes with Lukács, Schmitt, Benjamin and Adorno*. New York and Amsterdam: Brill and Rodopi Press.

Schopenhauer, Arthur. 1966. *The World as Will and Representation, Volume II*, trans. E.F.J. Payne. New York: Dover Publications.

Stangerup, Henrik. 1988. *The Road to Lagoa Santa*, trans. Barbara Bluestone. London: Paladin Grafton Books.

Zweig, Stefan. 1938. *Conqueror of the Seas: The Story of Magellan*, trans. Eden and Cedar Paul. New York: The Viking Press.

Index

© The Editor(s) (if applicable) and The Author(s) 2018
A. Falcato and A. Cardiello (eds.), *Philosophy in the Condition of Modernism*,
https://doi.org/10.1007/978-3-319-77078-9

CPSIA information can be obtained
at www.ICGtesting.com
Printed in the USA
LVHW04*1754060518
576196LV00008B/23/P

9 783319 770772